The Urban Organism

The City's Natural Resources from an Environmental Perspective

The URBAN Organism

Spenser W. Havlick

Department of Environmental Studies, San Jose State University

Macmillan Publishing Co., Inc.
NEW YORK

Collier Macmillan Publishers
LONDON

Copyright © 1974, Spenser W. Havlick

Printed in the United States of America

All rights reserved. No part of this book may be reproduced or transmitted in any form or by any means, electronic or mechanical, including photocopying, recording, or any information storage and retrieval system, without permission in writing from the Publisher.

Macmillan Publishing Co., Inc.
866 Third Avenue, New York, New York 10022

Collier-Macmillan Canada, Ltd.

Library of Congress Cataloging in Publication Data

Havlick, Spenser W
  The urban organism.

  Bibliography: p.
  1. Conservation of natural resources—United
States. 2. Cities and towns—United States.
I. Title.
S938.H38   333.7′7′0973   73-8583
ISBN 0-02-351810-3

Uncredited photos throughout the text were photographed and developed by the author.

Printing: 1 2 3 4 5 6 7 8   Year: 4 5 6 7 8 9 0

Foreword

We are all confused when we speak about our cities, which are becoming more and more overloaded with new forces that cause them to suffer, or about isolated towns and villages that suffer from abandonment and reduced forces. Confusion is the main reason we are not solving our new problems, and it also leads us to prefer crying about them as pessimists rather than attempting to solve them through a realistic optimism.

Why are we confused? Because the age-old ability of Man to solve the problems of his villages, towns, and cities in a successful way has been lost, as proven by history. Man's survival is often in question, and our admiration for ancient Athens, Renaissance Florence, Teotihuacan, and Peking has been tarnished.

Why has this happened? Because, following the first transfer of train passengers in northern England in 1825, human settlements changed radically from static to dynamic situations. The city or polis turned into a dynapolis, and the result was that, whereas Man could deal with his static, nongrowing village or his walled towns and cities, he found great difficulty in coping with dynamic expansion.

Is it impossible for Man to control and guide dynapolis? Not at all; however, in order to solve our new problems, we have to go back to the roots of our cities or, better still, of all our settlements, and try to understand them in a systematic and scientific way. This is the only way to solve our problems. To achieve this we have to remember the following: forty years ago speaking about cities really meant speaking about our buildings, about the beautiful and impressive monuments, and the slums. Twenty-five years ago it was more fashionable to speak about the cities as a problem of transportation. Ten years ago only the social aspects were fashionable, and now it is only those aspects involving energy and the natural environment.

But our cities and all our settlements consist of five elements: Nature, Man, Society, Shells (buildings), and Networks. This means that to "complete the crying cycle" we have to remember both the human values that have been forgotten and Man as an individual, Man who is the most important of all the five elements because he is the measure of all things, as Protagoras said so long ago.

When this is achieved, are we going to solve our problems? Definitely not, because our settlements are a system of the five interwoven elements. By doing our best for any single one of them we will not achieve anything at all if they are not brought into balance with one another. Think of any effort to support Nature alone, and try to revive the dinosaurs or fight for the survival of malaria-carrying insects. What will happen to Man?

What then is the road that we must follow? The only answer is that it is necessary to be able to understand all five elements and the total human settlements and their interrelationships. Only when we achieve this can we be led toward an equilibrium between them all and toward successful human settlements that, even if they are dynamic (and they will be, for a few more generations), can reach the phase of harmony that will satisfy Man, our great master, and make him happy.

Thus, this presentation is very useful for all those who are concerned about their system of life: it creates the connection between, on the one hand, the present and the emerging urban organisms and, on the other, the natural environment that is the basic element of Nature. Furthermore, it does not look upon this connection in a pessimistic way but covers both the problems and the roads toward their solution in a rather realistic manner. This approach helps us to understand the system of our life by making these necessary connections. Therefore we move from chaos, forming the settlements we suffer in, to harmony, which is planning the communities that are going to make us happy through a gradual process. Step by step these new urban organisms will serve us continuously and lay better foundations for our children and our grandchildren. Duly such an approach can really serve.

Athens, Greece   C. A. DOXIADIS

Acknowledgments

Only those who have undertaken to write a book or produce a similar effort recognize the multitude of people who are contributors in one form or another to its completion. An author, like a city, is sustained by innumerable other resources and persons. I owe a special debt of appreciation to certain individuals who as my tutors unknowingly served as special inspiration for the approach to this book—Stanley A. Cain, Provost, University of California, Santa Cruz; Justin W. Leonard, Professor of Natural Resources, University of Michigan; Gilbert F. White, Director of the Institute of Behavioral Science, University of Colorado; J. Carl Welty, Professor of Biology, Beloit College; Richard L. Meier, University of California, Berkeley; William B. Stapp, Chairman of Environmental Education and Outdoor Recreation, University of Michigan; and Constantinos A. Doxiadis, Chairman of the Athens Technological Organization, Athens, Greece.

I want to acknowledge the service and help that was given by Teaching Fellows of several courses that have been combined in the message of this book: Michael Schechtman, Michael Grear, Michael Long, and especially William Bryan, Jr., who was a dedicated colleague for three years. Many students from the University of Michigan and San Jose State University have also served as sounding boards for these ideas.

A special word of thanks goes to the faithful reviewers of the manuscript: Dean Bennett of the Maine Environmental Education Project; William Stapp, University of Michigan; Richard Cooley, Department of Geography and Environmental Studies, University of California, Santa Cruz; Mel Cundiff, Department of Integrated Studies, University of Colorado; William Bryan, Northern Rocky Mountain Environmental Advocate; and Paul Yambert, Southern Illinois University.

Photographic credits are due the Environmental Protection Agency, U.S. Forest Service, U.S. Bureau of Outdoor Recreation, U.S. National Park

viii Service, U.S. Department of Housing and Urban Development, U.S. Bureau of Sport Fisheries and Wildlife, the Athens Center of Ekistics, and several state agencies. The graphics and editorial staffs of Macmillan Publishing Co., Inc., have been of special assistance, and I salute Charles Stewart, and George Carr, editors, for their able guidance throughout the critical stages.

The most deserving and deepest gratitude is expressed to my wife, Val, who carried the entire load of internal editing and manuscript typing. In addition, Val mobilized the family's patience and understanding expressed by Scott, Jennifer, and David, whose support was generously given.

San Jose, California   S. W. H.

Contents

Foreword by C. A. Doxiadis   v

Acknowledgments   vii

Introduction   1

Section I   An Environmental Approach from an Urban Perspective

1   The Conceptual Framework of Urban Conservation   7
2   Integrated Resource Management and Urbanization   49
3   Recent Trends in Conservation Policy   69

Section II   A Survey of Resources: Regional Case Studies

4   Water Resources   107
    Case in Point: The Great Lakes States   110
5   Soil Resources   147
    Case in Point: The Mississippi Basin Region   151
6   Forest Resources   187
    Case in Point: The Gulf States   204
7   Atmospheric Resources   229
    Case in Point: The Eastern Seaboard   235
8   Energy Resources   261
    Case in Point: The Eastern Seaboard   262

ix

9 Mineral Resources   299
   Case in Point: The Rocky Mountain Region   309
10 Wildlife and Fishery Resources   349
   Case in Point: The Pacific Northwest   358
11 Recreation and Open Space Resources   389
   Case in Point: The Pacific Coast Region   389

Section **III** Mechanisms of Future Urban Resources

12 Ecumenopolis and Cities of the Future   437

Glossary of Terms   477

Bibliography   493

Index   501

Introduction

An author may never have asked you to put down his work, but that is just about to happen. At the end of this paragraph, I'm going to ask you to go to a window, open a nearby door, or get up and take a quick look at the world within your immediate view. Before you do, however, I want to propose that you are about to see a stop action scene of an evolutionary event that has been in motion more than a million years. Perhaps you and I have shared the realization that man has recently entered a new era by the creation of a new natural resource—new at least by geological time and in comparison with traditional resources such as minerals, wildlife, and other features of the landscape made useful to man by his application of knowledge and technology. You have participated in that creation and it has participated in making you whatever you are. This recently identified resource is a form of human settlement called an urban area. How was your city born? When? Listen to it! Is it fulfilling functions for you and its other members? Does your particular urban area have problems of circulation or traffic congestion? Breathe deeply, and smell the effects of urban respiration. Where do the by-products of urban metabolism go? Are they recycled or are are they passed on to a nearby suffering human settlement? Will your city live for thousands of years as some cities have done or has it begun to decay and atrophy? Go to a nearby vantage point, RIGHT NOW, and look at your city.

Let me share with you how this revealing experience first happened to me. Recently I climbed to the top of the acropolis above Lindos on the Greek island of Rhodes. Below me were the soils of the hillsides and valleys, the vegetation, the sea and the people, with paths and roads that, when mingled together, formed a total community. It was an insight into a fragment of the human ecosystem that embodies man and his related

1

physical, social, and biological interdependencies. I was struck by the universality of the concept that an urban area is a recently evolved natural resource; I realized that I must add the *urban area* to the list of traditional resources such as water, soil, forests, air, minerals, and wildlife.

I invite you to test this concept in human settlements where urbanization has become widespread in the 1970's. I have repeated this observation in Tapiola, Finland; Athens, Greece; London, England; Portland, Maine; Kansas City, Missouri; Denver, Colorado; and Los Angeles, California. It appears that the concept of an urban area as a natural resource helps us to understand a second order of complexity that is derived from the traditional stock and flow resources also discussed in this volume.

Of course, I tried to anticipate what you, the reader, would see, smell, hear, feel, and think when you looked out upon your particular urban area resource. I could be sure of several circumstances confronting most readers:

1. You have an urban area to gaze upon. (Today nearly 80 per cent of Americans live in urban environments.)
2. You are curious and/or concerned about the quality of urban-influenced environments (which includes almost all of them).
3. You are an undergraduate student or an inquisitive graduate student from another discipline related to environmental affairs. Or you are an active housewife or professional woman, an hourly wage earner, a businessman, or a governmental staff member.

The messages are intended for this kind of readership. An objective of the book is to provide an inventory of national resource problems and practices under a conceptual framework that places the *urban area in the center of attention as a new synthesizing resource.* This fresh approach needs to be understood by the nonprofessional resource manager (which includes all of us), the blue- and white-collar worker, as well as the conventional manager of a forest or a fishery. It is incumbent upon every citizen in every community to become knowledgeable about the environmental imperatives that make his urban resource either lethargic and decadent or dynamic and satisfying to himself and other human inhabitants.

Most of us who come from or have been exposed to the biological sciences are familiar with a biotic community. It is accepted as a changing and dynamic system. A pond, a *chapparal,* or a beech-maple community is understood in its succession toward a predictable equilibrium or climax condition under certain environmental and biological constraints. But I daresay most people have not understood the phenomena that make their urban environment acceptable or unacceptable as a place to live. Responding to part of this challenge is our task in the chapters ahead.

Woven through many of the descriptions of urban resource problems are implicit challenges to the *reader* to become an active participant in the affairs that determine the direction and evolution of his own human settlement. Many action strategies for resolving pollution problems at local, state, or national levels are yet to be invented. You as a reader are called upon to be a doer either in inventing, modifying, or implementing mechanisms that, in the light of increasing understanding and sharpened sensitivity, will enhance the quality of what might be considered the world's most recent and dynamic resource—a human settlement.

After reading part or all of this edition:

If you become angered from your past complacency . . .

If you have become motivated from new information or a slightly different approach . . .

If a sense of urgency mixed with a sense of hope has been kindled . . .

and

If you have made a commitment to take appropriate and effective action . . .

then our mutual effort toward increased understanding of, greater involvement in, and continued dedication to the difficulties of urban conservation will have been successful. If only some of these suppositions would hold true for you, at least a beginning has been made.

Perhaps a word or two should be said about the philosophy behind this presentation that distinguishes it from other books—especially those that could be used as textbooks. Traditionally a volume such as this is used as a reference for an ample supply of dates, events, names of places, and other inventories of facts. By the same tradition the instructor or professor who uses a traditional text is viewed as a facilitator of resources, a raiser of provocative questions, and one who proposes alternatives and hints at questions that encourage a student to synthesize and move into the area of problem solving. This book tries to fulfill some of the responsibility traditionally given to professors. I hope the perspective is one that may be a fresh approach to resource management and environmental problem analysis. The vast storehouse of factual material will need to be obtained from other sources where constant updating is carried on. But some of the new and necessary questions are raised by one who has always lived in cities, used their resources, and expects that whatever improvement in the quality of life that is possible will also evolve out of our present urban organisms, which are the cities of the world and their inhabitants.

Even though the emphasis here is on American cities and resources, it should be understood that the problems and opportunities of managing urban systems are of worldwide dimensions. In fact, you, the reader, are encouraged to remember that most large human settlements in the United States are especially dependent upon an international supply of resources and that these cities have considerable influence on all of the passengers of Spaceship Earth.

An Environmental Approach from an Urban Perspective

The Conceptual Framework of Urban Conservation

Our Current Dilemma

Prior to the 1970's, the conservation of natural resources was a collection of practices primarily removed from the urban scene. *Conservation* as a philosophy or attitude was essentially envisioned as sustaining or increasing the yield of various resources that lay beyond the jurisdiction or concern of the urban dweller. For the first two centuries of its development, America's scattered and relatively small population put no more than a modest strain on the rich resource base. The *carrying capacity* of the environment in terms of water supply, land productivity, mineral deposits, availability of wildlife, and other biological and physical factors encouraged various forms of human settlement.

When the population was small or scattered, the resource base of water, soil, wildlife, air, open space, and the other essentials for human existence was not taxed beyond its physical capacity to deliver an expected product or service. In addition, the technology for severe and massive resource depletion remained at a miniscule level compared with the massive engineering potential for resource exploitation that is available today. It was not until the midtwentieth century that the sheer numbers of people and the consumption rate joined together to form environmental crises of worldwide dimensions. As *urbanization* and *suburbanization* increased, the burdens of urban wastes, along with the rapidly rising social costs that were imposed upon the metropolitan environment, exceeded the traditional delivery systems. That is, the *metabolic by-products* of immense human settlements were difficult to manage once the urban organism grew to metropolitan size without appropriate funds and technology to undertake

7

Figure 1-1. During the 1970 London garbage workers' strike, solid wastes accumulated in parks and along residential streets. Ordinarily citizens of metropolitan areas are not aware of the amount of metabolic wastes generated by a large human settlement.

Figure 1-2. The ghost town of Independence, Colorado. This settlement supported a population of 1500 people in the 1890's. Timber and minerals were exploited and the transient residents, typical of "extraction" communities, moved on. (U.S. Forest Service)

Figure 1-3. Hobart Hills, California, was abandoned at the end of a logging bonanza in what is now the Tahoe National Forest. (U.S. Forest Service)

Figure 1-4. Many towns dependent on a single resource base boom and die and then revive again. Such has been the case with Silverton, Colorado, shown in this 1957 photograph, east of Main Street. Recreation resources now bolster the town, once a center for gold and silver mining. (U.S. Forest Service)

the ponderous jobs of metropolitan solid waste disposal, air and water pollution control, and transportation and energy supply.

A phenomenon contributing to the saturation of natural support systems is the disassociation of urban man from his traditional resources. The early American homesteader and other pioneers were able to make reasonably good estimates of their land and water needs. When the residents of an early fishing village, logging town, or mining town realized that the major resource base of the community was dwindling, they did not usually become instant conservationists. However, they were aware that the resource was diminished, and after following the normal trend of wringing the last bit of "juice" out of whatever resource was left, they moved on. With the spread of industrialization, a strain was placed on the natural environment that resulted in an apparent separation or isolation of urban man from his sustaining environment. In most cases, the consumer of the resource physically was no longer near the resource being used. Today most citizens of a large city have very little idea what the condition of their resource bases are or if and how something is being done to increase or sustain their yields over time.

Perhaps the very definition of a resource needs updating. Almost automatically the doomsday ecologists of the early 1970's fell into the habit of promoting depletion-oriented definitions of resource use such as the degree of renewability or *nonrenewability*. Considerable attention was given to the stockpiling of scarce, exhaustible, and nonreusable commodi-

Figure 1-5. Mercur, Utah, as a bustling gold-mining town in 1893 experienced its greatest boom. This same site was founded in 1869 as Lewistown, and thrived until 1880 while about $1,000,000 in silver was taken from nearby mines. Since that time, the town has boomed and died periodically. In 1953 all that remained were shells of rock buildings, mammoth ore dumps and tailing piles, a few cabins, and two inhabitants. (Utah State Historical Society)

Figure 1-6. Families of this Greek fishing village on the island of Sifnos are constantly aware of their resource base—the sea.

ties or parts of the natural landscape that are or might be essential for human welfare. Human welfare, in earlier days, usually meant the isolated and provincial caretaking responsibilities for United States citizens instead of a concern for all the passengers on Spaceship Earth who might rightfully wish to share strategic resources. Rather than scarcity being the only criterion in a resource definition, another approach appears to be more rational. A resource becomes a resource only when information about it can be combined with technology to yield something of value to man. Futurist Richard L. Meier has said that most of the so-called natural resources in the world are not worth the expense involved in extracting or making use of them, and are therefore relegated to the submarginal class. They became a true resource only when the scarcity of the primary commodities or services produced from such resources has increased, and the price rises have occurred, or when a significant improvement in technology has been established. However, some of our most important resources involve no consumption and no price as defined by economists. Under other analysis the price of use is in social or ecological denominators not commonly used in the economic marketplace.

Television documentaries, newspaper and magazine articles, papers at scientific meetings, and university lectures on conservation of natural resources have forecast future crises as a result of horrible waste and accelerated exhaustion of rich natural resources. These projections are

11

12   inadequate because they do not consider an acceleration in technology and knowledge. Of course, faulty technology is an ever-present potential pitfall. The collection and use of knowledge are uniquely human activities. Most indications point to potential increases in the efficiency of utilizing and applying knowledge and technology that affects the allocation, use and reuse of natural resources for human needs. Whether or not, and when, that potential increase is realized will be more of a political decision than a biological or physical imperative. Additional knowledge by itself will not solve resource problems, but it will give the citizen and the decision-maker a broader base upon which practices can be implemented to minimize the hazards of resource scarcity. Conservation and its related resource management strategies began when scarcity of a resource met head-on with the scarcity in technology and a knowledge about the resource in question.

Beyond the technology and knowledge consideration, there is the equally critical issue of man's value system. (A value system is the basis on which decisions are made.) The value system of a society is a primary motivation for whatever technological innovations are produced and used. If a value system promulgates consumption of resources beyond a physical capacity to reproduce those resources, eventually depletion will occur. A resource crisis involves value orientation, resource base, knowledge application, and technological innovation.

The major question now is whether the value system, knowledge and technology, and whatever persuasive skills are required to apply them are stronger in the direction of abusing a given resource or in the direction of conserving that resource.

A Period of Exploitation

Near the beginning of the twentieth century, the conservation movement began as a protest against certain logging, wildlife, and mining practices that were going on far beyond the city limits. Conflicts in the management practices of lumbermen, water developers, fish and game managers, and land speculators were increasingly common. Clearly, conservation of resources was not perceived as an urban problem. It was considered even more absurd to think of an urban area as a resource. You, the reader, are asked to consider a city or town as a transformed combination of resources. Perhaps the city or town can be appraised as a "second order" resource inasmuch as it is providing benefits to its inhabitants and to its region or nation. When disadvantages, costs, or turmoil mount beyond the yield of benefits, a city as an urban organism (or as a resource) is usually abandoned. In fact, the major goal of urbanization was to convert the resource base into cities. As a result, early settlers utilized the soils, minerals, wildlife, grasslands, forests, and water with vigorous abandon. As one studies the historical events, he is left with the impression that people believed that the resources at hand were either infinite or scarce enough to justify rapid exploitation before the supply had to be shared among competitors.

Seldom, if ever, during the first two hundred years of United States' expansion was the city seen as a unique system that was directly dependent upon not only the traditional natural resources of land, water, air, and minerals but also upon a continuous yield from the basic human natural resources. Indeed, the time has yet to come when most urban dwellers will perceive their town, city, or metropolis as a recently evolved natural resource whose very survival depends upon successfully competing for human talents as well as for other resources. The private sector and, to a lesser degree, public agencies are competing for qualified personnel. Each employer serves as an unofficial agent for the urban area involved. Thus, in the final analysis, the situation emerges where one city with its respective agents is competing against another city for individuals. That process, in turn, requires that urban areas in competition for human resources (for example, labor force) must then also compete for the increasingly scarce or poorly distributed natural resources that are expected by individuals. In the United States, these traditional resources have a lengthy history of exploitative competition by individuals as well as by public agencies and private corporations.

For example, at an early point in American colonization, wild animal resources reeled under the blow of exploitation. In addition to demands for *trophy animals* for private and public display, Eastern cities and European markets were supplied with vast quantities of furs, hides, and food from the white-tailed deer, elk, beaver, marten, and mink. Human predation was very heavy on the wild turkey, ruffed grouse, heath hen, Canada goose, and the passenger pigeon. As each frontier was opened, no matter whether it was through the St. Lawrence River Valley or over the Cumberland Gap, waterfowl, fish, fur-bearing mammals, and other wildlife were harvested. Perhaps the frontiersmen felt the supply was limitless. The annual slaughter of 250,000 American bison to feed the railroad crews is somber testimony to this perception of a "renewable" resource.

The example of the reduction in quantity and quality of many animal resources (with certain exceptions such as the white-tailed and mule deer) can be shown with all the basic natural resources in the face of unmanaged urbanization. In order for human settlements to thrive, they must take on a *commensal* or mutualistic role of commensalism instead of becoming *parasitic* upon the biological and physical foundations of the environment that sustains an urban organism.

Relative *ecological stability* (which is always in a dynamic flux), is achieved by struggles throughout the period of community succession and by a type of cut-throat competition with the biggest or fiercest coming out on top of the *biological pyramid*. The ironic feature about a quasi-equilibrium condition in any biological community at the climax or "terminal" successional stage is that once the interrelationships of biological factors, soils, temperature, moisture, nutrient availability, and the multitude of others are in dynamic harmony (if we can call it that), a shift in one of the major elements puts the systems into new motion. Ecological stability is a misnomer on one hand; on the other it describes a relative condition over great periods of time when successional changes tend to be a little less gradual. Even towns and villages in their pioneering era tend to exhibit rapid changes in population and function compared with a city or metropolis that has matured or become balanced through economic and cultural diversity over many centuries of competition with other semistabilized urban centers. If the diversity of species is to be maintained, it is imperative to insure the vitality of the various habitats that constitute an *ecosystem*. *Habitat* deterioration is the most forceful element in species elimination. When the decrease in numbers of species begins, one can be relatively certain that the spiral of instability is in motion. Unfortunately, the lesson of ecological succession has not been learned well or experienced widely by urbanites. The long time it has taken for the forest resources to be integrated into our daily residential and commercial activities is indicative. For three hundred years forests were cleared or burned back from the edges of towns to accommodate agricultural land required by growing cities. In later chapters details of the impact of urbanization on specific natural resources are discussed. But at the outset it can be shown that in an effort to conserve the two very scarce factors of production, namely labor and capital, the early settlers naturally turned to the exploitation of land and all its resources in order to accumulate capital.

In turn, part of the capital was utilized to provide machines and other labor-saving schemes for extracting, processing, and using natural resources to accomplish the Herculean task of permanent settlement. When mechanization in urban areas was widely used at an early date, the evolution of cities was accelerated. However, the rapid growth of cities in selected parts of the United States was less a function of mechanization than it was a mix of good agricultural land, a skilled labor force, an invigorating

Figure 1-7. 20th century suburban developers clear forests as ruthlessly as early settlers. Rock Creek watershed, Montgomery County, Maryland appears treeless and grassless, prime factors contributing to topsoil loss and subsequent sedimentation of the Potomac River. (USDA—Soil Conservation Service)

Figure 1-8. Flooding is a natural inundation of the flood plain; too often permanent human invasion of the natural high water area causes property damage as shown in this 1965 Sevierville, Tennessee, flood. (TVA)

climate, an ample water supply, and vast energy and mineral resources, as well as other factors.

In almost every case, exploitation of key resources in or near the vicinity of a human settlement took place without internal regulating mechanisms that could forecast the eventual environmental crisis. More frequently than not, the demise of a specific resource such as the passenger pigeon is explained away by the excuse of "progress." Talismans of careless resource management such as the *Dust Bowl,* excessive air and water pollution, and pesticide residue buildup were hardly heeded by the urban dweller because he assumed he was protected from ecological disaster by technology.

Perhaps one of the most dramatic examples of exploitative resource use over a short time is the settlement of *flood plains.* Depending upon one's point of view, the resource in question is soil, land as open space, land as residential and commercial sites, or human lives. In spatial terms, the flood plain is the land that has been inundated by water that has exceeded its regular channel capacity. Records indicate that under various conditions of *soil porosity,* precipitation, channel characteristics, temperature, and the like, flood waters rise to a given contour line with a statistically predictable frequency but with no forecast about when the high water will occur.

The tragic paradox of the flood plain is easy to visualize. Because of flatness, fertility, and proximity to major transportation systems such as roads, railways, and shipping, man has settled on river *bottomlands.* He has farmed the rich soil deposited by floodwaters since the first signs of

15

Figure 1-9. The losses incurred in the March 1963 flood of Sevierville, Tennessee, were not prevented by federal flood management programs. (TVA)

civilization in Mesopotamia, Greece, and Africa. Even the earliest cities were built in flood hazard areas. Civilizations seem to have come and gone with droughts and floods (although not necessarily in that order). The curious observation that one can make about flood plain settlement is that man has switched from awe and respect to disdain and ignorance about the changes and exploitation of the bottomland as a natural resource.

Valley residents of the Nile, Mekong, Amazon, Congo, Yangtze Kiang, and Ganges rivers have accommodated their life styles to the periodic inundation of flood waters. On the other hand, American flood plain residents have ignored or resisted the limits imposed by natural events of runoff. In the United States, an assumption exists that technology can protect the person who builds in a high hazard flood zone.

Exploitation of the flood plain by agricultural, residential, and commercial interests became common after the damaging waters of the 1920's and 1930's. Before that period, people were not dependent upon federal policy or program for protection from devastating floods. Bottomland dwellers had to fend for themselves, which resulted in a tragic loss of life and property. Even *after* passage of the *Omnibus Flood Control Act of 1936*, flood losses continued to climb from several hundred thousands of dollars per year to over $1 billion in *annual* flood losses in the 1970's. This trend

Figure 1-10. Despite massive federal investments in flood protection, annual losses continue to increase. Here is a devastating flood of February 1966 that struck Gatlinburg, Tennessee. (U.S. Army Corps of Engineers)

continues in spite of nearly $24 billion of public funds that has been invested for flood protection structures since 1936.

Several explanations exist for the rising costs of flood damage, which are given in dollar figures corrected for inflation. As urbanization takes place in the flood plain, much of the natural storage and *absorption* capacity of the soil is lost through the process of draining or filling a wetland. With less of the surface land available for infiltration, an increase in volume and rate of runoff is generated from roads, rooftops, driveways, parking lots, and other "hardened" surfaces. Development after some structural device is installed is perhaps the most serious mistake in flood plain exploitation. Speculative land acquisition downriver from a dam or levee has resulted in increased residential and commercial buildup in areas of high hazard. No amount of protection can guarantee the safety of persons or structures from a flood that exceeds the "highest flood on record." Without a decrease in precipitation and with continual flood plain development, there will always be a chance to have or exceed the "project flood"—that is, a flood that is 10 per cent greater than the highest water level in the historical past.

Some typical figures demonstrate the folly of continual flood plain buildup and exploitation. In 1950, the U.S. Army Corps of Engineers completed flood control projects for the industrial and commercial districts of

Figure 1-11. Urbanization in the watershed and flood plain increase the risk of rapid runoff from hardened surfaces. The tragedy of this scene is that residents probably never knew the location of the flood plain or the degree of hazard that existed in the past. (U.S. Army Corps of Engineers)

Figure 1-12. In Morgan City, Louisiana, it was difficult to find the floodwall (at the left) under water during high water flood conditions on April 14, 1973. Too frequently residential and industrial land uses have encroached on the flood plain far beyond our capacity to guarantee protection. (U.S. Army Corps of Engineers)

Kansas City, Missouri, for a project flood of 170,000 cubic feet per second. The following year, 1951, a flood of 700,000 cubic feet per second inundated the "protected" area. In Klamath, California, a 1955 flood inflicted heavy damage to the community. Federal disaster relief was rushed in and the town was rebuilt on the same flood plain. In 1964 Klamath, California, was hit by flooding again, and all but two of the previously rebuilt structures were washed away in what amounted to almost total devastation to the

town. Man seems to learn very painfully and very slowly about the results of his high-hazard flood plain exploitation.

The larger picture of soil conservation is equally pessimistic over the long term. Consider the millions of years that were required to build up the deep rich soil deposits of the Midwestern United States. A complex interaction of flora and fauna in Silurian, Devonian, and Ordovician seas provided the building blocks for the rich corn belt *loams.* For thousands of

19

Figure 1-13. In Kansas City, Missouri, June 1950, there was an average daily flow past the central industrial district of 6,600 cubic feet per second and an operating flood project designed to handle *170,000 cubic feet per second* had been completed. In this photo, Kansas City, Missouri, July 1951, the central industrial district is submerged by a flood *exceeding 700,000 cubic feet per second!* (U.S. Army Corps of Engineers)

Figure 1-14. Klamath, California, December 1955. Community of approximately 1000 people suffered major flood damage to buildings, roads, structures, and utilities. Federal disaster relief assistance helped rebuild the town. Nine years later another flood destroyed all of the town except two structures. (U.S. Army Corps of Engineers)

Figure 1-15. In addition to the losses suffered by these businesses and the inconvenience of clean up, one must also consider the inches of good topsoil that have been lost to farmers up river. Note the mud on this Main Street the morning after floodwaters receded. (U.S. Army Corps of Engineers)

years since Pleistocene glaciation, the biogeochemical cycles in collaboration with the *biota* and climate produced Midwestern soil deposits of over three feet in depth. Man's incredible ravage and exploitation have sent all but a few inches of the original *topsoil* to the bottom of modern seas and rivers. Graphically illustrating this loss of topsoil is the Mississippi River delta's growth rate of one mile every sixteen years. The exploitation of the soil resource in the flood plain and in agricultural and urban areas will eventually result in a layer of topsoil so thin or so unusable (from increased salinity, *lateralization,* and pesticide accumulations) that strikingly different forms of land-based agriculture will be required. (This is further discussed in Chapter 5, Soil Resources.)

Whether these soil changes took place under the label of flood plain protection or *monospecies* agricultural practice, it is evident that the field practitioners placed an unreasonable amount of faith in technology, and too many of them could not envision the ecological impacts that beset

Figure 1-16. Severe erosion has been the result of clear cutting and copper smelting near Ducktown, Tennessee.

us today. Exploitation of forests, air resources, and minerals, including energy resources, is aggravated by the concentration of people in suburbs and cities. Later chapters outline how the separation of the consumer from the raw material or resource origin also seems to decrease the appreciation and recognition of resource misuse and scarcity. At the same time, situations of excessive mineral waste, air pollution, or reckless logging practices go unheeded and unchallenged as exploitation continues to plague urban Americans and third-world people.

Wilderness and open space, both recently recognized as assets, were subjected to abusive overuse as a result of inappropriately conceived recreation developments. After settlers had established towns and cities and after the industrial revolution had run its course, wild-land resources felt the midtwentieth century blow when urban exports in the form of tourists and campers began to use up, in a very literal sense, the state and national parks. Even though many of the park areas are remote from the massive human settlements that have grown throughout America, parkland and wilderness suffer the spatial pain of overconsumption. Today, places of virtual seclusion and solitude (aside from a different kind of isolation common in cities and suburbs) are so few and far between that most Americans find costs of traveling to them prohibitive.

The City—A Second Echelon Resource

Analogies may be drawn between the biological sciences and the events of human settlements. Some of these analogies are coincidental but at the same time hopefully very instructive. Consistent with the definition of a biological *analogy*, these urban analogies are also descriptions of arrangements that are similar in function but dissimilar in structure and origin. This analogous concept must be distinguished from the *homologous* condition where there may be a difference in type and function, although both structures are derived from a common primitive origin: to illustrate, the wing of a bat and the foreleg of a mouse have mutual embryonic beginnings with their ultimate form dictated by their evolutionary adaptations.

In the perspective of geological time, a city is a very recent evolutionary occurrence. For hundreds of thousands of years, man, in his habit of hunting, gathering, and cultivating, was attracted to the resources that yielded his livelihood. Prairie-dwelling Indian tribes stalked the bison; islanders of various seas plied the coral reefs for their marine harvests; miners established towns that boomed and died on the motherlode; and loggers went where the timber was abundant and left when the forest was cut away without thought or hope of regeneration.

The "harvesting" form of human settlement can still be found today at or near every traditional resource site. But these single resource ranching towns, logging towns, oil or mining towns, "corn belt" towns, or others of the same genus have become minor urban developments in comparison with the large urban centers that are major recipients of many basic resources and raw materials extracted from the hinterlands. Within the last

Figure 1-17. Salida, Colorado, is an example of a human settlement that prospered from basic resource utilization. This community is situated near logging, ranching, and mining activities near the San Isabel National Forest. (U.S. Forest Service)

Figure 1-18. Some "harvesting" types of villages are located in hinterland regions as evidenced by this aerial view of Beaver, Alaska. This extraction form of human settlement is located on the north fork of the Yukon River six miles south of the Arctic Circle in an area with resources that include fish and wildlife, forest products, and minerals. (U.S. Forest Service)

two to three thousand years, every major city has become a resource in its own right—a *second echelon resource* that uses, synthesizes, homogenizes, and concentrates the basic resources supplied by smaller settlements in order to produce goods and services in magnitudes undreamed of by mankind as recently as two hundred years ago. (In such an urban area, no longer does man build his home where the needed natural resources are found, but rather the resources are shipped, sometimes thousands of miles, from their source to the city where they are used.) Even a town that may have begun as a primary resource extractor has, in many cases, evolved in function and in *morphology* into a larger, more diversified, more dynamic urban area—literally a newly created resource.

For instance, the availability of an abundant energy resource, waterpower, determined the location of a majority of early New England towns. Most of the first settlements grew at the *fall line* where the gradient of the river was abrupt enough to produce rapids or falls. When a dam was built, a waterwheel (and later the hydroelectric turbine) harnessed the head or pressure of water created by the pond. Waterpower was one of the essential ingredients in the growth of logging towns. As a bonus to the sawmill and grist mill operations, the town's proximity to the sea enabled easy transportation of raw materials and finished products. The reciprocal phenomena of more immigrant labor and more manufacturing jobs encouraged the growth of paper and pulp, textile, leather, and other manufacturing activities at or near the hydropower site. Diversification took place over time, and several major fall line towns stabilized even after local sources of raw materials and local markets diminished. Some towns such as Waterville, Maine, and Gardner, Massachusetts, do not have resource diversity and therefore undergo periods of severe economic instability. The development of hydroelectric power generation gives flexibility and stability to commercial operations through a broadened base of support. Ordinarily an urban organism founded on renewable resources undergoes more certain evolutionary steps at a more rapid rate than settlements based primarily on exhaustible or nonrenewable resources.

The intent here is to demonstrate that the city, as a totality, is a mixed cultural and natural resource albeit a second order of complexity one *"trophic level"* above the traditional resources described in most textbooks and references written before the 1970's. Instead of viewing an urban area as a static portion of the landscape or as a dead-end dumping ground for

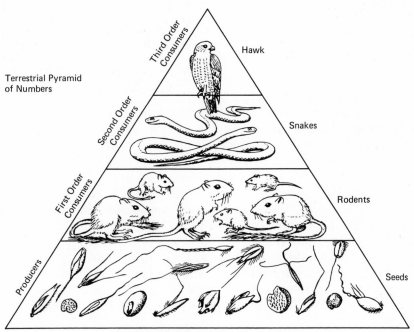

Terrestrial Pyramid of Numbers

Third Order Consumers — Hawk

Second Order Consumers — Snakes

First Order Consumers — Rodents

Producers — Seeds

Marine and Terrestrial Pyramids of Numbers

Figure 1-19. Here is a terrestrial pyramid of numbers showing trophic levels with predators or secondary and tertiary consumers at the top. [Reprinted with permission from Elna and Gerhard Bakker, *An Island Called California* (Berkeley: University of California Press, 1972), p. 17]

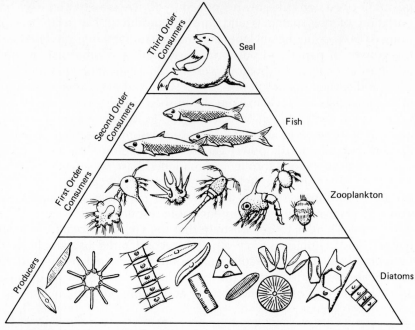

Figure 1-20. Marine trophic levels are shown in this schematic diagram with upper level consumers supported by producers in the form of diatoms and other phytoplankton. [Reprinted with permission from Elna and Gerhard Bakker, *An Island Called California* (Berkeley: University of California Press, 1972), p. 17]

biological and mineral cycles, a large urban area is considered here as a continually resynthesizing component of the human ecosystem.[1]

The "trophic level" concept is borrowed from *ecology*—the study of interrelationships and consequences of an organism, the species population (*autecology*) or a community of organisms (*synecology*) affecting an environment and vice versa. Different members of a biological community occupy different positions or trophic levels of production, consumption, energy transfer, and energy loss. The most fundamental members, known as *primary producers,* contain *photosynthetic* pigment (for example, chlorophyll a and b) These primary producers provide foodstuffs basic for the next trophic level, which in turn provides it for the next.

In the presence of sunlight, water, and carbon dioxide, these producers photosynthesize a potential food supply for organisms unable to manufacture their own. This basic or primary trophic level is occupied by plant

[1]U.S. Bureau of the Census, *Statistical Abstract of the United States, 1970,* 91st ed. (Washington, D.C., 1970), p. 15. In 1950 the Bureau of the Census adopted the concept of the urbanized area and delineated boundaries for unincorporated places. All the population residing in urban fringe areas and in unincorporated places of 2,500 or more is classified as urban according to the current definition.

kingdom members ranging in size from the unicellular algae to the towering *angiosperms* and *gymnosperms* of the Pacific Northwest forests. The urban analogues of producer representatives are, of course, the fishing, farming, logging, or mining towns whose major activity is making basic resources available to larger urban areas at the next highest trophic level.

Just as there are *herbivores* or organisms that depend directly on the primary producers, so there are larger urban areas that are not involved in extractive activities but act as consumers of raw materials. The raw materials are "produced" by primary producer-type settlements such as the ranching, mining, logging, or fishing villages.

Figure 1-21. In urban trophic levels, urban primary producers provide the foundation for the pyramid of numbers. "Extraction communities" that center around mining, ranching, fishing, and logging are examples.

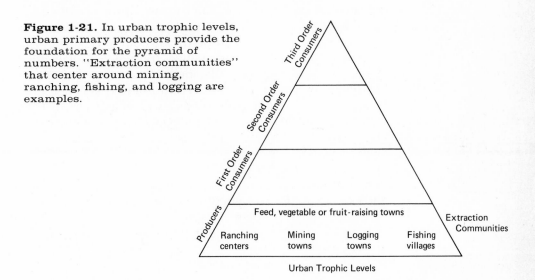

Figure 1-22. Directly dependent on the "producer communities" are the first order or primary consumer towns that carry out primarily functions of meat processing, smelting, milling, canning and other prewholesaling and wholesaling activities.

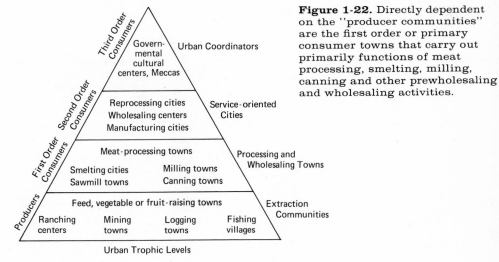

28   As the second trophic level of urban organisms evolves, many employment activities shift toward service, reprocessing, wholesale operations, and
other middleman functions. With the growth of this kind of urban organism, diversity of production and complexity increases. Illustrations that
immediately come to mind include Atlanta, Boston, Chicago, Denver, New
Orleans, Minneapolis-St. Paul, and Omaha. These are all cities whose
primary raison d'être has changed and expanded through the years. Second,
third, and fourth level transformation activities become common as food,
fiber, metal, and other commodities are reprocessed, refabricated, reused,
and then used again. In a considerably more thorough transformation,
biological communities recycle and lose energy as one predator is eaten
by another predator who in turn falls victim to perhaps a parasite and
eventually a *decomposer* in the form of bacteria or fungi of decay.

Thus the fate of natural resources can be traced from original sites of
extraction or production to secondary and tertiary consumers. Usually the
first step of refinement takes place near the origin of the resource; fish are
cleaned and frozen; petroleum is deemulsified; iron ore is sintered and
upgraded; trees are cut and scaled; and gravel is washed and sorted. The
next step in the utilization of a resource produces an array of specified
processed raw materials in the form of fish meal, paraffin, ingots, lumber
or fiberboard, and concrete mix.

Up to 90 per cent of the resources extracted from the hinterland eventually find their way to urban areas as the city becomes a concentrator of
resources. As the resources are converted from their raw form into commodities such as automobiles, frozen TV dinners, and Touch Dial tele-
phones through a series of reprocessing steps, considerable waste of the
basic resource takes place. This resource waste occurs from rust and corrosion, from the disposal of packaging materials and losses from other non-

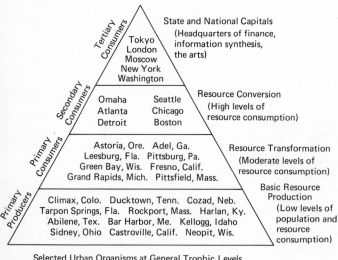

Selected Urban Organisms at General Trophic Levels

Figure 1-23. The
concept of urban
trophic levels is more
clearly visualized if
one identifies specific
urban organisms that
carry out the major
producer-consumer
functions mentioned
in the narration. The
cities and towns listed
here were selected as
convenient
illustrations from
various areas.

cyclical procedures, and is similar to the matter lost through nonrecycling in natural systems. The increased knowledge and sophisticated technology required to produce such commodities form information resources that can be used to prevent breakdowns in the biophysical, economic, and social systems that produce and use the highly processed original resources.

Man himself demonstrates the result of energy transformation as he participates in a predator role in the world's natural food chains. It is impossible to avoid loss of energy as carbohydrates, fats, and proteins move up through the trophic levels from producer to consumer. The Second Law of Thermodynamics shows that no energy transformation can be 100 per cent efficient. We always end up with less usable energy after the transfer, with most of the lost energy being transformed into heat.

The example of one predator eating another will serve as a dramatic illustration. With the salmon or any high-level *carnivore,* a rather complete sequence of energy loss can be shown from primary producer to ultimate consumer. Let us assume that 1 per cent of the solar energy that is available to the algal "food factories" on the ocean's surface is converted or incorporated into the plant. Inasmuch as the algae require some energy for "housekeeping" functions such as respiration, growth, and reproduction, an immediate energy loss begins with the primary producer. It should be noted that terrestrial plants are usually somewhat less efficient in their use of radiant energy than fresh water or marine vegetation. Most aquatic plants, especially the floating and submergent species, are spared the need for extensive supporting structures as well at the work needed to acquire and transport nutrients; that is, they require less energy for maintenance functions than terrestrial relatives whose leaves, roots, trunks, bark, and attractive floral parts are specialized accessories not required by the *phytoplankton* of the lakes and oceans.

To continue with the "biological pecking order," the algae are eaten by members of the next trophic level such as the snails and other mollusks. Vast numbers of invertebrates from the protozoa to the crustaceans are also primary consumers who feed upon primary producers. The taxonomic group, however, has nothing to do with who eats whom or what. Vertebrates from almost all families have some members who are primarily vegetarians. Some of the largest mammals, the baleen whales, sift and screen *zooplankton* and phytoplankton from the sea, illustrating how the intermediate steps of the food chain (and subsequent trophic level energy losses) are bypassed. The more common energy route is for the algae to be eaten by *microcrustaceans.* The microcrustaceans in turn may be eaten by other crustaceans or small fish who are eaten by larger fish who eventually feed the predacious salmon species. Energy loss takes place during normal activities. Obviously when the salmon is consumed by the fisherman or the gourmet, it is a miniscule fraction of the energy originally synthesized by the algae that served as primary producer. A fair estimate is that about 10 per cent of the total energy consumed by one trophic level is synthesized into one biomass of the next.

30   Too often the illustration stops at this point. The important factor to remember is that regardless where one consumer is on the food chain, there is another link. The chain is a continual loop where the decomposers are always available or waiting to perform the vital task of reconverting and recycling inorganic elements as a part of the decomposition process. Perhaps it is misleading to speak of a biological pyramid because regardless of whatever or whoever is at the top of the pyramid, that individual salmon, man, or hawk eventually succumbs to the relentless consumers or decomposers who prepare the basic ingredients for use by the primary producers. Thus the endless loop continues with *entropy* taking its gradual harvest from the total system. When a given genus no longer plays an active role as producer and consumer, *atrophy* sets in.

Similar catabolic processes affect the urban organism. Net loss of population, diminution of the percentage of young adults, a decrease in new business development, and increased residential and commercial vacancies are among factors that over long periods of time determine the viability of a community. In some cases, the city becomes a nonfunctioning vestige; in other examples it becomes a vital producing organism.

Conservation and Its Recent Extension—
Urban Conservation

Thus far the discussion has centered on traditional natural resources and biological implications of resource use. Having introduced man as a key figure in the urban resource and before beginning a presentation of urban conservation's basic concepts, it is helpful to review the use of the term *conservation*. The evolution of the definition itself is a reflection of an increased emphasis upon urban man and his relationships with the total environment.

The word *conservation* was first used by Gifford Pinchot in a nationwide context during the early part of the Theodore Roosevelt administration when the movement of conservation was implemented as part of a political platform in 1902. Although during the past seventy years conservation has held different meanings, for most people, the word probably stimulates the image of preservation. However, preservation should not be synonymous with conservation. Dean Emeritus Samuel Trask Dana of the University of Michigan's School of Natural Resources was quoted in a February 1970 issue of the *Michigan Journalist* as saying, "When I was young, conservation was the cause," but he was quick to point out that "conservation has changed its meaning. Now anything the speaker likes is conservation and anything he doesn't, isn't." Dean Dana is justifiably perturbed by the vague use that is so often made of the word. He goes on to say, "Now the preservationists say the utilizers aren't conservationists anymore. I'd just as soon see the word abolished." However, the word has not been abolished. In fact, instead of disappearing, the definitions of conservation have proliferated. As a documentation of the most commonly used concepts, a three-way classification of terms is now given under the categories of General, Physical, and Ecological definitions.

General Definitions

The first definitions of conservation were of a general nature, leaving much of the interpretation of the term in the hands of the individual. This type of definition has continued to be popular to the present day. Because of the historical interest in the definition of "the greatest good for the greatest number" and the confusion over the origin of this definition, several of the earliest versions are listed.

1. ". . . McGee . . . defined the new policy as the use of the natural resources for the greatest good of the greatest number for the longest time." (W. J. McGee, Head of Bureau of American Ethnology.)[2]

2. ". . . where conflicting interests must be reconciled, the question will always be decided from the standpoint of the greatest good of the greatest number in the long run." (Quotation from letter of James Wilson, Secretary of Agriculture, to Gifford Pinchot, Forest Service, Feb. 1, 1905, the letter actually having been written by Pinchot.)[3]

3. "Conservation means 'the greatest good to the greatest number—and that for the longest time.'"[4]

4. "Conservation seeks to insure to society the maximum benefit from the use of our natural resources. It involves the making of inventories, efforts at preservation, the discovery and prompt employment of methods of more efficient use, and the renewal and even restoration of resources."[5]

5. "And Conservation is more than the wise use and ecological preservation of natural resources—mineral, soil and water, plant and animal, human. It may well be the foundation of new social philosophy. Our public land policies, anti-trust regulations, tariffs, and related laws were developed around the exploitation of natural resources, and they helped materially to promote our present economy. Is it not reasonable to suppose, then, that laws and regulations which promote the conservation of resources will help to build a new attitude toward the environment in which we live? And from this may well develop a way of life as different from the prevailing one as that is different from culture of the past."[6]

[2]Gifford Pinchot, *Breaking New Ground* (New York: Harcourt Brace Jovanovich, Inc., 1947), p. 326.

[3]Ibid., p. 261.

[4]Charles R. Van Hise, *The Conservation of Natural Resources in the United States* (New York: Macmillan Publishing Co. Inc., 1910), p. 379.

[5]A. F. Parkins, and J. R. Whitaker, et al., *Our Natural Resources and Their Conservation* (London: John Wiley Sons, Inc., 1939), p. ix.

[6]Edward H. Graham, *Natural Principles of Land Use* (New York: Oxford University Press, 1944), p. 231.

32   Economic Definitions

Economists frequently define conservation in specific terms of use rates over time for physical resources. The following definitions are selected examples.

1. ". . . the heart of the conservation problem 'is the determination of the proper rate of discount on the future with respect to the utilization of our natural resources.'"[7]

2. "Conservation is any act reducing the rate of consumption or exhaustion for the avowed purpose of benefiting posterity."[8]

3. "Conservation is tied to a particular aspect of use; it is concerned with the *when* of use. . . . In conservation, the redistribution of use is in the direction of the future; in depletion, in the direction of the present."[9]

Ecological Definitions of Conservation

This group of definitions emphasizes man's interrelationships with natural resources.

1. "Conservation is a state of harmony between man and land."[10]

2. "Conservation in the broadest sense is probably the most important application of ecology. Unfortunately, the term 'conservation' suggests 'hoarding', as if the idea were simply to ration static supplies so that there would be some left for the future. The aim of good conservation is to insure a continuous yield of useful plants, animals, and materials, by establishing a balanced cycle of harvest and renewal."[11]

3. In the last several years ecologist Stanley A. Cain has proposed an operational definition of conservation, which also embodies its historical development. Eight terms are used to provide a framework for making the definition explicit: preservation, restoration, beneficiation, maximization, reutilization, substitution, integration, and allocation.

Professor Cain acknowledges the pitfalls of the partial understandings portrayed in the oversimplified definition. In his teaching and in the syllabus for his University of Michigan course, Natural Resource Ecology, Cain preferred to describe what people do when they say conservation:

a. *Preservation.* The conservation movement started with the preservation of certain natural resources from destructive use. It included the protection of plant and animal species from commercial use, the avoidance of spoiling magnificent scenery and natural wonders, and the leaving intact of natural

[7] L. C. Gray, "Economic Possibilities of Conservation," *Quarterly Journal of Economics* Vol. XXVII (1913), p. 499; by Arthur C. Bunce, *Economics of Soil Conservation,* (Ames Iowa: Iowa State College Press, 1945), p. 2.

[8] Erich W. Zimmermann, *World Resources and Industries* (New York: Harper & Row, Publishers, Inc., 1951), p. 807.

[9] S. V. Ciriacy-Wantrup, *Resource Conservation, Economics, and Policies* (Los Angeles: University of California Press; 1952), p. 51.

[10] Aldo Leopold, *A Sand County Almanac,* (New York: Oxford University Press, 1949), p. 207.

[11] Eugene P. Odum, *Fundamentals of Ecology* (Philadelphia: W. B. Saunders Company, 1953), p. 317.

ecosystems. This type of conservation results in the establishment of wildlife sanctuaries, wilderness areas, and parks. It also includes the removal from immediate use of timber stands without implying permanent reservation.

b. *Restoration.* Much of conservation is the restoration to high productivity of abused and misused natural resources. This has been called 'repairing the biosphere,' and consists of correcting man's inadvertent or heedless mistakes in handling natural resources.

c. *Beneficiation.* This term originally referred to the several processes that permit the economic use of low-grade ores of iron, copper, etc., but it has been extended to include the upgrading of any natural resource so as to yield more of a desired good or service.

d. *Maximization.* This aspect of conservation is the avoidance of waste through efficient use of natural resources, and the production of the most possible utilities.

e. *Reutilization.* Many natural resources can be used in such a manner that they can be used again, as water that is cleaned of pollution and used again, or the reaggregation of scrap metals for use. Much recycling of matter goes on in nature; reutilization as a matter of conservation refers to what man does to enable the reuse of a natural resource.

f. *Substitution.* When a resource gets scarce its price tends to go up. A conservation practice in this sense is the active search for substitutes of common for scarce and renewable for nonrenewable natural resources.

g. *Integration.* Because natural resources are interrelated and interacting in nature, and because man's actions are interrelated, single-purpose use of a natural resource may maximize a given use but not maximize the net benefits which could be had from a group of related resources. The principle of integrated use takes these facts into consideration and plans for the greatest net socio-economic utility.

h. *Allocation.* A single resource or a resource complex can be used in more than one way. Economic systems combine the allocation of natural resources by the price system in a free economy with a certain amount of social allocation. When the general good over-rides individual or private interest, there is a public determination of the use to which a resource is put. This is social allocation. Much of the governmental role in the field of natural resources is concerned with the social allocation of their use."[12]

At the risk of adding still another definition to the collection, the author submits his version as follows: conservation is an operational collection of ecological knowledge and skill applied in a way to understand and manage as many consequences of an environmental activity as possible in keeping with the expectations of all participants—plants and animals including man. The array of resources at man's disposal can be conserved through appropriate management under that definition that stresses comprehensive, harmonious management based on a value orientation of social equity.

[12]Stanley A. Cain, *Natural Resource Ecology—Class Syllabus* (Ann Arbor, Michigan: University of Michigan, 1965), mimeo; pp. 129–131.

34   An urban conservation philosophy is needed to give the urban resident in America or elsewhere a new hope and efficacy about the metropolis as a resource. The concept of urban conservation requires a comprehensive knowledge and understanding of the urban area and it should provide incentives for creative experimentation with the relatively young resource. Perhaps no other nation in the world has the capability to do the job better than the United States. However, if the American engineering and economic and political expertise fail to provide wide-scale opportunities for quality urban environmental livability, there is no place where that failure would be more humiliating.

In question are the resources such as air and water that affect and are affected by a massive urban complex. Yet individual resource practices have never had an overall synthesis or integration. The need for a comprehensive urban conservation approach becomes apparent when one appreciates the increasingly heavy demand that huge human settlements impose on the natural environment. Innovations in technologies that consume natural resources seem to outweigh and outpace technologies that conserve urban-dependent resources such as air, water, and open space. For example, cities give priority to water purification systems; considerably later attention is directed to proper waste water treatment facilities. In many cases, the time lag for dealing with input considerations (for example, water, foodstuffs, and raw materials for industry) and output realities (for example, waste water, garbage, and solid or gaseous wastes) may be thirty to forty years.

One explanation for the lack of comprehensive urban-related resource management is that each specialist is working diligently in a specific area of expertise. Neither the private sector nor most forms of urban government provide an overview that would consider interrelationships between various resource decision-makers. As an ecologist studies or manages a biological community, he does his best to analyze the array of physical, social, biological, and *synergistic factors* that are in concert to achieve certain results. The best way for urban ecological considerations to be used for management is to undertake an analysis of the critical elements of a human settlement and then devise management strategies that take into account the vital urban elements and their interdependencies.

In order further to understand the concept of urban conservation, it is helpful to dissect the urban organism into its most fundamental elements or systems. Years of medical research have produced a wealth of knowledge on mammals, and so the task of separating the different mammalian systems for study is relatively simple. Textbooks are available on the circulatory, nervous, skeletal, muscular, reproductive, and endocrine systems of man. The physiology, morphology, and taxonomy of maples, for example, is also well understood and documented. But biological, physical, and social sciences have not gathered a workable body of knowledge on the functioning of a human settlement and have hardly gathered enough data and knowledge to fully understand the functioning of a "natural" community.

Even with the information that does exist, it has yet to be used in any **35** substantial way to prescribe and direct improvements in the redevelopment of old cities or in the creation of new communities in the United States.

An Anatomy of Human Settlements

An anatomy of the urban settlement reveals five elements: nature, man, society, shells (buildings), and networks (communications, canals, electrical transmission lines, transportation, and sewerage lines). C. A. Doxiadis, in his study of *ekistics,* or the science of human settlement, has elaborated on how the five elements, even though they arise at different times, even-

Figure 1-24. The five ekistic units of Nature, Man, Society, Shells, and Networks provide a new approach for an analysis of the problems of all human settlements. (From C. A. Doxiadis, *Ekistics,* Hutchinson of London, 1968.)

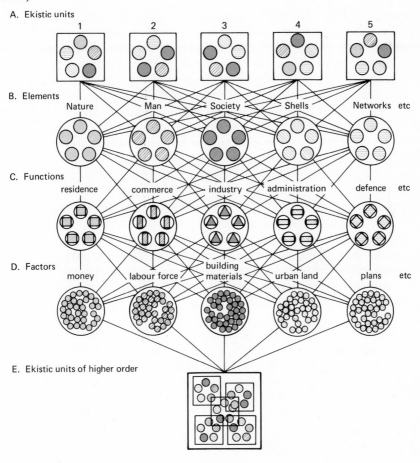

36   tually become interconnected into one system that can be called the "molecule of the city." He goes on to say that if we break the molecule into atoms and subtract or fail to recognize one of the parts, there is no longer a city. The heavy emphasis in the Doxiadis approach to understanding human settlements of all sizes is to appraise the interrelationships or forces that exist between the five basic elements that he has identified. The descriptive paragraph for each of the urban elements will be enhanced if each reader applies illustrations from his personal experience.

Nature

All of the primary resources mentioned earlier are included in this category. Water resources, mineral resources, soil resources, air resources, even the plant life and animal life exclusive of man make up the raw materials that are prerequisites for a human settlement. Other subdivisions of the Nature element are the geomorphology, the weather and climate. Included also are the chemical cycles that are in operation, and the other biological and ecological forces that are at work.

Man

In listing the five basic elements of a settlement, there is a temptation to suggest that one or two elements may be dominant or more important. But this temptation is avoided in the subcategory, Man, with special caution and bold apologies to fellow *Homo sapiens*. Such an anatomy of an urban area, at least at the outset, should give each element equal weight and importance. "Man" brings to attention individual human needs of security, aesthetics, space, light, air, and emotional requirements. Personal attitudes, perceptions, and the five human senses are fully represented in addition to man's biological needs.

Society

Man's proclivity to congregate for various reasons dictates the need to consider social and cultural imperatives of urban formations. Under the societal element one should include economic development, educational provisions, population density, composition, and cycles, plus the institutional inventions of religion, courts, government, general health, and welfare. Subunits of group value systems, social stratification, power structure, and racial interactions need to be known.

Shells

Frequently when the elements of Nature, Man, and Society evolve in synchrony, the shells of housing and public structures stand as logical outgrowths of a process instead of idiosyncrasies of an architectural period. Shells or the structures that house families, public activities, and regional operations include houses, schools, town halls, centers for shopping, recreation, medical facilities, performing arts, industry, or transportation facilities such as an airport or bus terminal.

Networks

The circulation of goods, services, and people are analyzed under Networks. The physical or electronic facilities that provide the lifeblood of the urban organism are classified as a unique denominator. Specific examples include water supply and sewerage systems, runoff or drainage works and flood protection structures, communication and mass media systems; oil, gas, and electrical pipelines and grids; and the various transportation systems of air, water, highway, and rail. Networks portray the linkages established between inhabitants of an urban area with special reference to function, scale, and location of interaction.

The reader will observe that there is parallelism lacking in this division of knowledge about urban organisms. That is, instead of a consistent or systematic taxonomy, the listing of urban elements becomes more complex from one element to the next. Every subsequent category builds upon ingredients of the preceeding element; but at the same time each additional element adds a special contribution to the total. For example, the category, Man, has evolved from the systems of Nature and added the emotional, psychological, and moral values to the classification. Or in the case of Networks, connections are made between units of the previous category, Shells. In addition, Networks should take into account ecological implications (Nature), emotional, psychological, and other needs of individuals (Man) and cultural, legal, and social considerations raised in the element called Society. Unfortunately, the specialists in each of the five elements have seldom collaborated on a plan for a new urban area. A simultaneous study of all elements is imperative for future settlements.

It is assumed that too often the dissection of a city takes place with attention given to only one or two of the elements. Let us say, that transportation (Networks) and commerical or residential buildings (Shells) are emphasized by a particular city developer. The life-sustaining qualities of the city will undoubtedly suffer when several of the elements are provided for without equal consideration and provision for the other elements such as Nature with its biological and geographical implications, Man with all of his psychological and individual attributes, and Society with the social and cultural implications. A discussion of this kind of imbalance will come up later in remarks dealing with urban metabolism.

Hopefully, the assumption is reasonably clear that human settlements have been and are evolving. The clumping together of man, his physical structures and social linkages, becomes increasingly complex. The organism, metropolis, emerges as a resource, and as a part of the total ecosystem that yields certain utilities to man in the form of goods and services including reservoirs of information. The goods and services are understood to be greater personal and economic security, better education, better medical services, more leisure time, a greater variety of human contact, and a generally higher level of amenities or a better material standard of living than was available in the scattered habitations of rural or hinterland settlement. This concept of an urban area as a resource fits many of the tradi-

38   tional definitions, but seldom is any mention given to the city as a resource in the current literature. Table 1-1 is a typical listing of various resource categories with the human settlement conspicuously absent. The author hastens to add that his citation of Table 1-1 does not reflect his endorsement. He disagrees with several points including the notion that exhaustion is a certainty for glass and sand in the nonreusable category. Also it is disappointing not to find the concept of a "flow resource" used in the category of renewable resources.

The traditional resources in the twentieth century are equally if not more important than they were hundreds of years ago. Much of the soil of the Great Plains has become depleted. Americans, in an effort to conserve and allocate their own mineral resources over time, are using minerals of other

Table 1-1. Natural Resource Classification[1]

I. *Inexhaustible*
    A. *Immutable.* Seemingly incapable of much adverse change through man's activities.
        1. *Atomic energy.* Vast quantities of fissionable materials available in granitic rocks.[2]
        2. *Wind power.* The result of climatic conditions.
        3. *Precipitation.* An unlimited supply. Man, however, will very likely alter the distribution pattern in the future. Weather modification.
        4. *Water power of tides.* Resulting from sun-moon-earth relationships.
    B. *Misusable.* Little danger of complete exhaustion, but when improperly used their resource quality may be impaired.
        1. *Solar power.* The total amount received by growing plants has been reduced by air pollution caused by man.
        2. *Atmosphere.* Local and world-wide pollution because of smoke, exhaust fumes, nuclear fall-out, and so on.
        3. *Waters of oceans, lakes, and streams.* All currently being polluted at increasing rates as a result of human activity.
        4. *Water power of flowing streams.* The reaction of water to gravity.
        5. *Scenery in its broadest sense.* Aesthetic values subject to impairment by human activities. Examples: Mt. Rainier, Blue Ridge Mountains, Oregon and Maine coastlines, Grand Canyon.

II. *Exhaustible*
    A. *Maintainable.* Those resources in which permanency is dependent upon method of use by man.
        1. *Renewable.* The living (biotic) or dynamic resources whose perpetual harvest is dependent upon proper planning and management by man. Improper use results in impairment or exhaustion with adverse socio-economic consequences for man.
            a. *Water in place.* The quantity and quality of water in specific places of use: streams, lakes, subterranean sources.
            b. *Soil fertility.* The ability of soil to produce plant substance desirable to man. Renewing soil fertility takes time and money.
            c. *Products of the land.* Those resources grown in or dependent on the soil.
                (1) *Agricultural products.* Vegetables, grains, fruits, fibers, and so on.
                (2) *Forests.* Source of timber and wood pulp.
                (3) *Forage land.* Sustains herds of cattle, sheep, and goats for the production of meat, milk, leather, and wool.
                (4) *Wild animals.* Deer, wolves, eagles, bluebirds, bullfrogs, spotted salamanders, sphinx moths, fireflies, and so on.

nations. Only recently has forestry become a farming practice in order to sustain yield over long periods of time. Fish and animal wildlife are being artificially propagated or stocked in order to withstand the increased fishing and hunting pressures from urban sportsmen. This presentation is not deemphasizing the long-recognized resources but is simply taking an additional step in suggesting that the large dynamic city is another resource, in fact a mixture of first- and second-order resources, to be added to the list of natural resources available to man.

During the industrial revolution, the resource we know as a city was considered by many to be evil, suppressive, and something to be distrusted and avoided. This feeling undoubtedly became prevalent because several of the elements were ones developed or overemphasized at the cost of

Table 1-1. (continued)

---

      d. *Products of lakes, streams, and impoundments.* Freshwater fish: black bass, lake trout, catfish.

      e. *Products of the ocean.* Marine fish: herring, tuna. Marine mammals: porpoises, gray whales, Pribilof fur seals.

      f. *Human powers.* Physical and spiritual.

  2. *Nonrenewable.* Once gone there is no hope of replacement.

      a. *Species of wildlife.* The passenger pigeon, great auk, and Carolina paroquet have become extinct. They represented the end products of perhaps a million years of evolution.

      b. *Specimen wilderness.* Within several human lifespans wilderness values cannot be restored even with the most dedicated program.

B. *Nonmaintainable.* The mineral resources. Total quantity is static. Mineral resources are regarded as wasting assets. When destroyed or consumptively used, they cannot be replaced.

  1. *Reusable.* Minerals whose consumptive usage is small. Salvage or reuse potentialities are high.

      a. *Gem minerals.* Rubies, emeralds, and so on.

      b. *Nonconsumptively used metals.* Gold, platinum, and silver; some iron, copper, and aluminum. These metals can be extracted and reworked into new products: jewelry, silverware, vases, and so on.

  2. *Nonreusable.* Those minerals with a high or total consumptive use. Exhaustion is a certainty.

      a. *Fossil fuels.* When consumed, gases (potential pollutants), heat,[3] and water are released.

      b. *Most nonmetallic minerals.* Glass sand,[4] gypsum, salt,[5] and so on.

      c. *Consumptively used metals.* Lead in high-octane gasoline and in paint, zinc in galvanized iron, tin in toothpaste containers, iron in cans, and so on.

---

[1] Oliver S. Owen, *Natural Resource Conservation: An Ecological Approach* (New York: Macmillan Publishing Co., Inc., 1971), pp. 10–12.

[2] and fusionable materials in the sea. Man may be very capable of seriously reducing the fissionable materials available on earth. Atomic energy through fusion is another story for it would appear that there is an almost inexhaustible supply of the hydrogen isotope, deuterium, in the sea.

[3] Heat is also a potential pollutant.

[4] At the present rate of consumption, the sand used for glass is estimated to last 3 billion years.

[5] Salt in the ocean would also seem practically inexhaustible.

40   man, nature, and a special faction of society. But during this postindustrial period in American history, the uniqueness of the urban resource is that a synthesis and transformation of basic resources takes place. Energy is concentrated by a large city as are intellectual, spiritual, and cultural expressions aggregated with special intensity in cities.

The Challenge of Urban Conservation

A major question looms: can the planner and builder of cities and its suburbs link the use of traditional resources with the new resource, the city itself? This question clearly poses the dilemma of resource allocation and human satisfaction. Man is both the guinea pig and the potential research director of the urban conservation challenge that lies ahead.

It has been suggested that the recently evolved dynamic human settlement is an organism of tremendous complexity that is bidding for survival. Whether *megalopolis* and other forms of human settlement make it or not in the centuries ahead may depend on our present efforts to redirect the physiology, morphology, and genetics of the urban organism. Whatever replication of settlements continues must be in synchrony with the physical and ecological imperatives that are at work on Spaceship Earth. To do less than this puts the social, physical, and biological futures of the largest cities in serious question.

Undoubtedly, there will be man-created environmental tragedies in the years ahead in addition to the natural catastrophes that have historically plagued man. The task at hand is to reduce the severity and frequency of man-created environmental disasters as we continue to urbanize. In order to be preserved as a system that achieves goals for its residents, the urban resource is in need of better design and management. There is a critical need for a citizenry that is more knowledgeable, more motivated, and more concerned about the urban resource and its traditional counterparts. Such increased motivation might begin to foster changes in behavior, changes in attitudes of the citizenry, and eventually changes in the urban condition itself.

Prescriptions for Action

The first building block in conceptual foundations of urban conservation, is a description of the physical and biological features that comprise the urban system. The second consideration deals with how an urbanite can move to the level of prescribing and implementing changes in a given urban situation once he has identified and understood the problems of his community or settlement. Simply stated, "action" is the second ingredient of urban conservation as presented here. The third step is an effort to monitor what actions have been attempted and determine which have succeeded or failed and why. This third feature, testing the effectiveness of various urban conservation practices, has been overlooked at very high costs. Most innovative and successful strategies for managing urban resources have survived by chance or have been "rediscovered" time after time. If any rational guidance or direction is to be given to new urban areas (or to the restoration of present ones), the citizenry can ill afford to ignore the successes and failures of previous or present urban resource experiments such as Peking, China; Constantinople (Istanbul), Turkey; Athens, Greece; Rome, Italy; Florence, Italy; Paris, France; London, England; Stockholm, Sweden; Salt Lake City, Utah; Los Angeles, California; Radburn, New Jersey; Columbia, Maryland; Reston, Virginia; or Valencia, California.

Urban conservation, like water conservation or wildlife conservation, is a management strategy. In this approach the problems of an urban area are systematically identified. Alternative solutions to the problems are presented, and the application of solutions is initiated through various public and private mechanisms. But before any of these steps can take place in a programmed way, the concept of how man can best be provided for in his urban "container" must be clearly understood and valued.

Walls in Biological Organisms and Urban Organisms

Man's experimentation with the containers of human settlements is limited. As urban builder Constantinos A. Doxiadis and historian Arnold Toynbee have pointed out, man has lived in urban configurations for more than five thousand years. One must compare this time against several million years that *Homo sapiens* has frequented the earth's landscape. As nomadic wanderers temporarily gathered together, the experiment of human groupings began. The theory that security and general welfare are increased by clumpings of people was tested countlessly from the settlements of Mesopotamia to the cliff-dwelling, apartment-building Indians of the American Southwest.

Despite the problem Jericho had with its walls, man used revetments around his cities on a trial and error basis for three thousand years. The concept of a definite boundary between an organism and its external environment is, of course, not the invention of urban organisms. The creation of a cell wall and cell membrane is one of the most profound and earliest biological inventions. The cell membrane is a differentially permeable membrane and has at least four fundamental tasks: (1) to keep the interior in, (2) to keep the exterior out, (3) to enable that which is inside to get out, and (4) to allow that which is outside and needed inside to get in.

For a moment think of how a cell membrane performs these four tasks with specific examples. Consider the extensively studied *Chlorella*, a unicellular alga. Or use the specialized *sclerenchyma* or *chlorenchyma* cells

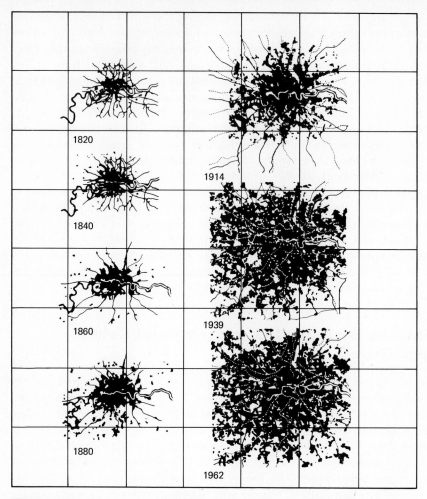

Figure 1-25. The pattern of London's growth and expansion, superimposed on a grid 20 × 20 kilometers, dramatizes how cities with or without walls, with or without greenbelts often expand beyond an "urban container." (C. A. Doxiadis, *Ekistics*)

found in woody shrubs. The osmotic gradient can be shifted out of equilibrium by the presence of high salt concentrations exterior to the cell membrane. Water passes through the porous wall toward high salt accumulations. Consequently the cell becomes limp and the plant wilts. If through dilution of the high salt concentrations the *osmotic* differential is returned to normal before the plant dies, *turgidity* is restored.

Of course, the reverse of the event just described is possible. If, through the manipulation of the interior or exterior environment, the passage of water into the cell is excessive, the cell could burst from the pressure built up within. Animal membranes exhibit considerably more resilience. In fact, the membrane of the common *Amoeba* demonstrates unusual abilities of engulfing food particles and changing its shape as it moves in an aqueous medium with its everchanging *pseudopodia*. As one makes observations about membranes and cell walls up the *phylogenetic* ladder, it soon becomes obvious that specializations that are common among the protozoa and colonial algae generally become more specialized in more advanced phyla. The outer skin (or body wall) of mollusks, echinoderms, insects, fishes, and amphibians exemplifies unusual design and function for the accomplishment of these four tasks described.

Mammals rank very high in skin specialization with the various dermal layers that provide thermal regulation, sensory stimulation receptors of tactile, chemosensory (taste and smell), visual, and auditory qualities. The indented and deeply convoluted surface areas of the digestive and respiratory systems illustrate how materials (food, oxygen, and carbon dioxide) are exchanged between interior and exterior environments of man. Highly specialized lung tissues in the alveoli have a two cell separation between the atmosphere and the hemoglobin-rich red blood cells, which are the vehicles that transport carbon dioxide and oxygen to and from one of nature's specialized "loading docks."

If the notion of a living organism's wall (membrane or skin) has stirred some curiosity, make the transition from the epidermal wall of the human individual to the structural wall of the human family. In different places, climatic and cultural conditions help determine the raw materials used in wall construction of various shells: for example, homes, offices, and schools. But do not the four fundamental tasks remain inviolate? Walls of adobe, plasterboard, hide, fiber, plywood, glass, or concrete perform the same fundamental functions for the occupants: (1) privacy (keeping the interior in), (2) security (keeping the exterior out) from the elements or other persons or animals, (3) and (4) permitting commodities (raw materials as well as waste products), friends, occupants and pets moving in or out of the house as the occasion requires. Waste products, instead of moving through the stomata of the leaves and stems of plants or through differentially permeable membranes of Henle's loop of the nephrons of a kidney, leave a home via a sewer pipe, a chimney flue, a door, or a window.

The less courageous reader may give up, but let us take the final leap and extend the concept of the container or wall beyond the dwelling unit to man in his neighborhood, in his city, in his region, in his megalopolis, or in whichever dimension of human settlement seems manageable. The author suggests that inhabitants of early city-states built walls for the four basic tasks mentioned. However, wall building and parameter establishment are expressed in numerous forms.

The forms of walls often change over time as cities spill over the walls and into the countryside. Some of the most noteworthy examples of how walls have changed are certain Parisian and Viennese boulevards that were once medieval walls built to protect and contain the city. One of the best known streets in the world was once a wooden wall. The history of Wall Street is seldom remembered (if ever known) by most Manhattan com-

Figure 1-26. A previously fortified gate stands out along the ancient and formidable wall of the City of Rhodes.

Figure 1-27. A crumbling memento of the past is seen in the walls near the Greek city of Lindos founded in the tenth century B.C. on the island of Rhodes.

muters as the site of a walled barricade that was supposed to keep Indians separated from the northern limits of the New Amsterdam settlement. Stockades are highly modified carryover from the walls and boundaries of old Amsterdam. The earliest plans for Manhattan called for canals across the community. Bedrock formations forced the engineers and planners to reconsider the differences between Dutch polders and Manhattan substrata. Nevertheless, in many cities reminders of walls still persist in the form of portals, gates, or other special entranceway designations, as evidenced in Istanbul, Rome, Paris, Frankfurt, and Madrid. In old towns and small cities that have not experienced excessive growth, the walls remain as crumbling mementos of an era replaced.

As cities and countries evolved, the complexity (and subtlety) of the wall increased. The Berlin Wall or the Great Wall of China exemplifies the ramification of a totalitarian government confronted with a more laissez-faire system. Historically, urban morphology suggests a trend for a clearly defined perimeter. Archeologists have recovered from early Athens the carefully spaced stones that read, "I am the Agora." The walls of Athens and Piraeus become more substantial as events are traced from Mycenaean to Medieval times. Moats were added and then several hundred years later came the British greenbelts, the American "incorporated city limit" signs, and now the automobile beltway that defines an urban boundary.

Recent Separators and Integrators

As the walls become more and more complex physically and socially, so do the questions about them. Will the beltways be swallowed up as they strangle a city after megalopolitan growth sets in? Where is the line to be drawn? At what point does the urban organism reach a carrying capacity for its total interior and exterior surroundings? How rigid should the "container boundary" be?

Ebenezer Howard was an early spokesman for the concept that continued expansion of an urban area would add to confusion, congestion, and chaos in the absence of limitations on population and area. His book *Garden Cities of Tomorrow* (first published in 1898 in *Tomorrow: A Peaceful Path to Reform*) sought to: (1) outline methods of relieving London of slum conditions, (2) preserve attributes of rural and urban landscapes, and (3) provide social, economic, and cultural advantages to residents of the new town or "garden city." Howard envisioned the "Garden City" as a compact, rigorously defined community protected from encroachment by a sur-rounding greenbelt and autonomous through the provision of industry to furnish nearby employment for residents.

The British experience produced Letchworth and Welwyn Garden City between World Wars I and II. Then after the New Towns Act of 1946, Parliament gave authority to the Minister of Housing and Local Government and the Secretary of State in Scotland to designate land area in their

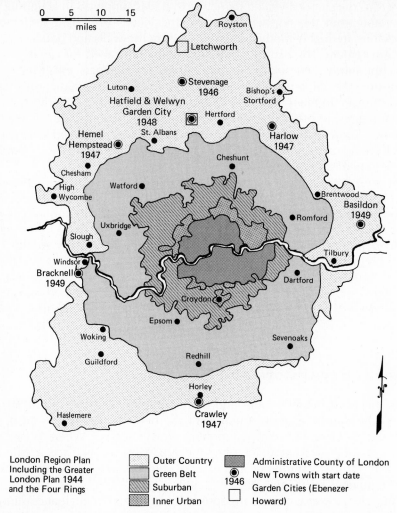

0   5   10   15
miles

Royston

Letchworth

Stevenage
1946

Luton

Hatfield & Welwyn
Garden City
1948   Hertford

Bishop's
Stortford

Hemel
Hempstead   St. Albans
1947

Harlow
1947

Chesham

Cheshunt

High
Wycombe   Watford

Brentwood

Uxbridge

Basildon
1949

Slough

Romford

Windsor

Tilbury

Bracknell
1949

Dartford

Croydon

Epsom

Woking

Sevenoaks

Guildford   Redhill

Horley

Haslemere   Crawley
1947

London Region Plan
Including the Greater
London Plan 1944
and the Four Rings

☐ Outer Country
☐ Green Belt
▨ Suburban
▨ Inner Urban

▨ Administrative County of London
◉ New Towns with start date
1946
☐ Garden Cities (Ebenezer
Howard)

Figure 1-28. London Region Plan including the Greater London Plan
1944 and the four rings. Note that the official "Green Belt" is shown as
the clear ring beyond the suburban ring. [Adapted from Royston Landau,
New Directions in British Architecture (New York: George Braziller, Inc., 1968),
p. 18]

respective geographical jurisdictions as sites for new towns. Also power
was given to appoint development corporations for development and
implementation purposes. The entrance requirements for Stevenage, as an
example, specified that in order to qualify for residential accommodations,
the family breadwinner must find employment in the Stevenage area, and
that the household, prior to its move to Stevenage, live in the center city
of London. Even with these stipulations, a two-year waiting list for apartment occupancy exists. This suggested that the boundaries were not only

given meadows and hedgerows. Socioeconomic considerations played a key role in applicant acceptance.

Regardless of the kind of wall or the specifications of the urban container, the succession and growth of a healthy urban area has several parallels with the succession of a strictly biological community. Pioneer species invade an area in the first steps of a long succession. Members of a biological community establish territory and home ranges in a way that is strikingly similar to the method used in human settlements. Specialization and division of labor among community members become common. Even when one community blends with a nearby urban area with different commercial activities, a continuum can be diagrammed to show a gradual blending of two cities over time and space. It is not unlike a *biological continuum* first described by plant ecologists Clements and Weaver. They spoke of a gradual change in the biota as a reflection of the gradual gradients in moisture, species present, soil conditions, and climate. There are also parallels to be fully researched concerning materials recycling and efficient energy use if time will give us a chance.

Perhaps it is by coincidence that the speed of blood flow in the circulatory system of mammals has a ratio of movement of $400:1$ between the aorta and capillary networks. Man's circulation (his transportation) in megalopolis has yet to link up the same ratios of speed evidenced in the supersonic transport of twelve hundred miles per hour to the three miles per hour walking speed of pedestrians. Urban pathology created by the automobile continues to be a menace to the urban organism in terms of respiration, dispersed circulation, elimination of wastes, and even the lack of decomposition of those Detroit cadavers that fill junk yards. Man has not yet achieved the integration and separation even in physical design that is demonstrated in systems other than human.

Urban Conservation and Its Role in the Future

The biological sciences provide a valuable storehouse of information about how man and his inventions work. Man might profit well to analyze more carefully these biological phenomena than he has in the past. The concept of the cell membrane has important analogous lessons when we talk about containers of cities. Disciplines in the biological sciences such as morphology, genetics, physiology, and ecology have direct application to one of the world's newest resources, the urban organism.

Out of the traditional practices of conservation as it has applied to individual resources comes a new integrating concept, urban conservation. The reader is invited to consider the idea of a city or any human settlement as a second-order resource. This chapter has also proposed that since cities are integrators and concentrators of all resources including human resources, more attention should be given to the carrying capacity of the urban environment. Furthermore, the residents of cities need a better

48   understanding of their dependency upon and interrelationship between the resources that come almost for granted into daily use. Approximately 180 million people, in the United States alone, live in such massive human settlements. Occasionally an example from another part of the world is used not as a panacea but in hopes that it may offer perspective and a vision. Once the citizen is informed about the physiology, morphology, and ecological imperatives of an urban area, his chances for influencing its future, if not its evolution, are somewhat improved. Even though human settlements of the million population scale have only recently emerged, the task of making those metropolitan complexes livable for humans is awesome. Some urbanists question the possibility; too little experience exists in managing and conserving the urban resource. But the task must be undertaken with a vigor that civilization has seldom mustered. To not attempt the task at all will certainly jeopardize the very survival of the urban resource that has so recently been created by man.

Integrated Resource Management and Urbanization

The intent of this chapter is to present a description of resource management in an urban area. The discussion will be general in order for the reader to check out or try to make appropriate application of the presentation to his own city. Some of the examples of how specific resources are managed or should be managed come from current cases in the United States; other illustrations are presented as hypothetical situations that the reader is invited to test against whatever local reality is available. The early premises in the chapter suggest that very little integration of resource management takes place in a community, large or small, even when a problem develops that is related to resources affecting each other. Present management and administrative strategies for coping with resource problems are given and then suggestions are offered on how more effective urban resource management might be instituted.

The Role of Advocates in Resource Management

For every issue, regardless of whether or not it is resource-oriented, there is an advocate, a spokesman, a defender, a promoter, or, if one prefers to move toward action, a change agent. Without some kind of advocacy, a subtle event seldom comes to public attention. This fact in itself sets the stage for our discussion of how resource advocates become established. That "event" could be a long-standing traffic problem, an air-or water-pollution menace, or an excessive amount of service given to one part of the community and denied another part. Changes in such events do not come about without an individual or organization who for civic, personal, or other interests makes the event an issue. Some of the very earliest   **49**

50   participants to bring an essentially unnoticed event to the public eye are the "information filters" along the line, such as the wire service editor. Many news releases, with the exception of disasters and very unusual events, are submitted to the wire services, the newspapers, and other mass media by advocates of various causes. Political candidates, industry, large governmental units, athletic organizations, and universities all have a public information office or news service. The people who write news releases compete against each other for air time or inches in the press. Since all news releases cannot be transmitted to the public in their entirety, each advocate of a given organization does his best to package the information in a way that the wire service editor or newspaper editor permits all or part of a release to be made "public."

When the conservation movement was led into the political arena by Gifford Pinchot and Theodore Roosevelt at the turn of the twentieth century, various waves were whipped into public attention and public action by advocates in important national offices as well as at various state and local levels. The recent efforts of certain Secretaries of the Interior such as Stewart Udall and public protectors such as Ralph Nader and Joseph Sax cannot be overemphasized. Several like-minded people have been promoters of specific projects: a change in American forestry practice, the establishment of a park or a program, a change in corporate behavior toward safety and consumer products, or the creation of new environmental legislation. An important observation is that each individual advocate usually serves as a change agent for a very specific task. In this situation, the danger of tunnel vision looms as a weakness to be guarded against. When the specificity of an objective is so precise that it does not consider other impacts, then the dilemma of urban resource management takes form.

In an urban community, especially one of one-hundred thousand inhabitants or more, the resultant concentration of the various human and other natural resources (such as energy, metals, fiber, and building materials—limestone, gravel, sand, and clays) creates great complexity. As this complexity is unscrambled, one often discovers that a single person or a small number of people have jurisdiction over one resource. Ordinarily the purview of such responsibility does not extend beyond that one resource that may be parks and open space, atmospheric resources, or water resources. Sometimes there are completely different individuals serving as advocates for the same resource at different stages of use in the city. To illustrate, most commonly one person and his staff have the responsibility for an urban area's water supply and water purification system. The water commissioner plays the advocate role in building wells or reservoirs for water supply purposes. His responsibility also includes that of water purification and distribution of the water supply to homes, schools, business, and industry. But after the water leaves the tap and is used, it then becomes the responsibility of another person, often another municipal agency.

In most American cities, as soon as water begins its journey down the drain it comes under the jurisdiction of the waste-water treatment and collection people, often headed up by a sewerage commissioner. In some situations both tasks are under a department of public works, but characteristically in cities over one-hundred thousand there is usually competition, particularly at budget time, between the water managers—one who is on the water purification and distribution side—the other who is on the collection and waste-water treatment side. To avoid an oversimplification of the water resource management picture, one must remember that there are counterparts at the county, state, and federal levels of each advocacy position. Sometimes the titles change, but the similarity of function continues, be it a drain commissioner, a water-pollution control officer, or a water quality administrator.

The complexity of *pollutants* and the multiplicity of jurisdictions are usually more than one manager or one staff can handle in a large urban area. Let us assume there is a need to consider the various impacts of a given pollutant on the environment. If that pollutant is brought to the attention of the water managers, they will have little basis on which to make a judgment about comparative impacts on resources other than water; they may have no knowledge about the impact of the given pollutant if it were to be disposed of in sanitary landfill (a chance of land pollution) or via incineration (a chance of air pollution). How are the tradeoffs between the three potential receiving resources—water, land, or air—to be evaluated, and by whom?

The concept of a pollutant varies depending upon the frame of reference. A pollutant for one person or for one portion of the urban public may very well be a valuable ingredient in a manufacturing process or a helpful household commodity. Let us assume that pollution is an act of consciously or unconsciously passing costs on to another party. The act can be performed by an individual, a governmental unit, or a corporation. For the polluter to reuse his "potential" pollutant, a new use or new value needs to be found that has benefits in excess of those that encouraged him to pollute. If the polluter is not motivated to internalize the costs[1] imposed by pollutants, a pollution control agency may impose negative incentives to reduce pollution by unfavorable publicity, injunctions, or penalties in the form of fines and prison terms. Of course, according to this definition, every person, family, organization, and community is a polluter. However, there are tremendous variances in the levels of polluting or passing costs on to others.

Case Study: Litter and Solid Waste.

Let us consider the problem of litter, which costs several Eastern states an estimated $.32 for each piece that is picked up along state highways and costs the nation annually $500 million. According to a national survey

---

[1] To internalize the cost of pollution, a polluter would make the cost of abating pollution part of the normal cost of doing business. If adequate pollution control is not provided, the pollutant moves into someone else's realm. If the pollution has to be treated by someone else downwind or downstream from the source, the cost has become external to the original polluter.

of roadside litter taken in 1969 sponsored by Keep America Beautiful, Inc., an average of 1,304 pieces of litter per mile is dropped on America's highways each month—nearly 16,000 pieces per mile per year.[2] On an individual basis, certain people because of ignorance, temperament, or both, litter more than others. Some "litterbugs" may not be aware of the offensive unsightliness that is created by their cumulative acts. They may not regard their own physical and social impact on the total environment, or singly on other people as substantial; therefore, they underestimate their potential even as paper polluters. Others who litter simply forget. But there is also a small number who cast their scraps along the streets or across the countryside intentionally. They are the environmental arsonists who pollute with malice of forethought. Last, but not least, are those who really don't want to litter, but—because there is no container nearby—or because their pockets are either overflowing, nonexistent, or full of holes—or because they are a little lazy or very much in a hurry—they litter. Such behavior resembles that of a little child just *before* he is toilet-trained.

If the problem of littering is expanded to an urban scale, it is clearly an issue that has a number of mild antilitter advocates and very few adversaries. The man in the street, although he may not be aggressively *for* beautification or an antilitter campaign, is certainly not against it. In nearly every city, the Department of Public Works has such a busy work schedule that it normally would support an antilitter campaign if for no other reason except to make its job easier through the centralization of litter pickup locations. The city business manager is supportive of a litter cleanup campaign because private individuals do for a while what public servants have had to do in their urban custodial chores.

It is important to remember that prior to the time the object becomes "litter," it fulfilled some purpose. A paper or foil wrapper may have kept a stick of gum hygienic. A throwaway bottle or can once held some beverage or fluid. A discarded wrapper or box may have had the sole function of luring a buyer through establishing a specific link of appeal between the purchaser and the package. Once it is used, the item, if not consumed or recycled, becomes a candidate for littering.

By managing the distribution route of a can, a bottle, or a bundle of paper, the material can either become a cost to a city (economic and aesthetic) or a revenue if it is routed to a commerical *recycling* operation. For example, the collective annual cost to the New York City area of disposing of the seven pound Sunday edition of *The New York Times* is approximately $5.5 million. If the disposal of used Sunday editions of the New York Daily News is also considered, the total annual cost to the citizens of the area just for the disposal of their Sunday papers approaches $13.26 million![3] If those who purchased these papers would take them to paper recycling centers, consider the savings. In addition to eliminating or at least greatly reducing the $13.26 million collection costs incurred by the

---

[2] A.P. Wire Service; New York; November 23, 1969.
[3] Elizabeth Barlow, "Cut the Garbage" *New York* (January 18, 1971), p. 41.

city, according to Paul Swatek in his *User's Guide to the Protection of the* **53** *Environment,* equally important factors would be conserved.

Since a ton of newsprint represents pulp from about 17 trees, recycling a stack of newspapers about 36 inches high saves one tree. Recycling a ton of newsprint also eliminates a major portion of the pollution associated with producing new pulp. For the sulphite pulping process, this pollution includes 275 pounds of sulfur, 350 pounds of limestone, 60,000 gallons of water, 9,000 pounds of steam, and 225 kilowatt-hours of electricity, per ton of unbleached pulp.[4]

According to the Association of Secondary Materials Industries, a trade group, of the 58.5 million tons of paper used in the United States in 1969, 11.5 million tons were recycled—meaning that 200 million trees did not have to be cut. But if 50 per cent of the paper had been recycled, the cutting of another 300 million trees could have been avoided.[5]

Until recently, the advocates of recycling litter and large volumes of solid wastes were not heard or seen. In large metropolitan areas wastes were not perceived as potential products because those officials or persons involved in trash pickup were specialized to do the specific job of collecting and disposing of whatever debris the urban area produced. Economic incentives for recycling solid wastes were nonexistent, and public attention was seldom focused on the possibility of "materials reclamation" at a metropolitan scale. Eliminating litter has had modest cleanup *advocates* and no substantial *opposition* except human inertia, which, of course, can be a formidable veto by the act of apathy. In contrast, improving urban solid waste disposal has had few advocates, but a large number of communities is waiting to see if newly developed technology offers any economies over present methods such as landfill and incineration.

In 1969 United States municipalities spent about $4.5 billion to collect and dispose of nearly 350 million tons of solid wastes. By 1980 solid discards are expected to exceed one-half billion tons annually. Incredibly, ordinary municipal wastes now contain an estimated 10 million tons of iron; 1 million tons of nonferrous metals such as aluminum, copper, nickel, tin, lead, silver, gold, and zinc; and 15 million tons of glass, together worth nearly $1 billion.[6] In addition, approximately half the bulk of urban refuse consists of paper and wood products—more than 35 million tons of wood fiber annually. Reuse of only half of this wastepaper would in effect reduce the drain on our wood resources each year by 30 million cords—an amount equivalent to the total timber production from a million acres of forest. At present, most of these resources are incinerated, buried in dumps, and lost, to create, in many cases, new health and pollution problems. This is a clear challenge to the official custodians of our urban water, land, and

[4] Paul Swatek, *The User's Guide to the Protection of the Environment* (New York: Ballantine Books, Inc., 1970), p. 125.
[5] David Gumpert, "Efforts to Save, Reuse Waste Products Slowed by Variety of Problems," *The Wall Street Journal* (June 23, 1970), p. 1.
[6] Ibid.

54   air to integrate the management and the reclamation of our solid wastes.

The root causes of the waste generation problem are complex. Many of the same fundamental difficulties involved in urban pollution of any kind are traced ultimately to the American frontier philosophy, the Judeo-Christian ethic, the political economic system based on a profit motive, lack of a spaceship viewpoint, and a nonexistent human and land ethnic, all of which culminate in the so-called American life style where values of people are out of harmony with ecological imperatives of the long run. Other authors have elaborated on these root causes of environmental problems, but I mention them here as an important point in our discussion on solid wastes.

Some humble beginnings have been made. In Madison, Wisconsin, a pilot project finds the U.S. Departments of Agriculture, Interior, and HEW cooperating on research to recycle the resources from Madison's solid waste. The Bureau of Mines has developed systems that can efficiently separate and recover the glass and metallic wastes; the Forests Products Laboratory has been developing ways to recover and convert the wood fiber into boxes, corrugated board, and tissue paper. Their joint objective is to reprocess these wastes into an acceptable state and at low enough cost for reuse by manufacturers.

This federal experiment is not the first time such comprehensive recycling efforts have been attempted. In 1964 an entrepreneur in Houston, Texas—Victor Brown—conceived the idea of an operation that was capable of shredding and mechanically sorting trash into its basic components. The recovered materials were to be resold to industry for reuse. Brown executed a contract with the City of Houston to process 25 per cent of the city's garbage at a charge of $4.11 per ton. Unfortunately, his experiment has been economically disappointing. In 1970 Brown was losing $2 per ton on all garbage he handled because he couldn't sell most of the materials he salvaged.[7] Only $\frac{1}{6}$ of the collected paper found a market—and that with the construction industry for building materials rather than his anticipated market with the paper companies. For multiple reasons including their heavy investment in woodlands and pulp-making equipment, the paper companies have shunned Brown's reclaimed wood fiber. Of the sixty thousand tons or more of compost that Brown's Metropolitan Waste Conversion Corporation can turn out each year, only five thousand tons have found a market in agricultural uses. Brown's only success, of a modest sort, has been in the sale of metal to the copper industry for use as a catalyst in its production process.

New technological processes for reclaiming solid wastes are increasingly successful and numerous. Many of those active in recycling argue that once the economic problems are overcome, the technological obstacles will easily fall. Some have suggested that the federal government should begin creating markets for recycled products by confining its own purchases to recycled goods. In addition to economic and technological restrictions,

[7] Ibid.

there is the problem of regulatory restrictions. Zoning keeps recycling dealers and their "unsightly" businesses out of municipal centers, markets are restricted by exportation limits on materials such as copper and nickel, and a 10 per cent depletion allowance provides a tax break to timber growers. Inequities also exist in transportation where, for instance, freight rates for iron ore and pulpwood are currently lower than those for scrap metal and scrap paper.

It seems that forms of uncoordinated or unilateral decisions about present waste disposal methods will continue until a strong new advocacy emerges to challenge the current procedure. The complexity and difficulty of integrating resource management requires strong advocates on all sides, in addition to an integrated policy among the resource managers who must correlate technology, economics, and governmental arrangements in the best interests of an urban region.

Garbage and solid waste have as many sources or control points as there are residents and business operations. When one variable with a single point of control, such as salt on streets, is the focus of an environmental debate, the resolution of the dilemma is often considerably easier.

Case Study: Salting Streets

During the last twenty-five years, salt has been used with increased frequency for winter road maintenance in freezing climates. At first salts of sodium chloride and calcium chloride were used to prevent freezing of sand stockpiles and to improve abrasion on slippery streets. As it was discovered that salt melted snow and ice on roadways, the volumes of salt application increased not only on curves, hills, and intersections, but also on most city and county thoroughfares and interstate highways. A report from Wisconsin indicates that in 1955–56, 7,355 tons of salt were used on state highways.[8] Nine years later (1964–1965) 165,000 tons were applied to Wisconsin's state highways. Today many Midwestern cities average 25 to 30 tons of salt applied per mile of street during one winter. The increase in the use of salt has been accompanied by an increase in protests by advocates of less salt or no salt. The lineup of spokesmen on different sides of an issue follows a common pattern in large urban areas where individuals and groups of conflicting goals, or methods to reach certain goals, come into confrontation with each other.

One of several events could initiate the use of salt on streets: a street department official may attend a meeting of municipal personnel and be impressed by an example of successful winter road maintenance where salt is employed; a member of the driving public or a snowplow operator may suggest the idea of salt application to a councilman; or possibly a mere visit to the appropriate city officials from a salt company representative, a citizen's letter to the local newspaper, a suggestion from an automobile insurance company, or an advertisement or notice in a trade journal read

[8] F. H. Schraufnagel, *Chlorides*; Report of the Commission on Water Pollution; State of Wisconsin; mimeo.

by public works personnel may stimulate sufficient interest to give salt "a try." Whatever the origin, some advocacy is established for salt application. Once an advocate for the idea exists, the next step must be faced—how is a policy decision to be made or changed in regard to the particular issue at hand. The successful promotion of any idea to the implementation stage necessarily includes the elimination of the most substantial opposition that must first be identified. If the objections are satisfied and dismissed, a departmental administrative request is submitted to the committee for budget review or perhaps directly to the municipal legislative body for approval.

Often, when a new resource management policy is introduced, the suggestion is made to try the practice (such as salt application) on a pilot or experimental basis. This approach gives the public an opportunity to test the concept and, at the same time, gives advocates a chance to smooth out difficulties as they consider objections to the deicing practice. Once the salt application program has begun, potential opposition is always present. Internal negativism may arise from inconvenience of storage or handling, difficulty with spreading equipment, increase in undesirable working hours under unpleasant working conditions, or increase of health hazards that may be perceived or real.

Resistance external to the Department of Public Works or the Road Commission may also emerge at unknown times in the future and for unpredictable reasons. The concern about environmental pollution in the United States is a case in point. Here is where the single-function resource manager such as the road commissioner or street department engineer is most vulnerable. He is expected to be an expert in his special area of responsibility. But the complexity of urbanization requires that the consequences of one department's resource management policy be evaluated in terms of its ecological impacts on other resources. To fulfill the kind of overview function that is prescribed takes special training, different administrative arrangements, and a broadened attitude of resource stewardship by government and the general public. Compounding the difficulty, major resource allocations must be appraised in terms of economic, technological, social, administrative, and political and environmental considerations. Who could have predicted the surge of interest and concern among the general public in environmental quality at the beginning of the 1970's? This was an external factor, which, in addition to many other public outcries about environmental abuse, helped to crystallize the challenge put to urban street managers regarding the widespread use of salt as a deicing agent. Environmental impact reports are supposed to inform interested parties about possible environmental consequences of a given project such as a citywide salting program.

The "ban salt" advocates gather support by listing some of the disadvantages of salt application:

1. Excessive corrosion to the automobile and damage to other materials.

(Automobiles operated in western states where sand and cinders are used in place of salt last many more years than automobiles of the Midwest and Northeast that are exposed annually to the corrosive action of salt.)

2. Deleterious effect on pavement surfaces.
3. Lethal effects on roadside vegetation including trees in urban areas.
4. Damage to lungs from airborne particulate material.
5. Increased water pollution from meltwater runoff.
6. Reduced visibility from salt film on mirror and window surfaces.
7. Cost increase over sand and other abrasive materials.
8. Increased sodium concentrations in water supplies, constituting a potential danger to persons on salt-free diets or those subject to hypertension and heart disease.

As a result of this intensified concern for environmental impacts, some city officials and more numerous "ecological watchdogs" were inspired to ask questions about the environmental costs of salt use versus the presumed safety benefits. Advocates of salt reduction programs urged that alternative measures to salting such as the following be used to reduce snow-induced accidents:

1. Lower speed limits for snow or ice conditions.
2. Snow tires with cleats or studs.
3. Emergency driving and parking regulations at times of heavy snowfall.
4. Incentives for greater use of public mass transit during snow periods.
5. An education and information program to caution winter drivers about risks.

If the antisalt advocate wishes to undertake a campaign to reduce or eliminate salt use, several strategies are at his disposal for influencing the resource manager (in this case the Road Commission or the highway or street department). The challenge is strengthened if, in addition to the questionable arguments for safety, the severe impacts on other parts of the urban environment are stressed—impacts that result in increased salinity of surface and ground water, public health consequences, lethal effects on trees and vegetation, and unreasonably high costs to individual automobiles, fabrics, and even pavement surfaces. An antisalt group would probably try to discuss the dangers with public officials, call public hearings, and, if the effort is successful, scale down the use of salt. Instead of an immediate total ban on the use of salt, a gradual reduction in application would appear to be an effective change agent strategy. If the decreased amount of salt appears to cause a sharp upturn in the accident rate, the antisalt proponents face a new challenge of public protest. Instead of a complete salt ban, the revised practice may become a discretionary application of salt mixed with sand at steep grades, on curves, school bus routes, and major urban arteries. Then, depending on the countervailing forces,

58　a resource management policy is established that takes into account impacts on the resources of vegetation, soil, air, water, people, metals, and the mix of these and others. Needless to say, interdepartmental cooperation is imperative in cases that involve multiple resources.

The Need for Regional Coordination

The consequences of a single decision at the local level may be significant at a regional level. For example, if one city or county bans or reduces salt application, others nearby will also undoubtedly weigh the merits and disadvantages of such a ban. This carryover from a local to a regional issue is especially true when there is a mutual and shared resource in question, such as air, water, a transportation network, or a metropolitan park system. If nutrient levels are excessively high in a drainage basin that encompasses a large urban area of many governmental jurisdictions, the issue may be excessive phosphate, nitrate, and potassium buildup in the receiving water. One community may consider an ordinance against high phosphate detergents. However, if upstream communities take no action to ban such detergents, the citizen downstream may feel undue martyrdom and futility as he cooperates with antiphosphate advocates.

Integrated resource management needs coordination among departments at the local level as seen in soil and water conservation districts. However, it is equally, if not more imperative, that coordination or integration take place between levels of government in the same or overlapping geographical areas. It is absurd for one political jurisdiction to permit a certain kind of aircraft noise level, air quality standard, or pesticide use to prevail whereas quite different standards exist in neighboring units. Without regional resource coordination where free movement exists across political boundaries, severe injustices can occur. When urbanization becomes widespread in a watershed, airshed, or other naturally defined resource region, it is especially unreasonable for adjacent cities, townships, or counties to enact inconsistent effluent standards.

Management districts are not new in the United States. Today's challenge is the need for more of them that will function better. Conservancy districts in Ohio for flood control, soil and water conservation districts, and western ranching districts preceded the more recent watershed councils, river basin associations, and regional park or recreation authorities. The "grass roots" approach made famous by the Tennessee Valley Authority's (TVA) basin-wide effort at coordinated resource management is a unique example of integrated resource management.

One Success Story: The TVA

The unusual economic, political, and social climate of the early 1930's permitted the establishment of the TVA. Prior to this period, the creation of a separate federal authority to enhance the development of a region was without precedent in a laissez-faire economy. Before 1933, the Tennessee River basin was plagued by poverty that was directly related to an excessively depleted resource base. Poor logging practices had denuded the mountainsides and very little attention was given to reforestation. Without forest cover, the natural consequence was for soils to wash away excessively. Poor grazing practices accelerated soil erosion, flooding was aggravated, and agricultural productivity dropped as general economic deprivation became widespread.

When resource problems of the Tennessee Valley reached crisis proportions during the severe national economic depression, it became clear that local and state agencies were not equipped to reclaim exploited resources. The repair job could not be done on a resource by resource basis. The interrelatedness of the resources and the people was tragically graphic in this situation. It was obvious that highly coordinated and integrated management of soils, forests, fertilizer production, water supply, navigation, power production, credit extension, and other services was essential to the development and future of the Tennessee River basin. More than forty years later, the TVA continues as an example of coordinated resource management to other regions and countries of the world—but it has never been duplicated in the United States. The TVA has, in recent years, fallen into criticism for being exploitative and top-heavy with its bureaucracy.

Coordination of Water

Incentives for local authorities to manage resources do not appear persuasive enough to deal with the magnitude and severity of resource problems that today face large metropolitan regions. A metropolitan regional conscience has never emerged to put the wheels into motion for comprehensive resource management policy because the majority of people do not become involved in the actual decision-making process. The only direct participation that emerges at a metropolitan scale is during an emergency or crisis. The prevalence of local autonomy strongholds has slowed man-

Figure 2-1. An overgrazed pasture in Warren County, Tennessee, that is suffering from erosion. (TVA)

Figure 2-2. A few years ago these two fields in Madison County, North Carolina, were equally gullied. The owner of the field at left entered TVA test demonstration program and by proper fertilization produced cover that checks erosion and permits livestock production. (TVA)

agement consolidation for a resource, even one as vital as water. For example, the tendency of each municipality is to acquire its own water supply, and a strong propensity for individual municipalities to treat their own waste water and dispose of their solid wastes exists as well.

The most frequent explanation for city autonomy over water supply or waste-water treatment is that it gives a community control over rate structure. If a city wishes to raise water and sewer rates, it is a local decision predicated by local needs. If, however, a municipality contracts with a metropolitan water and sewerage authority, the individual municipality has less voice and less control over decisions about rate increases. On the other hand, economies of scale are purported to bring considerable savings to participating governmental units because being linked into a large system eliminates the need of separate, even though smaller, investments by each town in duplicate facilities such as wells, reservoirs, and purification plants.

Logically, the state government might assume leadership in providing incentives for communities to coordinate resource management activities that tend to overlap or duplicate. However, with few exceptions, the metropolitan areas grow with such speed and strength that coordinated efforts that would require difficult negotiation and compromise are left by the wayside. The difficulties of each unit doing "its own thing" have been anticipated and warned against by political scientists and farsighted planners. Nevertheless, the development of cooperative, intergovernmental management of resources never becomes widespread until the persuasion by the federal government begins. The government's most effective persuasive weapon is the federal treasury and its promise of matching federal grants to local units of government who can work out differences and come up with metropolitan-wide water-supply park district and waste treatment systems. Additional bonuses are available if planning includes state participation.

Unfortunately, merely establishing federal jurisdiction does not, by itself, solve the many difficulties of uncoordinated resource management. For every natural resource, there are usually several competing federal agencies and bureaus involved. The classic example is the management of water resources at the federal level. Every Cabinet member has a hand in the water picture. Most people immediately think of the Department of the Interior, the Department of Agriculture, and the Department of Defense (especially the U.S. Army Corps of Engineers) when a reference is made to federal water managers. But Justice; Commerce; Health, Education, and Welfare; Housing and Urban Development; Department of Transportation; and the other departments, new and old, have a vested interest and an active claim. Even the State Department is involved through international water-related treaties, compacts, and projects such as the Rio Grande irrigation allocations, the Columbia River power production, and the transportation arrangements of the St. Lawrence Seaway.

Figure 2-3. After the resource base was eroded away in the forms of mineral depletion, forest elimination and soil erosion, this eastern Tennessee community suffered human resource depletion. Most of the 30 million Americans in the poverty category (less than $3000 annual income) live in resource eroded and exploited areas such as the one shown in this 1973 photograph.

Figure 2-4 [OPPOSITE]. Waterfowl flyways of North America. By returning bands found on banded ducks and geese, thousands of people all over America help wildlife biologists determine the routes, or flyways, used by our waterfowl between their northern nesting grounds and southern wintering areas. Banding records are maintained, and results analyzed, by the Fish and Wildlife Service. (U.S. Bureau of Sport Fisheries and Wildlife)

Coordination of Pesticide Usage

The regulation of pesticides touches on a resource management problem that illustrates the controversy that rages far beyond local and state units of government. Unfortunately, within one federal department many conflicting stands may exist regarding the management of a single resource problem. The Department of Agriculture serves as a good example, for within its jurisdiction the Food and Drug Administration may have held one view about pesticide use, the Soil Conservation Service or the Agricultural Research Service another, and the U.S. Forest Service still another.

Even with pesticide dosages given exactly as prescribed by directions, severe environmental consequences may take place. In the administration of present regulations, a basic understanding of "biological magnification" is usually not considered. If it has been taken into account, negligence in labeling prevails. When various consumers of plant or animal material ingest *"hard" biocides* (those that resist biodegradation), amounts of the chemical begin to reside in fatty tissues and strategic organs. This phenomenon takes place regardless of whether it is a caterpillar chewing a leaf sprayed with an *herbicide* or a cotton stalk illegally sprayed with DDT.[9] If another consumer, this time a higher level predator, takes the biocide-laden victim, a magnification of the biocide concentration takes place. Therefore, the widespread disaster signs of biocide use—even when applied according to directions—are seen at the top of the trophic levels where carnivores and exclusive predators reside.

Since most carnivores do not confine themselves within a specific township, county, or state political boundary, a biocide regulation policy needs to be coordinated over multiple political subdivisions. In fact, the migratory patterns of several mammals (including aquatic forms), many fish, and most bird species cross international boundaries. For example, if Canada and Mexico had strong biocide legislation to control pesticide buildup in migratory waterfowl and the United States had weak legislation, threatened species would lack appropriate protection. Many migratory species nest and breed in Canadian provinces. Twice a year the journey is made across the United States to winter feeding grounds. If protection against excessive biocide accumulation is not provided by all nations enroute, the danger to the species increases. An international treaty precedent has been set regarding hunting bag limits and seasons for threatened species; similar restrictions on pesticides are also in order.

[9] A federal ban on DDT use was intended to eliminate DDT use in 1973.

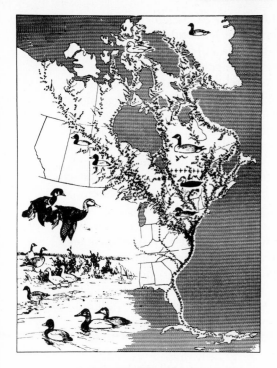

Atlantic Flyway

Mississippi Flyway

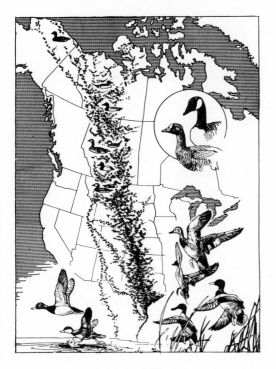

Central Flyway

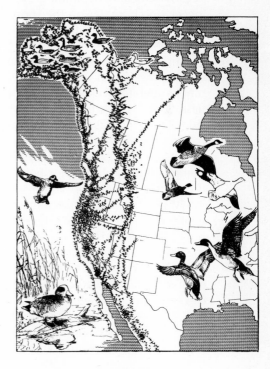

Pacific Flyway

64   ### Other Inequities of Uncoordinated Resource Management

In a competitive industrialized society there is a tendency for any given jurisdiction *not* to impose costs upon itself, particularly if the benefits from such costs accrue to "outside" persons or neighboring jurisdictions. It is very easy to say a steel mill town should clean up its air and water pollution so that the cities downwind and downriver can have a more pleasant environment. The "more pleasant environment" means that costs in the form of jobs and dollars need to be incurred by the industry in the steel town. Like safety devices, pollution-control costs tend to erode the margin of profit, unless increased costs are passed on to the consumer. Generally, there is an economic incentive to avoid pollution control activities unless new profits or special advertising benefits are available. Treating operational wastes thoroughly is very discomforting to a steel mill manager or steel-worker when he knows, in effect, what he is doing is reducing the cost of an operation for a nearby competitor by providing him with a cleaner air or water supply. Further, it seems inequitable for strict pollution control regulations and enforcement to be imposed in one county or state without equal application of the law in an adjacent unit. Actually, with the relative ease of managerial mobility and plant expansion or relocation, pollution-control regulations and enforcement should be consistent throughout all fifty states. A set of worldwide standards is obviously the ultimate objective.

External effects or "spillovers" of resource management have positive and negative impacts depending on the location of the observer. Consider a logger who operates on the short run. (Here a short run means a planning horizon shorter than the time it takes for the tree to grow from seed to maturity.) He may remove all the valuable timber and ground cover instead of employing the more expensive selective cutting and replanting procedures. Without an integrated resource management policy, the careless timber operator will not have to bear the costs of silt or sediment pollution, flash floods, and other disparities imposed on contiguous land. The "other side of the coin" is for expensive flood protection works or waste control facilities to be built without all beneficiaries being charged a fee that reflects the true costs of installation and operation. Perhaps an even better example is the lighthouse whose operation benefits any passing ship, even though the shipowner whose vessel was guided past a reef or beckoned safely into a harbor does not share part of the costs for operating that lighthouse. A more equitable resource allocation process takes place when political boundaries or other institutional arrangements include and link the beneficiary and cost bearer.

Another major urban resource management problem arises when one resource, such as water, has different or overlapping geographical areas as use changes in a single metropolitan region. The pressures of urbanization may eventually force private and public sectors to coordinate their inter-related functions of flood control districts, water supply and waste treatment systems, recreation authorities, transportation networks, and other resource utilization operations. If these and other necessary services do not keep the urban ecosystem in quasi-equilibrium, problems of massive human settlements of today will become cataclysmic disruptions in the cities of the twenty-first century.

Instituting More Effective, Coordinated Resource Management

At the outset of this chapter, a promise was made to move from the descriptions of urban resource management situations to a discussion of how more effective coordinated resource management might be instituted. Before widely accepted changes in environmental management can be implemented, there must be a basic understanding among the general citizenry about environmental problems and the available solutions. The author believes that environmental education should be an important ingredient in the primary and secondary school curriculum if any widespread changes are to take place. Such a program is a logical synthesis and extension of the biological and social sciences that are presently being taught. A prevocational or precollege exposure to environmental problems helps to increase the environmental awareness of the general public as an advocacy for environmental issues becomes a natural outgrowth of the educational system. To provide the refined concepts and some comprehensive practices for environmental problem solving remains essentially the responsibility of American higher education. However, much of the initial practice can begin at primary and secondary levels.

A college education has not completed its mission if it has only equipped the student with a large storehouse of knowledge filed neatly in lecture notes. What is needed is an education that develops an environmentally literate person with a special sensitivity to human equity and the third-world nations. The real payoff of an investment of time and money in a college education lies in the student's ability to utilize whatever knowledge he has accumulated, including the area of daily resource management. Furthermore, putting that knowledge (in the form of theories, facts, and ability to interpret and analyze data) to use should not wait until after graduation. Rather, experimentation with coordinated resource management in urban settings can and should begin while the student is in school. Part of that objective can be achieved through simulation and gaming activities; much of it should be accomplished by direct involvement through work-study experience in the urban ecosystem, using current local issues that demand an application of coordinated resource management principles.

Possibilities of an Urban Resource Seminar

It may be helpful to the reader if the author gives an illustration from his experiences and current practice in an urban resource seminar. The intent here is to show how a college or a university class can be organized in a way that builds competence in students who wish to become more effective change agents of urban resource problems. Similar neighborhood

66 opportunities exist for community-level workshops that deal with environmental problem solving.

First of all, the professor or coordinator needs to "advertise" the class in a way that will attract students from a wide variety of disciplines. In addition to students in biology, political science, engineering, economics, and sociology, it is advantageous for reasons of diversity to recruit persons from as many programs or departments as possible. The perspectives offered by people from art, prelaw, journalism, anthropology, and other areas strengthen the students' learning experiences and their work capabilities far more than a seminar composed entirely of students from a single discipline. If large numbers of students seek admission, it is suggested that application forms be used so that two or three of the most promising students from each of the departments or discipline areas can be selected.

Unusual interest and motivation is generated when an invitation is extended to the students to identify major resource-related problems in their immediate urban environment. The search for problems is intended to produce a list of case study topics. In the process, local or regional environmental problems are identified and analyzed in a way that will ascertain if there are adequate data, learning value, applicability to other urban areas, and general manageability in the time that is available. From the list of ecologically related problems typical of large human settlements, the students select a topic or issue that they will pursue for the duration of the experience. The author asks the students to trust the experience of the professor in narrowing to one or two topics if the selection process becomes too lengthy. The natural tendency for students from various disciplines is to select a theme that is very familiar to them. However, for an optimum learning situation, a student is encouraged to align himself with an unfamiliar topic. At the same time, he is encouraged to serve as a consultant or peer resource for the students working in the area of his strong competence.

One of the most effective ways for the college level student to become knowledgeable about the need for coordinated resource management is to actually involve himself in the "real-world" problem-solving mechanisms. Instead of performing traditional "library research," the students interact with actual persons involved in the problem; data are collected from original sources and interviews are conducted to document attitudes and perceptions from many sides of the question. Sometimes part of the seminar assignment is to move toward the actual resolution of the problem under analysis but time is usually a severe constraint. The author believes that ordinarily the implementation stage should not be a part of the class activity.

The chronology of the overall approach begins with the class nominating a sizable list of local resource problems that might serve as class projects. A preliminary search is then undertaken by class members to determine the feasibility of each proposed project. Next the list is narrowed to the number that is appropriate for the size of the class (four to six persons per project is a workable group). Subsequently, each student "signs up" for the project on which he wishes to work. This might be done by ballot with each student indicating first and second preferences. Once the teams have formed around each topic area, students map out objectives, plan strategy, establish a division of labor, and indicate what consultative resources from the faculty or the community may be required. At subsequent plenary sessions the various teams compare their successes and setbacks and make a critique of each other's progress. The final activities of the seminar include preparing a diary of procedure and results evaluating achievement, problems of entry, timing, degree of commitment, and, if a summary of activities is presented, inviting the officials, citizens, and participants who were involved in the field experience to make a critique of the presentation.

Regardless of the specificity of the projects that might include flood-plain zoning, air-pollution ordinance enforcing, acquiring open-space land, or instigating action for waste treatment in a particular subdivision or factory—the student team is forced to consider the ecological, political, economic, and technological implications. The team discovers internal problems inherent in any committee effort. They also find that their internal work problems are a microcosm of those of the professional resource manager as he works along on a daily basis. The student enthusiasm and occasional impatience is tempered by a firsthand exposure to the complexity of coordinating resource problems in a larger human-physical system. Out of the experience comes a deeper appreciation of how the governmental or private systems can work more effectively and where and how certain institutional mechanisms should be replaced. The need for a common philosophical or political ideology is seen as an artificially combined group struggles with value questions. In addition, students usually learn the need for advocacy mechanisms to help complete the jobs. There is usually the problem of one or two individuals wanting to, or being asked to carry the major burden of the team. That is one of the many events of group dynamics that comes into the life of a team. Even if full success is not achieved as a part of the class project, valuable understandings develop that produce citizens, regardless of vocation, who are more skillful in identifying environmental problems and moving toward their resolution.

This kind of exercise need not and should not be confined to a university or college biology or sociology class. Adults in every city must become involved in an informed way with problems and issues that determine the survival and quality of massive urban settlement. The task cannot be relegated to the professional resource manager alone. Even the most conscientious, best informed, most skillful administrator desperately needs vigorous, supportive public advocates to press for sound programs. The forces that are working consciously or unconsciously to dehumanize the human settlements of America have acquired and developed stout public

68   defenders. Those persons wishing to implement policy and practices that enhance the human dimension of urban areas in a coordinated manner will be most successful if they have had practice along the way. If a person has not had that practice he has been denied an important learning opportunity that American higher education should provide.

Recent Trends in Conservation Policy

A gradual realization about the difficulty of national and worldwide environmental management has swept over the new generation of "environmentalists" or "conservationists." Today's Americans who are swelling the ranks of environmentally committed citizens have a dedication and intensity that resemble those conservationists of the two preceding generations. However, a marked contrast exists between the large number of people who are "token environmentalists" and the small number who are making deep personal sacrifices and dedicating their influence and energy in the direction of constructive social and institutional change. Other people fall somewhere between these two positions and serve like the few "voices in the wilderness" of previous decades who had a watchdog position primarily on nonrenewable or slowly renewable resources. This recent awareness of the ecological implications of resources and related problems of massive human settlements can be understood when it is realized that the actual condition of the environment is encountered by those who live in it, or by those who depend on it directly for certain expected amenities, goods, and services. Indeed, many conservationists who have been caught up in the environmental movement of this decade have undoubtedly lost sight of where roots of the conservation movement began, and where its branches are today.

The Philosophy of American Natural Resource Use

There have been at least four major philosophical outlooks that have described the modus operandi of American natural resource managers over

69

the last two hundred years. These four general outlooks of *exploitation, preservation, regulation,* and *management* have been expressed in the behavior and attitudes of those who hold them. In the last fifteen to twenty years, the policy of comprehensive or integrated management has been regarded as a synthesis of the earlier traditional resource utilization approaches of exploitation, preservation, and regulation. Resource management, used in the generic sense, is exemplified by the multiple use philosophy of the U.S. Forest Service, or by the early philosophy of the TVA, and the recent application of integrated systems analysis in the area of urban and regional planning. The reader is cautioned that there may be a tendency either in the private sector or in the public agency to label its operation "comprehensive resource management" when upon close inspection one may discover that preservation, or in another case, regulation, really dominates the operational policy and practice. More often than not a specific issue of national concern such as the supersonic transport, an effort to create or salvage a wilderness area, or a challenge to national park or national forest use draws public attention to a resource utilization dilemma. Subsequently, once political strength is mustered, a given position takes the form of either an administrative policy, a legal guideline, or a managerial procedure. Too many writers in the past have argued or at least implied that these positions of the conservation movement have evolved in a particular chronological order. It seems clear, however, that in the complexity of these times no one disagrees that the threads of exploitation, preservation, regulation, and management are intimately interwoven. It is only at specific times and in parts of the nation or the world that one position seems to predominate over the others.

Exploitation

The predominance of one general conservation policy over another can be traced to the first settlers in America. Whether one documents the approach used by the Spanish conquistadors in the Southwest or the immigrants who stepped off the Mayflower in 1620, their actions exploited the environment. In the past, man has not always been exploitative as he interacted with his natural environment if the archaeological evidence is translated accurately. Pictographs and various decorated artifacts from the Old and New World portray man's subjugation to nature. Living creatures, celestial bodies, and numerous physical resources were deified and held in considerable awe. Oriental religions promulgated a reverence for life that was seldom duplicated in religious policy or practice of Western culture.

Inasmuch as the concept of creation or an established beginning was incompatible with many Oriental and Near Eastern philosophies, man's catastrophic intervention into the affairs of a *pantheistic* system was taboo even if he had had the technology to do so. The cyclical notion of time with the likelihood that reincarnation might place a human being into the form of another member of the animal kingdom—presumably another genus—gave the "resource manager" of those times quite a different perspective. And, of course, nearly 95 per cent of the population were resource managers of one kind or another as they interfaced directly with the raw materials and agricultural setting. Today, only about 5 per cent of the U.S. population is involved directly in livestock, grain, vegetable, and fruit production activities.

From Judaism, Christianity borrowed a strikingly different approach in dealing with nature. Early Christians believed that amphibians, reptiles, fishes, birds, and plants were created as spiritually nonrepetitive organisms. In breaking with earlier tradition, it was taught that with the exception of man, these creatures had very little spiritual lineage at all. Fragments of divinity were purported to be distributed on a "people only" basis except through the eyes of maverick theologians such as Saint Francis of Assisi and Albert Schweitzer. Lynn White, Jr., has characterized Christianity as the most *anthropocentric* religion that has ever been devised. So, departing from the ancient paganisms of Africa, Oceania, South, Central, and North America, and the Asian religions, people in the United States have employed rather different religious foundations to rationalize their rejection of man's dependence on his environment. One predominant American tradition that had its roots in the Christian Crusades has been that man has dominion over the beasts, the waters, the fields, and the forests.

And God said, Let us make man in our image, after our likeness; and let them have dominion over the fish of the sea, and over the fowl of the air, and over the cattle, and over all the earth, and over every creeping thing that creepeth upon the earth.

Genesis 1:26

An eighteenth century version of the Crusades was launched as the settlement of North America began. The colonists came, they saw, and they conquered with varying degrees of success and vengeance. The conquest did not take place in a spirit of idolatrous elimination as the forests were cut and burned and the bison butchered. If one chose Christianity, there were simply fewer theological constraints on ravaging whatever resources were available as long as God, through his sinful mortals, was the beneficiary. Presumably man, with the grace of God, had dominion and power over all his landscape and its creatures. However, enough evidence is piling up against the attitude of expecting nature to serve man without any reciprocity that is seems clear that the continued exploitation of American resources is nearing, or in some cases passing, the point of diminishing returns for man the omnipotent. This is not to say there were no preservationists or multiple use proponents in the United States until 1900; as one looks at the landscape, however, it is apparent that the exploitative philosophy predominated well into the twentieth century. Some argue that it continues today. The author believes the American extravagance with regard to energy consumption is a good example. Even in mid-1973 when

72 concern was rising about perceived shortages, the major thrust by the White House and the energy companies was to import more oil and gas, develop more offshore oil and oil shale resources, and get more coal, with hardly a mention about ecological safeguards or the need for reduced energy consumption.

Preservation

The historical roots of the conservation movement are sketched out with clarity in Stewart Udall's *The Quiet Crisis.*[1] Even though the environmental crisis is getting noisy today, very few of the visceral, intellectual, and philosophical underpinnings are altered in terms of the rationale for resource use. Despite the unchanged or only slightly changed notion of man subverting and controlling nature, another backlash from the rape of the landscape has begun. In the latter half of the nineteenth century, a group of preservationists convinced certain public agencies that unique high quality samples of the landscape should be set aside for the enjoyment of future generations. Some preservationists received criticism for being elitist as relatively inaccessible wilderness was put aside and used by the wealthy. Here it should be said that preservationists are not for total nonuse of the designated areas, but rather for a use that is amenable or aesthetically enhancing to the land. Geological wonders were the prime reason for the establishment of reservations in what are now known as Yellowstone National Park, Yosemite National Park, Carlsbad Caverns, and others. In subsequent years forest "reserves," wildlife sanctuaries, and eventually wilderness areas were set aside.

Conservation, as a political password, first paid off for President Theodore Roosevelt. His choice for the first head of the U.S. Forest Service, Gifford Pinchot, proposed a scheme to manage forest resources at a national level. More than that, Pinchot recognized the interrelationship of forest, water, mineral, wildlife, human, and other resources. For the first time in American history, the conservation movement had an advocate in the White House and a spokesman among other highly placed governmental officials. President Theodore Roosevelt, on March 14, 1907, appointed the Inland Waterways Commission made up of representative congressmen, a forester (Gifford Pinchot), a geologist, an engineer, a statistician, and an irrigation chief. In its first report to President Roosevelt, the Commission stressed the ecological character of the natural resource problem, pointing out how the control and use of water could conserve coal, iron, and soil. The findings of the report also recommended the maintenance and preservation of vast forest resources as an alternative to exploitative lumbering practices of the previous three or four decades. Perhaps even more noteworthy was the organization of a White House Conference on Conservation held on May 13, 1908, by the Inland Waterways Commission. Never before or since

[1]Stewart L. Udall, *The Quiet Crisis* (New York: Holt, Rinehart and Winston, Inc., 1963).

has the United States seen gathered at the White House a more influential and representative group of individuals: the President, the Vice-President, seven Cabinet members, the nine justices of the Supreme Court, the governors of thirty-four states and representatives of the other twelve, many members of Congress, delegates from sixty-eight national societies, four special guests, forty-eight general guests, and the nine members of the Inland Waterways Commission. This epic "environmental state of the union" conference heard startling papers that documented the extravagance and reckless waste of the past and cautioned that the foundation of the Republic depended on the conservation of all our natural resources.

The conservation impact of Pinchot and Roosevelt makes efforts of all subsequent administrations look meager at best. During his administration, President Theodore Roosevelt withdrew 234 million acres of land from private entry, including 148 million acres that were created as national forests. Another 84,700,000 acres of coal, phosphate, and other mineral-rich lands were denied access by private developers until the areas could be studied by the Geological Survey and a recommendation made as to their value and general management.

Any recent environmentalists who were impressed by the *1972 United Nation's Conference on the Human Environment* held in Stockholm should remember on February 16, 1909, President Roosevelt requested that the major nations of the world convene at the The Hague, Netherlands, to consider the conservation of the natural resources of the globe. What these prefatory paragraphs say is simply that the conservation of resources has meant a wide variety of things to various groups who had dealings with the environment—including the first colonists. The first substantial political emphasis came during the first ten years of the Theodore Roosevelt regime when the fear of resource scarcity enabled the President to take wide sweeping action in the name of resource preservation and wise management.

Regulation and Management

The period just before, during, and after World War I was characterized by public policies that were insensitive to wide governmental management of natural resources. The holding companies that were gaining power did not unfurl the banner of conservation. World War I, World War II, the Korean War, and the Vietnam-Indochina War diverted public attention and strategic resources to the war efforts. Wars are always anticonservation, extremely wasteful, and always seem to sabotage serious long-range resource management practices. After World War I there was a sharp rise in industrialization, mechanization, and automation with its concomitant rise in the use of metals and fossil fuels. The fact that many renewable resources were undergoing excessive exploitation paved the way for a period of conservation legislation and policy in which regulation of resources was emphasized.

The backlash from exploiting the use of replenishable and nonreplenish-

74   able resource use picked up momentum in the late 1920's and mid-1930's in conjunction with the trend of antitrust, antimonoply legislation. Perhaps the land resources in the form of range, topsoil, and general habitat suffered the most critical damage of the twentieth century during the 1930's. The economic despair of the Great Depression joined forces with the failure of the resources in this period of disastrous floods, Dust Bowl "days," and dwindling wildlife populations. The author offers the suggestion that the interrelationship of economic, ecological, and social forces combined to produce the sad state of affairs in the flood plains, the prairies, the forests, and in the industrializing cities. It is important to note here that President Franklin D. Roosevelt, faced with the overwhelming combination of re-source exploitation and the severe economic depression, got down to the business of management through a vast public works program that not only provided employment to large numbers of people but also improved the country's natural resources. Beginning with the Civilian Conservation Corps, President Franklin D. Roosevelt quickly tackled everything from forest protection to soil erosion control to lake and stream surveys to recreational developments. A fuller discussion of the policy and practice on a resource by resource basis is given in Section II. An unprecedented series of regula-tory and management bills were passed by Congress during the 1930's—the decade of the most vigorous natural resource legislation. These bills touched upon the most severe resource problems of that period as national concern and crises helped push through the TVA in 1933 (the Norris Act), the *Prairie States Forestry Project in 1934,* the *Soil Conservation Act in 1935,* the *Omnibus Flood Control Act in 1936,* the *Guffey Coal Act in 1936,* and the *Wildlife Restoration Act in 1937.*[2]

A classic example of a clash between public conservationists and private speculators was the controversy of public power versus private power epitomized by the Tennessee Valley Authority (TVA). New York-based holding companies who owned controlling stock in Southern and Mid-western utility companies bitterly fought the establishment of federal power production facilities in the seven-state watershed of the Tennessee River. Most observers such as Phillip Selznick and Judson King (for an incredible account of this controversy read King's *The Conservation Fight,* Public Affairs Press, 1958) agreed that the effect most feared by the private sector, in addition to "creeping socialism" as President Dwight Eisenhower once labeled the TVA, was the "yardstick" effect. In other words, a measurement and example of low-cost power production set in the TVA region had visible benefits against which neighboring privately owned utilities could be measured. With the perspective of time, one gets the impression that Congress created a public monopoly in natural resource management to provide competition for private resource monopolies that were taking

---

[2]Many of these acts are discussed in Section II under their appropriate topics and are described in the Glossary.

possession of various resources such as timber, oil, coal, gas, metals, and other minerals and marine fisheries.

Perhaps the most interesting feature about the TVA for this discussion is the revelation that here was the last comprehensive federal conservation policy decision implemented by Congress that favored the nonurban American. Certainly, flood-control benefits, reduced electrical rates, increased navigation possibilities, and improved recreation facilities were among advantages enjoyed by the residents of Chattanooga, and other urbanites in the TVA, but the major thrust of the TVA Act signed by Franklin D. Roosevelt was to provide direct help for the rural population whose resource base had been critically eroded away. The rural electrification program was a subsequent project that helped the rural dwellers. Almost without exception, federal resource legislation and conservation policy from the mid-1930's to the present have given preference to urban resource problems or to urbanites who tend to create problems in the hinterlands. Of course, during this time period, an exodus from rural areas was underway that eventually shifted much of the political power base to urban decision makers. But the transition of political muscle that is exercised by urbanites and surbanites over "ruralites" in the form of resource management policy is neither rapid nor complete. The one man, one vote has shifted the balance of power but substantial blocks of power are still produced by nonurbanites in debates and votes that affect all rural or agricultural interests.

But with the transfer of political leverage to metropolitan interests, it became clear that the resource manager, whether he was a biologist or an engineer, had to do more than regulate. The regulation of a single energy source, or one migratory bird species, or a recreation site fostered dangerous tunnel vision. Managerial skills were thin, and ecological evidence was incomplete about the consequences of single use or single resource development and management. The day to day fluctuations and the seasonal crises kept the game biologist, the soil conservation agent, and the public health officer busy. When a crisis struck, the policy for dealing with a given problem was hammered and patched together in a crisis workshop. Needless to say, the policies and practices that grow out of such a setting usually leave much to be desired. The author contends that policies and legislation emerging from a crisis or traumatic atmosphere are worse resource management strategies than doing nothing at all.

The Emergence of a Comprehensive Policy

In the midtwentieth century the pendulum continued to swing from the exploitative (particularly in wartime) to the preservationist position and back. With each sweep of the pendulum, the "comprehensive management" outlook became part of the resource manager's philosophy at a

76   doubling rate. A *total systems approach* of solid waste, water pollution, and air pollution management is currently used in the most progressive metropolitan areas. Instead of a *watershed* or *airshed,* the new emphasis is on the "problem shed" that stresses the concept of regionality.

The factors that influence a national position on conservation policy are too complex for a thorough discussion here. But a glimpse at several major influences would help the reader understand what has happened in the most recent decades and what may take place in the years just ahead.

World War II took priority over nearly all environmental interest that had been created in the previous decade. Production for the military effort took precedence over every conservation practice. But even then, interesting spinoff effects were created during the four years of World War II. If the TVA and its tremendous electrical generation capacity had not been created, some doubt exists whether or not the Atomic Energy Commission's efforts at Oak Ridge, Tennessee, would have progressed to the point it did with a competitive advantage over similar German and Japanese efforts. Recycling metals in the form of cans and iron scrap was encouraged. New ways of lengthing the life of wood were discovered. Paper was reused, and "strategic commodities" such as gasoline, rubber, and even leather were conserved through reduced use and the development and use of substitutes.

The Mid-Century Conference of 1953 was the first major national conservation conference since Theodore Roosevelt's National Governor's Conference (1908). It was sponsored by Resources for the Future, a private educational and research organization focusing on environmental matters. Funded heavily by the Ford Foundation, Resources for the Future made its name in the conservation movement by sponsoring the conference that called attention to President Truman's Materials Policy Commission report and mustered broad support from natural resource users and conservers.[3] The political climate was not conducive for the insertion of teeth into legislative or administrative steps that dealt with resource management and regulation. But the time was fast approaching when the total environment and the interdependency of pollution costs were going to be considered. An environmental assessment was to include not *just* the soil problem, the recreation problem, the atmospheric problem, or the water problem. Instead of a narrow, tunnel-visioned environmental assessment a comprehensive view of resource management with an array of alternatives slowly became dominant in resource planning policy. In fact, fifteen years later, the congressional background paper for the 1968 hearings on National Policy on Environmental Quality stated:

Lack of national policy for the environment has now become as expensive to the business community as to the nation at large. In most enterprises a social cost

---

[3] A 1953 inventory to determine the status of available resources and projected demands after a period of nearly fifteen years of no strong conservation legislation and a world war.

can be carried without undue burden if all competitors carry it alike. For example, industrial waste disposal costs can, like other costs of pollution, be reflected in prices to consumers. But this becomes feasible only when public law and administration put all comparable forms of waste-producing enterprises under the same requirements.

The abuses of water and air resources during the war production effort were so aggravated that the first federal water pollution control mandate was launched in 1948. Even though it was very mild at first, this federal involvement was the beginning of a trend that usurped much of the previous state responsibility in the water pollution control area. More federal dollars, more federal assistance, more federal standards, and more federal enforcement came to pass as the *1948 Federal Water Pollution Control Act* was amended, strengthened, and supplemented by sister legislation in 1953, 1956, 1961, 1962, 1965, 1966, 1967, 1969, 1970, and 1972.

The air pollution control effort came fifteen years after the first water pollution control legislation appeared. The *Clean Air Act of 1963* put the federal government into the air pollution control business. Only a few major metropolitan regions (such as Los Angeles, Pittsburgh, and San Francisco) had previously been active. As a result of interurban and interstate airsheds, costs and other disadvantages created interjurisdictional difficulties that were unresolved under municipal and state institutional arrangements.

The solution of resource problems is becoming increasingly the responsibility of the federal government. Undoubtedly international controls eventually will become widespread. In fact, in 1973 the World Bank began asking that environmental impact statements be filed for its major projects. The trend for nationalized control has been demonstrated with essentially every resource problem as seen by looking at the chronological list of the following legislation. Notice how the early emphasis was on forests, soils, and water, and how in recent years the focus has broadened to incorporate air and recreation resources and even endangered species.[4]

1911   Weeks Act (forests)
1924   Clarke-McNary Act (forests)
1948   Bureau of Land Management established (soils)
1948   Water Pollution Control Act (water)
1954   Small Watershed Act (soils)
1954   Atomic Energy Act (minerals)
1955   Minerals Multiple Use Act (minerals)
1956–60   Soil Bank Program (soils)
1960   Multiple Use-Sustained Yield Act (forests)
1963   Clean Air Act (atmosphere)

[4]Many of these acts are discussed in Section II under their appropriate topics and are also listed in the Glossary.

1964 Urban Mass Transportation Act (urban open space)
1964 Wilderness Act (recreation)
1964 Land and Water Conservation Fund Act (recreation)
1965 Water Resources Planning Act (water)
1966 Demonstration Cities Act (urban open space)
1967 Air Quality Act (atmosphere)
1968 Housing and Urban Development Act (urban open space)
1968 Wild and Scenic Rivers Act (recreation)
1969 Coal Mine Health and Safety Act (minerals)
1970 Clean Air Amendments (atmosphere)
1972 Water Pollution Control Act Amendments (water)
1972 Marine Mammal Protection Act (wildlife)

The Current Trend in Environmental Concern

It is appropriate to take note of trends in the conservation movement that have moved out of the purview of the public agency. What efforts have been made by the private sector? What efficacy does the student interest in environment hold? Will the environmental teach-ins that began in the 1970's entrench a broader awareness of resource problems and solutions among the American public? It is apparent that a new trend in environmental concern has been launched on American college and university campuses and has spread into secondary education.

American colleges and universities have been the breeding grounds for several social movements in recent decades. The relatively open forum for the expression of ideas that a university provides has served as a springboard for the civil rights movement, the Peace Corps, and Vista in the 1960's. Numerous antiwar, antipollution, and other antiestablishment campaigns have been generated at American campuses and then spread through political and other institutional channels. We can only speculate about the cause of the environmental concern that took on nationwide dimensions in 1969 and 1970, picking up massive momentum on university campuses with "*Earth Day*" celebrations in the spring of 1970. However, its uniqueness as a contribution to the contemporary conservation movement merits a detailed discussion.

In the fall of 1969, the Nixon administration offered assurances that troop withdrawals from Vietnam would begin on a prescribed, although unannounced schedule. A general "Vietnamization" of the war was designed to replace American fighting personnel with South Vietnamese troops. The draft lottery was then initiated and served to placate some campus unrest. Overtures by the federal government to get out of Vietnam as well as a general increase in activism at that time certainly must have been an incentive for campus activist groups to focus on another issue. It was the "in" thing to be politically active. Thus the concern about the survival of

Figure 3-1. Ralph Nader was one of the most popular speakers at Earth Day gatherings. Here he is shown addressing one of the first large campus "teach-ins" on the environment at the University of Michigan, March 1970.

the biosphere grew as a student movement. The sputtering torches of perturbed scientists such as Barry Commoner, Paul Ehrlich, Garrett Hardin, John Bardach, and Rene Dubos were picked up by youth and spread like wildfire nationwide.

The surge of interest in environmental issues undoubtedly was also stimulated by the abundant evidence showing that defoliation by potent herbicides in Southeast Asia was producing severe biological changes in that area. Environmental degradation in the United States resulting from careless consumer and industrial behavior is another "bone of contention" for many activists.

As racial injustices, dramatized by the urban riots of 1967 and 1968 in Detroit, Watts, Newark, Philadelphia, and elsewhere appeared to be superficially bandaged, the ecosystem survival campaigns emerged as additional causes behind which student as well as adult involvement heightened. It is assumed, however, from the experience of the first years of the environmental movement that other issues will continue to take precedence. Even by 1973 and 1974 the enthusiasm for environmental activity among youth has cooled in comparison to 1970 and 1971. Racial injustices, poverty, American involvement in the Middle East, Indochina, Africa, and Latin America will undoubtedly be major targets of students in protest. There are also other battles being fought in women's liberation and consumer disenchantment with workmanship.

The pervasive feature about the environmental movement is that as long

79

as man inhabits the earth with his present ecological recklessness and ignorance there will always be fuel for the torch carried by the doomsday ecologist. The new conservation awakening does not have as its target a single resource problem as was the case in conservation battles of the past. Furthermore, the crisis of Spaceship Earth affects every socioeconomic bracket, every gender, every race, every religion, and every culture. By its very magnitude and its almost incomprehensible complexity, the movement also has obvious built in copouts for those who consider the task far too monumental to tackle. Yet the skirmishes have begun, and the youth in grade schools, high schools, and colleges are stepping up to the firing line. Interestingly, members of the business community and persons over thirty are joining the ranks either because of personal initiatives or because of image-building pressure.

Most minority groups resist involvement in the environmental protest because they feel participation will dilute what are, in their opinion, more urgent issues. Instead environmentalists argue that the ills of the total ecosystem are exemplified and ramified in social sores and physical blights that affect every urban or rural dweller—yellow, brown, black, and white. It appears to the author that those who are the most economically, politically, and socially disenfranchised are always the groups who suffer the heaviest environmental costs.

The Teach-in and Earth Week

One major instrument of the recent conservation movement was an action-oriented teach-in. The prime objective of the environmental teach-in was to identify, diagnose, and resolve local, regional, or national problems. The procedure often used in these teach-ins involved an increase in motivation among the teach-in participants who tried to work out alternative ways of solving whatever problem was in question.

The teach-in concept was born in 1965 at The University of Michigan when attention focused on the American involvement in the Vietnam War. Organizers attempted to inform the students and the adult public about the inequities of the situation in order that the national government could be persuaded to withdraw its military operations from Vietnam. Various forms of political action were used including marches to Washington, pickets, boycotts, and other protests. Efforts were made to involve religious leaders, minority group leaders, prominent figures in the entertainment and athletic world, and even conservationists. The conservationists were reminded that prolific bombing and the use of herbicides in jungle defoliation have severe and long-lasting effects on the people, the soil, the water, the wildlife, and the total environment thirty to forty years hence. Thus the war in Indochina on sheer environmental evidence seemed to have more serious effects (in addition to the traditional social, economic, and political evils of war) than any previous Armageddon.

The 1970 environmental teach-in approach borrowed heavily from the antiwar teach-ins. Several improvements were made, however; student organizers of the best environmental teach-ins brought to the community and college campuses both offenders and those who felt offended by environmental deterioration. Industrial polluters came together with labor leaders, citizens, governmental agency personnel, and ecologists. As a result, an educational "quantum jump" took place among many Americans, young and old, in regard to the environmental state of the union.

Earth Day and Earth Week events in the early 1970's put facts and fears in issue after issue of almost every nationally read magazine and journal. For some time after the first environmental teach-ins, magazine cover stories alerted and sensitized readers who never had heard the words *ecology, ecosystems,* or *eutrophication* before. Headlines about "Earth Day" events appeared in all metropolitan newspapers. Prime time was used on all major television networks, in newscasts, feature programs, and documentaries to portray what no biology course ever tried to do but should have been doing as a regular task. Some of the messages about severe environmental disruptions and possible future biological disorders (with some of the possible remedies) began to be heard by Americans of every economic category and every political persuasion. America was "ecologized," but could the real payoff of the environmental teach-ins—namely personal and public commitment to environmental stewardship—ever materialize? Would individuals, corporations, and public agencies make the sacrifices that would produce a nation or a society living in harmony with its environment and its counterparts around the world?

The Role of the Citizen in the Post Teach-in Era

The payoff is, of course, to translate the information, concern, and knowledge begun by the teach-in into significant action that will maintain some degree of *mutualism* or commensalism in the total ecosystem. To put it in more common terminology, can postindustrialized society "save the earth" or even at best "give earth a chance?"

The conservation movement of the 1970's has an advantage (or perhaps an "Achilles' heel") over previous conservation campaigns and other major social protest movements because more individuals are encouraged to participate in a very personal way of direct action. No matter how subtle or complex, most environmental problems are identified with urban areas where 90 per cent of the problem makers are or will be. However, it is an open question whether or not conservation groups marching under the ecoflag, living in ecocommunes, or attending ecology center workshops will produce policies, programs, and practices as influential as the Pinchot-Roosevelt machine at the turn of the century. Will the new ecotactics be as far-reaching as the New Deal conservationism of the 1930's? Probably not. Considerable skepticism exists about the outcome even among some of the early and most avid crusaders. However, everyone attached to this most recent wave of the conservation movement agrees it is well worth the effort if there is to be any reduction in personal consumption as a nation or better yet if there is to be a significant reduction in corporate pollution

82   and the corporation effort to get consumers to buy more ecologically disruptive, nonessential products.

Most biologists agree that with the additional loads of food additives, pesticides, *radio-nucleides,* herbicides, toxic by-products of commercial and industrial life, and sheer numbers of people, the biological equilibrium of the ecosystem is in serious jeopardy. Past slogans of traditional conservationism warned about the elimination of nonrenewable resources, but that cry had been used countless times before. Now the slogan of the new conservation movement says more than that. It warns in devastatingly convincing documentation that the eradication of the *renewable* resources is the additional price that man will pay unless his life style is changed.

The youth who were alerted to the new environmental hazards in schools and colleges during the early 1970's are now becoming part of the decision-making public. These young adults have new roles as voters, as household consumers, and as young leaders in their communities. Environmental education and conservation education courses are becoming common in primary school curricula and as high school and college courses. Organic gardening and organic or health food stores are found across the United States. Cooperative living and cooperative gardening experiments are becoming more commonplace than was the practice ten years ago. Whether or not these and other stirrings of the conservation movement will influence policy directions at the national level is a question that can be answered only over time.

Recent trends in conservation policy have taken form at national and state echelons in addition to or in complementarity with more environmentally sensitive individual behavior that is in evidence. The *Environmental Protection Agency* began cracking down in 1971 and 1972 on large industrial polluters and various governmental offenders that were in violation of antipollution regulations. Early targets of the EPA compliance activities were the Reserve Mining Company in Minnesota for dumping taconite tailings into Lake Superior; General Motors for balking at the strict carbon monoxide, carbon dioxide, and nitrogen oxides automobile emissions for the period 1971 to 1976; Wyandotte Chemical Corporation for mercury pollution, and several national airlines for emissions and noise pollution. The extension of automobile emmission deadlines in 1973, the difficulty of providing federal funds for urban rapid transit, and a dilution of environmental impact statement efforts combine to suggest that some large industries and small-visioned individuals are weakening laws and procedures that were intended to improve environmental management.

The Role of the Federal Government in Two Urban Crises

Perhaps two of the newest and most significant trends in environmental affairs at the national level are federal involvement in solid waste management and rapid mass transit. It is not at all surprising that both of these problems have a record of federal involvement very similar to that of water and air pollution control. The difficulties of urban solid waste, urban transportation, and urban water and air pollution in their early stages were almost totally local concerns. Only when the severity of the air and water pollution problems reached gargantuan, multicounty, and interstate proportions did the state and eventually the federal governments get involved.

Solid Waste. As we envision the metabolism of an urban organism as discussed in Chapters 1 and 2, the massive human settlements of our postindustrialized society are literally huge chemical, physical, and energy sinks. Until recently, the flow of the innumerable commodities and nutrients had been managed in only one direction—*to* the urban area. The tonnages of food, for example, are shipped hundreds if not thousands of miles on a year-round basis. The nutrients, in the form of proteins, fats, and carbohydrates are chemically unlocked and reshuffled during the transforming process of human consumption and use. After heat loss, the remaining mass in a changed form is released into or near the urban complex via waste treatment plants, smokestacks, dumps, and sanitary landfill sites with small fractions of the energy stored temporarily in the tissues of the urban residents. The city is then a mammoth chemical and physical sink not only of nutrients and energy but of all the containers and packages that comprise the multitude of goods and products.

Historically, it is a municipal responsibility to carry off the metabolic residues of urban household activity. Even though private collectors now cart off the majority of commercial and industrial wastes, the burden of residential solid waste disposal on financially struggling cities is staggering. This country spends over $4.5 billion annually for collecting, processing, and depositing domestic and industrial urban wastes. The cost of solid waste management, even with the primitive procedures in general use, is surpassed only by urban expenditures for education and highway construction.

Very basic policy changes need to take place for the problem of urban solid waste to be resolved. Americans need to reduce the production of waste-creating materials. There is a strong need to systematically reclaim useful materials that are now discarded. Also, the availability of long-lived products or comparable substitutes is characteristically unpublicized in a capitalistic system where profits are made on wasteful, useless items or on products with built-in obsolescence. As in the air and water management activity, the beginning of federal solid waste management was very modest. The *Solid Waste Disposal Act of 1965* was the first step. Even the name of the legislation "Waste Disposal Act" left much room for improvement. The emphasis should be and has become more on the recovery, reuse, and recycling of valuable resources in the form of minerals, metals, fibers, and other reusables as a result of domestic, commercial, industrial, agricultural, and mining activities. Five years later a companion piece of federal legislation was properly called the *Resource Recovery Act of 1970.*

Not only has the label changed; the policy and practices are beginning to catch up to the problem. Before the 1965 Solid Waste Disposal Act only

84 two states assumed any responsibility for solid wastes. Five years later forty-two states had completed surveys on solid waste management needs and were working on comprehensive plans to meet them. Only recently has the federal government geared up to be of any substantial help to an old but local problem. The policy recommendations by federal agencies directed toward urban areas have taken a great variety of approaches; some include a ban or tax on disposable containers, others place a tax or *surcharge* on durable consumer items that will require ultimate recycling. New federally sponsored incentives for recycling metal, glass, paper, and other reusable materials is forthcoming. Grants-in-aid for technical assistance and solid waste management training have grown to begin to meet the magnitude of the problem. Other federal financial incentives encourage the operation and regionalization of recovery and recycling centers with an overview of the problem that is more comprehensive than in the late 1960's and early 1970's. The Madison, Wisconsin, pilot project discussed in Chapter 2 is one such incentive. Other barriers that remain include differential freight rates favoring new ore over scrap material, consumer ignorance about packaging disadvantages, and the traditional citizen's maladies of apathy and nonchalance about a problem that is not in full sight. Trash mashers, sanitary landfill, and municipal incineration are temporary efforts that precede the real solution of total reuse and recycling at the urban scale.

The relatively recent federal policies of custodianship of urban land, air, and water wastes have special significance relating to how, where, and how fast urban areas flourish. Once the appropriation of federal funds are available, state and local considerations take on decreased importance. Some political scientists observe that because special bonuses go to a metropolitan waste treatment or garbage collection system, urban growth is subsidized at the cost of rural or outlying areas that could not or care not to qualify. Urban transportation systems dramatize this point. The question of urban mass transit subsidized by the federal government also serves as an instructive illustration of new federal involvement and policy intended to relieve urban environmental problems.

Transportation System. The recent urban transportation policies have emerged out of crisis and wasteful expenditures on earlier networks that did not properly serve the cities of today. The pattern of original private custody of roads, canals, and trains, followed by increased federal regulation, heavier subsidy, and eventually almost complete federal control, is not unlike the chain of events that transpired for other urban-dependent resources. The painful implementation of urban mass transit programs is better understood when we see what an integral part the transportation system is to any urban organism. It has similarities with the circulatory systems of higher animals: major arterial and venous systems in the form of inner city expressways, interspersed with secondary roads and eventually laced with a gridiron pattern of capillaries or neighborhood streets (see Figure 3-2). The social, physical, ecological, and financial pain to a metropolitan area is considerable when the vehicular transport system is changed.

Networks

In plants and animals the circulatory or nervous systems and networks end towards one centre;

In human settlements there are two types of circulatory systems: towards the centre and between the parts

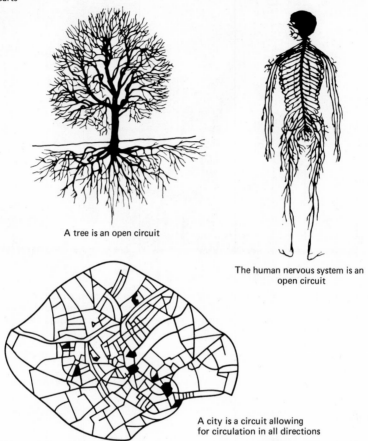

A tree is an open circuit

The human nervous system is an open circuit

A city is a circuit allowing for circulation in all directions

Figure 3-2. Networks in plants, animals, and human communities or urban organisms serve comparable functions. In human settlements there are two types of transportation networks or circulatory systems: one in and out of the centers of activity, and another among the residences of the city. (*Ekistics,* C. A. Doxiadis)

If the present rate and magnitude of urban growth had been anticipated, it might have been less traumatic to integrate mass transit systems into the present tissue of the city. It is ironic that transportation routes, in large measure, determine where and when urbanization takes place (see Figure 3-3).

In man's first settlements simple paths connected one person's house with his neighbor's house, and in the successive buildup of the community

Figure 3-3. The presence of major intersections, round-abouts, and traffic circles serve as magnets of human activity and commercial development such as this platz in the Berlin borough of Charlottenburg. (German Information Center)

Figure 3-4. Picadilly Circus in London is a famous crossroads of human activity.

Figure 3-5. In a living city of antiquity such as Lindos on the island of Rhodes, paths between residences form a tight network within the town with a single road leading off to another human settlement.

paths between individual dwelling units connected the village well, town square, or marketplace. Man's movement between villages generally followed a linear pattern. As networks are established, additional growth develops along the major route and at nodes or intersections of other routes. The growth at a four-corner intersection is usually less vigorous at a five or six road intersection of equally busy streets. A rapid transformation of land use occurs at most expressway cloverleaf interchanges in a rural area. Within a few years after construction, the land use adjacent to an expressway cloverleaf changes with the establishment of service stations, restaurants, and other service accessory installations.

The various kinds of networks, specifically transportation systems, had an overwhelming influence on the other ekistic elements (Man, Nature, Society, and Shells), which formed future urban development. In the formative stages of the United States, stagecoach routes and the distance covered by horse in one day often determined the placement of county seats of **87**

Figure 3-6. On the Greek island of Mykonos, residences are in close proximity to each other. Networks are short and compacted, which gives an opportunity for a kind of communication not available across broad streets or expressways.

government. Railroad construction and operation provided major arteries for development as drainage patterns were changed, rights of way were cleared, and wildlife habitat was disturbed by fires started from steam engine sparks in the forested and prairie regions of the country. Canals also had long-range influence, first in the Eastern states and more recently with the vast water diversion projects of the Western states. One economically and biologically adverse impact of a large canal project in North America was demonstrated by the invasion of the sea lamprey and later the alewife through the St. Lawrence Seaway. Both of these *anadromous species* penetrated the Great Lakes only after the Welland Canal and other navigational works permitted easy access to the Great Lakes system.

In the years ahead automobiles and jet aircraft represent major threats to environmental and human tranquility in the author's judgement. The private car also looms as a serious environmental menace. The price Americans pay for their personal privacy, convenience, and potential safety provided by the automobile must be balanced against the very substantial toll levied on the natural and physical environment and on man himself. The preparation of the roadbed and site modification usually has serious implications on drainage, local wildlife, and vegetation. Altering drainage patterns and cutting roads into hillsides and mountains produce potential erosion hazards whereas moisture *absorption* is significantly reduced in multilaned highways with huge cloverleafs. However, initial construction of such roadways may not be as detrimental as the effects caused by maintenance and daily uses of streets and highways listed in these examples: (a) The application of calcium chloride, sodium chloride, and other chemical ice retardants influence vegetation up to 150 feet from the shoulder of the road. (b) Oil and gas spilled on the pavement usually are carried off by storm water into drains and local surface waters. (c) Microscopic particles of asbestos from brakeshoe linings have been shown to be carcinogenic, and other atmospheric contamination from automotive emissions is well known. (d) Vibrations from trucks and other heavy vehicles have adverse structural effects on dwellings and physiological effects on residents. This negative impact is in addition to the decibel levels produced along heavy-use highways, which are usually in excess of acceptable noise standards. The automobile has done more to spread the protoplasm of the city beyond its manageable boundary than any other force. The city limits of American communities seldom catch up with the suburbs whose sprawl is encouraged by the automobile and expressways.

The major policy milestone that diluted and dehumanized the American city was formalized in the *Public Highway Act of 1956* and its invidious *Highway Trust Fund.* The principal purpose of this fund is to provide revenues to build the interstate highway system. It is also the source of all federal funds for federal aid to primary and secondary roads. The highway trust fund currently has a claim on about 71 per cent of all federal excise taxes related to highway use including tire rubber, trucking tonnage,

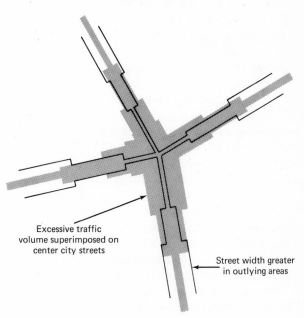

Figure 3-7. In most old towns the first main streets were built to accommodate a small community and modest traffic flows. As the town grew to a city, the outlying streets were built with considerable width. As collectors of traffic the suburban arteries seem to be oversized compared with the traffic they carry and compared to the downtown streets which carry great volumes of traffic at metropolitan crossroads.

Excessive traffic volume superimposed on center city streets

Street width greater in outlying areas

and most notably the motor fuel tax. Revenues to the fund in fiscal 1973 totaled $6 billion, but this increases as tax revenues rise. Over $8 billion are anticipated in 1975. For bankrupt cities, who years ago lost money (and still do) on bus transportation authorities and other municipally managed transit systems, this 90 per cent federal contribution has special appeal. Even though trains, buses, and subways carry many more people, there is patently unfair differential pricing in those cities and states that prefer mass transportation facilities. The local burden for mass transit construction is from $.33 to $.50 on the dollar as compared to the $.10 on the dollar for interstate highway construction.

A few years ago the total cost of the interstate highway system was estimated at $56 billion. In 1973 as a result of a variety of factors, the estimate was up to $80 billion and will go even higher because of cost escalation. About $3.4 billion of the increase is attributed to the additional 1,500 miles authorized for the system in 1968. The present completion date for the interstate highway system is 1975, when the United States is expected to have and is limited under the present legislation for the interstate highway system to 44,500 miles.

The only glimmer of hope on the horizon for a change in America's road-building approach can be seen when people begin to consider that building highways is a completely different notion than moving people and goods. On May 5, 1970, Maryland enacted a law, that not only created a new department of transportation but also gave the secretary of the department responsibility for the development and maintenance of continuing comprehensive and integrated transportation planning process, including the state master plan for transportation. With this kind of provision, there is a possibility that instead of building roads, funds will be diverted to urban mass transit. The Maryland law created a transportation trust fund and allocated to it most of the highway user revenues previously earmarked for highway uses. There are stirrings in other states to take similar action or else to divert highway user funds for other modes of transportation.

For the automobile advocates and the highway lobby, several clear and direct statements must be made to substantiate the claim that automobile use in the center city is the antithesis of wise urban conservation practice. Nearly 95 per cent of all travel in urbanized areas is by car; yet between one fourth and one half or the urban population do not drive an automobile. In the center of most large U.S. cities up to 60 per cent of the population do not own a car. Detroit's inner city residents serve as an ironic example; it is the "Motor City" center city residents who are also without any rapid mass transit system. Clearly the choices for personal conveyance are severely restricted among the poor, the young, the elderly, and the handicapped. In 1980, there will be 100 million people in the United States from these categories who will not have ready access to an automobile.

This anticonservation practice of urban automobile use becomes more obvious when one looks at how the policy decisions are made for investing in automobiles and highways instead of in less discriminatory transportation. Trains, buses, subways, and other modes are not that much more costly; we just got off on the wrong vehicle. That mistake cannot perpetuate itself much longer. How did it happen? Simply stated, there were very poor criteria for past transportation construction projects. The comprehensiveness, the synthesis, and the integration that a transportation system performs or can perform for an urban area demands that the system utilized be one whose output can contribute the greatest benefits to the total urban organism. This did not occur. Difficulties now arise because city planners, economists, and policy strategists have no adequate ways to trace the multitude of specific outputs produced by a given transportation investment.

Somewhat understandably, highway engineers are led to believe that projects yielding the lowest user cost or the lowest capital cost are the best designed projects. Thus the highway engineer and affiliated transportation planners, in the absence of being able to identify the flow of costs and benefits throughout a complex urban area, settle for more concrete, short run, transportation-specific indicators of success. Only in recent years have *environmental impact statements* been required for federal projects such as highways, airports, harbors, and other public works. Of the tens of thousands that have been submitted, most project statements appear to be attempts at project justification that are woefully narrow-visioned, principally because of the view of their authors who represent considerably less than a broad understanding of social and ecological costs. As a result, the full range of public costs and associated private losses seldom enter into the policy formulation and decision process. An indicator such as improved traffic flow is not necessarily a surrogate for the real payoff, which is increased contact potential for people and business activities.

Thus the frequent costs borne by the urban public (public usually means unorganized individuals) include twenty-four hour noise pollution, air pollution (with all its automobile by-products from blood lead levels to carcinogenic asbestos particles in lung linings), natural drainage and groundwater disruptions, and water pollution attributable to vehicles including roadside salt accumulations that are toxic to vegetation, corrosive to metals, and abusive to surface water supplies. There is also the preemption of public parkland that could have captured other higher value uses. Furthermore, when the acreage consumed by highways is removed from the local tax rolls, the compensatory costs of human relocation, wildlife habitat destruction, water supply recharge and absorption losses, sound buffering, and destruction of aesthetic values are seldom covered over the life of the expressway.

The calculated use of transportation to meet the anticipated needs of a community relies heavily upon long-range projections of travel demand that combine sophisticated statistical and model-building techniques. Often when a new policy is under consideration, a question is asked about

92   what will happen if the present policy is not continued. Although answers to this question are rather scanty and poorly publicized, it may be interesting to see what actually did happen in one American city that has resisted or been denied (depending upon your point of view) ample expressway networks.

A mass transit study done in the late 1950's projected Washington, D.C., travel demand for 1965, 1970, and 1980.[5] In the ensuing years, it has been possible to check some of the projections against actual travel growth. The factors believed to generate travel between downtown Washington and the suburbs all increased more than had been projected. That is, the population outside central Washington was 15 per cent higher than forecast, and central city employment was 18 per cent higher than projected. However, a discrepancy in the projections is obvious when further statistics are viewed. Despite the growth of suburban populations and center city employment, weekday transit trips were 23 per cent lower than the figure projected in the study cited. Equally surprising was the finding that average weekday traffic crossing the District of Columbia line was 40 per cent less than the projected figure.

The inaccuracy of the study's projected figures seems to have a three-part explanation: (1) Because of the efforts of conservation groups and others, anticipated major expressways were not built in the period studied (1955 to 1965), (2) Suburban areas matured quickly, providing services and goods comparable to or better than those found in the central city, and (3) People arranged their lives differently when faced with a lack of transportation facilities; they switched houses, jobs, and shopping places to take covenience and liveability into account.

What are the implications of all this? Perhaps travel-demand projections may be leading to an overinvestment in the wrong kind of urban transportation facilities because understandably not all projections are accurate. Certainly people are somewhat flexible and when they are deprived of convenience, they may readjust their style of living. In 1958 it was believed that the development and prosperity of Washington, D.C., and its surroundings depended upon the building of an adequate transportation system. Fifteen years later, despite these very costly transportation facilities not all being built, the region was apparently no less prosperous or developed or contented. In fact, it may have been better off in that the large amount of choice landscape that would have been sacrificed to transportation was left for the area citizens to enjoy.

As originally planned, the U.S. interstate highway system was patterned after the German Autobahn and the Italian Autostrada, and justification for all three was similar—national defense. The interstate highway's initial aim—to connect major cities—maximized the use of the automobile, which

---

[5] Lyle C. Fitch, "Goals of Urban Transportation Policy," *Ekistics* Vol. 29 No. 170 (January 1970), pp. 20-24.

Figure 3-8. Electrified trains serve the Greater London region as seen by this station in Nottingham. Train arrivals and departures tend to be frequent and very punctual.

serves best in indirect intercity travel and on vacation trips. When later the purpose of the interstate highway system was expanded from building interstate highways between cities to the construction of limited access highways through the hearts of cities as well, the effect was catastrophic on metropolitan areas. Not until many years later did people begin to realize that the term *limited access* was figuratively and literally true, for gaining access to the road and *to the forces* that kept building those roads in the face of proven better alternatives was indeed very limited.

European cities such as Paris, London, Barcelona, Stockholm, Rome, and Vienna pioneered and improved efficient, clean, economical, and pleasant urban rapid transit systems, whereas the United States has struggled with modest experiments in electrified commuter trains (Los Angeles, Detroit, Milwaukee), subways (New York, Boston), and elevated urban trains (Chicago). Some of them failed; some mass transit systems were even forced out by automobile manufacturer conspiracies. And so the typical U.S. city continues to choke and commuters travel bumper to bumper on roads and expressways every rush hour every day.

One unlikely consolation about the oppression of the automobile in the hearts of American cities is that perhaps human settlements in other parts of the world will see the human and ecological costs before new urban communities become "automobilized." In 1972 the mayor of Munich, Germany, visited Los Angeles to inspect the freeway system because his city was about to make a decision concerning several transportation alter-

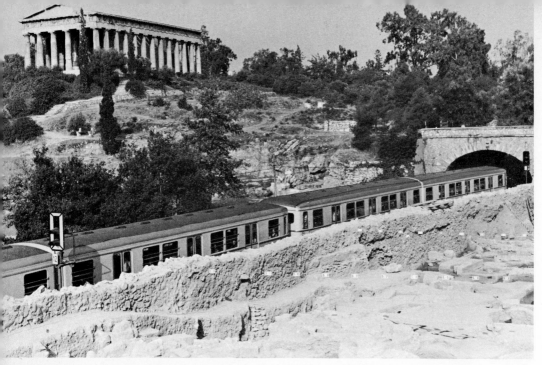

Figure 3-9. The Mass Transit System in Athens, Greece, takes the commuter past the ruins of antiquity. Most large European cities have outpaced American cities in providing high speed mass transit for their urban residents.

natives. He returned to Germany horrified at what he had seen, and urged that his city build a (nonautomobile) rapid transit system.

The use of the automobile in the center of our cities is a most anti-conservation practice; however, it has become almost universal in the

Figure 3-10. Usually the American subway schedules cater primarily to the rush hour commuter. This potential MTA customer in Boston seems prepared for a wait of some duration. (Massachusetts Bay Transit Authority)

Figure 3-11. Urban automobile traffic seems to fill expressways at rush hours faster than engineers and road builders can widen them. Perhaps there is a more effective solution to this problem? (U.S. Dept. of Housing and Urban Development)

twentieth century. The reasons behind this resource tragedy in terms of human dislocation (55,000 automobile-inflicted deaths in 1973), health, safety, open-space consumption, strategic mineral waste, and low-energy efficiency have been given in detail in many other references. San Francisco's Bay Area Rapid Transit (BART) was the first American mass transit system to be built after more than twenty-five years. Subsidies paid by Bay Area communities are presumably justified by increased property tax revenues expected from land contiguous to or in the vicinity of the rapid transit system. However, despite all of the publicity, BART links up only a rather small portion of the California megalopolis.

Only through a shift in federal policy and financing can urban rapid mass transit be provided that will enable cities to have a circulation of people and goods without the annihilating effect or urban cars, expressways, and storage lots. It is believed that urban dwellers have been exploited by a strong and special set of interests representing the automobile manufacturers, the highway construction companies, the petroleum companies, large land speculators, roadside motel and restaurant chains, and organizations such as the International Brotherhood of Teamsters, the American

Figure 3-12. The Bay Area Rapid Transit (BART) system was the first major regional mass transit venture in 25 years of unsuccessful dependence on the auto for high speed urban transit. (Bay Area Rapid Transit District)

Trucking Association, and the American Automobile Association. Where could one find more impressive adversaries? Yet it is in the hands of the American public to encourage the federal government to redress the policy for urban transportation systems including airport expansion programs that have human and ecological impacts second only to the highway system. Air travel represents larger and larger percentages of travelers and poses one of the largest environmental problems in the twenty-first century. The policy must provide linkages for the pedestrian as he moves from one mode to another without despoiling his landscape, his cityscape, or himself. One of the critical tests of the efficacy of the citizenry and the federal government will be to see how well the federal agencies move to coordinate and

Figure 3-13. The San Francisco area BART system gives commuters in a metropolis of 5 million people a clean, efficient, and environmentally sound alternative to the automobile. MacArthur Station shown here is the main transfer point in the system. (Bay Area Rapid Transit District)

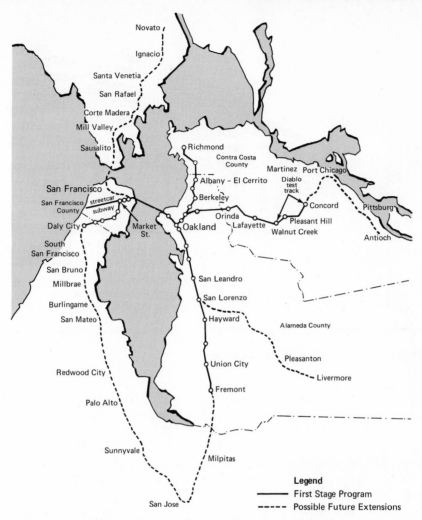

Figure 3-14. Map of the San Francisco Bay Area Rapid Transit System. The totally urbanized corridor along the southern part of San Francisco Bay from Fremont to Daly City (San Mateo, Redwood City, Palo Alto, Sunnyvale, San Jose, etc.) elected not to participate in BART. Many second thoughts exist today about not joining in with the original system. (Bay Area Rapid Transit District)

manage the vast resources that make up and depend upon the transportation networks of urban areas. The federal influence in the management policies of water resources, air resources, and recreation resources has been handled with modest aplomb and hopeful effectiveness. Very critical decisions regarding the most effective policy for moving people and goods and maintaining the natural environment among urban areas will be made in this decade. The outcome will be a conservation practice that will affect the habitability and survival of megalopolis and her scattered predecessors.

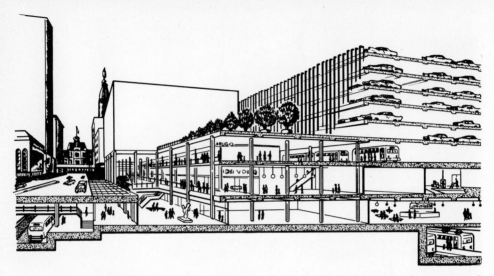

Figure 3-15. The schematic cross section of a Philadelphia urban renewal project shows potential for federal influence in the coordination of urban transportation networks. (C. A. Doxiadis, *Ekistics*, Hutchinson of London, 1968)

Projection into the Future

If the past is prologue, the mid-1970's will experience variations of the earlier conservation policies. When exploitation produces serious public conflict, a new surge of regulation and preservation policies will occur. The regulation of automobile oligopolies will be in the form of safety devices, emission standards, and challenges to the internal combustion engine itself. Presumably one result will be a diversification of the automobile industry into the area of urban rapid mass transit. If the large airline companies also grow insensitive to the public's desires to regulate service, rates, and environmental pollution, the affected public will insist upon more stringent management. Corporations involved in food preparation, mining, fishing, ranching, and lumbering can also expect demands imposed on them that would have been considered a clear infringement of private rights in the 1950's, 1960's, and early 1970's.

Environmental reform, if forced upon monolithic corporations, will certainly result in increased costs for goods and services and a reduction in choices for consumers. Specifically, the cost of such items as buried electrical transmission lines will be passed on to the customer. The car buyer may have only ten models to choose from instead of sixty from one automobile manufacturer. It is almost as chic to recycle glass and paper today as it was patriotic to smash and recycle metal cans, collect rubber tires, and grow victory gardens during World War II. Despite all the logical environmental incentives to establish resource management policies for strict pollution control and austere consumer behavior, another stark factor,

Figure 3-16. A 1973 photograph shows 230 KV cable being pulled underground on Bryant Street in San Francisco. Several progressive American cities and utilities have embarked upon programs to bury high voltage transmission lines for aesthetic and economic reasons. (Pacific Gas and Electric Co.)

the freedom to consume, poses a formidable hurdle in the path of a nationwide conservation ethic.

The freedom to consume has been a basic unwritten right in American history as long as that consumption did not injure or threaten to damage another person or other property. One reason why the federal government or the most vigorous conservation organizations have not seriously wrestled with this basic dilemma is that in this Country an equal opportunity for achievement is an understood goal. In a laissez-faire economic system,

Figure 3-17. Reduced labor costs, less expensive equipment required, year round protection from damaging weather (ice, wind, and snow), improved safety with no surface poles all add up to lower installation and maintenance costs for underground residential distribution lines. Does your community insist upon them? (Pacific Gas and Electric Co.)

Figure 3-18. Underground transmission facilities for electric power lines are required in most new subdivisions and gradually utility companies are being forced to bury higher voltage lines in urban centers and in outlying areas to avoid visual blight and maximize (surface) land uses more effectively than in the past.

Figure 3-19. "Before" photograph of overhead wires in the vicinity of an historic village church which benefitted from an underground conversion project, as seen in Figure 3-20. (Pacific Gas and Electric Co.)

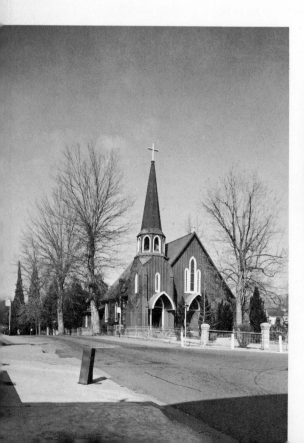

Figure 3-20. The "after" photograph to show how an historic church site appears without overhead wires, following an underground conversion project. (Pacific Gas and Electric Co.)

1. Metropolitan Belt	9. Twin Cities Region	18. Southern Coastal Plain
1.a. Atlantic Seaboard	10. Colorado Piedmont	19. Salt Lake Valley
1.b. Lower Great Lakes	11. Saint Louis	20. Central Illinois
2. California Region	12. Metropolitan Arizona	21. Nashville Region
3. Florida Peninsula	13. Willamette Valley	22. East Tennessee
4. Gulf Coast	14. Central Oklahoma—	23. Oahu Island
5. East Central Texas—Red River	Arkansas Valley	24. Memphis
6. Southern Piedmont	15. Missouri—Kaw Valley	25. El Paso—Ciudad Juarez
7. North Georgia—South East Tennessee	16. North Alabama	
8. Puget Sound	17. Blue Grass	

Figure 3-21. Urban regions have been established for the United States. If current trends prevail, the urban pressures on the total resource base will originate from these metropolitan areas as projected for the year 2000. (From *Population and the American Future,* The Report of the Commission on Population Growth and the American Future, 1972.)

inhibiting the freedom of the public to consume is antithetical to free enterprise. So even the most fervent conservationist, if exiled to an inner-city ghetto for many years, might be willing to compromise some pollution, some wilderness, and some low-level waste by-product for decent housing, decent food, decent education, decent job opportunities, and decent dental and medical care. It is not an "either or" situation. No national conservation policy has accepted the status quo of human or other natural resources. It would appear that regardless of which outlook prevails—exploitation, preservation, regulation, or management—the influence of conservation-related agencies and organizations will increase. For with increasing numbers of people in the United States and on Spaceship Earth, the nonreplenishable resources will approach exhaustibility. Even with *substitution* and other rational resource policies, preservation, regulation, and management must eventually supercede exploitation as a permissible option in dealing with human and other resources such as the urban area.

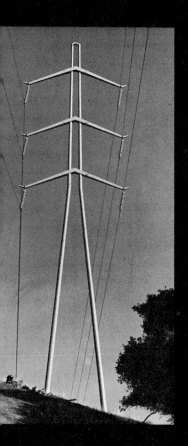

A Survey of Resources: Regional Case Studies

In an effort to sort out important details from the constant barrage of stimuli that comes to him, man has created categories for information storage and presentation. Trying to understand the complexity of natural resources and how they are affected by man, most authors in conservation and resource management have dealt extensively with one resource, or in the general conservation texts have created a list of basic resources and discussed them without the reality of fundamental interrelationships. In the past this approach may have served a useful purpose, alerting readers to apparent scarcities and inequitable distribution of resources and the historic exploitive policies of natural resource management. However, today's urban man lives in an increasingly vast network of synchronous interrelationships and complexity. An effort follows that attempts to describe some of that complexity. It will be more difficult to read than a traditional survey of resources and it may fall short of reality. Yet the presentation of regionality in resource use and management should give the reader a more straightforward notion of the dilemmas that lie ahead in the urban organism as it grows.

Some aggregation of resource problems will be required by the reader if he desires to have an accurate impression of reality. Therefore, instead of discussing each resource such as soil, water, or minerals in a vacuum, different geographic regions of the United States are presented with an emphasis on a specific resource and its affiliated problems of management, policy formulation, and attempted conservation practices. Even though energy resources and atmospheric resources are discussed in the context of the Eastern Seaboard region, it is abundantly obvious that the Eastern portion of the United States has soil resource problems (discussed in the Mississippi basin), forest resource problems (discussed in the Gulf States region), and water resource problems (discussed in the Great Lakes region).

Water resources was chosen as a lead topic for the Great Lakes region because of the pervasive influence that water has in that area. Similarly selected resources are discussed in context of a region where a given resource plays an especially important role. Granted, water is an integral part of any region—obviously it is one of the most critical in the Pacific Southwest—but the Great Lakes region lends itself particularly well to a discussion of water-resource management because Great Lakes residents have assumed this resource to be highly abundant. Such an assumption is more common when technology separates people from their fundamental resources.

A useful way to look at a resource is to observe its status and function in the absence of man's intervention and then compare the condition of the resource after man has incorporated it into "his" system. It was and continues to be very difficult to realize how each personal activity has a specific impact on the natural environment. Each breath, each visit to the bathroom, and each trip to the shopping center has a measurable impact on the primary resources of soil, atmosphere, and water as well as on the dynamics of the urban resource.

At this point, an invitation is extended to each reader to participate as fully as possible in a special series of "field trips." Many Americans have visited a number of the field trip sites that are suggested, but those visits were made without the special task we have before us. We must identify, diagnose, and contemplate the urban-related resource problems that face the population residing in the areas considered. If the reader has never been to one of the geographical areas described, this presentation may arouse his interest and serve as a unique guide: if the reader is a resident or previous visitor he may enjoy checking out the reality of the description. Most important, however, is the degree to which the reader can take the general discussion and then move toward the identification, diagnosis, and resolution of whatever urban-oriented resource problems are most familiar or most vexing to him.

Many qualifying statements should undoubtedly preface this section but let us try to agree on a few basic principles that guide our thinking and observations.

1. Large human settlements can be defined by using several kinds of boundaries. A word of caution is given here to avoid the topographic and political boundaries that have been commonly used for the identification of city limits. Consider a boundary describing a zone of maximum influence that is exerted over the resources required for the maintenance and survival of the urban organism under discussion.

2. The boundaries, or extent of influences, change continually and this presentation of urban resource problems by megalopolitan and geographic regions is exceedingly arbitrary.

3. Human settlements, regardless of their size and previous independence, are no longer closed systems biologically, socially, or politically. A firm realization of this principle will ease the implementation of rational international and interregional growth and human enhancement. The success of *ecumenopolitan* life depends on the appreciation by a world citizenry of the relatively closed system known as Spaceship Earth.

CHAPTER 4

Water Resources

Here we are—urban people, almost unconsciously connecting the proverbial but misleading cycle between the sky and the earth. We turn the faucet, push a button, or flip the lever linking the water supplied and the water disposed.

From earlier encounters, urban dwellers have somehow accepted the fantasy suggesting that there is a continuous *hydrologic* cycle ever-circulating, ever-purifying water in limitless abundance. The fairy tale of water as a "free" good, which talks about water as a flow resource must be retold as a serious resource problem facing every major urban conglomeration in the United States. We are the judge as well as the accused every time we walk past a drinking fountain needlessly flowing or a dripping faucet in the home, school, or office.

Water traditionally has been considered a renewable resource capable of being recycled either through waste-water treatment systems managed by man, or in larger, natural systems operating beyond man's control. If one assumes that thirty inches is the mean annual United States' rainfall, approximately 5 billion acre feet of water come down on the country every year. It is estimated that one-half of it evaporates without ever being captured; one-sixth is lost in runoff, although some of this may be temporarily used enroute to its ultimate destination—the sea. The remaining two-sixths is equally divided between that which is used by plants and that which percolates into underground water supplies.[1] The flow in an unmanaged system is usually inconceivably slow (for example, artesian percolation) and the frequency and volume of delivery is highly variable.

[1]Shirley W. Allen, and Justin W. Leonard *Conserving Natural Resources* (New York; McGraw-Hill, Inc., 1966). Adapted from W. J. McGee, "Water as a Resource," *Annals of the American Academy*, Vol. 33 (1898), pp. 521–534.

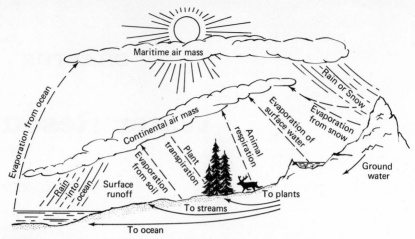

Figure 4-1. The water cycle. The interchange of water between the atmosphere, land, and sea is a major factor in producing the soil so necessary to most land plants and the seasonal changes that affect all organisms. Water is evaporated from the oceans and carried over the land where it becomes precipitated as rain or snow. Water is also evaporated from the soil and from the bodies of plants and animals to be later precipitated over the land or sea. (From *General Zoology* by Tracey Storer, Robert Usinger, Robert Stebbins, James Nybakker. Copyright 1972, McGraw-Hill Book Company. Used with permission of McGraw-Hill Book Company.)

In order to receive the full value of a renewed water supply, the price tag of time and redistribution *or* the price tag of sanitary engineering technology must be paid in full.

The shortcoming of the legendary water cycle is that the water disposed of today may be our or our neighbor's water of tomorrow. Most urban Americans drink and excrete water that has been drunk and excreted nearly a dozen times previously. The intensified reuse and shortening of time and space for water "recovery" helps to explain the dilemma in water-resource allocation and management in human settlements of the present and future.

Urban water problems have always involved the issues of quantity and quality. If demands on the available supply of freshwater were modest and spaced judiciously over the seasons in accord with the natural precipitation and ground pressures, no severe water quantity problems developed. However, if the attractiveness of the settlement in terms of water supply, economic activities, pleasant natural surroundings, or other factors brought an influx of population, eventually certain predictable strains were placed on the natural environment's ability to produce the volume of water required for a burgeoning population.

Villages, towns, and cities experience definite warning signals when water withdrawal exceeds the immediate local supply. Groundwater tables recede, well levels drop, and it is difficult for deep aquifers to constantly produce heavy pumping. As in the *domino theory,* when one water source dries up, other producing sources are subjected to added pressure, increasing the possibility that additional wells and springs will go dry. The resident of more arid regions of the United States may be surprised to learn that even urban areas of the Great Lakes region have had serious drawdowns of the water table as a result of rapidly expanded water use that outstrips the ground supply.

Table 4-1 depicts the estimated sources of the earth's water supply. The situation in the United States and typically in the Great Lakes is that 80 per cent of the water used comes from surface sources. The Ground Water Resources Institute in its March 1972 news release stated that there is about thirty-five times more underground water than surface water. The report said, "The U.S. ground water resources that are less than one-half mile under the surface constitute 97 per cent of our total supply at any one time. This 'hidden reservoir' amounts to 47.5 billion acre feet—a supply that will last the United States about 7,800 years at the current rate of depletion." What the report did not point out was that out national per capita consumptive rate of 158 gallons per day is increasing. Also, as we notice the "complexion" of ground water, it usually has high levels of

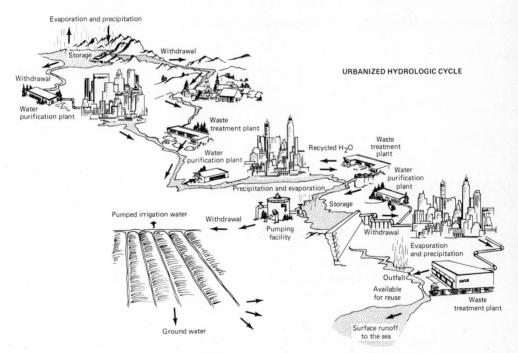

Figure 4-2. The urbanized hydrologic cycle. Large cities tend to short-circuit the traditional water cycle by various diversions, treatment facilities, and recycling. Increasing volumes of water are rerouted for urban uses today as engineering technology promotes ground water recharge, recycling, advanced treatment and other innovations that circumvent the slower natural processes which preindustrial man depended on.

110   Table 4-1. Breakdown of World's Water Supply*

	Water (thousand cubic miles)	Total Water on Earth
Surface		
I. Icecaps and glaciers	7,300	2.25%
II. Fresh water lakes	30	.009%
III. Saline lakes,		
(Caspian Sea, Dead Sea)	25	.008%
IV. Streams	.28	.0001%
		2.26
Ground Water		
Root zone (near surface)	6	.0018%
To depth of $\frac{1}{2}$ mile	1,000	.306%
Below $\frac{1}{2}$ mile	1,000	.306%
		.61
Oceans	317,000	97.1%
Atmospheric moisture	3.1	.001%

Note: Groundwater down to a depth of one-half mile (.3%) is many times the amount of freshwater readily available (.0091%) on surface.

*K. A. Mackichan, and J. C. Kammer, "Estimated Use of Water in the U.S., 1960," Geological Survey Circular 456, 1961.

hardness or other impurities that must be dealt with even if the pressure from underground sources can be maintained by recharging, controlled withdrawal, and other groundwater conservation practices.

CASE IN POINT: THE GREAT LAKES STATES

The Historical Role of Water

It is most appropriate to consider water resources in the geographical context of the Great Lakes region for several reasons. Sixteenth-century trading posts, missions, and military outposts of the Great Lakes basin have grown into metropolitan centers totaling over 30 million people. The megalopolis of the Great Lakes is well underway in its formation from Milwaukee and Chicago across northern Indiana and southern Michigan to Detroit with one arm reaching toward Toronto and Montreal in Canada, and another arm sweeping the southern shoreline of Lake Erie through Cleveland and Buffalo, plus fingers pointing toward Rochester, New York, and Pittsburgh, Pennsylvania. This area contains the greatest volume of freshwater in the world along with some of the most chronic examples

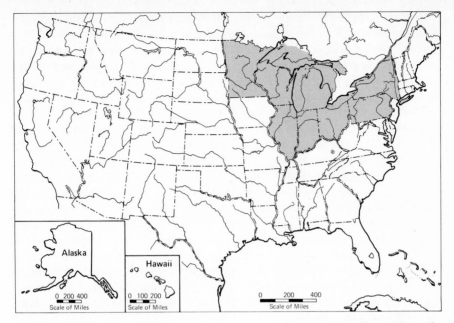

Figure 4-3. The Great Lakes states serve as a focus for the discussion of U.S. water resources.

Figure 4-4. The Great Lakes megalopolis has arisen in the presence of an abundant mix of human and other resources, one of which is the largest supply of surface fresh water in the world.

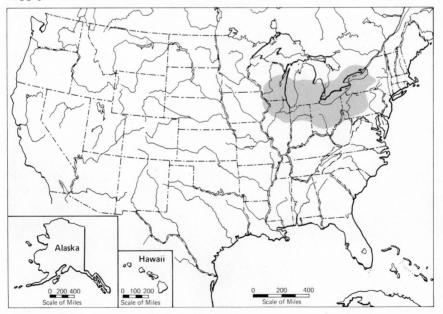

112   of urban water pollution and supply shortages for agricultural and domestic consumption. All of the typical uses of water are illustrated in the Great Lakes basin as well as the problems and procedures to cope with those problems. As we shall see, the very bounteous supply of water as a natural resource coupled with the concept of the traditional hydrologic cycle was in large measure responsible for the partial devastation of this once unique, urban-sustaining resource of America's inland freshwater seas.

Early settlers took water resources for granted in the humid regions of the Eastern United States, and eventually this led to one of the root problems of present water management difficulties—the presumed abundance of water in quality and quantity.

As in every part of the United States, the early Great Lakes settlers sought out establishment or development sites that offered an advantageous mix of land and water. Military forts were located at strategic narrows in the rivers and lakes or at access to or junctions with early transportation routes. Cities in the Great Lakes basin that have the urban heritage of being at one time either a military post or a trading center because of the advantage of water for commerce and communication inclued Green Bay, Detroit, Buffalo, Toledo, Sault Sainte Marie, Duluth, Toronto, Milwaukee, Cleveland, and Chicago, to name just a few.

Historically, human activity has centered near sources of water. As individual families sought out new homesteads or whenever commercial oper-

Figure 4-5. Heavy industry favors locations (as seen here on the Detroit River) with water nearby for cooling, processing, and transporting raw materials and finished products. The Detroit River, which connects Lake Huron and Lake Erie, gets thoroughly exploited for these uses plus waste disposal and other urban-oriented uses.

Figure 4-6. Chicago's North Avenue Beach as photographed in 1968, showing how the Lake Michigan beach was used as a dumping ground. Chicago skyline is in the background. (Environmental Protection Agency: photo by John Hendry)

ations relocated, water supply was an important consideration. When man was nomadic, if his water supply and/or food supply became exhausted, he simply loaded up his travois or packed up his tents or wagons and moved on. Unfortunately, as his settlements grew larger, more ponderous, and more permanent, it became more difficult to move to another location. Eventually, "other locations" that were highly desirable settlement sites became occupied. Such settlements often clustered around springs, wells, or surface waters that would provide for transportation, energy, industrial, agricultural, and domestic uses. For years individual waste disposal systems of privies or outhouses sufficed as long as residences were widely scattered. Over time the concentration of new residents began to fill the interstices of the villages and towns, and the "honey wagon" that collected human wastes from the various dwellings became a common sight in many Great Lakes cities as well as in other cities around the world such as London and Paris. Such primitive methods eventually proved inadequate, and municipal water supply, waste water, and water collection systems developed.

The idea of an enclosed sewer, one waste-water collection system, originated in the midnineteenth century to collect storm runoff from the urban land area and shunt the potential floodwater into a local water course. The convenient feature about the big storm drains was that they could be used to carry off sewage as indoor plumbing came into vogue and toilets were brought inside from the backyard privy or outhouse. During the drier periods of the year, the so-called sanitary wastes from toilets and sinks were collected and slowly carried away, untreated, in the large sewers. Of course, when a cloud burst or any appreciable rain occurred, the flush of surface runoff from buildings and pavement combined with the "sanitary waste" and sent a slug of rather potent material down to the receiving river or lake. The waterborne, raw wastes of these larger and larger human settlements eventually began to exert tremendous pres- **113**

114 sures on the natural carrying capacity of the receiving waters. It is interesting that despite such dependence upon surface waters for removing the wastes of human settlements, man has yet to adequately consider the waste assimilation ability of local water resources as an important criterion when locating new towns or even adding suburbs in America. Ironically, the urban growth in the Great Lakes and elsewhere is probably going to be dictated more by this factor of waste-water collection and treatment than any other stimulus of human settlement in the twentieth century. With the assumption that waste-water collection and treatment systems are going to exert great influence in urbanization patterns, it would be useful to know how they serve urban man.

The Origin of Municipal Water Treatment

The primitive sewer served its purpose to carry waste away from centers of relatively small human activity. As population and density increased, the springs, wells, and individual surface water sites were no longer dependable for providing uncontaminated water. Gradually the ecological imperative of an aquatic carrying capacity became noticeable to urban organisms that had exceeded the ability of their water resources to assimilate the wastes imposed by the huge sewer systems. Less obvious to many is the reason why only limited amounts of raw sewerage can be accommodated by the aquatic community in natural waters.

The city-originated organic material attracts a team of bacteria, algae, and invertebrate organisms that attack the sewage and other organic wastes, breaking them into elemental chemical constituents. For the most part, this team of biological converters or transformers is the same group of living organisms that attacks the various natural organic additions to a stream or lake such as dead fish, logs, and even the tremendous tonnage of leaves that drops or is swept into the water courses each autumn. But this multitude of decomposers can convert only specified amounts of nontoxic organic material in a given time and only under specific "working conditions." When the waste load is exceeded and/or when the "working conditions" or environmental climate are not within certain thresholds of temperature, pH, dissolved oxygen, and other limiting factors, a breakdown or collapse of the natural purification system occurs.

Cleveland, Detroit, Toledo, Milwaukee, Buffalo, and Toronto are notable examples of Great Lakes cities whose combined sewer systems poured directly into major lakes or tributaries. However, during rainy periods the sewers flushed rainwater *plus* raw sewage and industrial waste into the receiving water course, which was also the major source of drinking water for the burgeoning metropolitan populations. Every large city in the United States disposed of its waste water in a similar manner—Boston, New York, Washington, D.C., Miami, New Orleans, Los Angeles, San Francisco, Seattle, St. Louis, and on down the list. The major difference in Great Lakes cities was that by withdrawing drinking water from the same water that received sewage, the hydrologic cycle was detoured before those urban populations could benefit from the *evapotranspiration* and long-term natural water purification systems.

Apparently the least cost route was followed with the hope that no negative consequences would result. Ample warnings were sounded from those who had some ecological insight or training. One caution came from the President of the United States concerning the degradation of the Great Lakes region. He said, "I want to say just one word to you men along the lakeshore. I want the people of Michigan, Ohio, Pennsylvania, and New York to aid in the campaign for pure drinking water from the lake. You can't get pure water and put your sewage into the lake. I say this on behalf of your children."[2] The children of the people to whom he spoke are now those who are shocked to realize the simple truth that he put forth. The year was 1910 and the President was Theodore Roosevelt. Today the President would need to broaden his plea and also call upon the people of Indiana, Illinois, Wisconsin, Minnesota, and Ontario—in fact the urbanites of the entire Great Lakes basin—for the next pure water campaign, as most large cities along the Great Lakes coast tap their doorstep water supply for industrial and domestic uses.

Eventually, public health officials began to realize that increasing instances of amoebic dysentery, typhoid, hepatitis, cholera, and other waterborne diseases were attributable to larger volumes of human excrement entering the same body of water that was used as the municipal water supply. To prevent the cities' waste overburden from having disastrous environmental impacts, the technologies of sanitary engineering were employed. Thus in the early 1900's, most cities in the Great Lakes region were required to chlorinate (disinfect) and apply other treatment methods to the raw water before it was distributed in city water mains.

In a typical Great Lakes city, the lake water is sucked into a huge intake pipe fifty-five feet below the surface. Less than ten years ago the intake was usually about fifteen hundred feet offshore, but now it is at least six thousand feet offshore. (One wonders why the city water department had to extend the intake pipe so far into the lake?) After a gentle ride through the intake line, the raw water is brought up into huge tanks that look like indoor swimming pools, where calcium carbonate and sodium carbonate are added to precipitate the suspended particles. Subsequently, raw water is filtered through sand beds, rinsed again before the addition of various chemicals such as fluorine and chlorine, and then the treated water is pumped to reservoirs or high-standing water towers around the city. Gravity carries the treated water into the water mains and eventually to the homes and factories of the citizen who pays on the average less than $.25 per thousand gallons. Curiously, larger volume users such as industries pay considerably less per unit of water. This is a rather strange practice if clean

[2]Senator Frank E. Moss, *The Water Crisis* (New York; Praeger Publishers, Inc, 1970), p. 32.

116   water is an increasingly scarce commodity. Even with the apparent abundance of surface water in the Great Lakes region, many communities supplement their surface supplies with well water. Worldwide, there is a breakdown of total water availability (see Table 4-1), which shows the percentage of groundwater versus surface water (that is, after we subtract "surface water" in glaciers and the oceans).

Waste-Water Treatment

It was not until 1925 that the first city of some size in the Great Lakes region—Milwaukee, Wisconsin—started plans to build a progressive metropolitan waste-water treatment plant. The idea behind this pioneer effort was to return the waste water to Lake Michigan totally disinfected from pathogenic bacteria and also to prevent a large percentage of the nutrients (phosphates, nitrates, and the like) from entering the lake that did serve and still today serves as the city's source of potable water.

After used water leaves apartment buildings, factories, or single family homes, it flows to a main collection line that is buried underground. If it is in an old section of the city, the water and its waste load probably enter a combined sewer that also accommodates rainwater from rooftops and pavements. In the combined sewer there are small weirs or dikes that divert the sanitary waste water toward a waste treatment plant in dry weather. However, when it rains or when there is heavy groundwater infiltration, the rush of waste water and other excess water cascades over the low diversion dam in the pipe and heads for the river or lake.

In newer subdivisions or in cities where combined sewers have been separated into storm and sanitary sewers, the waste water goes into the sanitary waste-collection network and is carried by gravity to the waste-water treatment facility. The mention of gravity feed is very important because most urban waste collection systems depend on gravity to carry the waste water throughout the urban occupied watershed to a major collection point for treatment. The degree of treatment varies from city to city, but in the Great Lakes general guidelines have been established for all municipal facilities. All of the Great Lakes are connected and the lakes further downstream are directly or indirectly influenced by the quality of lake water above. Therefore, *secondary waste-water treatment* has been requested at interstate-federal hearings where federal water pollution control authorities have made recommendations.

The waste treatment procedures are borrowed, for the most part, directly from naturally occurring events. The major differences are that the sanitary engineer telescopes the time of the process and controls biological and physical conditions to achieve specific results.

Primary Treatment

In the initial steps of *primary treatment* the solids that settle and floating materials are removed in a grit chamber. Garbage grindings, cigarette butts, prophylactics, paper, and other materials that can be removed by mechanical devices are thus extracted. Almost 30 per cent of the American population has primary treatment or less for its waterborne wastes. Too often this process consists of skimming or settling of solids with a dose of chlorine added before the effluent is returned to the local receiving water. Primary treatment represents about a 40 per cent reduction in *biochemical oxygen demand (BOD)* and a 60 per cent reduction of suspended solids. The 1972 Amendments to the federal Water Pollution Control Act require at least secondary treatment for municipal and industrial wastes by 1977. Theoretically no primary treated wastes will be permitted in navigable waters. The law in effect says there will be no more pollution control by natural dilution. The reader should take a moment right now to call his local city or county public works department and inquire what kind of waste-water treatment is given the material sent down his toilet and drain.

Secondary Treatment

The *secondary treatment* process is essentially biological treatment. In order to cope with the growing immensity of urban water pollution, sanitary engineers took a clue from the processes of aquatic ecosystems. They discovered that bacteria, algae, and the invertebrate populations could be brought into controlled environments and be used to rapidly transform and decompose human wastes under optimum conditions of oxygen, light, temperature, pH, and other factors. The waste effluent is brought into contact with bacteria, algae, and various invertebrates such as rotifers, ciliates, flagellates, and microcrustaceans that transform the organic material into its inorganic constituents. In a trickling filter arrangement, the waste water is trickled over rocks and gravel that are coated with organisms that expedite the absorption and adsorption process of organic conversion. In an *activated sludge technique,* the effluent is mixed and aerated in large tanks that contain populations of bacteria and other organisms whose task is to literally remove the suspended solids and reduce the BOD up to 95 per cent before the waste water enters the nearby river or lake. Up to 90 per cent phosphate removal can be accomplished with the application of ferric chloride. Biological breakdown of wastes for small towns is possible in lagoons where specific organisms are introduced to transform waste products to inorganic salts. In all of the variations, the treated water is given a final dose of chlorine to try to eliminate pathogenic bacteria from entering the receiving water. This disinfection helps prevent outbreaks of dysentery, typhoid, and cholera. However, hepatitis and other viruses can pass through the secondary treatment process that is used by the majority of American cities.

Muskegon Project. In a discussion of waste-water treatment in the Great Lakes region, attention should be drawn to the large experiment that Muskegon, Michigan, has launched to try to prevent urban waste water from entering Lake Michigan. Seventeen thousand acres of level sandy soil located five miles east of the city limits have been obtained by the city.

Figure 4-7. In Muskegon, Michigan, more than 10,000 acres of open space were required for the "living filter" waste treatment facility. The cost of the project exceeds $36,000,000. Most urban areas do not have the open space or soil conditions for this kind of waste treatment. (Muskegon County Dept. of Public Works: photo by Teledyne Continental Motors)

After initial sedimentation, sanitary and storm runoff is sent to several large lagoons. After settling, the waste water is applied (using irrigation techniques) to the sandy soil that has been cleared of trees and graded for agricultural production. Nutrients in the form of phosphates, nitrates, and organic material plus other necessary elements for plant growth are available for terrestrial crops instead of fertilizing the aquatic vegetation in nearby Lake Michigan. Special water collection lines are installed under the sand to catch percolation water for further treatment when necessary before the used water is released to surface sources or recharged into groundwater supplies.

It is not certain how effectively the sandy soil will accept the nutrient-rich waste effluent over a long period of time and during the cold winter months of the Great Lakes region. It is an ambitious experiment. However, even if it is successful, most metropolitan areas in the Great Lakes region and elsewhere do not have tens of thousands of acres of sandy flat land available, not to mention the funds required for land purchase.

A 1977 goal is for most American communities to adopt secondary sewage treatment, although within the next twenty years it is expected that tertiary processes will be required.

Tertiary Treatment

Tertiary treatment uses rapid sand filters, distillation, chemical adsorbtion by activated carbon, and other advanced procedures that clarify the waste water beyond the biological treatment steps, removing all nutrients including phosphates and nitrates and producing a perfectly acceptable potable water source. However, it is very expensive and with a few exceptions such as Santee and Lake Tahoe, California, Warren, Michigan, and Chanute, Kansas, tertiary treatment is not common in American cities. A basic reason for the trend from secondary waste-water treatment to tertiary treatment is the increased volume of poorly treated waste water getting into natural waterways, even with 90 per cent removal of suspended solids and biochemical oxygen demand in carefully operated secondary plants. The federal Water Pollution Control Act Amendments of 1972 established a

Figure 4-8. 1972 photo of Muskegon waste treatment facility under construction with settling lagoon at center and three aerated biological treatment ponds in the background. After about 80% BOD removal the effluent is discharged to storage basins and the liquid portion is eventually used for agricultural irrigation. Note clay lining delivery truck leaving outlet lagoon in the foreground. The population served is about 200,000. (Muskegon County Dept. of Public Works: photo by Teledyne Continental Motors)

120 program with a national goal of eliminating the discharge of all pollutants into navigable waters by 1985. The legislation's goal by mid-1983 is for municipal treatment plants to utilize tertiary and other advanced treatment including, if practicable, recycling and reclaiming waste water.

No longer is it acceptable to use dilution in navigable waters as an alternative to waste treatment. In-plant process changes, more efficient reclamation, and physiochemical treatment of primary-treated wastes will supplement the tertiary treatment facilities in the immediate future. Costs of tertiary waste-water treatment are estimated to be approximately $.26 to $.30 per thousand gallons in addition to the primary and secondary treatment operating costs that are in the $.15 to $.20 per thousand gallons (3.8 cubic meters) cost range. Gasification of organic waste is another alternative currently being explored. Instead of transporting waste to large treatment facilities, gasification digesters in homes or small communities are a step toward the realization that what were once wastes are becoming urgently needed raw materials. Tertiary and other forms of advanced treatment are steps toward a society that recycles and reclaims resources.

Federal Role

The pressures put upon local communities to upgrade regional water quality fluctuate with the severity of pollution conditions and the availability of funds to improve waste treatment conditions. The Ninety-Second

Figure 4-9. A modern waste treatment plant at Lake Tahoe, California. (Environmental Protection Agency)

Congress enacted far-reaching legislation to improve municipal waste treatment facilities. Federal percentage contributions for municipal waste treatment facility construction was raised to 75 per cent, which begins to approach the 90 per cent matching federal aid to highways program. However, after Congress passes the authorization, substantial dollars are usually lost at the appropriations step. The White House took even bolder action by withholding $6 billion that had been allocated by Congress for 1973–1974 municipal waste treatment plants. It is fortunate that the natural system is able to provide some waste assimilation capacity—especially in the Great Lakes region.

The Physiology of a Lake

Has the reader ever wondered how the typical lake, river, or estuary deals with the waste load we impose from our daily activities? One of the reasons that human settlements of the Great Lakes region have not paid closer attention to waste water disposal is that the lakes themselves offered tremendous purification possibilities without man's technology. It is a fascinating story to discover how the major freshwater lakes assimilate the wastes they do and how man in his ignorance has begun to destroy that capacity.

To have an appreciation for the natural purification capacity of a lake, it is useful to remember how most of the lakes in the Great Lakes region were formed. In four separate advances and subsequent retreats, the *Pleistocene* glacial activity gouged huge basins from the soft sedimentary rock. The deepest basins eventually became linked as a huge chain of lakes that initially flowed south through the present valleys of the Illinois, Wabash, Maumee, and Susquehanna Rivers. Eventually when the melting ice mass retreated from Lake Ontario and the northerly portions of the Saint Lawrence River, the flow moved northerly into the Atlantic Ocean. Glacial geologists suggest that as the unimaginable weight of the ice sheet was lifted from the land along the southern shores of Lake Michigan and Lake Erie, there was a gentle upwarping of the land that shifted the drainage of the Calument, Saint Joseph, Maumee, and Cuyahoga rivers to a northerly direction and into the Saint Lawrence drainage basin.

After a lake is freshly carved out of bedrock either by an alpine glacier or a continental ice sheet, the water tends to be relatively free of organic nutrients. Often the young lake is deep, clear, cold, and very sparse in biological organisms. Limnologists or students of lakes label this phase of a lake's *succession* the *oligotrophic* stage. It is low in nutrients and therefore unable to sustain a large *biomass*.

However, if there are surges of nutrients and sediments after a rainfall or spring melt period, there is the likelihood of a temporary pulse of algal growth. Because of the cold temperature of oligotrophic lakes, a very high dissolved oxygen content is the rule, and modest amounts of waste organic

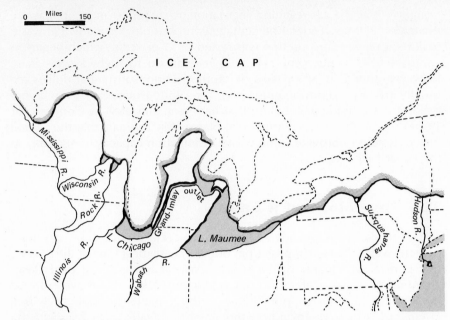

Figure 4-10. In the early stages of the late Wisconsin ice sheet of the Pleistocene Period, natural drainage proceeded in a southerly direction by way of the Wisconsin, Rock, Illinois, Wabash, Maumee, Susquehanna, and Hudson River drainages. (U.S. Geological Survey)

Figure 4-11. As the ice front retreated to the northward, Lake Chicago occupied the southern half of the Lake Michigan basin and extended over adjoining territory. The waters of Lakes Huron and Ontario were combined to form Lake Warren and extended to the forming Finger Lakes. Note their westward drainage across the southern peninsula of Michigan by way of the present valley of the Grand River. (U.S. Geological Survey)

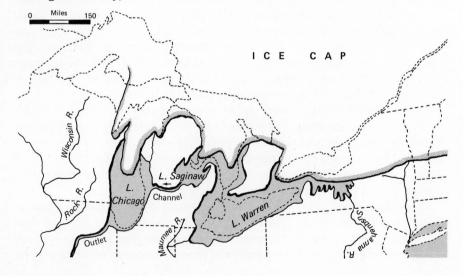

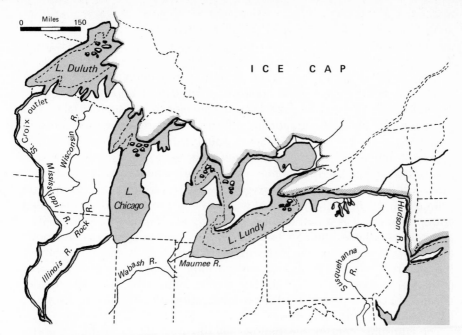

Figure 4-12. As the lakes' shorelines continued to change with the receding ice sheet, Lake Duluth appeared and Lake Chicago became approximately the size of Lake Michigan today. The drainage across Michigan disappeared, being replaced by the Mohawk outlet, which drained Lake Lundy eastward to the Hudson and to the Atlantic Ocean. (U.S. Geological Survey)

Figure 4-13. Due to the retreat of the ice cap north of Hudson's Bay and the upwarping of the lower Great Lakes region, the St. Lawrence River became the only outlet for the entire system. Today, the ancestral outlets are occupied by the largest cities and industrial centers of the Great Lakes region. (U.S. Geological Survey)

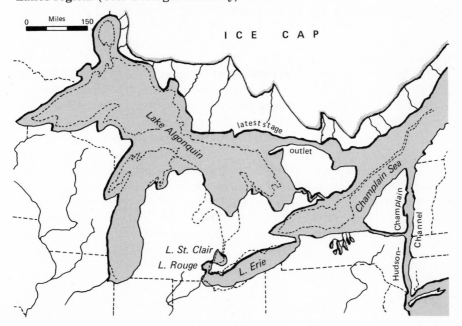

124 materials can be satisfactorily assimilated. Cold water holds higher concentrations of dissolved oxygen than warmer temperatures: this means that
more oxygen is in the "bank" when organic waste is introduced. In warmer
water the vulnerability to exceed the oxygen supply is greater and, of
course, the chances for anaerobic decomposition increase with warmer
water and more wastes. Lake Superior is the largest and most dramatic
example of an oligotrophic lake. Even the species of fish such as lake trout
and whitefish and other aquatic life reflect a very early stage of succession
compared to the greater percentage of rough fish found in the other Great
Lakes. As the water chemistry changes over geological time, organisms
appear that are adapted to warmer water, more nutrients, shallower depths,
more turbidity, and depressed oxygen levels. This gradual transformation
from a sparsely nourished body of water to a well nourished lake is called
eutrophication. It is a natural biological process but as man builds cities
along rivers or lakes, the concentration of nutrients (from urban metabolic
activities) placed into the receiving waterway speeds the nourishment
process from an oligotrophic or *mesotrophic* situation to the eutrophic
condition best portrayed by Lake Erie and, in many ways, by Lake Ontario.
Localized pockets of accelerated eutrophication are also clearly visible in
Lake Michigan and Lake Huron.

The eutrophic condition is biologically the most active during the entire
aquatic succession. Much more biomass is present in the eutrophic lake
than in any other but additional loads of biochemical oxygen demanding
material such as urban or agricultural runoff, municipal, and industrial
wastes create severe problems in the ability of the aquatic community to
assimilate additional materials. The natural purification and decomposition
processes become less effective as pollution becomes severe. The natural
propensity of the life in a pond or lake allows various decomposers to attack
introduced materials. These chemical transformers or decomposers convert
the organic material into the elemental building blocks of protoplasm, and
in doing so, use the dissolved oxygen present in the water.

Let us assume that one of the Great Lakes or any pond or lake has been
exposed to the warm sunlight of late spring or early summer. Presume that
the body of water borders a large city. As the upper levels of the lake are
heated by the sun, temperature stratification takes place. At the same time
and throughout the year for that matter, waste water from various industrial
and other urban uses is coming into the lake with its load of heat and
other pollutants. The *stratification* of the water actually creates barriers to
horizontal circulation of whatever heat and other wastes are emptied there
from the metabolic activities of the urban organism. Consequently, large
plumes of heated water fan out over the upper level of the lake. As the
temperature differential becomes greater, the potential for mixing nutrients
or dissolved oxygen from the lower depths is greatly reduced. Thus the
waste assimilation capacity of lakes in the vicinity of urban areas is curtailed. Even with urban wastes after primary or secondary treatment, the

Figure 4-14. The southern portion of Lake Michigan is heavily polluted, as shown by this photo in the Indiana Harbor area. Thermal pollution and industrial wastes conflict sharply with recreation use of shorelines especially in a metropolitan area like Chicago. (U.S. Dept. of Housing and Urban Development)

phosphates, nitrates, and other nutrients have a tendency to be restricted to the upper levels of the receiving body of water.

Temperature stratification in lakes and large rivers, like eutrophication, is a natural phenomenon that takes place with or without cities. Cities, however, accentuate or accelerate both of these natural processes. In the Northern states, winter street salting practices produce similar stratification in lakes and rivers that receive salt-laden runoff. This is explained by different density levels with the saline water at the bottom. Natural and man-induced heat loads produce stratification conditions year-round everywhere. And as one might expect, natural forces are at work to mitigate the difficulties created if temperature stratification were to persist for several years. The reader can imagine what a vertical picture of an urbanized lakeshore would look like after several years if waste materials entered without mixing. It should be remembered that a layer of wastes could stay relatively intact depending upon the density of the material and the amount of vigorous mixing by surface winds or severe internal turbulence from upwelling. Of course, the warmer the water, the lower is its density; thus the likelihood is greater that warmer water will be near the surface—except at 4°C.

Figure 4-15. Bodies of water that receive heavy melt water from salted streets and highways tend to accumulate denser saline water at pond or lake bottoms which result in biological deserts during the entire year, once stratification becomes established.

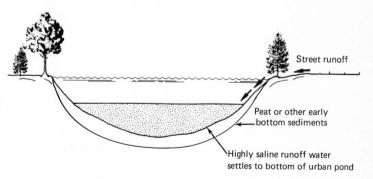

Street runoff

Peat or other early bottom sediments

Highly saline runoff water settles to bottom of urban pond

Lake Overturn

As the summer turns to autumn and the upper level (*epilimnion*) of the lake begins to cool, the temperature gradient becomes less pronounced. The shorter day length, the sun's smaller angle of incidence, and other cooling tendencies will eliminate the zone of sharp temperature difference (*thermocline*) and the temperature of the upper level of the lake will resemble that of the *hypolimnion* or portion of the lake below the thermocline. In the fall as the lake temperature is dropping because of colder environmental conditions, the surface water is the first to reach a temperature of 4°C. Since this is the most dense water, it sinks and pushes the warmer, less dense water to the surface. No wind is necessary, but it can assist in the mixing when uniform density conditions prevail. This overturn or mixing of the lake water is an important step in enabling nutrients freed by bottom dwelling decomposers to be distributed throughout the lake. Also important is the redistribution of oxygen from the surface or epilimnion layer to the deeper hypolimnion, whose cold summer temperatures enable the lake to have an additional storage of dissolved oxygen. With the fall and spring overturn, the deepest portions of the hypolimnion would undoubtedly suffer oxygen depletion since the hypolimnion is ordinarily below the summer photosynthetic range. Thus residual supplies of oxygen would be lost, and that becomes critical for large lakes (such as Lake Michigan) and even more critical for smaller bodies of water contiguous to urban areas.

Miraculously the lake water temperature nearing freezing (0°C. or 32°F.) has a lower specific gravity than the heavier 4°C. water; the 0°C. water filters to the surface. If water had its greatest specific gravity at freezing, 0°C., lakes would freeze from the bottom up. Happily for aquatic life and for that matter probably all life on earth, the freezing level begins at the surface and seldom freezes to a depth of more than forty-eight inches.

Winter-Summer Kill

If wastes, treated or untreated, from urban areas enter a body of water under the ice, nutrients and potentially decomposable matter incur an oxygen demand. As winter progresses in the Great Lakes region, the snow cover begins to blanket the layer of ice on the lake. Winter sunlight penetrating the ice can activate some photosynthetic activity and therefore provide some dissolved oxygen after the fall overturn. But if the snowcover reaches a depth that reduces or eliminates photosynthesis under the ice, the "stored" dissolved oxygen will quickly be expended by the fish and other organisms including the fleet of bacteria and invertebrates that are "working on" the waste material. The total depletion of oxygen produces a *"winter kill"* of fish and other aquatic life.

Even after a long winter with several months of snow cover, healthy lakes have an oxygen reserve to last until the spring overturn. As the surface waters absorb heat with increasing day length, the temperature of the upper levels warms from 1°C. or 2°C. to at least 4°C. or 5°C., which is the early spring temperature of the hypolimnion. When a relatively uniform temperature exists at all levels or at least at the upper levels, the lake mixes or overturns, often in the presence of a strong wind. As the warming of the upper layer continues, temperature stratification begins to define circulation cells that are somewhat analogous to atmospheric inversion layers commonly observed in all large American cities.

Summer kills have been reported when the biochemical oxygen demand exceeded the lake's ability to produce dissolved oxygen in summer months. Factors promoting summer oxygen depletion include high water temperature (which reduces the amount of dissolved oxygen available), high turbidity (which reduces sunlight penetration), accelerated rates of decomposition, and bacterial growth, which increase internal oxygen needs even before BOD-producing materials are added to the pond or lake.

Natural Aging

After several years for a small farm pond and several thousand for one of the Great Lakes, there are symptoms of the normal lake-aging process that become serious threats to the continued use of that resource. The health and welfare of individuals in a large metropolis become very dependent upon a major water body. The dependency may include industrial and domestic water supply, waste disposal, shipping, food supply (such as a fishing community), recreation, and the amenities of commercial and residential site location contiguous to a desirable body of water. Long-term effects of large lake aging can be profound enough to influence the climate of a region. The filling of San Francisco Bay is an illustration of where a large estuary with reduced water surface area affects local climate. Trends indicate that there is an increased temperature differential with decreased water surface area; that is, higher mean temperatures in summer and lower mean temperatures in winter plus reduced moisture-laden fog and increased atmospheric stagnation. In a heavily polluted area such as nearby San Jose, California, very serious air-contamination conditions are thus created. In the last 200 years, the area of San Francisco Bay has been reduced from 680 square miles to less than 400 square miles by fill operations stimulated a desire for short-run profits for a few at the long-term costs of millions of people in that California megalopolis. In the Great Lakes states the shoreline filling on smaller inland lakes of the region is as serious as on the Great Lakes themselves.

Aquatic Succession

In addition to the decrease in water quality, a lake regardless of its size is involved in geological and biological processes that tend to transform the lake into a terrestrial or marshlike habitat. The physical forces of erosion and sedimentation are constantly at work filling the lake bottom. As siltation renders the *estuaries* and *littoral zones* more shallow over time, bio-

Figure 4-16. Shoreline properties are threatened when structures are built near the constantly changing shoreline of the Great Lakes. Storm waves gnawed 25 feet of lawn and bank away in one year from this cottage owner near Empire, Michigan. Even with protective structures it will only be a matter of time (and several high water years) before this Lake Michigan residence succumbs to physical forces of the natural system.

Figure 4-17. Protective structures appear along the shoreline of the Great Lakes during years of high lake levels associated with heavy precipitation. Most efforts of this kind are not successful over the long run.

logical forces are at work on a seasonal basis adding organic tonnages and additional sediment via autumnal decomposition. Occasionally, there are natural forces both biological and physical that set back the eutrophication-sedimentation-aging process. *Seiches* that violently rock the lake water back and forth in its basin destroy shoreline properties and create flooding similar to the action of a small tidal wave. Prevailing westerly winds tend to erode the eastern shorelines only to deposit the clay and sand on a new spit or sandbar. Rivers dump their silty loads on a perennial schedule with deceiving interludes of late summer water clarity.

Consecutive years of abnormally heavy precipitation will raise the levels of the Great Lakes four to six feet above a long-established mean. Lengthy periods of high water create havoc for property owners and particularly those with recreation facilities and summer accommodations. Almost without exception, during "wet" years requests for increased shoreline protection are made throughout the Great Lakes states. Usually the cycle swings back to a series of drier years and the public outcry subsides. Dune formations, such as those in the Sleeping Bear Dunes National Lakeshore Recreation Area, are eroded away at the edge of high waters and blown by the prevailing westerly winds when wide sand bars and beaches are exposed during the sequence of years of reduced rainfall. However, every vested interest is not unhappy with high waters; presumably every extra foot of high water means millions of additional dollars to the shippers whose freighters and ore carriers can be fully loaded and not become grounded in harbors, canals, and rivers during high-water periods.

Curiously, all the forces that transform a lake from an open body of water to a marshy or terrestrial ecosystem seem to gang up near the end of the

Figure 4-18. Dune construction and destruction as an ongoing process is always in evidence in areas of the Great Lakes such as Sleeping Bear Dunes National Lakeshore Recreation Area. Waves, rains, sun, wind, gravity, human activity, and biological forces create an awesome symphony of change along a sandy Great Lakes shoreline.

Figure 4-19. Only a tiny percentage of the Detroit metropolitan waterfront is dedicated to public use and recreational access for the four million residents of the region. (U.S. Dept. of Housing and Urban Development)

job. The "job" may take five thousand or fifty thousand years, but the sublety of the aquatic succession becomes less disguised as emergent vegetation takes over a beachhead and as algal blooms cloud the open water during most of the summer.

Sanitary engineers try to extract the nutrients from waste effluent. Dredges try to scoop sediment out of rivers and harbors at an increasing rate. The U.S. Army Corps of Engineers dredges and relocates seven million cubic yards of polluted spoil from the Great Lakes each year and contaminates new sections of the water in the process. Dams are constructed to control the level; bulkheads are established to stabilize the shoreline. Far-sighted citizens and planners try to prevent waterfront "reclamation" activities that reduce aquatic open space and eliminate biological activities of the littoral zone. But the natural incessant transformation of freshwater lakes to terrestriallike habitat continues triumphantly over geological time. It is ordinarily in the best interest of an urban population to understand what assimilative capacity exists in their local surface waters and then make a commitment that enables a given water resource to produce the desired various benefits (of water supply, recreation, and waste disposal) for the the foreseeable future. At present, cities built upon the shores of lakes and rivers tend to speed up the enrichment process. Even with sophisticated secondary and tertiary treatment, the total eutrophication event continues; only the rate is changed.

Urban Water Pollution Problems

America as a nation of cities has generally turned its back on its waterways. Urban rivers and lakes more frequently serve as sewers and alleys than as proud promenades of human activity and reflectors of architectural splendor. The Great Lakes megalopolis is no exception to the national pattern of urban waterfront neglect. The urban hydrologic cycle is characterized by a once-through cycle that is once through one city and then the used water is sent downstream or downlake for the next city to worry about its quality and quantity. Green Bay, Wisconsin, withdraws water from Lake Michigan twenty-six miles to the east of the city, and then dumps the waste effluent in a nearby downstream swampy vestige of Lake Michigan. Milwaukee takes its water supply from upcurrent offshore cribs and deposits the effluent where Lake Michigan currents carry the waste prob-

Figure 4-20. The downriver area of Detroit illustrates how Americans have historically regarded rivers as sewers and alleys rather than as proud promenades of human activity and reflectors of architectural splendor. Looking south from the Ambassador Bridge in 1972, the plumes of pollution are blowing to Canada, immediately to the left in the photo.

lems south toward Racine, Kenosha, and Chicago. Chicago extracts Lake Michigan water and sends its "sanitary" wastes after treatment down the Illinois River for urbanites to deal with in the Mississippi drainage system. Detroit has its water intake in Lake Huron, and its waterborne wastes, treated or not, are delivered downstream to the Detroit River and Lake Erie. The pattern is duplicated in one metropolis after another. The pollutants in the surface and groundwaters become more challenging to water purification facilities as the size of the human settlement grows.

Degradation of water quality in the Great Lakes region and throughout the United States has taken place with far greater speed in localized pockets of metropolitan regions. This phenomenon has conveyed the false impression to the general public that all of Lake Erie or all of Lake Michigan has been polluted to death. The truth is that there is more biomass now than before, but the dominant species usually consist of organisms that are of less commercial value than previous species. Considerable confusion exists between natural eutrophication and the pollutants and other man-generated wastes that contribute to aquatic succession processes.

In the Great Lakes region, industrial pollution contributes more than 50 per cent of the entire pollution load in various forms including heat, dissolved metals, alkalies, acids, salts, and organic compounds and suspended inorganic and organic wastes, oils, and fibers. It is estimated that 45 per cent of the municipal waste-treatment plant load comes from industry. In the Great Lakes states paper, petrochemical, steel, food processing, and automobile-related manufacturing are major contributors to pollution problems. Agricultural runoff carrying pesticides and heavy loads of nutrients makes large contributions to Midwestern waters. Sediment loads from urban-related construction areas stripped of plant cover carry up to one hundred times the sediment load of areas with natural vegetation. Physical debris makes up another category of pollutants; the obnoxious floating material is usually the result of careless dumping into rivers or deposition on urban flood plains. Most inland lakes and rivers in the Great Lakes states such as Minnesota, Wisconsin, and Michigan are troubled with improperly treated sanitary wastes. The nutrient-speeded eutrophication approaches serious proportions in many other bodies of water in addition to Lake Erie and Lake Ontario. Direct ramifications most common to urban water users are the pathogenic bacterial and viral contaminants and the algal growths that build up to "boom and bloom" proportions with the addition to nutrients that are always concentrated in urban areas. The bacterial inhabitants in urban areas are important for several reasons: (1) they influence the use of natural beaches for swimming and other recreational activity, (2) survival of bacteria in water serves as an indicator or a summation of biological, physical, and chemical factors present, and (3) species or classes of bacteria present may yield information as to the environmental history of the water.

Organisms used as indicators of pollution include *pathogens* of the *enteric group*, spore-producing cells (*anaerobes*), *Escherichia coli* and other

members of the coliform group, the salmonella group, and fecal strepto-
coccus. *Cladophora* species are one of the most common algal indicators
of polluted water. Of course, in some of the heavy industrialized rivers
such as the Cuyahoga (Ohio), the Calumet (Indiana), the Fox (Wisconsin),
and the Rouge (Michigan) critical limitations for survival exist for even the
common pollution indicator flora and fauna. The domestic and industrial
wastes often rival the toxic conditions of *acid mine drainage,* which, of
course, is a chronic problem not in the Great Lakes basin but rather in
other parts of the Great Lakes states as characterized by the strip-mined
portions of Pennsylvania, Ohio, Indiana, and Illinois.

Radioactive wastes in water resources have not received the scrutiny they
deserve. There is a steady increase of industrial, medical, and commercial
uses of radioactive materials, in addition to nuclear-fueled electric plants
in the Great Lakes area and the nation as a whole. Perhaps the attention
given to thermal-pollution problems associated with nuclear power plants
has diverted necessary research and public attention away from *low-level*

Figure 4-21. *Cladophora*
and other algal
growths serve as
biological indicators of
polluted or
well-nourished waters.
Without excellent
phosphorus and
nitrogen removal from
urban waste water,
accelerated algal
growths destroy
aesthetic features of
beaches and taint
water supplies.
(Environmental
Protection Agency)

134   radiological pollution and the *duration* of the widely dispersed radio-
nucleides. Talking about the incomprehensible 24,000 year *half life* of a
plutonium-239 obscures the need for an equally serious discussion about
low-level emissions that accumulate from cobalt-60 (half life more than
5 years), strontium-90 (half life 28.8 years), iodine-131 (half life 8 days),
carbon-14 (half life 5,730 years), krypton-85 (half life 10.76 years), cesium-
137 (half life 30.23 years) and zinc-65 (half life 243.6 days). With the widespread peacetime uses of radioisotopes proposed under the Plowshare
program and others, the environments of air, water, and land are no longer
immune from these ubiquitous pollutants that over time become concentrated in the large metropolitan areas.

Water Pollution Control Legislation

The responsibility for controlling urban caused water pollution traditionally rested upon the shoulders of local and state governments. State
Departments of Fish and Game dealt with the pollution problems of
waterfowl and wildlife, and local and state Departments of Public Health
looked after bacterial problems of water supply and swimming safety.
However, over the last twenty-five to thirty years, most of the incentives
and financing of urban water pollution control have shifted to the federal
government. Ironically the first federal involvement came as the result of
unmanageable clutter and a threat to shipping in urban harbor waters,
specifically New York City.

The *Refuse Act of 1899* outlaws the discharge of pollutants into navigable
waters without a permit from the U.S. Army Corps of Engineers, but municipal sewage is exempted. Of course, with more and more civil and
criminal suits being filed against industrial polluters, more industries are
attempting to contract with municipal waste-treatment facilities so that
they will not need to qualify for a permit. Most permits require the attach-
ment of an environmental impact statement under the *National Environmental Policy Act.* It was not until December, 1970, that the White House
required firms and individuals to file for Refuse Act permits. In the first
two years after the ruling, 20,000 applications were received and about 2,500
had been processed and referred for certification.

The federal role of water pollution control evolved primarily because of
local inaction and jurisdiction disputes at several governmental levels. The
1948 Federal Water Pollution Control Act was modest and experimental.
Technical assistance, research program planning, and grants to community
sewage treatment works were encouraged from the earliest legislation and
continued through the 1956, 1961, 1966, and 1972 acts up to the present.
The federal involvement in pollution abatement has become more ambitious as depicted in the following trends:

1. Federal contribution in matching grants for municipal waste-water
treatment has risen from 30 per cent to 75 per cent.

2. Federal responsibility has broadened from interstate rivers to all navigable waterways in the United States and to the twelve-mile limit as it affects ocean dumping.

3. Enforcement proceedings that began with a cumbersome and ineffective three-step conference-public hearing-court action procedure have been speeded up through the use of direct court action with the help of the Freedom of Information Act, the Administrative Procedures Act, the National Environmental Policy Act (NEPA), and the opportunity for a citizen to acquire standing for class action proceedings against federal or other governmental administrators. (The 1970 Michigan Environmental Protection Act authorizes any private or public entity to sue any other private or public entity for equitable relief from pollution destruction or impairment of the air, water, and other natural resources.) The revival of the 1899 Refuse Act has also increased the involvement of federal agencies even though critics claim it can be used as a "license to pollute."

4. A single and presumably coordinated federal agency, the Environmental Protection Agency, has been established to deal with water pollution problems (and most other environmental concerns) as well as an advisory arm for the President called the *Council on Environmental Quality*. Many states have followed the federal pattern established by NEPA in terms of legislation and administrative or management procedures.

5. The establishment of national water quality standards and required statements by the appropriate state agency for present and future water uses now encourages the improvement of water quality conditions in the future instead of accepting the status quo. The national water pollution control situation has evolved slowly during the last thirty years. For those who wish to inspect the multitude of water problems that face the Great Lakes and the rest of the nation, one source is the 1971 account presented by David Zwick and Marcy Benstock called *Water Wasteland*.[3]

Many loopholes need to be closed, and present legislation must be more rigorously enforced if water quality is going to improve. Sediment control in nonagricultural land-disturbing activities needs more federal, state, and local support. The problem of toxic and hazardous substance disposal has only partially been addressed. Marine and federal facility discharges into waterways pose vexing problems of enforcement and regulation. Water pollution in small but compacted portions of wilderness areas such as the Boundary Waters Canoe Area, Sleeping Bear Dunes National Lakeshore, and in portions of Isle Royale National Park, or other even more remote aquatic habitats are shocking to discover but much easier to control than the massive agricultural runoff into America's freshwater lakes and streams. In the botanical world a weed is a plant out of place; it it not so that in the aquatic ecosystem pollution is a resource out of place?

One general observation is offered as a concluding thought about the relationship between urbanization and water pollution management. A

[3] David Zwick, and Marcy Benstock, *Water Wasteland;* (New York Grossman Publishers, Inc., 1971).

136   megalopolitan pattern is established in the eight Great Lake states and Ontario, which, among other factors, is partially promulgated by federal financial incentives for urban waste-water treatment and water supply systems. This pattern is even more pronounced in the more arid regions of the United States where interbasin transfers, irrigation, and water-related electrical power generation facilities (that, of course, includes almost all of them) are funded with heavy federal subsidies. The net effect of giving federal dollar bonuses to communities and cities that are tied into metropolitan sewerage systems is that a federal incentive is provided for urbanization without assurances that water quality conditions improve with larger urban populations to serve. New industries and other people-generating activities will tend to locate where sewer lines can be extended and where waste-water treatment plants can be expanded under the recently increased federal matching grants. Urbanized river basins in the Great Lakes and elsewhere will tend to promote massive waste water collection systems that conform to the gravity flow of the watershed. The success of these ventures will depend on whether or not the overall water quality improves (including the final receiving water body) and how river flows are augmented after urban or agricultural withdrawals divert large percentages of river water for use and treatment downstream. Southeastern Michigan, southeastern Wisconsin, and northern Ohio are large urban areas that have contemplated enlarged regional waste collection and treatment systems in the Great Lakes basin. If one is looking for an institutional mechanism to curb future excessive growth in heavily urbanized, heavily polluted areas, one solution is, of course, to deny the extension of sewer service as well as the expansion of federally funded waste-water treatment facilities. Another tack is to eliminate the federal expansion of interstate water supplies to huge human settlements that have exceeded the carrying capacity of their regional urban environment, and consequently, are failing to deliver nationally established standards for a healthy, satisfying life.

Flood Control

One last area should be examined in our chapter on urban water resources, for urban flood control has provided a controversial if not disgraceful example of how cities of the twentieth century have yet to find a harmonious relationship with environmental constraints that pertain to urbanization. Many other regions in the United States provide more dramatic and certainly more devastating illustrations of flood losses than the Great Lakes. Nevertheless, the problem can be adequately described using the tributaries of the Great Lakes. Hopefully, the reader will try the described model on whatever major river he lives near.

Long and heavy periods of precipitation often saturate the absorption capacity of a watershed or river basin system. In the collecting streams of the upper Great Lakes states and Canada, heavily forested areas of conifers

Figure 4-22. Flood plains are for floods, not homes. This flooded subdivision built on the flood plain experienced a flood in 1964 that was *12 feet lower* than a flood recorded at the same site in 1937. (U.S. Army Corp of Engineers)

Figure 4-23. Farm homes near Council Bluffs, Iowa, were inundated by this 1944 flood of the Missouri River. (W. Pottawattamie Co., Iowa; photo by W. H. Lathrop)

and a forest floor thick in humus, mosses, ferns, and shrubs constitute a huge sponge layer to prevent excessive runoff in periods of "surplus" water. Soils and vegetative cover that are less conducive to water retention encourage rapid runoff during snow melt or heavy rain periods. Every Midwestern river has a natural waterway to carry off the waters that spill beyond the normal stream channel. This surplus waterway between the normal flow channel and the highwater mark is called a *flood plain*.

If one were to look at a river channel and its flood plain in the perspective of recent geological time or even over a planning horizon of several hundred years, it would appear foolish to build homes, stores, factories, and other flood-vulnerable activities in the natural path of periodic deluges. Yet this is precisely what is happening in most American cities. Even worse, as the flood plain continues to be developed, the outlying portions of the watershed are frequently being converted from agricultural uses to residential and commercial activities. Understandably, with increased pavement and speedier runoff mechanisms such as roofs, gutters, and storm drains, a much larger volume of water is forced to move through the natural channel (often encroached upon) in a similar amount of time.

The "remedy" to the problem of flooding in America has actually aggravated the problem as we look to urban systems of the future. After several years of devastating floods (in the 1920's) in the Mississippi, Ohio, and Missouri River basins, Congress paved the way for the U.S. Army Corps of Engineers to become a major custodian of the flood problems in America. The Corps of Engineers and a sister western flood control agency, the Bureau of Reclamation, approached the problem quite predictably with a set of engineering remedies. It was believed that dams, dikes, spillways, levees, stream straightening, and channelization could cope with the problem that man created by building his structures in the natural flushing zone of every major river.

The record of achievement in reducing flood losses since the 1936 Omnibus Flood Control Act is dismal at best unless one asks the Army Corps of Engineers. Since a systematic engineering approach to the problem was begun at a national level, and despite the more than $17 billion that has been spent on flood control efforts, the average annual flood losses continue to rise. And most of the losses are due to the fact that urban populations have not acquainted themselves with an environmental imperative that says that the primary purpose of the flood plain is to permit the flow of surplus water to pass.

By building a dam, a levee, or a flood wall, the land developer speculates that previously flood-prone land is now safe for residential or commercial occupancy. The developer, the city zoning board, and the general public have apparently been misled by the label of the flood management agencies: the label usually reads "flood control" district, "flood control" program, or "flood control" project. It is not economically feasible to try to control all floods in urban areas. Instead it is reasonable to protect a city from excessive damage by certain proven solutions. The most effective measure is to empty the flood plain of uses that are in direct conflict with the natural events of seasonal or annual flooding. Instead of a housing development on the flood hazard site, the riverine area should be developed for recreational and open space uses.

In the Great Lakes region, the highest flood hazard season is in March and April when sudden rainstorms or rapid snow melts occur on a soil that is still solidly impervious from the winter freeze. The major portion of water rushes downstream often jammed by huge cakes of ice that block downstream movement of the surplus water. The backwater fills the floodplain. If structures are present, inundation is certain. This pattern is very common every spring in the Great Lakes basin, especially with rivers of summer and winter flows under six hundred to eight hundred cubic feet per second. The same river with the coincidence of a series of fast snow melting days and several inches of rain could experience at least ten times the low flow average.

Another misconception about flood control—let us correct the labeling right here to flood protection—is that if a house or business is swept away in a flood that has a stated frequency of once in fifty (or one hundred) years, it will be another fifty years before another flood of that magnitude will occur. Nothing is further from the truth. That fifty-year flood could occur again tomorrow or even three times in one week. The reason it has that misleading flood protection label is that statistically a flood of that magnitude occurs on an average of once every fifty years with no assurances when it will occur. Of course, as more and more urbanization occurs with its soil compaction, pavement construction, and speeded runoff, the severity and losses from flood waters will continue to increase with exactly the same amount of "preurbanization" rainfall.

Another rationale for zoning flood plain "open space-recreational" is the increased need for uncommitted reserves such as parks and golf courses in the center of our cities where most rivers are to be found. Where ponds, lakes, and streams have been drained or put underground in pipes, the city eventually thirsts for the valuable amenities of urban water surface and ends up paying a very dear price for artificial reflecting pools, lagoons, fountains, streams, and waterfalls.

Other certain measures to reduce flood losses in urbanizing areas are found in administrative and management solutions, not engineering devices alone. Why not provide flood protection insurance that would have premiums that reflect the true degree of risk? After one tries unsuccessfully to obtain insurance from a private company, it occurs to him that a well-managed industry that knows the true risks could not stay in business holding policies in America's flood plains. Mortgage rates should automatically reflect the degree of risk for structures in high hazard flood areas. *Flood proofing,* an effective flood warning system, and elevated foundations all help to reduce flood loss.

Flood hazard areas should be routinely marked in fairness to those who are seeking to rent or buy a home or an office. The public highway right

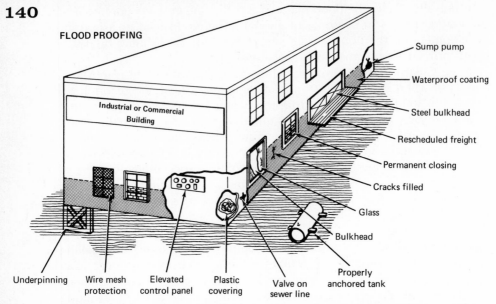

FLOOD PROOFING

Industrial or Commercial Building

Sump pump

Waterproof coating

Steel bulkhead

Rescheduled freight

Permanent closing

Cracks filled

Glass

Bulkhead

Properly anchored tank

Underpinning

Wire mesh protection

Elevated control panel

Plastic covering

Valve on sewer line

Figure 4-24. "Flood proofing" or "flood control" are misleading labels because the most severe floods can never be *totally* controlled or protected against. Urban flood plains of high hazard should be developed for recreational and open space use. (U.S. Army Corps of Engineers)

of way is used to warn citizens of falling rocks, gusty winds, curves, and steep grades. Some city streets warn people of low flying aircraft. Surely, it would be fair and proper to alert prospective buyers or tenants of flood hazards—even if environmentally conscientious road builders or scrupulous developers had previously filed environmental statements about flood hazards. Undoubtedly the environmental impact report was buried in the dusty shelves of a planning department.

Figure 4-25. It would be in the public interest to mark public buildings and erect highway signs that show serious flood hazard areas so that prospective tenants and buyers of real estate would be informed of flood dangers. This May 1973 photograph shows a house flooded seven miles north of Vicksburg, Mississippi. The area was closed to traffic on March 21, 1973 and homes were inundated shortly thereafter. (U.S. Army Corps of Engineers)

Figure 4-26. Had this community marked its flood hazard areas, perhaps the damage suffered by this property owner could have been avoided. (U.S. Army Corps of Engineers)

The metropolitan areas of Minneapolis, Milwaukee, Chicago, Detroit, and Toronto have programmed and in most instances built excellent "greenways" or recreational parklands along flood prone areas. These blue-green corridors of multiple use honor the environmental imperatives superimposed on urban organisms. Furthermore, they become more profitable over time as they provide recreational benefits and protect against property damage and loss of human life. When we try to control floods, we lose in every way; when we urbanites step back and let the hydrologic cycle express itself and find a symbiotic relationship, our dividends continue to flow.

Cities of the Great Lakes region, as they continue to develop into one of the major megalopolitan regions of the United States, will predictably try to exert more control over the lakes and streams in this massive watershed of the Saint Lawrence River. Some of the schemes for management and control are short term such as constructing shoreline retention walls, fish stocking, and harbor dredging. Other ideas such as tertiary waste-water treatment for all cities, a year-round shipping season, and regulation of all lake levels are engineering dreams that are quite within the reach of reality.

One imaginative proposal more than ten years old was to dam the major river systems of the Pacific Northwest, divert water to the arid Southwest,

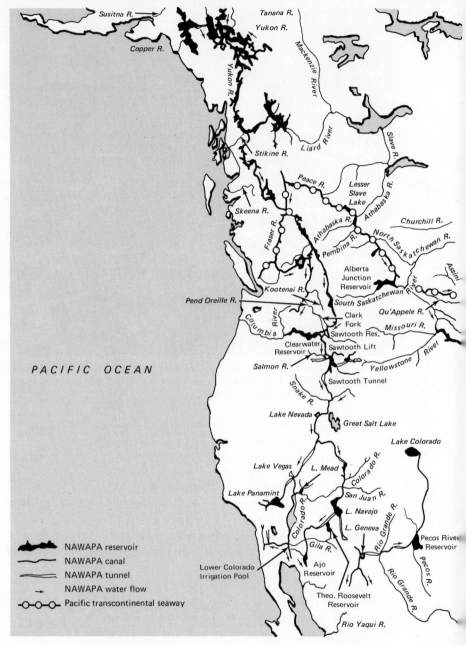

Figure 4-27. The North American Water and Power Alliance (NAWAPA) proposal involves the Great Lakes region in terms of flow augmentation, power generation, and the "far away" pacific transcontinental seaway. (Adapted from Guy-Harold Smith, *Conservation of Natural Resources,* New York: John Wiley & Sons, Inc., 1965)

and to the Great Lakes for major recharge and flushing. Of course, if barge canal connections are made from Lake Erie to the Ohio River, the holding ponds of the Great Lakes could also be used to help supply and flush the urban populations of the Ohio and Mississippi river valleys. These grandiose plans seem farfetched when they are first unveiled. Usually, for reasons

144   sometimes good and sometimes bad, they get shuffled from the spotlight of public attention to dusty shelves and back again. The ambitious North American Water and Power Alliance is now in hibernation but bits and pieces are revived from time to time. The same cautions must be heeded with other massive water diversion, flood control, irrigation, or navigation projects: planners and citizens, engineers and ecologists can hardly envision all of the important ecological or environmental forces that would be affected. A rigorous analysis of alternative projects to achieve the same goals is usually the most rewarding exercise that citizens and water resource developers can embark upon before the start up of a project that eliminates future options.

The Future of Urban Water Use: Time for a Change

Treated water is used for almost every purpose in urban homes across the country—

for drinking and washing clothes.
　for sprinkling the lawn and washing the car.
　　for fighting fires and cleaning streets.
　　　for air conditioning and cooking.
　　　　for taking baths and running garbage disposal units.
　　　　for flushing toilets.

People may soon begin to recognize that a separate water supply system for high quality uses and another for less critical needs is practical for cities with growing shortages and decreasing water quality. Vast quantities of water for fighting fires, washing streets, flushing toilets, garbage disposal units, and domestic or industrial cooling do not require the sophisticated treatment that they presently receive. As surface waters become laden with more nutrients and general urban contaminants, the cost of treating every drop that is used may be unreasonable and unjustifiable. Eventually the combined storm sewer and sanitary sewer will be separated and the contents of each will be treated separately. It makes similar sense to provide new urban areas with dual water supply systems. The very concept of water as a vehicle for waste carriage and waste disposal may come under strong challenge in the cities of the future.

In the meantime, water in the urban hydrologic regime is priced in a way that seems antithetical to wise water management. Those who use the least pay the most. This approach to pricing renewable as well as nonrenewable resources must be challenged. Instead of fostering water conservation practices, the economic incentives for water, electrical energy, and most other primary resource commodities is to use greater volumes so that the average unit cost will be lower. When it becomes widely recognized that larger volume water users have lower rates than single family residences, a change to remove this inequity may be forthcoming. In one Michigan city of 100,000, the water rate is $.37 per 100 cubic feet (750 gallons) up to 1,500 cubic feet, and then the rate is decreased in increments to $.18 per 100 cubic feet when the user exceeds 500,000 cubic feet.

The scrutinizing water consumer should ask, why do the largest users pay the lowest per unit rates especially in face of increased treatment and distribution costs, increasing demands, and growing water scarcities?

The answer frankly stated is that the largest users of water should not be subsidized by the smallest consumers. The larger users should not be permitted to pay lower rates per unit for large volumes of water used. This pricing procedure does not encourage process changes, recycling of water, or other water-saving measures. On the other hand, in the same Michigan city, the charges for sewage treatment are quite rationally fixed at a constant rate regardless of the volume involved.

The very instant water is used, two very profound changes take place that effect its future in the urban hydrologic cycle. The first event is a biological, physical, or chemical change. The water has become a solvent, a carrier, or an assimilator of waste. Or it has become a coolant and the heat load that is carried away affects biological activities. Metabolic action doubles or triples with each 10°C. increase in temperature. As mentioned earlier, warmer water is able to hold much less dissolved oxygen than cooler water. There is a long list of physical and biological changes taking place according to the various uses of the water.

The second critical change is a psychological one in the form of a human attitude about the "used" water. After its use it is disposed of, and Great Lakes residents are no different from people in other humid areas, and even in the arid metropolitan areas where "modern" man resides—let the used water pass downdrain, downstream, downlake. There is a feeling of personal irresponsibility once the water has done its job. Water immediately becomes an orphan after use. If one lives in an incorporated city, the moment the water is used, the civic administrative responsibility ordinarily shifts from the water department to a less popular, more sparsely funded sewage or sanitation department.[4] But more importantly, instead of the intense individual citizen concern about the adequacy of water supply, there is very little interest or knowledge about waste water as long as it gets down the drain or out of sight.

---

[4] In a 1967–1980 projection, "the average annual expenditures by local government in the U.S. for operation, capital outlays over and above construction, and debt interest will be: about an average of $3 billion per year for water distribution and water treatment facilities and services; and an average of about $1.3 billion per year for sanitary sewerage and sewage disposal facilities and services." From *Urban Water Resources Research,* The American Society of Civil Engineers (September 1968), p. 13.

5

Soil Resources

When college and university students are asked to express their preferences about topics they would like to have discussed in a course in environmental affairs or resource management, the subject of soil depletion and soil restoration is seldom mentioned. General interest in the nutrient base for food and fiber has slipped into dangerous obscurity for the urbanite, both young and old. This section analyzes the soil resource as an urban support system with an importance that is equal to that of resources more conspicuous to urban residents such as water and air.

It is easy to justify a discussion of soil resources in the United States using the Mississippi River basin as a case in point because most major U.S. soil types exist in what is the second largest drainage basin in the world. Furthermore, this basin embodies most of the historical implications and efforts of soil conservation that are typical across the United States. An example of every major soil-resource problem is available in this region. The reader is asked to translate the soil resource problems often associated in a traditional agrarian context of the past to the present and future soil difficulties that face city residents. Curiously, in suburbanization the same soil problems occur such as erosion, soil depletion, flooding, and soil toxicity. However, new problems also occur in the form of improper septic drainfields, poor soil structure for residential construction, *subsidence,* and the ominous problem of paving over fertile topsoil. Selected urban-related soil problems mentioned here include the wind erosion of the Dust Bowl, the water erosion of the Cumberland plateau, the nutrient depletion of southern tobacco and cotton lands, the urbanization in the Corn Belt, and the chemical concentrations in the croplands of the Upper Mississippi basin where dairying, orchards, and other food crops are common. Our interpretation of what constitutes the Mississippi River basin or drainage area includes the watershed of the mainstream and its tributaries that reach from the continental divides of the Rocky Mountain and Appalachian Mountain chains to the southern rim of the Great Lakes basin.

It is important to realize that after several hundred years of man's influence throughout the basin, the relatively thin film of topsoil continues to erode off the hillside, the prairie, the cornfield, and the strip mine. Soil has been listed in other texts as a renewable, replenishable resource, but the living soil community is very hard to reestablish once it is buried under

147

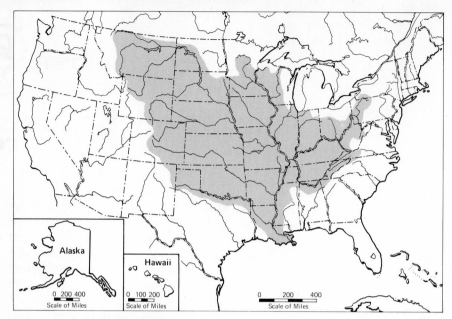

Figure 5-1. The Mississippi Basin region includes major tributary areas of the Ohio, Missouri, and Tennessee in the discussion on soil resources.

a gravel sand bar on the Missouri or poisoned by radioactive wastes, *persistent pesticides,* or other tenacious toxic substances, or deposited as a sloppy sediment in a Louisiana delta or carried off in the Gulf Stream current. Nearly 730 million tons of sediment per year are carried by the Mississippi from the wheatfields and farmlands of Mid-America. The delta advances on all fronts into the Gulf of Mexico at rates up to one mile every sixteen years.

Soil Profile and Soil Horizons

Curiously, most individuals never visualize soil as a living community. Yet productive soil is the result of many physical and biological forces tied together by chemical cycles. For example, one vital link in the nitrogen cycle is the fixation of the free gaseous nitrogen of the air into nitrates in the soil in the soil through the work of the nitrogen fixing bacteria that live in small nodules on the roots of leguminous plants. If we consider the carbon cycle—numerous fungi, bacteria, and insects contribute immeasurably to the decay of organic material back into useable soil.

The agronomist refers to a cross-sectional view of the earth, as seen in a road cut or a rock quarry, as the *soil profile.* Most soil profiles can be divided into four major layers or *horizons* that merge into each other: horizon A (topsoil); horizon B (subsoil); horizon C (parent material); and

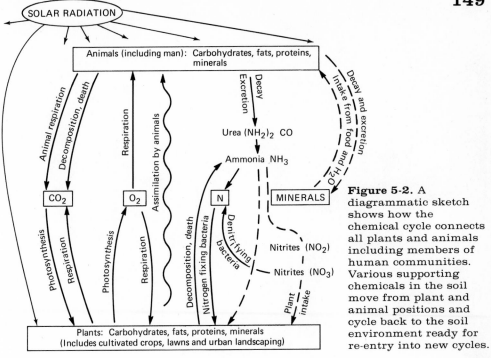

Figure 5-2. A diagrammatic sketch shows how the chemical cycle connects all plants and animals including members of human communities. Various supporting chemicals in the soil move from plant and animal positions and cycle back to the soil environment ready for re-entry into new cycles.

Figure 5-3. A soil profile from Logan County, Colorado. Most of the biological activity goes on in the dark-colored, well-drained loams of the A and B layers. Notice that below the light loam subsoils are the stratified calcareous sand and gravel parent material at about 20–40 inches. (USDA—Soil Conservation Service)

Figure 5-4. The silt loam (Class I) soil of this Missouri farm gives a reliable clue to its origin of previous silt deposition along a floodplain. (USDA—Soil Conservation Service)

horizon D (bedrock). (Refer to soil horizon figures and photographs). The transformations of the deep strata or bedrock of the D horizon with the blending of the minerals from weathered parent material in the C horizon combine with the down-leaching or percolation from above at the B horizon. At this point in the vertical cross section of the profile, tremendous biological and physiochemical activity goes on. Burrowing vertebrates, invertebrate animals, bacteria, fungi, and other decomposers who live in the organic material of horizon A, the topsoil, help the soil mixing and building process. The general kind of grassland or forest cover helps determine what mammals, amphibians, or reptiles are members of the soil building army. Some agronomists have suggested that the soil profile serves as an autobiography by which the observer can retrace the history of the soil community, its geological beginnings, the contributions of climate, and the influence of flora and fauna over the thousands of years that are ordinarily required to produce only a few inches of topsoil.

Most of us simply take the genesis and sustenance of our national or **150** local soil resources for granted. Even if one lives in one of the great cities that borders on a part of the Mississippi River system from Pittsburgh to Denver and from Minneapolis-Saint Paul to New Orleans, one has probably been seperated from an understanding of the dynamics of the soil as much as any American urban dweller. But as the barges load or unload, it is well to remind ourselves that the evolution of nearly every waterfront settlement was nourished in its early years (and many still are today) by a resource that most urbanites have forgotten.

CASE IN POINT:
THE MISSISSIPPI BASIN REGION

Basically there are two types of soil formation patterns, the regional and local. The regional pattern such as the Mississippi Delta region, which extends from the confluences of the Ohio and Missouri rivers to the Gulf of Mexico, is a result of the overall climate of seasonal flooding and deposition in which the soil and its associated organisms have developed. A local soil pattern is a smaller unit within a region and is defined and strongly influenced by local geological and topographical differences such as slope and drainage.

Figure 5-5. Floods occur at the upper layers of a soil profile in one location and add to the upper horizon when the current slows and the waters subside. What we see in this Mississippi flood of 1944 is a massive addition of silt and enrichment to a soil community while temporarily disrupting man, the invader and the benefactor of a flood plain. (TVA)

152   The so-called Mississippi Delta region—a 650-mile-long subregion of the lower Mississippi River basin with an average width of 70 miles—was formed from soil that was deposited in the area by the river and consists of three sections—namely, the flood plain, the *loessial terraces,* and the *deltaic plain.* Periodically, soil has been deposited on the flood plain, the land along the riverbank that becomes periodically inundated when a river is carrying water in excess of its channeled capacity. Of course, this soil buildup in the flood plain is at the sacrifice of soil removal from upriver areas throughout the drainage basin. Slopes with steep gradients tend to lose soil most readily, and soil loss is accelerated if overgrazing, poor cultivation, abusive logging, or large construction is in progress. The *loessial soils,* on the other hand, were originally wind-deposited mineral particles transported when the postglacial muds dried and became airborne. As riverbank erosion cuts into the ordinarily deep loess deposits, the river channel is carved deeper and the valley shows loessial terraces where previous river levels once eroded the banks. The loessial terraces along the Mississippi rise from twenty to fifty feet above the surrounding flood plains. The delta bottomlands or deltaic plain, consisting of 35,000 square miles or three and one-half times more area than the Nile River delta, is characterized by soils deposited from the continual precipitation of river sediments. Drainage helps to reclaim the ordinarily water-logged silty loam soils.

As more permanent trading posts, forts, and other early settlements were established at the confluences and along the rivers of the basin, the annual flooding posed increasingly serious problems. More of the flood plain of the Mississippi River and her tributaries became developed either for agricultural purposes or for urban land use. The inundation of the lower Mississippi cropland was so severe during the 1973 floods that much of the region was proclaimed a disaster area. (Related flood management discussion is found in Chapter 4 and later in this chapter.) In the mid-1800's, the fertile loams of the flood plain and glacial *alluvial* areas were viewed as high priority sites for corn and other food production. Eventually, the highest demand upon the flat, water-contiguous flood plain shifted from cornfield to urban uses. The majority of urbanization in the corn belt portions of Iowa, Minnesota, Wisconsin, Illinois, Indiana, Ohio, Kentucky, and Missouri takes place on the venerable and sometimes vulnerable flood plain. Thus urban concrete, as in the Chicago metropolitan area, laid upon cornfields and other highly productive cropland pushes agricultural production to soils that are less suited for this purpose. Ironically, the need for larger quantities of food likewise increases with the ever-mushrooming population. Another previously unanticipated conflict with rich farmland is the urban demand for electricity that has put pressures on mining companies to strip away Midwestern agricultural soil in order to extract the coal reserves beneath.

In often false hopes of providing protection to the residential, commercial, and agricultural development of the flood plain, levees, *stream chan-*

Figure 5-6. Destruction of the vegetative cover on steep gradients makes the soil very vulnerable to erosion in areas of heavy rainfall and runoff. This 1973 photograph is in the watershed of the Tennessee River.

nelization, dredging, dams and other so called "flood control" structures were built. Yet, wherever man has had success in reducing flooding and soil redeposition, he has had to find other ways of refurbishing even the thick flood plain soils whose fertility becomes exhausted. If the traditional Mississippi basin crops of cotton, soybeans, corn, oats, wheat, barley, alfalfa, sugarcane, and rice continue to be grown, the struggle against waterlogging, summer drought, eventual infertility, and soil erosion will also continue, especially in the face of a growing national population and commitments to the hungry two-thirds of the world. Also increasing concern about unfavorable U.S balance of payments may encourage more agricultural production for export.

The Breakdown of Soil Communities

The soil resource problem is shared by both the rural and urban basin dweller. When the suburbanite carries his plastic bag of grass clippings out to the curb for trash pickup, he probably does not perceive his export from his lawn as a relatively recent form of soil erosion. And when the city **153**

Figure 5-7. Active gully erosion in an Iowa pasture. Urban consumers ultimately bear the cost of careless agricultural practices. (USDA—Soil Conservation Service)

dweller sniffs a garbage truck going to the incinerator or landfill dump, he does not ordinarily realize that the topsoil and water (in a modified form) of some farm or truck garden is being detoured from the mainstream of productive life support cycles. After the export of lawn clippings continues to the point of nutrient depletion, the naïve gardener buys peat and commercial fertilizers to try and replenish the soil he has exported or poisoned with his indiscriminate use of herbicides, insecticides, and other biocides. In some urban areas, space seems to prohibit the opportunity of a garden and natural vegetation. It is little wonder that the child who is deprived of a garden is also deprived of the knowledge and appreciation of one of the vital sustaining systems for urban life—the soil resources.

When one speaks about soil resources in an urban context, very few listeners have mental flashes of soil profile, sheet erosion (subtle removal of soil from barren lots and areas with a gentle slope, but limited vegetation), or even Public Law 566 (The Small Watershed Act of 1954), which is further discussed later in the chapter. Today in American metropolitan areas, the traditional discussion of soil and land management practices has very little meaning to the urban dweller because he has been remarkably and, in too many cases, disastrously separated from the soil that, in fact, is a major origin of his sustenance. Various soil components have been repackaged in garden store peat bags, truck-delivered topsoil, or Milorganite[1], and other multiple forms that the urban dweller seldom associates with the myriad complexity of the soil resource that was the life support system to the homesteaders of the nineteenth century and the Dust Bowl dwellers of the twentieth century.

Except for the scarce urban garden, metropolitan Americans have insu-

[1]Milorganite is a brand name for the dried sewage from the City of Milwaukee, Wisconsin. This by-product of an activated sludge waste-water treatment plant, naturally endowed with nitrogen-rich ammonia, is balanced with other nutrients and sold commercially as a fertilizer.

154

lated themselves from the earth in curious ways. Even in surburban developments where land is ample, the topsoil is often scraped or eroded away
during construction, leaving the claylike subsoil. The B horizon is quickly
laid over by a thin film of imported topsoil in a way that is carefully
designed to disguise the clay parent material or mask the landfill. If a marsh
is nearby, it is usually purchased but seldom regarded as valuable as a marsh
by the developer. Eventually the marsh is filled or drained to accommodate
more building sites. Man's shortsighted intrusion into the natural development of soil communities sets into motion imbalances of surface drainage,
nutrient recycling, water recharge, and many other soil-related services that
are bestowed upon the urban resident. Over the longest of time horizons,
it is appropriate to think of soil formation and depletion as a cyclic phenomenon. There is the chemical and physical weathering of the parent
material, the formation of the C and B horizons, and eventually the
humus-rich A horizon. Bulldozers and graders, rains and floods, and wind
and ice are common erodants that redistribute the upper soil layers. Thousands of years of soil buildup can be displaced in a single week or season.
Yet even after the erosion or depletion of the soil community, the persistant
environmental forces set the soil-building operation into motion with the
advances of pioneer soil-building species such as lichens, sedges, and
mosses. Their ultimate destiny, in addition to sustaining themselves, seems
to be to rebuild horizons A, B, and C from parent material in horizon D.
Far too often it is man's activity, not a glacier or a rainfall in a wilderness
area, that keeps the soil builders hopelessly busy. The soil community is
broken down by man faster than it builds itself up.

It is the urban man who applies the environmental cosmetic, a hybrid
grass named after a state or a landscape that is "greener than green." And
to keep it that way, the lawn and soil importer of suburbia is persuaded
to overfertilize, overwater, overweedkill, overinsecticide, and overremove
the grass crop by the manufacturers' instructions or by social pressures of
the neighborhood or both.

In what kind of condition is the U.S. soil profile with its horizons A, B,
C, and D? Horizons A and B in America are apparently on their way to
one of three places: the Atlantic Coast, the Pacific Coast, or the Gulf coast.
It is good, rich topsoil: the loams, silts, and sandy clays all mixed with ample
solutions of inorganic fertilizers rinsed off the farmlands, lawns, and greener
than green expanses of our countryside and cityscape. Perhaps in time,
several tens of millions of years at least, the upheaval or unwarping of the
earth's crust may bring horizon A above the level of the sea to complete
the cycle and prepare the soil for cultivation again.

In the southern portions of the Mississippi basin, an accelerated sedimentation rate, which is one measure of loss from horizons A and B, began
with the clearing of the forests by white settlers in the 1830's. In the cotton
planting and cultivation boom from 1830 to 1930, an estimated minimum
of five to eight inches of topsoil eroded from the uplands. This determination is based upon the accumulation of an average three and one-third

Figure 5-8. Serious gully erosion "can be stopped by check dams, fencing off of livestock and replanting." The one year later photo follows. (USDA— Soil Conservation Service)

Figure 5-9. Because of rich soils and ample moisture in most of the Mississippi drainage basin, proper soil conservation practices can correct small gully erosion caught at early stages. This photograph was taken one year later after careful soil erosion treatment. (USDA—Soil Conservation Service)

feet of sediment in the valleys of Northcentral Mississippi, with maximum sedimentation in some areas averaging eight feet thick.[2]

The C horizon of the soil profile is composed of weathered parent material derived from the nearby D horizon, which is often granite or limestone. The chemically and physically transformed but unconsolidated C horizon facilitates water storage and release. Most of the influence such

[2]C. Happ, G. Rittenhouse, and G. C. Dobson, *Some Principles of Accelerated Stream and Valley Sedimentation*, U.S.D.A. Technical Bulletin No. 695 (1940).

Figure 5-10. In the flood plain near Covent, Louisiana, sugar cane is grown after the deltaic soils have been drained and graded. The levee on the left is an effort to keep floodwaters out of the cropland. (USDA—Soil Conservation Service)

as alkalinity or acidity at this level is determined by the parent material, which is usually bedrock. For example, heavy organic peat soils with a low pH increase productivity when lime and potash are added. However, above this layer a greater influence is exerted by the vegetative and surface environmental factors. In the more humid portions of the Mississippi basin, about 30 per cent of the valley land has been damaged by sand deposition and swamping, another 35 per cent is not suitable for agriculture because of excessive flooding.

The extreme sensitivity of the living soil community is demonstrated wherever the living carpet of forest or grassland cover is removed or covered by acres of concrete and asphalt. The lumbering or paving action, if not done with utmost ecological replenishment, sets into motion a chain of potentially negative reactions: elimination of forest cover, planting of nutrient extracting crops, breakdown of organic soil layers, and eventual susceptibility of soil to water or wind erosion. The erosion in turn buries fertile valley soils with sands, clays, and other nonproductive components of the B and C horizons. During the season of maximum runoff, river channels fill with sediment, waterlogged soils become common, and the area becomes vulnerable to damaging floods.

Figure 5-11. Construction of subdivision near Omaha, Nebraska, without adequate controls from an erosion control ordinance presented this eroded appearance after a number of years. In contrast the area in the background with vegetative cover continues to be a healthy, productive living habitat. (USDA—Soil Conservation Service)

Figure 5-12. Highway construction and residential construction contribute the heaviest sediment loads to midwestern lakes and rivers. Several progressive cities in the Mississippi drainage basin have enacted subdivision sediment and soil erosion ordinances to prevent the economic and ecological loss pictured here. (U.S. Dept. of Housing and Urban Development)

Figure 5-13. Expensive "imported" topsoil is brought in to cover the B Horizon, which was exposed by erosion during construction or scraped and graded prior to building the homes.

Such a chain of events took place in the tributary systems of the Missouri, the Platte, the Arkansas, the Kansas, and the Red rivers, which fed the Mississippi mainstem from the Western prairies. The dark brown prairie and *chernozem* soils evolved over thousands of years as a mutualistic response to the rainfall patterns, the parent materials, and the anchoring effect of buffalo grass, the grama grass, the big bluestem and little bluestem. Antelope, bison, prarie dog, coyote, and other native members on the plains soil-maintenance team were forced out by ranchers, whose cattle and wheat began the decline of the soil resource. The prairie sod was turned to the sun. Drought years and high winds removed from eight to ten inches of topsoil in the black blizzards of the 1930 Dust Bowl days.

The Dust Bowl

The Dust Bowl phenomenon of the prairie and range states is the epitome of soil loss caused by winds, heat, and drought. Added to the natural hazards of the grassland community is man's insensitivity to the precarious soil-moisture-vegetation balance. In 1890, 1910, the late 1920's, the mid 1930's, the mid 1950's and the early 1970's a similar combination of forces permitted annual soil losses from the western Mississippi basin tributaries in excess of 200 million tons—almost all of them from the A horizon. Bankruptcy of the soil and the small western rancher of farmer went hand in hand as the latter headed for the city to find employment. The legacy of the prairie soil looked bleak indeed. Up to 75 per cent of the topsoil was depleted in a total affected area of 663 million acres—mute testimony to the need for improved soil conservation practices in the prairie states drained by the Mississippi.

Soil structure collapsed under compaction conditions when cattle ex-

Figure 5-14. Wind erosion is often the result of overgrazing, soil nutrient depletion coinciding with periods of drought and high wind. (USDA—Soil Conservation Service)

Figure 5-15. Wind erosion often scours away the upper horizons of the soil profile and continues to expose the subsoil and parent materials. They, in turn, are deposited elsewhere. A pioneer plant community is required before the re-establishment of the healthy soil environment and soil buildup can begin. (USDA—Soil Conservation Service)

Figure 5-16. After the carrying capacity of the soil community is exceeded, particularly under a stress condition of compaction or drought, the biological system that depended on the productivity of the soil resource also begins to collapse. Huge dependent human settlements become very vulnerable to food shortages when the soil resource is pushed beyond its capacity to produce. (USDA—Soil Conservation Service)

ceeded the carrying capacity of the land. The stage was thus set for the soil disasters in the form of flood, drought, nutrient depletion, and broken mineral cycles that continue today on the massive agricultural holdings of the Mississippi drainage basin, located in a country of perhaps the slowest learners of conservation lessons in the world.

Urban Implications

The city receives meat, grains, and fibers from the hinterlands and feed-lots, and the city dweller goes to the zoo to see farm animals and to the botanical garden to see hybrid wheat, corn, and cotton. And Americans read in their conservation textbooks that soils are "replaceable, maintain-able" natural resources!

Well, good old horizon D is still around. Hardly anybody in the city recognizes it anymore. In fact, parts of it are tied up in the building stone, the aggregate of roadbeds, highway surfaces, and the interiors and exteriors of buildings. Each particle of every shingle is a forgotten representative of horizon D. The parent material of our depletable soil resources has been assigned a new and economically more profitable destiny in the facades of structures and in the construction of roads rather than in the creation of soil itself. This comment is not registered as a complaint about the use of horizon D; the author does object vigorously to having no public awareness or understanding of the existence of the soil relatives in our everyday presence and no appreciation for their importance in our daily lives. One should never look through a window again without acknowledging that perhaps a sand dune or a beach was sacrificed for the manufacture of the glass through which his view is made possible.

Since the relationship of the soil to the survival and pleasure of a city is a little more clear, it would be fitting to examine how soil stability and soil nutrition can be practiced in urban areas. One part of the discussion is on the macroscale of metropolitan soil and land use. The second part is at the microscale of individual soil management practice.

Inasmuch as an urban area implies not only the physical boundaries of urban influence but also the region that serves as a support system for the urban population, it is appropriate to turn to the soil resources of the Mississippi basin. These resources in part supply the food needs for Midwestern and other cities. Of course, in almost every case the product of the land is converted to capital that enables a flow of food, goods, and services to come to a Midwestern town from all over the world. If the soil of Iowa, Illinois, or Minnesota is especially productive, a surplus of goods and services can be obtained beyond the levels required to sustain the local population. However, if the soils lose their nutrients or if the productive topsoil is eroded to the Gulf of Mexico, deprivation and collapse could come to the cities of the Mississippi basin just as surely as the same fate came to cities and civilizations of the Tigris and Euphrates and the prehistoric Indians of the American Southwest.

Soil management practices as rural sounding as *contour farming, strip cropping,* and *crop rotation,* shelterbelt establishment, *green manuring* and animal manuring, and gully reclamation must be understood as being directly related to the standard of living in the largest metropolitan cities of middle America. These cities include Chicago, Omaha, Kansas City, Cincinnati, Louisville, Saint Louis, Memphis, and New Orleans, which are by coincidence on a tributary or mainstem of the Mississippi. The Mississippi River basin's major breadbasket role for the nation, will continue only as long as the soil cycle of nutrients is sustained and the soil cycle of erosion is curtailed. Even in an especially near urban areas, the following practices of soil restoration should be utilized to the fullest extent possible. It should be kept in mind that most of these procedures can each be scaled down for application in a modest urban vegetable or flower garden:

Figure 5-17. Bricks and mortar, building stone, roads and sidewalks are the transformed soil horizon B (subsoil), C (weathered parent material) and D (bedrock) most visible to the inner city resident. (U.S. Dept. of Housing and Urban Development)

164 A. Contour Farming or Contour Gardening

The evidence in the agricultural literature is very clear about the advantages of soil retention when contour plowing is practiced. The crops are planted parallel to the contour of the slope, which in effect makes each row a holding area for moving water and moving soil particles. As the garden or crop rows ring a hillside, downward movement of water is diverted to the horizontal furrows from the previously vertical path. The objective is, of course, to slow the speed of water runoff that in turn reduces the amount of topsoil removed. Ground percolation is increased, which is beneficial to the recharge of groundwater for urban or dry weather agricultural use.

A modification of contour farming is to plow deep furrows at wide intervals along the contour of a slope. The purpose of the widely spaced trenches is to provide linear catchment areas, often in pastureland where sudden precipitation is retained and absorbed into the soil. An extreme modification, seldom used in the Mississippi River basin except along the steepest slopes and palisade areas, is terracing. Here an earthen steplike embankment is built to increase arable land as well as to check runoff. If the terraced areas are large, provisions must be taken to "walk the water" down the slope slowly enought to avoid sheet and gully erosion from getting started. Ordinarily sodded or heavily grassed pathways are provided for carrying excess water along the contour.

Figure 5-18. Contour planting is being practiced here to retard runoff and topsoil removal in hilly terrain. The same principle is applicable to a sloped urban garden. (TVA)

Figure 5-19. Terraces and crop rotation are demonstrated on this Iowa farm in the heart of the Mississippi basin "bread basket." Note the "producer-extraction type" community of Templeton, Iowa, in the background. (USDA—Soil Conservation Service)

B. Strip Cropping and Crop Rotation

In order to increase water infiltration on sloping land, "wide-row crops" such as corn, cotton, potatoes, and other vegetables should be planted on the contour, preferably in alternating strips that are interspersed by crops or vegetation that retain soil, moisture, and nutrients. Hay, alfalfa, clover, and some of the grains serve as intermediary strips. The advisable procedure is to annually rotate the highly nutrient-extractive crop such as corn, tobacco, or cotton with legumes that add nitrogen to the soil or with other cover crops such as oats, barley, and rye.

In the northern Great Plains wheat region where strips of wheat and fallow land, designed to conserve soil and moisture, dominate the land-scape, a recent and ominous problem exists called saline seep. Montana's Environmental Quality Council First Annual Report states that

"the moisture conserving capacity of this fallow system has surpassed expectations. Coupled with a geological situation where permeable, salt-laden glacial till over-lays a thick, impervious shale formation, moisture retention has resulted in a soil profile saturated with highly saline water. Water intercepted by the fallow ground, mostly during the spring months, moves rapidly through the soil profile, accumu-

165

lating salts along the way, and builds up on top of the shale, forming a 'perched' water table. This excess water moves downslope, accumulates in swales, and eventually breaks out at the surface where it evaporates and leaves the dissolved salts behind.[3]

Approximately 228,000 square miles of land in the Missouri drainage system have potential (geologic regime and fallow dry-land farming prac-tices) for saline seep development. This phenomenon affects soil productivity, ground water, and surface water. Reports from the Montana Environmental Quality Council show that there are regular discharges into the Missouri River watershed of seeps containing "manganese, lead, silver, sulfate, chloride, nitrate, and total dissolved solids . . . in concentrations exceeding U.S. Public Health Service drinking water standards and that quantities of dissolved solids, magnesium, sodium and lead surpassed recommended stockwater standards."[4] Continuous cropping and establishment of a sod cover over the land have been proposed as solutions to the saline seep problem but results do not seem to be encouraging. This area is excessively overgrazed and most of it is in need of treatment.

In the southern portions of the Mississippi River basin more than one hundred years of relatively intensive agriculture has been the pattern since the native forest cover was cleared. Where the typical southern pines (shortleaf, longleaf, slash, and loblolly) and lowland forest remain, so do the essential nutrients remain in cycle. But when nutrient-removing crops such as cotton and tobacco are shipped off the farm to urban processing centers, the nutrient cycles are jeopardized. Essential *macronutrients* include nitrogen, phosphorus, potassium (remember the fertilizer bag percentages of these three in that order?), carbon, hydrogen, oxygen, sulphur, and calcium. Trace elements of *micronutrients,* which are necessary in minute amounts for healthy crop growth, are boron, copper, chlorine, iron, manganese, molybdenum, and zinc. Without crop rotation between nutrient-adding and nutrient-extracting plants, the restoration of soil fertility becomes a very haphazard affair. Thus the southern plantations, after thirty to fifty seasons, came up with "worn out" soil. These cotton and tobacco farmers resorted to commercially prepared inorganic fertilizers when their efforts to reduce erosion and nutrient loss through strip cropping, manuring, and rotation of soil-building crops with "cash" crops failed over the years. Oliver Owen states that the direct application of anhydrous ammonia to soil was proved feasible in 1947 at the Mississippi Agricultural Experiment Station.[5] Today, the United States uses more than 8 million tons of this inorganic nitrogen fertilizer per year, which ranks as the fastest growing use rate of any fertilizer. Again, man tries to replicate what the soil community formerly did on its own over a longer period of time.

[3] State of Montana, *Environmental Quality Council First Annual Report* (October 1972), p. 87.

[4] Ibid., p. 88.

[5] Oliver S. Owen, *Natural Resource Conservation* (New York: Macmillan Publishing Co. Inc., 1971), p. 109.

Figure 5-20. Shelterbelts or windbreaks have special advantages in urban areas in the form of aesthetics, visual and sound barriers, and heating cost savings. In several years this Grand Forks, North Dakota, project will probably increase the value of the dwellings that are protected. (USDA—Soil Conservation Service)

C. Shelterbelts or Windbreaks

In western and northwestern portions of the Mississippi basin, wind erosion is a critical problem as was mentioned in reference to the Dust Bowl tragedies. Despite the regional nature of wind erosion on prairie soils in the semiarid western part of the basin, windbreaks are very effective at the local level. The objective is to reduce the wind velocity, which in turn reduces the evaporation of soil moisture, moderates temperature, and reduces soil blowing. Steel fences and selected kinds of crops or other vegetation are used. Rows are constructed at right angles to the prevailing winds.

The beneficial influence of a carefully designed shelterbelt of trees can extend 150 feet to the windward and up to 1,400 feet to the leeward. Research has shown that the protection in the *leeward* direction is equivalent to twenty times the height of the shelterbelt. Conifers such as spruce, red cedar, Scotch, Ponderosa, and Austrian pine provide year-round advantages but local conditions throughout the Mississippi-Missouri prairie region make possible the use of cottonwood, Russian olive, honey locust, burr oak, hackberry, green ash, and osage orange. While the shelterbelt

Figure 5-21. This North Dakota farm residence is well protected from wind and snow by this multi-row mix of coniferous trees and fruit-bearing trees and shrubs. (USDA—Soil Conservation Service)

Figure 5-22. On this Michigan farm, the highly productive organic soil requires protection from wind erosion. The aerial view shows windbreaks of black willow but the unprotected field in the left foreground has been wetted by sprinkler to prevent soil blowing. (USDA—Soil Conservation Service)

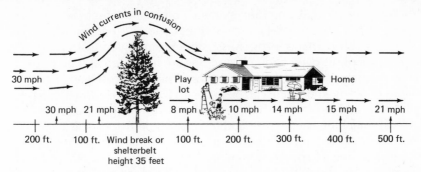

Figure 5-23. Influence of a windbreak on wind velocity in an urban area is substantial. Protection to people, structures and other urban activity extends up to 150 feet on the windward side and up to 1400 feet on the downwind side. (Adapted from the Kansas State Board of Agriculture)

vegetation is getting established, fencing and watering are usually required. After the nonnative species have created their own microhabitat including a soil profile different from the region, less attention is required.

In urban areas special kinds of shelterbelts have recently come into favor by informed residents and planners. A vegetational shelterbelt can buffer more than wind. For example, trees and shrubs serve as screens for unsightly areas such as expressways, expressway interchanges, and junkyards, and as barriers against noise and highway fumes. In addition to the use of vegetational buffers for local residential and commercial facilities, the concept of a shelterbelt has been practiced by Ebenezer Howard and other British and American town planners. The idea of a green belt that surrounds a town or city—even forming concentric rings—continues to be applied today. Special advantages of regional shelterbelts and tree-lined highways include the increased recreation land and habitat for wildlife in close proximity to the urban population. Good examples in the Mississippi basin region include the Cook County Forest Preserve system located in the Chicago metropolitan area and the Natchez Trace National Parkway connecting Nashville, Tennesse, and Natchez, Mississippi.

D. Green Manuring and Animal Manuring

In addition to the physical loss of soil, another major soil depletion problem is loss of soil fertility. The normal uptake of nutrients into crops and other vegetation reduces the availability of micro and macronutrients needed by plants. In the absence of agriculture, the leaf fall and organic decomposition returns most essential elements to the soil, but in the heavy-crop production areas of the Mississippi basin, nutrients are removed from the soil in the form of animals and crops that are shipped to metropolitan markets. *Green manuring* is the process of plowing under living plants to maintain a nutrient balance. Alfalfa, clovers, vetches, lespedeza, and soybeans are commonly used leguminous plants because of their high *nitrogen-fixation* potential. Turning under green crops and animal manures also improves the soil structure, increases organic content, and stimulates growth of soil decomposers such as fungi and soil bacteria. An average acre of agricultural land in the Mississippi basin region loses about sixty-five pounds of nitrogen annually as crops are harvested and up to twenty-five more pounds from the soil erosion. The deficit of eighty to ninety pounds of nitrogen per acre can be made up by green manuring of legumes, which can add up to two hundred pounds of nitrogen per acre. In city gardens, mulching the soil by adding grass clippings or soil enriched by compost-piling is a recommended procedure for soil improvement.

The spreading of animal manure has decreased in agricultural areas for several reasons. One, the concentration of livestock and poultry feedlots near urban areas has concentrated the supply of dung and urine from cattle, poultry, sheep, and pigs into facilities where extensive crops are not grown. Second, the ease of storage and application of commercial mineral fertilizers has displaced the use of animal manures on increasingly large consolidated cooperative farms.

If it would not be considered too remote an extension of animal manuring, some mention should be made of the revived practice of human

Figure 5-24. With thoughtful lawn and garden practices, the leaves or clippings are composted for mulch and humus supplements to the garden and lawn after a period of decomposition. (USDA—Soil Conservation Service)

Figure 5-25. Compost facilities provide an opportunity for the urbanite to recycle soil chemicals and nutrients. Specific compost pH, etc., can be produced by using certain species of leaves under particular composting conditions. This is a very economical way to build the A and B horizons in the urban soil profile. (USDA—Soil Conservation Service)

waste application in metropolitan regions. As noted in Chapter 4, Muskegon, Michigan, is a recent larger U.S. city pioneer in adopting this procedure. However, Germany, the Netherlands, and England have used treated human sewage as a soil conditioner for nearly a century.

Various techniques of spray irrigating activated sludge on cropland and forest land are now being practiced in the United States, predominantly in Gulf region forest plantations. In addition to returning nutrients to the soil and increasing yields, the sludge application on land tends to reduce the fertilizing effect on lakes and streams that ordinarily receive municipal waste effluents. Furthermore, if the nutrients are efficiently absorbed and utilized in the upper levels of the soil profile, groundwater recharge takes place. Potential drawbacks of this "human animal manuring" for large urban areas include the requirement of large expanses of open land, a need for highly permeable soil conditions, and the possibility that viruses, pesticides, or other toxic substances that find their way into major urban waste-water systems may accumulate in the soil to dangerously high levels.

Another soil improvement practice related to manuring that has seen a rebirth of popularity among urban residents is organic gardening. The "victory gardens" of the 1970's are personal victories against indiscriminate use of biocides on huge tracts of monocultural farmland and a resistance against high food prices in chain supermarkets. It is noteworthy to see that demonstration community organic gardens are being established to set examples for urban gardeners who wish to raise fruits and vegetables free from commercially prepared chemicals. This same educational strategy was used forty years ago in order to convince the farmer that inorganic fertilizers, hybrid seeds, and other agricultural innovations could increase his yield.

172   A new user of the Agricultural Extension Agent's free advice is the suburban gardener who seeks ways for biological control of insects. Consequently, natural predators such as ladybug beetles and praying mantises who feed only on scale insects, aphids, various flying insects, and caterpillars are increasingly being used. The strong smells of insect buffering plants such as chives, onions, and marigolds repel nematodes and other garden pests.

   Much of the advice about crop rotation, manuring, strip cropping, contouring, and shelterbelting has excellent application for the city-based gardener at the microscale. His soil throughout the Mississippi basin region was once grassland, forest, or swamp. With settlers coming through the Cumberland Gap, or migrating down from the Great Lakes or up the river from New Orleans, the choice land was converted to farms and orchards. Even though suburban growth is converting more than a million acres per year to residential and commercial use, small patches of the lawn are often reclaimed as garden soil. The productivity of a city garden is dependent upon the same basic soil conservation practices that are applied on the largest and most progressive farms.

Figure 5-26. Gully erosion with active bank cutting is shown on this Illinois farm. Even more serious erosion than this occurs in the eastern and western portion of the Mississippi basin region where the terrain becomes more rugged and the runoff is more sporadic. (USDA—Soil Conservation Service)

Figure 5-27. A strip-mined area in Fonde, Kentucky, was in need of vegetative reclamation, as seen in this "before treatment" scene. (TVA)

Figure 5-28. "After treatment," the same location (in Fonde, Kentucky,) several years later shows the difficulty of re-establishing cover and topsoil production on relatively level land. (TVA)

174   E. Gully Reclamation

When the topography of the Mississippi Basin region becomes sharply hilly and more rugged as it does in its far eastern and western tributary areas, gully formation is a devastating soil problem. Once the organic and root structure zone is torn away in a steep gradient area, the erosion of other soil horizons continues with great speed. In heavy thundershower regions, gullies can carve their way up a slope at the rate of nearly twenty feet per year. The extreme but instructive examples of gully formation are the Badlands National Monument, South Dakota, in the northwestern part of the basin and the Cumberland plateau and Copperhill, Tennessee, region in the far eastern portion of the basin. In the last example, indiscriminate logging of trees for open-heap copper smelting, sulfur dioxide smelter fumes, alternating rain and drought conditions, and steep slopes all contributed to vegetative killoff and subsequent excessive soil erosion.

Some of the best examples of gully reclamation are found in the Soil Conservation Service projects, the Ohio Conservancy Districts (which also are famous for flood damage reduction), and the TVA. In the drainage basin of the Tennessee River, forests were logged ruthlessly and in the Cumberland plateau strip mining continues to ravage the soil mantle.

Harry Caudill in his *Night Comes to the Cumberlands*[6] and more recently in *My Land is Dying*[7] dramatically portrays how the soil and mineral base are inextricably woven with the human settlement of Appalachia. The logging of steep slopes first exposed the humus of the deciduous forest carpet in this region. However, small-scale timber activities in western Pennsylvania, southern Ohio, southern Indiana, southern Illinois, West Virginia, Tennessee, and especially the Cumberland plateau and the rest of Kentucky were inconsequential in comparison to the ravages of strip coal mining in the same areas. With advances in surface mining equipment, stripping off the upper soil or overburden up to one hundred feet in depth became a very economical way to extract the bituminous deposits. Unfortunately, soil rehabilitation and gully reclamation were not major interests of the coal companies or their constituents. After the mining operations relocated, the exposed soil on the commonly precipitous slopes washed away during frequent downpours or moved into the valleys in the form of mudslides. Consequently, many years of soil plundering and sheet and gully erosion elapsed before pressures were mounted to halt the soil and land ravages typified by the Cumberland plateau and other nearby drainage systems of the eastern Mississippi basin. Predictably, in this area of up to sixty inches of rain per year, gullies once begun, cut deep into the hillsides. Up to 100,000 pounds of soil per acre per year are lost.[8] The best protection or rehabilitation for soil is reforestation, and the TVA has acquired an admirable reputation in this regard. Between 1933 (the year Congress

[6] Harry A. Caudhill, *Night Comes to the Cumberlands* (Boston: Atlantic Monthly Press—Little, Brown and Company), 1963.

[7] Harry A. Caudhill, *My Land is Dying* (New York: E. P. Dutton & Co., Inc., 1971).

[8] A. F. Gustafson, *Conservation of the Soil* (New York, Maple Press, 1936), p. 73.

Figure 5-29. Overburden from coal strip mine creeps down deforested hollow or valley in Letcher County, Kentucky. Disruption of the soil and pollution of the water supply from strip mining forced the abandonment of the home in the once productive valley.

Figure 5-30. The clearing of overburden—which means the removal of horizons A,B, and C in the soil profile—is accomplished by men and machines that were first introduced to this modern technology by the federal highway construction projects in Appalachia. (Bethlehem Steel Corporation)

Figure 5-31. Strip mining literally strips away the topsoil and exposes the bedrock that contains the horizontal seams of coal. Reclamation is almost impossible, as shown in this 1973 Kentucky photograph, inasmuch as the topsoil and other overburden are shoved down the steep mountainside.

Figure 5-32. Courageous efforts at strip mine reclamation on a modest scale have been attempted in several states of the eastern Mississippi basin region. This photo of hydroseeding a mined area with a mixture of grasses, legumes, fertilizer, and water shows how the letter of a law is being met. Unfortunately there is no penalty in the strip mine laws in case the seeds do not grow. (Bethlehem Steel Corporation)

created the TVA) and 1947, reforestation in the Tennessee Valley increased 115 times whereas the nation as a whole increased only 2.5 times during the same period.[9]

Reclaiming small gullies is accomplished with the construction of small check dams of fencing, brush, and rocks. Manuring and seeding of quick-growing species on the contours usually permits the establishment of pioneer species and other erosion resistant vines, shrubs, and trees. Reclaimed gully areas should, for the most part, be kept in heavy vegetation in order to curtail future severe soil and water loss and to provide food, cover, and habitat for wildlife.

The Mississippi and its major tributaries very dramatically illustrate the relationship between gully erosion and the lives of people and cities downstream. The effect of topsoil loss on local agriculture is obvious. But, in addition, when gully or other deep cutting erosion takes place, the less fertile B and C horizons wash or blow downstream or downwind only to be deposited on bottomland topsoil making it less productive. Furthermore, the heavy sedimentation process fills stream channels that in turn can no longer carry the normal river regime to say nothing of flood conditions. The very severe floods that occurred in the Mississippi basin region in the late 1920's and 1930's prompted the Omnibus Flood Control Bill of 1936, which gave the U.S. Army Corps of Engineers major responsibility for flood protection in rural and urban areas as well as the previously assigned and closely related chore of maintaining navigable waterways, harbors, and associated facilities.

Flood Control in the Mississippi Basin

Some of the institutional and managerial problems of soil conservation are easily portrayed in the Missouri portion of the Mississippi basin region. The skyline of the towns and cities across the ten-state Missouri River valley (17 per cent of the area of the United States) gives a clue to the direct dependency of cities upon the soil. The grain and feed elevators stand out and the earthy fragrance of the feed lots and stockyards add the exclamation point. The loessial or wind-deposited loam is predominant throughout the region ranging in depth from three feet to nearly one hundred feet. Rainfall is spotty and periodically sparse west of the one hundreth meridian; therefore, overgrazing and bad tilling practices quickly contribute to erosion and excessive sediment loads. The Big Muddy, as the Missouri River is nicknamed, floods annually with varying severity. On the average, $60 million of annual property damages are calculated on the mainstem whereas yearly losses on the watersheds of the smaller tributaries average

[9] TVA Division of Forestry Relations, *Tennessee Valley Forests,* Norris, Tennessee (1950), p. 10.

Figure 5-33. The Tennessee Valley Authority tries to promote a good record with flood management projects. This photo shows the site on which TVA's Fontana Dam now stands in western North Carolina. The picture was taken before construction began on that dam in January 1941. (TVA)

$77 million. When soil losses and other indirect costs are figured, the annual average damages soar to an additional $71 million.[10]

Thirty-three major dams comprise the TVA system, regulating the Tennessee River and its tributaries for flood control, navigation development, and power production. Of these, nine are on the main Tennessee River, the others on its tributaries. Together the dams have a combined storage capacity of more than 23 million acre feet of water, of which 13 million acre feet are useful for flood regulation and normal power production and 11 million acre feet for flood regulation alone. Through 1971 this control had reportedly saved nearly $350 million in flood damages in the Tennessee Valley, and additional amounts on the lower Ohio and Mississippi rivers. The system is capable of reducing the crest of Mississippi River floods at Cairo, Illinois, by as much as four feet, giving perhaps false security to 6 million acres of fertile Mississippi Valley land "protected" by levees, and presumably lessening the frequency and depth of flooding on an additional 4 million acres not so protected.

[10]The Missouri Basin Inter-Agency Committee; *The Missouri River Basin Development Program,* Washington, D.C.: U.S. Government Printing Office, 1952, p. 8.

Figure 5-34. TVA's Fontana Dam is a flood management and other multiple use model that creates a reservoir with a useful storage capacity of 946,000 acre-feet. Fontana is the highest concrete dam east of the Rocky Mountains. It is located on the Little Tennessee River in North Carolina and borders the Great Smoky Mountains National Park. (TVA)

Figure 5-35. Which side of the levee would you prefer? Vast areas of the Mississippi Basin suffered heavy flood losses as can be seen in this May 22, 1973, U.S. Army New Orleans District photo showing the Red River backwater between Marksville and Lock Site #1. (U.S. Army Corps of Engineers)

Figure 5-36. During the 1973 Mississippi River flood many people were left to their own resources. This homeowner near Valley Park, Mississippi, built a private levee around his house.

Figure 5-37. In this Monroe, Louisiana, subdivision barricades of sandbags are established around homes in hopes of fighting the flooding Mississippi River in 1973. (U.S. Army Corps of Engineers)

Figure 5-38. This photo looks downstream toward beginning of channel improvement or stream channelization on Deer Creek Watershed near Northwood, Iowa. Seedings were made daily following construction using hand methods. Seeding cover is crownvetch and bromegrass. The two year project was completed in 1971. (USDA—Soil Conservation Service)

Figure 5-39. The Omaha District of the Army Corps of Engineers built this one-half million dollar local flood protection project for the city of Hawarden, Iowa. The project consisted of a new diversion channel for Dry Creek skirting the southern portion of the city and emptying into the Big Sioux River. The completed project can be seen in this aerial photo. (U.S. Army Corps of Engineers)

Figure 5-40. Emergency flood protection takes the form of sandbags and elevated merchandise in Ottumwa, Iowa. Twenty-four hours after this photograph was taken, the main street was flooded. (U.S. Forest Service)

Figure 5-41. Silt-filled stream channels, heavy runoff and cities built on the flood plain create a situation like this in Ottumwa, Iowa, located on the banks of the Des Moines River. This was the second major flood within a one-week period. (U.S. Forest Service)

However, by mid-1973 the wire services had reported that nearly 15 million acres of the lower Mississippi Valley were flooded and damages were estimated to be over $450 million during the first six months of that year! In order to attempt a reduction of flood damages, the U.S. Army Corps of Engineers dredges stream channels (as does the Soil Conservation Service and other state and federal entities), and builds levees, spillways, dikes, and flood control dams. Too often they have forced speculation and in the long run increased flood damages.

Another powerful land and water development agency, the Bureau of Reclamation, approaches the plight of the farmer from a different tack. Reclamation has as a major objective the irrigation of arid land and reclamation of submarginal soil. The Gavins Point Dam, on the Missouri River, shows the unhappy overlap of agency jurisdiction. The Corps of Engineers dam at Gavins Point flooded 20,000 acres of land that the Bureau of Reclamation had opened up as good irrigated farmland.[11]

A somewhat more satisfactory arrangement for soil conservation on a watershed basis is practiced by the Soil Conservation Service under Public Law 566, which is often known as the Small Watershed Act of 1954. Some of the main purposes of this legislation are to reduce upper watershed erosion and flooding. There is an important proviso in the act that states that at least 50 per cent of the drainage area of a given project must be practicing sound soil conservation procedures as stipulated by the Soil Conservation Service. The critical impetus, therefore, is to obtain participation at the local level in soil management practices before additional federal funds come in to build dams or provide other assistance in watersheds of up to 250,000 acres.

Chemical Accumulations in the Soil

Although not confined to any specific part of the Mississippi basin, or any agricultural area in America for that matter, the problem of chemical and toxic substance concentration in the soil and in crops becomes increasingly serious. This is the most recent widespread soil resource problem in the United States. The northcentral Mississippi basin drainage areas of Minnesota, Wisconsin, Iowa, Illinois, Indiana, and Ohio portray the severity of the toxic substances that include radionucleides, *sterilants*, inorganic chemicals—especially fungicides, insecticides, herbicides, and other biocides including potent predator poisons.

In the upper Mississippi Valley area, truck farms, orchards, dairying, and other food and feed crops specialize in output for the nearly 40 million people of that six state area, 75 per cent of whom are urbanized. Of course, after initial processing, many of the agricultural products from this area

---

[11] Elizabeth S. Helfman, *Rivers and Watersheds in America's Future* (New York: David McKay Co., Inc., 1965), p. 126.

184   are shipped to urban markets across the United States and around the world. With the need for what they thought was increased efficiency and increased productivity, *monoculture agriculture* was promoted by agricultural economists and other farm advisors. This large-scale single crop approach imposed obvious problems on the unconsulted multitude of bacteria, fungi, algae, and other essential decomposers and soil builders that are accustomed to a somewhat more diversified vegetative cover that exists under natural conditions.

In 1962, Rachel Carson publicly raised the question about chemical side effects in *Silent Spring.*[12]

What happens to these incredibly numerous and vitally necessary inhabitants of the soil when poisonous chemicals are carried down into their world, either introduced directly as soil 'sterilants' or borne on the rain that has picked up a lethal contamination as it filters through the leaf canopy of forest and orchard and cropland? Is it reasonable to suppose that we can apply a broad-spectrum insecticide to kill the burrowing larval stages of a crop-destroying insect, for example, without also killing the 'good' insects whose function may be the essential one of breaking down organic matter? Or can we use a nonspecific fungicide without also killing the fungi that inhabit the roots of many trees in a beneficial association that aids the tree in extracting nutrients from the soil?

Our short-term applications of chemicals may impose long-term breakdowns in the vital mechanism of the soil communities. Carson states:

Under some conditions, the chemical conversions and transformations that lie at the very heart of the living world are affected. Nitrification, which makes atmospheric nitrogen available to plants, is an example. The herbicide 2,4-D causes a temporary interruption of nitrification. In recent experiments in Florida, lindane, heptachlor, and BHC (benzene hexachloride) reduced nitrification after only two weeks in soil; BHC and DDT had significantly detrimental effects a year after treatment. In other experiments BHC, aldrin, lindane, heptachlor, and DDD all prevented nitrogen-fixing bacteria from forming the necessary root nodules on leguminous plants. A curious but beneficial relation between fungi and the roots of higher plants is seriously disrupted.[13]

The problem of chemical concentrations then emerges as a twofold concern: (1) there is potential danger to the mechanisms that sustain soil fertility and productivity, and (2) there is alarming concern about the buildup of toxicants and radioactive materials in the plants (and eventually animals) that are ingested by man. Clearly there are not enough data available to make widesweeping proclamations about how much insecticide is permitted in an orchard or a bean field, how much radioactive waste can be sent into the environment before genetic or shorter term hazards are felt, but the very uncertainty coupled with the early clues about dan-

[12]Rachel Carson, *Silent Spring* (Boston: Houghton Mifflin Company, 1962), p. 56.
[13]Ibid., p. 57.

gerous effects over the long run make some of America's decisions of chemical use look premature at best. It appears that land-oriented disposal of urban waste including toxic substances will be an accepted practice, because of relatively more national interest and legislation that pertains to air and water pollution control. In other words, if stringent standards and enforcement exist for air and water environments and no federal or state regulations are effective for "soil quality control," then the land environments are going to receive many waste products that were not permitted in the atmosphere or the waterways. Even after soil and land protection legislation is passed, many of the toxic substances and accumulated *chlorinated hydrocarbons,* for example, will persist at "effective" concentrations in the soil for decades.

In some respects, soil poisoning from pesticides, herbicides, or other toxic substances that have fallen upon the soil may be an even more challenging problem than nutrient depletion and the physical loss of topsoil. The millions of urbanites in the breadbasket of America will undoubtedly become rather anxious as they await the research findings on the long-run impact of commercial chemicals on the dynamics of the soil resource. It was, it will be recalled, the urbanite whose numbers, whose "best interests," whose persuasions in collusion with the agricultural lobby promoted the kindergarten and myopic view of managing soil resources in the Mississippi River basin and elsewhere throughout the United States. Recently, we have come to learn whoever said "There is no such thing as a free lunch" was right. One needs only to stand at the very edge of the delta of the Mississippi River to understand. Even the lunches we paid for may have been purchased too cheaply once all the ecological and social costs are known.

CHAPTER

Forest Resources

Urban Americans relate in two fundamental ways to forest resources in contemporary metropolitan activities. The first way involves the living tree species on site in or near the urban or suburban area. The second way concerns the relationship between the urban consumer and the distant forest whose recreation sites, fish and game, watershed capabilities, and thousands of wood products including pulp and paper commodities are used by urban populations.

An urban citizen stands to gain from knowledge accumulated by the forestry profession as it is applied to the city setting. For example, the microclimate effects of trees in an urban area are substantial. Some of the poorly publicized benefits of urban forests include reduced summer temperatures and moderated winter temperatures, favorable humidity, reduced wind velocity as in a shelterbelt effect, noise and visual buffers, assimilation of air pollutants, and necessary habitat for popular urban dwelling birds and other wildlife. The aesthetic value of using native and introduced species is demonstrated in the most popular and most beautiful portions of charming cities. Seattle, Portland (Oregon), San Francisco, New Orleans, San Antonio, Minneapolis, Milwaukee, Atlanta, Boston, New York, Washington, D.C., and several other cities have distinguishing landmarks and appealing neighborhoods enhanced by forests or native tree species.

Extraordinarily practical applications of forest management in urban areas include the separation of vehicular traffic from pedestrians and vegetative screening of areas of heavy public use such as shopping centers, schools, and high-density residential neighborhoods. However, to have good survival growth rates for the urban tree, specific conditions need to be accounted for. Certain species of trees, such as locust and sycamore, survive much better than maple and oaks when plantings are scheduled near streets that have salt applications in the winter. Soil compaction is always a

187

188   problem for the urban forester. Chemical sprays, such as DDT in the attempted control of Dutch Elm disease, had deleterious effects on robins and other songbirds who frequented urban trees and forests. Other pesticides are in trial stages. Monoculture problems along (single species) tree-lined streets are common when disease or insect infestation takes place. Drought periods cause serious fire hazards in wooded residential areas, particularly in Western states. Improper pruning by utilities and underground trenching with the risk of severe root damage are other constant concerns of the urban forest experts. Most city governments are owners and managers of the majority of trees in their cities when one considers that the trees located between sidewalk and street are a city responsibility as well as the trees in parks, along highway median strips, and in urban forest preserves.

Chapter 6 asks the reader to take a moment to contemplate how his urban area is an integrator of all basic resources including forest resources. Forests play an increasing role in our daily lives, not only in producing paper and other forest products but in making a city a healthier, more pleasant place to be; that is, trees are seen as a special asset to the community. The synthesis of ekistic elements—Nature (of which forests are a part), Shells (buildings and other structures), Man, Networks, and Society is essential as more and more Americans fail to appreciate the biological forces that still operate despite man's decreased proximity to intact natural communities such as forests. As with soils or wildlife, there are regional differences in forest communities. Therefore, as regional forests are mentioned, the reader must make the transformation of principles to his or her geographical location.

Forest Regions of the United States

When the Pilgrims landed at Plymouth Rock in 1620, they were greeted by densely forested land, which at that time was typical of over half the country that later became the United States. That original 822 million acres of forest has shrunk to approximately 650 million acres today plus 16.5 million acres in coastal Alaska. As man left the oak, chestnut, beech, and maple trees of the New England states, he found great variety in species and habitat, for this country is rich both in the distribution of its forest volume and in the number of species of trees. Many ways have been devised for dividing the United States into forest regions. The U.S. Forest Service map (Figure 6-1) reflects one of the more traditional methods and seems reasonable and understandable, since each region is uniquely its own both in geographic location and species.

The Northern Forest
Primarily extending along the northern boundary of the eastern half of the United States, around the Great Lakes area, with fingers extending south

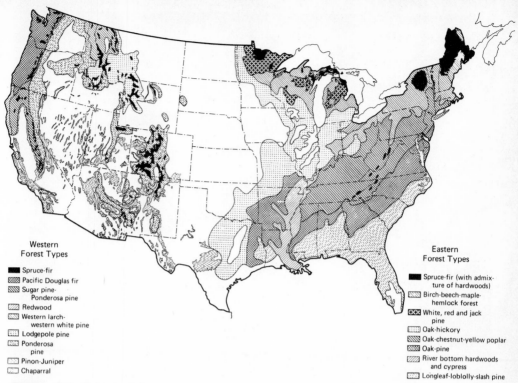

**Western
Forest Types**

■ Spruce-fir
▨ Pacific Douglas fir
▧ Sugar pine-
   Ponderosa pine
▨ Redwood
▨ Western larch-
   western white pine
⬚ Lodgepole pine
▨ Ponderosa
   pine
⬚ Pinon-Juniper
⬚ Chaparral

**Eastern
Forest Types**

■ Spruce-fir (with admix-
   ture of hardwoods)
▨ Birch-beech-maple-
   hemlock forest
▨ White, red and jack
   pine
⬚ Oak-hickory
▨ Oak-chestnut-yellow poplar
▨ Oak-pine
▨ River bottom hardwoods
   and cypress
⬚ Longleaf-loblolly-slash pine

Figure 6-1. Principal forest types of the United States as shown in the 48 states. (U.S. Forest Service)

Figure 6-2. The Northern Forest provided pines, spruce, and balsam fir for pulp and paper-oriented towns like International Falls, Minnesota, with pulpwood in the Rainy River. (Boise Cascade)

Figure 6-3. Most Upper Great Lakes communities such as International Falls evolved around forest product activities. Diversification of economic activities enabled many northern forest towns to survive and prosper after the timber supply was reduced. Fort Frances, Ontario, in the foreground with paper mill and International Falls, Minnesota, in background with fiberboard mills. (Boise Cascade)

into the highlands of Appalachia, this forest originally covered land that was more suitable for trees than crops. Rich in white pines, the forests of Michigan, Minnesota, and Wisconsin were terribly abused by loggers in the late 1800's and around the turn of the century. Today, although less extensive in acreage of forested land, the Northern Forest still contains white, red, and jack pine; white, red, and black spruce; paper and yellow birch; maple; beech; elm; ash; and aspen with some Eastern hemlock, white or balsam fir; white cedar and tamarack.

Central Hardwood Forest

One of the country's most extensive forest regions, the Central *Hardwood* Forest reaches from the Rio Grande River of Texas to the shores of Cape Cod to the southern portions of Michigan, Minnesota, and Wisconsin. Since the soil of this region is especially rich, it stimulated much tree clearing

Figure 6-4. The Central Hardwood Forest is the source of furniture, hardwood lumber, and other deciduous forest products. Wasteful cutting and poor management have occurred primarily because of small parcel ownership patterns. (U.S. Forest Service)

to enable its use for agricultural purposes. Here white oak, hickory, white ash, walnut, and tulip or yellow poplar reach optimum quality and quantity.

The Southern Forest

Continuing in a clockwise direction around the country, we next encounter the longleaf, shortleaf, loblolly, and slash pines of the Southern Forest, which follows along the coastal plain from southeastern Maryland to eastern Texas. Because of the long growing season and the abundant rainfall, huge volumes of wood are produced in record time in this region. In addition to the four characteristic pines, the forest includes pecan and hickory trees on well-drained soil, and cypress, gum, river birch, laurel, live oak, and the swamp chestnut oak in the swamps and river bottoms.

The Tropical Forest

Only the southernmost tips of Florida and Texas are considered to be in this region. The scrubby hardwoods, mangroves, and palms that inhabit this region are valuable for erosion control, wildlife habitat, and aesthetic purposes, but not as commercial saw timber.

Figure 6-5. The oak-pine forest is found from Texas, across the Gulf States north to Maryland and New Jersey. The best Southern Forest growth occurs in the good soils and warm climate of the Gulf States. This photo shows natural reproduction underway at Crossett Experimental Forest, Arkansas. After pine seedlings are established the "parent" overstory will be removed. (U.S. Forest Service)

Figure 6-6. Part of the Southern Forest includes the swamp species shown here in a Georgia cypress photo of 1903. (U.S. Forest Service)

Figure 6-7. Forest hummocks of palm and hardwoods dot the landscape of the Everglades. The tropical forest is more of wildlife habitat, water conservation, and aesthetic use than of commercial saw timber value. (National Park Service)

The Rocky Mountain Forest

Although not continuous, the Rocky Mountain Forests are interspersed from Canada to Mexico, the Black Hills of South Dakota and southeastern Colorado to the eastern slopes of the Sierra and Cascade ranges. Typical species include Ponderosa pine, western white pine, Douglas fir, Engelmann spruce, western larch, and lodgepole pine. The relatively short growing season and low rainfall of this forest impose modest restraints on timber growing in the region.

Figure 6-8. The Rocky Mountain Forest is portrayed by a stand of lodgepole pine in the Lewis and Clark National Forest, Montana. The clear-cut area in the foreground shows lodgepole reproduction in this photograph taken eight years after the original cut. (U.S. Forest Service)

FOREST RESOURCES

Figure 6-9. The high climber is perched seventy feet above ground in this **195**
typical Pacific Coast forest. (U.S. Forest Service)

Pacific Coast Forest

Some of the nation's largest single specimen trees that result in the greatest volume of valuable timber per acre are located in a region extending from Alaska and the northern border of Washington through Oregon and the northern two-thirds of California. Douglas fir, Sitka spruce, and western hemlock in the northwest, redwood in the coastal section of northern California, and Ponderosa and sugar pine in the mountain ranges of the Cascades and Sierras provide great volumes of *commercial timber.* Port Orford cedar and western red cedar and alder are also present in Washington and Oregon, although in lesser quantity. Much of the forest harvest in the Pacific Coast virgin stands requires extra heavy logging equipment. Along with the Southern Forest, the Pacific Coast Forest is a major forest-growing region that supplies a large portion of the nation's commercial timber.

Some mention must also be given to the large stands of western hemlock, Sitka spruce, and Alaskan red cedar found in Alaska. These trees, which

Figure 6-10. The nation's greatest volume of valuable timber per acre is located in the Pacific Coast Forest from Alaska to California. This photo shows redwood logging procedure in Del Norte County, California. (U.S. Forest Service)

196 grow primarily in the lower elevations, offer hope for a vigorous source of lumber for the paper industry.

The American History of Forest Management

Exploitation

Until about one hundred years ago, little thought was given to the benefits of forests, other than wood that was used in great abundance to provide logs for cabins, firewood, furniture, bowls, ax handles, bridges, railroad ties, fence posts, and many other uses. Much wood was wasted as settlers cleared their land of trees to obtain fields for growing crops and protection from Indian attacks. Probably people gave little or no thought to forests as an exhaustible resource as they focused on creating a new nation with its networks, settlements, trade, defense, and agriculture.

President John Quincy Adams had expressed some interest in reforestation, but no one heeded his suggestion. For many years, no legal way was

Figure 6-11. Considerable waste took place in early logging practices as this 1905 California redwood skidding operation indicates. (U.S. Forest Service)

Figure 6-12. Natural loblolly pine reproduction on badly eroded slopes in Mississippi. With fire and grazing protection, the southern pines illustrate the effectiveness of ecological succession after severely depleted soil conditions in southern agricultural areas. (U.S. Forest Service)

provided for purchasing timber stands without buying the land as well. States were usually less interested in the forests than was the federal government, but with no agency to coordinate forest-related activities and no trained foresters to educate others, trespassing on forests was severe.

William Penn required of those to whom he assigned land that one out of six acres was to be kept in forest. This could have been used as a crude forestry guideline, but unfortunately favor was given to agriculture and lumber production. For nearly one hundred years following the founding of the United States as a nation, the ownership of forested lands shifted between states, private interests, and the federal government. Often corporations would acquire large tracts of land, would strip them of all valuable timber, and then, to avoid paying taxes on what they considered to be worthless land, they would let their denuded land revert to state ownership. The importance of water conservation was not recognized, and, indeed, wasting natural resources was of less concern than the wasting of time. Most men who hunted and fished or simply explored the forests for recreation were considered time wasters. Land was generously given away for railroad, canal, and wagon road companies. Homesteaders and miners also received their share.

Figure 6-13. Most of the eastern private deciduous forest is in small parcel ownership. The woodlot owner sees little incentive for instituting advanced forest management practices if his major use is for occasional hunting and firewood.

Softwoods. The *softwoods,* the needle-leaved trees, usually grew in dense stands of fairly homogenous nature. The white pines were treasured for years by the British and colonists as a great source of wood for boat building. With no thoughts to future needs, nineteenth century men wasted at least 25 per cent of their harvest through hasty logging, blasting of log jams, fires, and careless management practices. By 1900, the pines of the New England and Great Lakes states had been so badly depleted by the loggers' clear-cutting methods that they were of little value. The loggers were forced to move on either to the Pacific Northwest or to the Southern states where long leaf, short leaf, loblolly, and slash pine had quickly appeared in the ecological succession following the abandonment of the southern soil-depleted tobacco and cotton farms. By 1940, most Southern lush pine stands were reduced to remnants.

Hardwoods. According to an interesting account by Oliver S. Owen, in contrast to the sweeping logging techniques of the softwood forests, the hardwoods, or those trees with broad leaves, were vulnerable to the dam builders, highway engineers, and farmers who again removed the trees in large numbers to make way for their respective projects.[1] The hardwoods, although many were of commercial value, grew in mixed stands as beech-maple, oak-hickory, elm-maple-basswood, and oak-chestnut, to mention

[1]Oliver S. Owen, *Natural Resource Conservation; An Ecological Approach* (New York: Macmillan Publishing Co. Inc., 1971).

a few combinations. They were difficult to log, because weed trees—those of no commercial value—were sprinkled in among the best timber.

Coordinated Forest Management—Before 1905

The major shortcoming of coordinated resource management has been that it is seldom put into practice until considerable difficulties are experienced with a given resource. Management of the forest lands of the United States were no exception. They were not managed at all for the first 150 years of the nation, and thus serve as a good example of how coordinated management is eventually put into effect.

A memorial (which in years past was a formal communication) was sent to Congress in 1874 by a committee of the American Association for the Advancement of Science (AAAS). This memorial emphasized the importance of federal lands in maintaining valuable water conditions in addition to traditional timber values. The report recommended the withholding from sale and the protecting of public lands. As a result, the Division of Forestry under the Department of Agriculture was established in 1887, although for some time thereafter the division had scant appropriations and no jurisdiction over forest reserves.

A second report by the AAAS was sent to Congress in 1890. Slowly it became clear that there were more values in a forest than was reflected in the price tag attached to board feet of timber. In 1891, a national law was signed by President Benjamin Harrison that authorized him to establish, by proclamation, reserves of public land for future uses, whether timbered or not. Some 13 million acres were promptly reserved, but were then left unattended for years. In 1896 President Grover Cleveland reserved 20 million additional acres.

Slowly the administrative machinery began to be assembled for managing the forest reserves. The *Organic Forestry Act,* signed in 1897, spelled out the administrative needs and obligations of a forest reserve, including the option of selling stands of timber independently of the land parcels. In 1905 the term *reserves* was changed to *National Forests.* Transfer of responsibility went from the Department of Interior to the Department of Agriculture, where the United States Forest Service was created to administer and manage the nation's public forests.

Of course, millions of acres of forest land in the nation remained unreserved, some being part of Indian reservations and others being part of vast railroad land grants. During this same thirty-year period, state forest land was suffering from neglect, although Maine, Michigan, and Wisconsin were beginning some studies as early as the 1860's. Between 1885 and 1891, fourteen states established forestry programs dealing with the protection and sale of state-owned timber. Privately owned tracts were managed to only a slight extent. Cities were almost total consumers of forest products during this period with very little attention given to managing the trees within city limits or reserving wooded parkland and wastershed beyond the municipal jurisdictions.

200   Coordinated Forest Management—1905 to Present

With its birth in 1905 and nurtured by President Theodore Roosevelt's keen interest, the U.S. Forest Service and its chief forester, Gifford Pinchot, created new national forests, received substantial appropriations, and in practice began a forestry profession. The conservation impact of the Pinchot-Roosevelt era was described in Chapter 3. However, during this time a series of important federal laws were enacted that dealt with forest management. Perhaps they should be noted here.

The Weeks Act of 1911 established two important principles: (1) the purchase with federal funds of lands to be managed as national forests at the headwaters of navigable streams, and (2) the cooperation in terms of finances, technical advice, and assistance between the federal government and states and/or private forest land owners in forest-fire control in the watersheds of navigable streams.

The Clarke-McNary Act of 1924 is often referred to as a milestone in American forestry because it expanded the federal-state cooperative principle. The act focused development of forest policy around three major objectives: (1) control of forest fires, (2) distribution of forest planting stock, and (3) educational and technical services for woodland owners.

The McNary-McSweeney Act of 1928 provided for a financial program authorizing forest research, especially a thorough and scientific inventory of the country's forest resources.

The Knutson-Vandenberg Act of 1930 authorized financing for reforestation of national forest lands. It also established policy that levied a "tax" on the purchases of national forest timber for reforesting or otherwise improving the particular sale area after cutting.

In 1933 President Franklin D. Roosevelt was inaugurated and was immediately confronted with an urgent need to create emergency labor organizations to help relieve the effects of the severe national depression. Since this period was described in some detail in Chapter 3, it is sufficient to note here that reforestation, timber-stand improvement work, building of fire-control, recreation, and other administrative facilities on both federal and state public lands all received unprecedented attention that yielded improved and expanded facilities that are still very much in use today.

Nearly half a century elapsed from the time that national forests were created until they were ruled by comprehensive, coordinated resource management. One is only partially correct if one assumes that the threat of having the forest resource completely eliminated by the lumber barons of the eighteenth and nineteenth centuries was resolved by the establishment of national forest reservations. The demand for forest products has increased at an incredible rate, with over 5,000 products worth $23 billion annually being available today. The United States uses more wood per capita than any other nation on earth. Each year, every American man, woman, and child uses about 204 board feet of lumber. Furthermore, the products of the forest are not only wood products; they also include water, grazing land, wildlife, wildlife habitat, minerals, and dozens of other new recreational facilities. The recreational demands are imposed primarily by urbanites who swarm to the state and national forests for camping, hiking, fishing, swimming, skiing, and snowmobiling. The Forest Service, needing to accommodate these expectations as they appeared and increased during the last fifty years, required coordinated management of the highest caliber. Fortunately, the U.S. Forest Service is noted for a strong *esprit de corps* and did a noteworthy job of mustering its forces to meet the demands of the urban public. It is aided by four other federal agencies who in a more minor role also help administer and manage the nation's forests.

1. *The U.S. Soil Conservation Service:* primarily concerned with farm management and their associated forest reservoirs.
2. *The Tennessee Valley Authority* (TVA): focuses on timberland management in the dam and reservoir vicinities along the Tennessee River and its tributaries.
3. *U.S. Bureau of Sports Fisheries and Wildlife:* works toward improving forest habitat for game and fish.
4. *U.S. Bureau of Land Management:* handles the former Taylor Grazing Act districts of seventeen western states that mostly include grazing land but also contain some timber.

Management efforts early in the twentieth century were devoted to fire control and prevention, research on disease, insect infestation, and water-supply production. Additional efforts were made to coordinate other multiple uses that included activities as diverse and seemingly incompatible as logging, mining, grazing, skiing, snowmobiling, hiking, and wilderness camping. The very heavy demand for forest products, the losses caused by disease (responsible for 45 per cent of total saw timber destruction each year), fire (accounts for about 17 per cent of the timber loss each year), insects (the cause of 20 per cent of all timber loss annually), and weather (causes about 8 per cent loss per year) compounded to create difficulties of chronic proportions for man. These losses might have been minimized if the forest had been left to the devices of its own capabilities. A sophisticated, computerized, and highly coordinated management program has evolved to promote a sustained yield of diverse forest products for posterity.

However, let us not forget that the incentive for coordinated management most frequently appears in the form of a crisis or a perceived crisis to be avoided. Hints of a crisis in forest products and especially the use of forested land are beginning to appear in the form of increasing costs and shortages in what we have assumed is a nonexhaustible resource. Indeed, of all the replenishable resources, it appears that forests, more than any other resource, are taken for granted by the urban dweller. The critical states of water, air, and wildlife have received considerable publicity in recent years, and the federal role in the management of those renewable resources has been conspicuous although not always successful. In contrast, relatively little is said about the diminishing state of out forest resource with isolated

202   exceptions such as complaints against U.S. Forest Service clear-cutting
activities in the Bitterroot National Forest of Montana and other localized
trouble spots where urban and rural leaders have united to raise vigorous
protests.

The Current Picture

Of the more than 190 million acres of forest lands in the Gulf State region,
approximately 80 per cent are privately owned. This situation contrasts
sharply with the western United States where 43 million acres of forest land
out of a total of 135 million acres or 31 per cent are privately owned.
Southern commercial timber and pulpwood producers such as Weyerhauser, International Paper Company, and Georgia Pacific own about 20
per cent of the south's private woodland. About one-third of this land is
in small woodlots of forty acres or less that is owned by farmers. Another
one-third is held in private estates or by gun clubs and other urban-oriented
owners.

Productivity of a forest, as with every renewable resource, depends on
how man uses it. Even before man began to utilize forest products, the
effects of insects, disease, storms, lightning, drought, and decay had taken
their toll. These troubles have often increased with man's intrusion. To
determine the volume of an annual forest crop of a given acreage, the
volume of wood lost to destructive agents is subtracted from the growth
for that year. In 1950 the U.S. Forest Service reported a deficit of about
1 billion cubic feet per year. By 1965, because of intensified forest management, for the first time in decades, timber growth exceeded timber cut
although much of the growth was of inferior quality. Today, of the total
666.5 million acres of forest area in the United States, including Alaska,
only 499 million acres are considered commercial forest land—that is, forest
from which merchantable wood products can be taken in paying quantities.
Of this acreage, 92 million acres are in national forest, 44 million in other
federal, state, and county lands; 67 million are owned by the private timber
industry, and 296 million (60 per cent) in private holdings that are mostly
farms.[2]

A Look Towards the Future

In late 1972, Forest Service officials said in their Demand and Supply Study
that with a 60 per cent increase in demand for timber and its products
anticipated between now and the year 2000, and only a 15 to 20 per cent
boost in timber supplies expected, the result will be a 30 per cent increase

[2]"A Forest Service Warning on Timber." *San Francisco Chronicle* (December 6, 1972),
p. 2.

in timber prices by 1980 and a 60 per cent boost by 2000.[3] The Forest Service also warned that the timber industry cannot find relief from the impending shortage by intensified cutting in the national forests in violation of the principle of *sustained yield.* Furthermore, it recommended that this nation should look chiefly toward the private forest holdings for added supplies as they are currently producing less than half of their potential. To realize this potential, however, the farmers and other private forest holders will probably request federal subsidization for thinning out stands and replanting other cutting.

The fact that United States citizens are apparently insatiable consumers of paper products is certainly a major contributing cause of this pending crisis. The present U.S. population is over 215 million and each American uses up over 530 pounds of paper annually or almost $1\frac{1}{2}$ pounds of paper every day. As our economy grows, so do our paper "needs." Predictions for the year 1985 indicate that American consumption of paper will reach a whopping 675 pounds per person per year. In Chapter 2, paper recycling was discussed. However, it seems appropriate to review here that a ton of newsprint represents pulp from about 17 trees; recycling a stack of newspapers only 36 inches high saves one tree.[4] In addition, if one-half of the paper and wood products from our total urban refuse were recycled each year, the drain on our wood resource could be reduced by 30 million *cords*—an amount equal to the total timber production from a million acres of forest.[5]

A good portion of the blame for this blatant waste rests on the urban dweller's shoulders. It is he who accepts extravagant packaging without complaint and who finds it easier to throw out the newspaper rather than stack it and periodically drive it a few miles to a recycling bin. It is also the urban dweller who watches supermarket clerks fill those nice brown paper bags only half full of groceries instead of bringing string or cloth bags from home, or at least old paper bags to be reused and filled to the top. However, perhaps more of a push would be put on recycling if there were more of a demand for recycled paper. Currently market incentives encourage using virgin materials. For example, a lumber company is taxed according to the number of trees it owns. Taxes decrease in proportion to how throughly the company exploits its resources. In other words, tax incentives make it more profitable to cut down trees that to conserve them.

Much construction timber is also wasted, as can be seen from the amount of scrap lumber that is discarded by workmen at a housing site. Apparently it is more economical to leave large quantities of usable timber behind rather than to move it to the next job. We are indeed the "wastemakers." In the future, Americans may turn to the use of substitute materials for

---

[3] Ibid.

[4] Paul Swatek, *The User's Guide to the Protection of the Environment;* (New York: Ballantine Books, Inc., 1970), p. 125.

[5] David Gumpert, *The Wall Street Journal,* "Efforts to Save, Reuse Waste Products Slowed by Variety of Problems" (June 23, 1970), p. 1.

Figure 6-14. Large quantities of lumber and other home construction materials are discarded in mass-produced subdivisions such as the tract in San Jose, California. Leftover cedar roof shingles, Douglas fir and redwood 2 × 4's usually end up as landfill or "bayfill" as is the case in the San Francisco Bay region.

building and construction. Paper may be made from the fibers of a strain of fungus. But more important, as the population increases and the amount of wood available per person becomes less, people may have to change their priorities as to the use of available timber.

CASE IN POINT: THE GULF STATES

History of Gulf States Timber Production

The Southern Forest of the Gulf States region is used as an illustration in the forest resource discussion because of the biological, social, and economic analysis that can be carried out. Even though there is less urbanization in the forest regions of the southeastern United States than in most areas, tremendous urban consumption of Gulf State forest products takes place.

From the tupelo, mangrove, and cypress swamps of the Carolinas to Texas, from the bottomland cottonwoods to the pine hills of the Ozarks and the Smokies, the Gulf region possesses a combination of rich soil, ample moisture, and moderate temperature that is unrivaled in the United States for timber production. The long growing season that such conditions create results in an annual wood increment of as much as one cord per acre contrasted to less than one-quarter cord per acre in the spruce swamps of the lake states. But urban Americans seldom pause to remember that the South produces about 25 per cent of the nation's softwoods and over 50 per cent of its hardwoods. Here, as with most resources that are vital

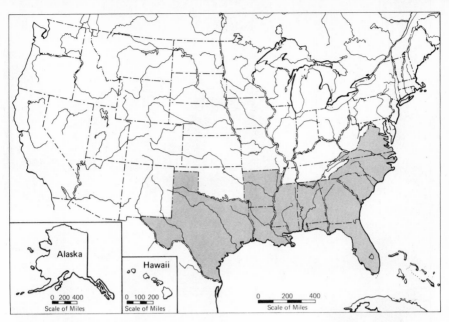

Figure 6-15. The geographical example for the forest resource discussion is the Gulf States region.

to the establishment and maintenance of any city, the source of our forest products such as newsprint, rayon fabrics, alcohol, plywood, particle board, lumber, veneer, furniture, and plastics has been forgotten by the urbanites who depend upon them on a daily basis.

There are several products of forest land that the city dweller takes less for granted today than in the past. They include watershed protection, wildlife production, recreation opportunities, potential second home sites, and scenic amenities. However, these forest land benefits are usually more typical of Northern, Central Hardwood, Rocky Mountain, and Pacific Coast forests. The forest lands of the Southeastern United States, especially the Gulf region states of Florida, Georgia, Alabama, Mississippi, Arkansas, Louisiana, and Texas appear to contain the "work horse" forests of the future in terms of timber production, diversified forest products, and pulp.

Since the early 1800's immense stands of longleaf and slash pine have yielded large amounts of pitch for resin and turpentine, thus creating the *naval stores* industry. In addition, the exceedingly strong live oak that thrives in the Gulf states region proved to be one of the best sources of wood for building ships in the 1700's. In the 1820's, as settlement continued in this area of the country, the forests were cleared in order to open agricultural land to tobacco and cotton. As the Industrial Revolution opened up new worldwide markets, a region-wide network of plantations, manned by black slave field laborers, arose. The nutrient-extractive crops in a matter of years rendered the soil infertile. However, land was so

Figure 6-16. Partial view of a 1925 portable logging camp near Laurel, Mississippi. Early use of southern pines was for naval stores and for urban construction in the eastern United States. (U.S. Forest Service)

abundant that the farmers simply left their worn out fields and moved westward in search of new planting grounds where more forest lands were cut over. Vast acreages of land were subsequently eroded, and were not restored for future agricultural use. When the Civil War began in 1861, the cotton industry was declining. The war further added to the ruin of the South. Not until the turn of the century was serious thought given to silviculture or scientific forestry practices.

During this same period in the Great Lakes states, lumber barons were clear-cutting white pine and the mixed deciduous forests at an alarming rate without any efforts at reforestation. It is important also to keep in mind that other resource bonanzas were going on almost simultaneously in the United States. The unmanaged harvests (that is a gentle or polite way of saying exploitation) included wildlife, most minerals, land of every kind, water, and, or course, timber. At the end of the nineteenth Century and into the early twentieth Century, the unscrupulous timber operators had exhausted the easy-to-get forest reserves of the Northeast, the Great Lakes, and the Pacific Northwest. Many then began intensive clear-cut logging in the Southern forested lands that were not earlier cleared for agriculture.

Louisiana hit her forest production peak year in 1913 with over 4 million board feet of lumber produced. Alabama had her peak year in 1925 with

2,235,700 board feet. Very wasteful logging practices prevailed as the cities of the Midwest, East, and South were built from the Southern oaks, the sweetgums, the pines, the maples, and the beeches. Unfortunately, these early loggers employed crude management methods to obtain their lumber. They moved into a wooded area, indiscriminately cut the trees burned the area over, and moved on to new forest land. These procedures mark a considerable contrast from the prescribed or controlled burning of well-managed longleaf pine forest plantations of today. Land was so abundant that conservation practices were neglected. As a result, over 80 per cent of the original 125 million acres of long leaf pine were carelessly destroyed. Timber production began to slump badly as early as 1915, and by the height of the Depression, virgin forest land in the Southeast was virtually non-existent. In addition, fire and subsequent erosion devastated so much of the land in the Gulf States region that by the time of the Depression, the 150 years of abusive one-crop agriculture, ruthless logging, frequent burning, and eroded topsoil had left 75 million acres of abandoned southern forest and farmland beyond any practical use. Agricultural and forest diseases and insect pests such as the boll weevil added to the South's state of environmental disrepair. Fortunately, in terms of timing, during President Franklin Roosevelt's administration two new federal organizations breathed fresh hope and life that affected the Southern forest region. The Tennessee Valley Authority was established, in the watershed of the Tennessee River and its tributaries, and the Civilian Conservation Corps (CCC) brought in federal assistance for soil reclamation and reforestation that still continues today.

The forest products industry took advantage of this fortunate series of events and, in the decade following World War II, completed the reforestation program begun by the CCC. It also followed the impetus of the CCC in establishing significant conservation and land management practices that included:

1. Fire prevention controls.
2. *Selective cutting*—a harvesting method in which selected trees are pruned from a forest stand. This provides maximum groundcover at all times, while allowing for enough timber removal to make such a program economically worthwhile. A stable, long-range management practice of this type is part of a sustained yield program.

Artificial props of many kinds (fertilizers, pesticides, and various economic assistance programs) were introduced and are still more prevalent in the South than in any other large resource region (with the exception of California) as efforts continue to rejuvenate the Southern forest resource base. The land that grew steady crops of cotton is slowly being returned to timber production. In managing the returning Southern forest resource, the administrative logistics are a vexing problem because of the South's unique kind of ownership patterns where a large percentage of the land

Figure 6-17. Fire moving through loblolly pine stand in South Carolina. (U.S. Forest Service)

Figure 6-18. A man-started fire in a Mississippi shortleaf pine forest. (U.S. Forest Service)

Figure 6-19. A massive longleaf pine fire in Florida. Up to 94 percent of U.S. "fire bug" fires occur in the southern states. (U.S. Forest Service)

Figure 6-20. South Carolina farmers cooperating in putting out a small pine plantation fire with rakes and pine branches. (U.S. Forest Service)

Figure 6-21. Because of the frequency of ground fires in the Gulf region forests, the tractor and Mathis fire plow are used as seen in this Ocala National Forest, Florida fire. (U.S. Forest Service)

is divided into small, privately owned woodlots rather than the large timber stands of the West.

Fire control also continues to be a greater problem in the Southern forest area than elsewhere in the United States. In the last several decades up to 94 per cent of all incendiary forest fires (fires set deliberately by "firebugs") occurred in the Southern States.[6] In proportion to other kinds of man-caused fires (for example debris burning, smoking, and camping)

[6]R. E. McArdle, "What the South is Doing Today," *American Forests* (April 1956), p. 24.

210 incendiary fires continue to be much more serious as they also burn acreages one to ten times larger than other human-caused fires.[7]

Much of the early state and federal forest activity centered around fire control. The enactment of the Weeks Act in 1911 encouraged states to expand their fire-control activities, and the passage of the Clarke-McNary Act in 1924 strengthened this involvement. Of course, fifty years ago it was not envisioned that the metropolitan areas would be growing out into commercial forest lands. The management of erosion, pests, disease, and fire has thus become a new and difficult problem for administrators of urban jurisdictions and managers of public and private forest lands whose various products are in increasing demand by urbanites.

Confronted by the expected growth in population and anticipated increased demands for wood and its products, the Southern Forest Resource Council, representing most Southern forestry organizations, studied the problem and produced a blueprint for the Third Forest—the forest of the future. Their views are less pessimistic (and also less realistic) than that of the U.S. Forest Service report that was previously mentioned. The Southern Forest Resource Council believes that through such methods as *monoculture forestry,* increased dependence on "wonder machinery" such as highly automated timber harvesters, tree improvement programs, and more efficient use of the whole tree, U.S. forests will be able to meet the demands of the year 2000.

Southern Monoculture Forestry Practices

Following World War II, a serious manual labor shortage hit the forest products industry of the South as higher wages and better jobs lured many workers to the North. This forced companies to adopt more fully mechanized planting and harvesting methods. The required large influx of capital investment dictated new land management practices. Increased timber volume per acre was stressed, both to take advantage of the harvesting ability of the new machinery and to offset its increased operating costs. As standardization of timber in both size and age was urged to minimize waste, two new production methods were formulated and put into effect.

1. Large wooded tracts were completely cleared of timber as clear cutting replaced selective cutting as the chief harvesting method.
2. Planting was limited to a single species of each economically valuable tree. These species were genetically bred to exhibit both a rapid and a highly predictable growth rate and other physiological characteristics of high economic value. Because of the short life cycle of these species,

---

[7]U.S. Dept. of Agriculture Forest Service, *Annual Fire Report for National Forests,* Washington, D.C., 1968.

Figure 6-22. Longleaf pine logs are removed from a rapid growth rate, mixed palm and pine stand in Florida. (U.S. Forest Service)

concentrated plantings could be managed to produce even-age stands of identically sized trees.

As forest products companies incorporate these new methods into a single-crop, monoculture production program, which allows them to regulate both the quantity and quality of their timber crops, the ecological and economic outlook of the industry is being radically changed. The company lands that are replanted with the same crop every year must rely more heavily on chemical fertilizer to stabilize their productivity potential, and each tree species must be sprayed with pesticides and herbicides to prevent

Figure 6-23. The future looks bright for the "work horse" forests of the Gulf State region typified by this longleaf pine reproduction. (U.S. Forest Service)

growth impairment by insects and disease that are especially devastating to one species crops. As the economists' voices continue to be louder than the ecologists' pleas, monoculture remains popular in this period of unprecedented economic growth and reduced diversity. It has substantially decreased timber regrowth time and consequently switched the emphasis to short-term profit programs.

However, the feasibility of monoculture cannot be calculated in economic terms alone. A program so far-reaching and yet so recently initiated must answer the following questions before its true value can be objectively judged: How ecologically sound are the land-management practices necessary to support monoculture? What is the long-range dependability of the single monoculture species? Does widespread monoculture allow for diversity in management methods if the need arises?

The ecological dangers of monoculture might best be represented by Figure 6-24. The single monoculture species is clear-cut for maximum yield per acre. This removes most of the source for organic groundcover that is supposed to decompose to enrich the soil. The bacteria that decompose this dead plant or organic matter release the important nutrients, nitrogen and phosphorus. However, without a sufficient nutrient supply or organic medium on which to live, the bacteria colony is depleted. This depletes the nitrogen and phosphorus nutrients in the soil, which reduces the soil's fertility. To counteract the drop in productivity, chemical fertilizers are added to the soil. These replenish the nitrogen and phosphorus supply, but also produce chemical changes that break down and deplete the valuable nutrient ion supply. Chemical fertilizers must be continuously applied to maintain maximum soil fertility, yet at the same time they exhaust the soil's nutrient supply. As the soil grows less productive, more chemical fertilizers have to be added. This is an irreversible cycle, which ultimately leads to a loss of groundcover and subsequent erosion.

Pesticides, herbicides, and fungicides are sprayed on crop lands to reduce losses from insect, weed, or disease damage. However, pesticides release

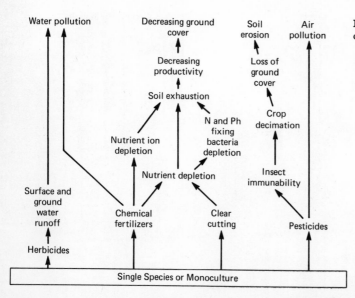

Figure 6-24. Ecological dangers of monoculture.

noxious hydrocarbons into the atmosphere that cause air pollution. Furthermore, herbicides and chemical fertilizers contain potentially toxic nitrates that enter surrounding streams as surface runoff or by soaking through the soil to the water table, or entering watersheds directly causing water pollution. In clear-cut areas this would be hastened.

Because monoculture species are rushed into seedling production shortly after they are *hybridized* (before a thorough, long-range testing program has been carried out), knowledge of the species' ability to withstand insect or other damage is speculative at best. In addition, insect pests may build up an immunity to the pesticides used, as has happened with DDT. An insect epidemic could wipe out an entire species, denuding large areas of land. As in the case of soil exhaustion, such a loss of groundcover would result in wholesale erosion. Therefore, it appears that the monoculture method of production is on ecologically tenuous ground.

Economically, widespread monoculture is very restrictive in long-range terms, particularly as the ecological consequences of monoculture take effect. Although it is the fastest, most efficient method of producing economically valuable timber, opening up a renaissance in forest products and spurring a concurrent rise in consumer demand, monoculture forestry dictates an influx of more sophisticated machinery and larger capital investments, which in turn necessitates increased output per acre to counteract spiraling costs. This vicious cycle exhausts the soil, and the only way

Figure 6-25. Forest tent caterpillar larvae congregate when at rest or during molting periods. Monoculture plantations are particularly vulnerable to insect infestation. (U.S. Forest Service)

Figure 6-26. A forest tent caterpillar outbreak in the Mobile Bay area, Alabama, defoliated 26,850 acres of water tupelo. (U.S. Forest Service)

to offset decreasing crop yields is to intensify monoculture production, thus further exhausting the soil. The cycle appears irreversible, and may ultimately lead to economic disaster.

Having introduced monoculture, the forest products industry is confronted by the same problems that wiped out the cotton industry. It will be locked into an unalterable land management program whose production demands and ecological ramifications will destroy its economic structure, unless drastic changes are instituted to save this aspect of the forest products industry.

In order to avoid such regional disaster, forest product company owners must be convinced that their "monoculture" management is unwise. In so doing, both future implications and present applications of forest management practices must be considered from ecological and economical viewpoints. Certainly, the United States Forest Service and the Society of American Foresters, which are the major policy-setting organizations of the forestry profession, could do much to inform both the industrial leaders and private woodlot owners (who are the chief suppliers of the forest products industry) of the long-range ecological dangers of one-crop production. The negative effect of ecological consequences on economic growth must also be cited. Undoubtedly, before changes can be instituted, both private and industrial interests will have to be convinced that a production program that pays heed to basic ecological principles will continually regenerate fertile, productive crop lands, which means stable, long-range economic profit. Following such an attitude change, viable, alternative management practices will need to be proposed and demonstrated by professional forestry consultants. Tied in with this attitude change, the federal government must provide the forest products industry with the economic incentives and/or mandates to switch management tactics. Subsidy programs whereby a company that changes to less intensive production methods would be reimbursed by the federal government for loss of profits and federal legislation to control production parameters on economically valuable timber land could both be useful. Production parameters to be regulated by federal legislation should include:

1. The timber yield per acre on company lands.
2. The amount of timber per acre on privately owned land that may be sold to industry.
3. The maximum percentage of a given area that can be clear cut.
4. The intensity of chemical fertilizers, herbicides, fungicides, and pesticides used per acre of forest land.

Tree Improvement

Since the first Southern Forest Tree Improvement Conference was held in 1950, the Gulf States have become deeply involved in tree improvement programs with important progress being made as they have become leaders in the field. Federal and state agencies cooperating with each other and with universities and industrial organizations to avoid duplication in their research have made available funds go farther. This combination and

Figure 6-27. Applying highly toxic, granular systemic insecticide, phorate (Thimet), for tip moth control in experimental slash pine planting on Olustee Experimental Forest, Olustee, Florida. (U.S. Forest Service)

Figure 6-28. Forest Service crew using a power sprayer to apply insecticide to loblolly pine infested with Southern pine beetle in South Carolina. Tractor in background is equipped with tanks and pump. Some trees are felled and sprayed. (U.S. Forest Service)

cooperation leads to the exchange of ideas, plant materials, equipment, and aid. Research findings are made immediately available to all concerned. This practice is unique in the world of business and has led to rapid advances in tree improvement.

There are two ways to bring about improvement of trees, environmental control and genetic control, each of which causes variations within trees.

Environmental Control

Forest trees retain all the inherited variability that is typical of wild populations. Within each species or among related species that can be crossed are potentially usable heritable characters such as diameter, height, straightness, and bole quality. Other variables that affect volume per acre and wood quantity are listed in Table 6-1. Since some of these variations are created by environmental conditions such as site, soil characteristics, differences in spacing, and competition by overtopping, the Southern foresters now are learning to manipulate some of these environmental differences.

Table 6-1. Traits Most Often Selected
in Tree Improvement Programs[1]

The variables affecting volume per acre are:
1. Height
2. Diameter at breast height
3. Form
4. Ability to compete
5. Disease and flood resistance
6. Drought and flood resistance
7. Temperature resistance (extreme cold)
8. Resistance to urban stresses
   a. salt in the soil (from salting city streets)
   b. soil compaction (deficiency of oxygen)
   c. toxic chemical air pollutants
The variables affecting wood qualities are:
1. Straightness
2. Specific gravity
3. *Tracheid* and fiber lengths
4. Cellulose content
5. Percentage of summerwood
6. Self-pruning
   a. branch angle
   b. branch diameter
   c. number of branches
7. *Oleoresin* yield
8. Bark and *tannin* yield

[1]Adapted from Charles D. Webb, "Juvenile-Mature Tree Relationships," *Proceedings of the Seventh Southern Conference on Forest Tree Improvement*, Gulfport, Mississippi, 1963.

The management systems in the South are also improving growing conditions by applying cultivation techniques. High yields of cottonwood along the Mississippi River are the result of careful site selection, thorough site preparation, cultivation during the first year, and protection from insects and deer.[8] Similar results in other Gulf states are being obtained from such cultural methods as "mechanized tree farming."

Cultivation and brown-spot control shortened the grass stage of longleaf pine in Georgia so that at four years their heights averaged about the same as third year heights of slash and loblolly pine. This will allow the rotation to be shorter and production to be more rapid which is another way in which improvement will help Southern foresters meet future demands.

Genetics

The key to success on southern tree plantations is to use genetically improved seedlings. Growing trees from the seed of superior trees, grafting,

[8]J. S. McKnight, and R. C. Biesterfeldt, "Commercial Cottonwood Planting in the Southern United States," *Journal of Forestry*, Vol. 66, No. 9 (1968).

218   and hybridization have been in experimentation in the United States since the 1940's. In recent years these methods have become popular in state and company-owned nurseries. Research indicates that disease and insect resistance is inherited and that disease and insect resistant trees can be reproduced genetically. There is also reason to believe that wood quality can be manipulated through genetics. Programs already exist where a tree farmer can order seedlings that will produce just the type of tree he needs. One example is the Georgia Forestry Commission, which produces an assortment of seedlings that may be ordered for definite purposes. Other examples include nursery sites owned by pulp and paper mills that reproduce seedlings primarily to be used as pulpwood. One company gives millions of seedlings away each year that it will in turn buy back when they have reached maturity.

To find the right twigs for grafting, forests are searched for superior trees. Twigs are cut from these trees and grafted to the rootstock of a nursery seedling. After about a year in the nursery, these seedlings are transplanted in seed orchards. These trees produce superior seed in ten to fifteen years and are the source of the Third Forest. Often the original seedlings in the nursery have been produced from the seed of superior trees that were found in the forest.

To further ensure that the end result is truly superior, progeny testing is carried out whereby "each parent is tested by control pollinating it with four known pollens." Then the seeds are planted separately and when they produce seedlings, they are compared with "the normal woods seedling." Those trees that do not measure up are eliminated.

Hybrids planted in central Louisiana are demonstrating desirable characteristics of both parent species. They closely resemble longleaf pine in form and branching habits, but start height growth immediately and grow almost as fast as slash pine. They appear less susceptible than their parents to the brown-spot needle blight of the longleaf and the fusiform rust of slash pine.

Figure 6-29. Grafting is accomplished by matching the cambium of the new or improved species with the cambium of the stock receiving the graft.

Figure 6-30. A huge "hand" on a crane unloads pine pulpwood bolts directly from rail cars to conveyor that feeds the ever-hungry Arkansas mill. (U.S. Forest Service)

Pitch pine was crossed with loblolly in Georgia. The progeny have much of the growth habit of loblolly pine and some of the frost resistance of the pitch pine parent. These substantial improvements could be highly beneficial to production in the future.

The timber industry seems convinced that selection for higher specific gravity can increase paper yields from 25 to 80 pounds of cord of wood cut. Assuming an increase of 40 pounds, a 400 ton per day paper mill would realize an annual increase of 4,200 tons of paper using no greater volume of wood. Greater increases in growth can be expected of possibly 30 per cent in height and diameter. Disease resistant trees may be among the earliest practical results of forest genetics research. Once a blight-resistant tree is developed, it will have a built-in control with no further manipulation required. Insect resistant trees will also decrease the need for pesticides in the forest environment.[9]

Mechanization

Although machines already play a major role in getting the tree from the stump to the pulp mill, they will have an exclusive role in the future.

[9]R. L. McElwee, "Genetics in Wood Quality Improvement," *Proceedings of the Seventh Southern Conference on Forest Tree Improvement,* 1963, p. 23.

A manager of a major pulp mill boasts, "We receive wood at the mill every day that has not been touched by a single human hand."[10]

Practically every recent issue of forest-related magazines contains articles about the superiority of "The Machine." The gamut includes the tree monkey that prunes trees as it climbs them, the slashmobile, the top loader, the tree crusher, the one-man logger, the chip harvester, and a score of others.

The "mechanization explosion" implies that fewer employees will be hired. After all, if two tree crushers can clear three hundred acres of forest per week, why should people, who are much slower be hired? To further economize on labor, the pulp and paper industry seeks trained persons who can both operate this complicated machinery and keep it in operation at the same time. Such persons are not easy to find.

Using the Whole Tree

Whereas twenty-five years ago the leftovers from sawmills were thrown away or used as fuel, today in cooperation with pulp mills, chip-making machinery at the sawmills convert this waste into chips. These chips make up approximately 12 per cent of the pulp used in making paper products.[11]

About 20 per cent of the wood presently used in pulp production comes from hardwoods. By using these sources that would otherwise be wasted, the drain on southern pines has been lessened.

Lignin, a sticky substance that holds fiber cells together and makes up a considerable portion of the tree, was long a wasted product of paper mills. Recently, ways of using this substance have been developed, including mineral tonics for crops, and countertops and tabletops; research is being conducted into the use of lignin as a food preservative and as an ingredient in suntan lotions.[12]

Many persons claim that cellulose is the key to the future, and paper and pulp mills would like as much of this cellulose to come from trees as possible. They are attempting to supply the cellulose needed for chemicals and other products such as rayon, which uses more pulpwood than any other nonpaper product; 85 per cent of the cellulose is provided by woodpulp. Maximum yields of cellulose are obtained in trees produced on short rotations. A significant source of cellulose can be obtained from the trees that have been thinned and previously discarded from a pulp-growing forest.

[10]Charles Eddington, "The Mechanization Explosion," *Forests and People,* XIX (Third Quarter, 1969), p. 6.

[11]"From These Trees," Southern Pulpwood Conservation Association, Atlanta, p. 11.

[12]Victor J. Sutton, "The Pulp and Paper Industry . . . A Look Into the Future," Southern Pulpwood Conservation Association, Atlanta, p. 8.

Figure 6-31. Much of this huge pile of pulpwood at Southland Paper Mills, Lufkin, Texas, came from national forest lands in East Texas. This mill, started in 1940, as the first newsprint mill in the South, now uses 600 cords of wood daily, producing 360 tons of newsprint paper, 70 tons of paper board, and 20 tons of Kraft. (U.S. Forest Service)

Figure 6-32. This covered conveyor moves chips from storage silo to the first step of the sulfate paper-making process at an Arkansas pulp and paper facility. (U.S. Forest Service)

The Southern People

The most significant obstruction to supplying the paper needs of the year 2000 is that approximately 75 per cent of the forested land in the Gulf Coast area belongs to city dwellers who lack money or interest to turn their land into pine plantations. There has always been a conflict between the pulp and paper industry and Southern people. Many rural farmers have treated trees in much the same way as they treat weeds. Forty per cent of wildfires in the Southern states are set by arsonists; these are often grudge fires aimed at getting even with pulp mills and paper mills for not selling their land. In order to get along with these arsonists, some pulpers have sold them small sections of their land, whereas others have included seeded and fertilized firebreaks in their forest acres that cattlemen could use for pasturage.

Many of these private landowners would like to see their land and other forested land put into recreation areas. The Southern Forest Resource Analysis Committee reports that the southern nonrural society is beginning to favor an antitree cutting philosophy. Consequently, in order to stay in favor with Southerners, foresters are trying to create a favorable attitude toward forest management and multiple use in such a way that the forest land base is not substantially decreased.

Figure 6-33. Forest resources provided an important economic base for Covington, Virginia, as seen with the pulp and paper company mill in the foreground. Uses of forest land for recreation, second homes, and other purposes are putting extra pressure on Southern forest product industries. (U.S. Forest Service)

Apparently the pulp and paper industry is making a sincere attempt to create the Third Forest and to satisfy recreation needs at the same time. However, in the past six years legislation has been impending against them at an increasing rate. For example, in Florida, legislation threatens to acquire private land to create more resort areas. In Mississippi, legislation proposes to limit the amount of land an individual or corporation may own. In Florida, Texas, and the Carolinas valuable forest land has already been flooded to provide more water-recreation areas and power sources for urban populations.

Whether the timber industry will achieve its goal for the future is yet to be known. Whether people will tolerate recreation in the midst of vast tree plantations is also an unknown. Supposing the Third Forest is a success, one cannot help but wonder what the pulp and paper industry will do when the year 2000 arrives and the industry faces the prospect of supplying our multiplying masses with paper for the year 2001.

The Everglades

The Everglades are a unique forest and natural area resource whose value will increase as a result of urban needs and expectations, not only in the

Figure 6-34. A cypress swamp in the Everglades of Southern Florida serves as an example of nontimber uses of the Gulf States forest resource. (U.S. Dept. of the Interior, National Park Service)

Figure 6-35. Roseate Spoonbills in Everglades National Park, Florida. (U.S. Dept. of the Interior, National Park Service)

South, but throughout the United States. Admittedly, the recreation experience offered by the Everglades National Park is different than one would expect to find in a loblolly, slash, longleaf, or shortleaf forest plantation. Nevertheless, it seems to provide a special balance to the discussion in this chapter.

A growing threat to the forests of the United States is the urban growth that is spilling onto forest lands as people seek a rural environment "to get away from it all" meaning the noise, pollution, and pace of the cities. The South has fewer choice recreation areas than almost any other part of the country. Thus the outstanding and unique forest habitats that do exist should be protected and enjoyed. Without national population stabilization, people from popular national recreation areas and parks will eventually spill into other habitats. If the recreation-carrying capacity of the Everglades is exceeded and entrance to it is eventually denied to some of the millions who annually visit there and hope to in the future, greater recreational demands will be placed on the southern tree plantations and other forest lands.

The rich wildlife of the Everglades National Park is a biological montage unmatched anywhere—roseate spoonbills, anhingas, snowy egrets, wood ibis, manatees, raccoons, alligators, great puma cats, crocodiles, and white-tail deer to name a few. And still, this national park is also one of the most beset by forces both from within and outside its boundaries that could destroy its natural ecology and turn it into a polluted wasteland.

One such force, which has been building up for years, involves the impoundment and diversion of the "river of grass" flowing from Lake Okeechobee to multiple outlets of the Shark and Harney River systems. The flow of freshwater into and through the park is essential to the entire ecology of the area, and yet the natural drainage of water has been seriously altered (see Figure 6-36) as the levels of Lake Okeechobee have been manipulated and controlled. Vast areas south of the lake have been converted to agricultural lands, as canals and dikes to drain the land have been

Figure 6-36. Map of southeastern Florida showing directions of surficial drainage in the area of the Everglades and the Big Cypress Swamp.

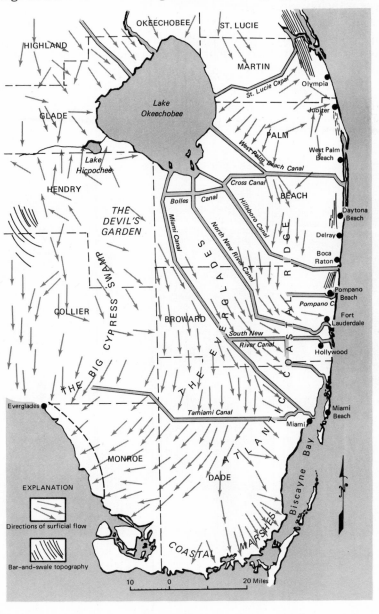

226 built in abundance by the Central and Southern Florida Flood Control District.

Within the last ten years, the National Audubon Society launched a campaign to alert the nation to the harsh fact that man-made water diversions and barriers were killing the park by shutting off the flow of freshwater from the north. The National Audubon Society commissioned the noted ecologist and author Peter Farb to study the problem and write an article for *Audubon Magazine,* an article that was later reprinted in *Reader's Digest.* At about the same time the Corps of Engineers requested and received authorization by Congress to make a new study of the design and operations of the Central and Southern Florida Flood Control Project with a view to improving facilities for delivery of water to the park. The National Audubon Society supported the new study. When its study was completed in the mid 1960's the Corps asked Congress to approve a plan that included storage of additional water in Lake Okeechobee from which, via the new and improved canals, the essential freshwater could be supplied. Again the National Audubon Society supported the plan in a statement presented

Figure 6-37. An aerial view of Everglades National Park, Florida, showing waterfowl in mangrove forest. (U.S. Dept. of the Interior, National Park Service)

at hearings held by the Corps in Florida. The plan was approved in the Omnibus Rivers and Harbors Act of 1968.

For several years another major threat to this area has been the Dade County jetport. Its proposed construction and operation would have spawned an industrial, commercial, and residential complex equivalent, when fully developed, to a city of at least a quarter-million people. The metabolic by-products of the complex, the combustion outfall of the jet engines, and the noise of the big jets would have been an environmental depressant over much of the park. Airport facilities are needed to accommodate the growing travel economy of southern Florida, but the Everglades site was only one of five alternatives. As of 1973, many of the airport runways were built, but as a result of a fight waged by several conservation-minded groups with the Dade County Port Authority, construction of the facility has been frozen and its use is limited to training flights for commercial airlines. However, the threat remains, and it is probably only a matter of time until rapid mass transit links the airport up to Miami over the many miles of unique habitat.

Forests and Future Urbanites

If a trend is set into motion that results in a long-term cutting of timber in excess of the biological productivity of the United States forests, several mechanisms are available to sustain the yield over greater periods of time. It is aasumed that forest products like most other goods show elasticities of demand according to cost. That is to say, when prices increase substantially for lumber, paper, or other wood products, the propensity will be reduced for urban dwellers to consume amounts that by the next decade could average three pounds of paper per day. Durable or reusable substitutes would come into vogue. The use of recycled paper and cardboard would become more common. Imports of logs or partially fabricated wood materials can provide interim relief to forest production shortages over supply. Development of "super" trees with straighter boles; fewer limbs; appropriate lignin content; disease, pest, and fire resistance; and other hybridized features could provide relief to the apparent shortages. But the crux of the demand over supply problem is the irrational waste that accompanies nearly every step of forest production from the initial fertilization to the millions of tons of "scrap" lumber that is hauled from construction sites and the daily metropolitan newspapers, two thirds of which are never recycled. But few realize that it requires no less than ten clear-cut acres of forest per day for each edition of out largest urban daily newspapers. An entire essay could be written on the prodigality of packaging materials, most of which were once forest resources.

Another treatise could be developed on the negative impact of preventing *all* fires in the forest. The Smokey the Bear information campaign to help alert Americans to the hazards of the careless use of fire and cigarettes has had at least one adverse result. When urban-based tourists and campers travel to forest areas where prescribed or controlled burning is underway, there is a conditioned response to object to any fire in a forest, especially in a national park where the forests are thought to be unmanaged. What the metropolite has forgotten is that in most forest communities, fire caused by lightning is a very natural event. Without periodic controlled burning, the understory fuel builds up to dangerous levels. Several forest communities such as jackpine and lodgepole pine increase yields with ground fires that open heat-resistant cones, prepare a seedbed, and eliminate competitive vegetation. Even the best long-run waste prevention for the California Sequoias and coastal redwoods is for the Forest Service to carry out controlled burning.

In addition to the subtle (and in some cases conspicuous) problem of forest product waste, there is an equal if not greater menace ahead in terms of forest *land* use. Urbanization is making heavy inroads in the Gulf States region and in nearly every forest production area in the United States. The forested areas of metropolitan areas qualify as prime targets for subdivision development. Second and third home sites are being developed in wooded areas three to six hours from the metropolis. In 1973 it was estimated that over 2 million Americans owned a second (leisure) home. Condominium and other recreation-oriented forest land use is often in conflict with traditional logging operations.

The critical challenge for the urban dweller and the forestry profession will be to discover ways in which the renewable features of the forest resource can be sustained in the face of a wide spectrum of increasing demands including scenic and wilderness opportunities, wildlife production, watershed protection, intensive recreation facilities, mining and mineral extraction (especially in Western forest and grazing lands), and the traditional output of paper, lumber, and wood derivatives. For thousands of years villagers and cityfolk looked upon the forest not as a resource but rather as a threat, a vast obstacle to be overcome. The major task now will be to overcome the cultural inertia that assumes limitless abundance from a renewable rewource and update the perception—or improve the perception accuracy—of urban forest users. Even "biologically flowing" resources have a carrying capacity beyond which renewability cannot be sustained in the presence of the multitude of urban consumptive patterns on forest resources in the Gulf States region and other American forest resources.

Atmospheric Resources

Of all the resources critical to the survival and metabolism of a human settlement, the atmosphere has been the most recently recognized. For thousands of years, settlements in North America and the rest of the world were scattered and sparsely populated. Even with the advent of industrialization, local pockets of air contamination were viewed as necessary costs of progress, and it was assumed that the general population was not adversely affected. Much of the apathy toward air resource management could be explained by the lack of understanding about the costs of air pollution to urbanites. In fact, the full range of effects are still not fully known except that people who live in urban areas are bearing disproportionately heavy health and property costs compared to those who have resisted the lure of migrating to large metropolitan regions with air-pollution problems.

The reciprocity of atmosphere and city—forces inherent in a city that have an effect on the atmospheric environment and forces unique to the atmosphere that have direct influence on the urban environment—is an area of urban ecological research that has just recently begun.

Never before has urban man known so much about a vital resource and yet so little in relation to what he must know. Air, which is the collection of gas and materials that make up the atmosphere, is a *flow resource* and is renewable. By precipitation, oxidation, and absorption into the oceans, the atmosphere can cleanse itself of all known pollutants, given sufficient time. Its renewability, unlike water or timber, is subject to the uncontrollable variables of local meterological and larger climate conditions. An urban area's carrying capacity for water, timber, and soil can be managed in various degrees using transbasin diversions, techniques of silviculture, and soil management practices. In contrast, the conditions under which a healthy, productive air resource is maintained is dependent not only on

229

230 the human pressures placed on the resource but also upon the vagaries of temperature *inversions,* wind direction, humidity, sunlight, local topography, proximity to land and water masses, and other physical factors. Natural processes in the form of terpenes (the airborne hydrocarbon released through plant stomata to form haze); the eruption of Krakatoa and Tambora, which spewed 50 million and 220 million metric tons of particulate material, respectively; forest fires; and decaying vegetation have always contaminated the air. Most air pollution, however, is man-made. The United States spews over 250 million tons of gaseous, solid, and liquid garbage into the air annually (see Table 7-1). Comparing the figures in this table with similar figures for 1968 reveal that total U.S. emissions have increased by 50 million tons in the two-year span. When comparing the per cent of the total emissions from the five sources, transportation has increased its contribution of total emissions into the atmosphere by 12.2 per cent whereas each of the other sources have managed to decrease their per cent of the total.

Gaseous pollutants produced by man's activities are by greatest weight, carbon monoxide, sulfur oxides, hydrocarbons, and nitrogen oxides. Solid and liquid airborne particles such as fly ash, dust, fumes, and mist are referred to as particulate matter. These gases and particles, when washed out of the air, damage plants and buildings on which they fall. Table 7-2 indicates many of the known effects of these specific airborne pollutants. Fluorides and heavy metals should be added to the list in Table 7-2 because of their presence in the emissions of large electric power generating plants, especially those that burn coal. Very little technology exists on how to control this increasingly large source of air contaminate stimulated by urban power demands.

Table 7-1. Estimated Nationwide Emissions, 1970[1]
(in millions of tons per year) Environmental Protection Agency

Source	Carbon Monoxide	Partic- ulates	Sulfur Oxides	Hydro- Carbons	Nitrogen Oxides	Total	Per Cent of Total
Transportation	111.0	0.7	1.0	19.5	11.7	143.9	54.5
Fuel combustion in stationary sources (power generation, industry, space heating)	.8	6.8	26.5	.6	10.0	44.7	16.9
Industrial processes	11.4	13.1	6.0	5.5	.2	36.2	13.0
Solid waste disposal	7.2	1.4.	.1	2.0	.4	11.1	4.1
Miscellaneous (agricultural burning, forest fires)	16.8	3.4	.3	7.1	.4	28.0	10.5
Total tons	147.2	25.4	33.9	34.7	22.7	263.9	100.0
Millions of tons change since 1968	+47.1	−2.9	+1.1	+2.7	+2.1		

Total Increase 1968–1970 23.4%

[1] Adapted from: *Environmental Quality 1972,* The Third Annual Report of the Council on Environmental Quality, (August 1972), Washington, D.C.: U.S. Government Printing Office, page 6.

Table 7-2. Effects Attributed to Specific Pollutants[1]

Air Pollutant	Effects
Particulates	speed chemical reactions; obscure vision; corrode metals; cause grime on belongings and buildings; aggravate lung illness
Sulfur Oxides	cause acute and chronic leaf injury; attack wide variety of trees; irritate upper respiratory tract; destroy paint pigments; erode statuary; corrode metals; ruin hosiery; harm textiles; disintegrate book pages and leather
Hydrocarbons (in solid and gaseous states)	may be cancer-producing (carcinogenic); retard plant growth; cause abnormal leaf and bud development
Carbon Monoxide	causes headaches, dizziness, nausea; absorbed into blood, reduces oxygen content; impairs mental processes
Nitrogen Oxides	cause visible leaf damage; irritate eyes and nose; stunt plant growth even when not causing visible damage; create brown haze; corrode metals
Oxidants: Ozone	discolors upper surface of leaves of many crops, trees, shrubs; damages and fades textiles; reduces athletic performance; hastens cracking of rubber; disturbs lung function; irritates eyes, nose, throat; induces coughing
Oxidants: PAN (peroxyacetyl nitrate)	discolors lower leaf surface; irritates eyes; disturbs lung function

[1]League of Women Voters of the United States, "A Congregation of Vapors," *Facts & Issues,* Washington, D.C. (September 1970). (Adapted from: (a) HEW, National Air Pollution Control Administration, "The Effects of Air Pollution," No. 1556, revised (1967); (b) NAPCA, *Air Pollution Injury to Vegetation,* No. AP-71 (1970); (c) American Association for the Advancement of Science, *Air Conservation,* Pub. No. 80 (1965); (d) National Tuberculosis and Respiratory Disease Association, *Air Pollution Primer* (1969).)

Inadequate Air-Resource Information

One of the most vexing problems about atmospheric resource management until 1973 was inadequate information. In order for rational air management to take place, the citizenry and the regulatory officials must have adequate information in quantity and quality to make proper decisions. The very brief list of comprehensive volumes for the general public began with Harold Wolozin's *The Economics of Air Pollution*[1] and is highlighted by John Esposito's indictment called *Vanishing Air.*[2] Wide differences of opinion exist regarding the effects of pollutants, their origins, and the best way of reducing the problem. Agreement cannot be reached on the

[1]Harold Wolozin, *The Economics of Air Pollution* (New York: W. W. Norton & Company, Inc.; 1966).
[2]John Esposito, *Vanishing Air* (New York, Grossman Publishers Inc., 1970).

amounts of pollutants that occur or on the current expenditures for air-pollution abatement. Considerable differences exist when comparing figures of the National Industrial Conference Board, the Mitre Corporation, the International Research and Technology Corporation, McGraw Hill, and the Center for Political Research, all of whom publish fairly comprehensive air pollution lists. Information from these and other privately and publicly supported organizations is used by the federal Council on Environmental Quality and the Environmental Protection Agency.

It would appear that the American public becomes anesthetized when the yearly totals are announced. We are told that somewhere between $16 and $30 billion are lost annually by air-pollution effects on human health, vegetation, materials, and property values. There is always the caution that "these cost estimates only crudely approximate the damage from air pollution." The individual is further numbed by the aggregate annual tonnages put into the atmosphere by manufacturers—at least 70 billion pounds, and by automobiles—approximately 290 billion pounds.

The figures hardly mean a thing, for they are too large to comprehend. Let us lean back and visualize 290 billion pounds, if we can. Therefore, instead we must ask specific questions about the costs that we as individuals are imposing on our urban environment. For some effluents, the

Table 7-3. National Ambient Air Quality Standards[1]

Pollutant	Primary	Secondary
Particulate Matter		
Annual geometric mean	75	60
Maximum 24-hour concentration*	260	150
Sulfur Oxides		
Annual arithmetic mean	80 (.03 ppm)	60 (.02 ppm)
Maximum 24-hour concentration*	365 (.14 ppm)	260 (.1 ppm)
Maximum 3-hour concentration*		1,300 (.5 ppm)
Carbon Monoxide		
Maximum 8-hour concentration*	10 (9 ppm)	
Maximum 1-hour concentration*	40 (35 ppm)	same as primary
Photochemical Oxidants		
Maximum 1-hour concentration*	160 (.08 ppm)	same as primary
Hydrocarbons		
Maximum 3-hour (6-9 am) concentration*	160 (.24 ppm)	same as primary
Nitrogen Oxides		
Annual arithmetic mean	100 (.05 ppm)	same as primary

(All measurements are expressed in micrograms per cubic meter except for those for carbon monoxide which are expressed in milligrams per cubic meter. Equivalent measurements in parts per million (ppm) are given for the gaseous pollutants)

*Not to be exceeded more than once a year.

[1] The Conservation Foundation, *A Citizen's Guide to Clean Air,* 1972. Reprinted in League of Women Voters of the United States publication "Toward Cleaner Air" (April 1972).

atmosphere is a sewer worth considering. However, that consideration must include the social, ecological, political, and other externalities or impacts that are put into motion. Equally important is the physical and biological condition of the receiving environment for every given pollutant at specific times and locations. For instance, a stable primary pollutant such as particulate matter requires certain kinds of abatement procedures. The substitution of fuels that have cleaner combustion and electrostatic scrubbers and precipitators also play an important role. Secondary pollutants are produced by photochemical or physiochemical interactions between primary pollutants within the atmosphere. The objectionable contaminants of this type arise from oxidation (often produced by ozone, which is generated by the photochemical reaction between organic substances and oxides of nitrogen) of hydrocarbons that are present in incompletely burned fuel fumes.

One of the reasons why there is an information gap between what the engineering and air regulatory professions know and what the urban public knows is that no widely used texts in general biology, geography, urban studies, government, sociology, political science, civics, conservation or other natural resource or urban resource related topic ever carried a chapter on atmospheric resources until the early 1970's. National air-pollution legislation was never passed until 1955 and that was a very humble and tardy beginning when one considers the magnitude of the problem.

A Brief Chronology of Atmospheric Resource Legislation

After the 1955 legislation that authorized the federal government to conduct research and provide technical assistance to states for the control of air pollution, eight years went by before much else happened. The 1963 Clean Air Act helped the states set up air pollution control agencies and opened the way for federal involvement with interstate air polluters. The automobile was never mentioned in federal legislation until 1965 and those amendments mapped out modest emission control programs. The State of California set the pace for the nation. The Air Quality Act of 1967 finally encouraged the states to establish air quality standards in severly polluted regions. When the Clean Air Amendments of 1970 were passed, a big step forward was taken by enabling the federal Environmental Protection Agency to set national ambient standards (See Table 7-3), issue implementation plan guidelines, set stricter 1975–1976 automobile emission standards, propose lead additive regulations, and set national performance standards and proposed hazardous emission standards. As expected, Chrysler, General Motors, Ford, International Harvester, and Volvo applied for extensions and exemptions in 1972 and 1973 that would postpone the enforcement of the 1975–1976 automobile emission standards. Many citizens hoped that statements made by several other European and Japanese automobile manufac-

234 turers that they were able to meet the American emission standards would serve as healthy stimuli for American automotive ingenuity. However, on April 10, 1973, the United States Environmental Protection Agency conceded to the pressure of U.S. automobile manufacturers when it announced a postponement for one year of the controversial 1975 emission standards. The postponement set an 83 per cent reduction from 1966 standards in hydrocarbons and carbon monoxide emissions in all states except California. Because of special atmospheric conditions in the Los Angeles basin, the California standard was set at a 90 per cent reduction. The original 1975 standards were established as 95 per cent reduction.

Instead of challenging or memorizing the national averages of costs and aggregate tonnages put into the national atmosphere (which in fact is not national but global), we must look at the problem of atmospheric resources in a more personalized and localized way. Whichever community or metropolitan area we live in, we should become familiar with the meteorological and topographic conditions that determine the carrying capacity of our particular airshed or urban atmospheric resource region.[3]

When meteorological and topographical conditions prevent air movement, the airborne pollutants concentrate. The natural tendency is for air near the earth's surface to rise when it is warmer than the air above it. If a higher, warmer layer of air is present, it acts as a lid, keeping the cooler surface air immobile, and an inversion exists. In some areas, inversions occur almost daily as the surface air, cooled at nighttime, is confined until it is warmed by the sun. In mountainous regions, cool air flows down mountainsides and is trapped in the valleys until warmed. Sometimes an extensive, high warm-air mass remains stationary for several days, prolonging atmospheric stagnation over a broad area.

We should be generally aware of the periods of the day and times of the year when stable temperature stratification is most likely. The inversion phenomenon usually occurs in conjunction with the following weather conditions:

A. During calm, clear nights when radiational cooling is able to lower the surface air temperature below the temperature at a higher level, for example, one hundred to four hundred meters. This type of inversion is the most frequent and hence it can be predicted several days in advance.

B. During large scale meteorological systems an inversion will occur whenever a stable air mass, usually a polar or arctic air mass, moves into the region. Along the northeastern seaboard region this type of air

[3]On April 30, 1971, William Ruckelshaus, administrator of the EPA, announced ambient air quality standards for the nation's six major air pollutants. For each pollutant two standards were set: primary standards to protect the public health and secondary standards to protect public welfare.

mass frequently moves over the area but other factors can become dominant such as massive mixing, convection currents, and other instabilities that could reduce the probability of an episode or a widespread air mass inversion.

The cities of Baltimore, Philadelphia, New York, Washington, and Boston are located in airsheds where the inversion frequencies are small compared to the frequency for Los Angeles and Denver.

The inversion layers and accompanying smog suffered by residents of Los Angeles, Denver, and many of the Western U.S. cities of dry, sunny climates varies greatly from the weather conditions and chemical reactions inherent in the smog of the urbanized eastern seaboard. The smog typical of the dry sunny climates is a yellowish brown haze caused by a photochemical process in which hydrocarbons and nitrogen oxides from automobile exhausts and other sources interact, in the presence of sunlight, to produce a variety of secondary pollutants. Among these are ozone (which in natural, minute levels very high in the atmosphere shields the earth from ultraviolet radiation) and peroxyacetyl nitrate (PAN). Another type of smog is fostered by the climate of eastern U.S. cities whose humidity and precipitation require many months of fuel burning. The sulfur-laden smoke from these burning coal and oil fires reacts with the atmospheric moisture to produce sulfuric acid.

In order not to be guilty of his own criticism about national averages and aggregate air pollution figures, the author uses a case study approach for a discussion of specific sources of air pollution, their effects on the total urban organism, and what measures of abatement and control are available. Again the reader is reminded to assume that many of the specific principles discussed here in relation to the Eastern Seaboard region apply with reasonable accuracy to wherever one lives. The reader should incorporate the local, physical, political, and other factors in order to check out the degree of applicability to his community.

CASE IN POINT: THE EASTERN SEABOARD

The Eastern Seaborad region of the United States with its problems of noise, particulate matter, sulfur, nitrogen and carbon oxides, hydrocarbons, radioactive wastes, and heavy airborne metals provides a convenient example of a megalopolitan area entangled in the typical complexities of managing atmospheric resources. The Eastern mountain, Piedmont, and coastal cities demonstrate most of the problems and attempted solutions that modern technology has provided.

236   Without exception, the vigorous corrective measures for air-pollution control have been preceded by a period of apathy, a crisis event, and then remedial action to try to prevent a recurrence of the crisis or perceived crisis. Almost everyone has been reminded of the Meuse River Valley, Belgium, disaster where sixty died in 1930; or Donora, Pennsylvania, where seventeen were killed and twenty thousand made sick in 1948; or the Ducktown-Copperhill, Tennessee, elimination of vegetation as a result of copper smelting; or the London killer smog that claimed four thousand lives in 1952; or the New York air-pollution episodes that have claimed hundreds of lives beyond the expected mortality rates in a series of chronic air inversions over the last twenty-five years.

Figure 7-1. "Plumes of progress," which emitted from industrial smokestacks, had a positive connotation in the 1940's and 1950's in the United States. (National Air Pollution Control Administration)

Figure 7-2. Smaller industrial operations have faced financial hardships to reduce air pollution under air emission standards. However, many air and water polluters broadcast pollution regulation as a reason for closing whereas, in fact, the plant has been phased out of operation for reasons of efficiency and other management decisions long before Air Quality Act regulations were contemplated. (U.S. Forest Service)

Figure 7-3. The air resource section centers on the Eastern Seaboard states.

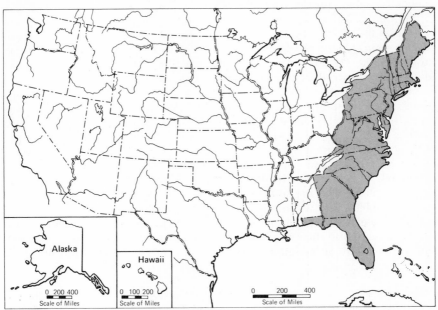

237

Boston's Early Air Pollution

It is often overlooked that Boston, Massachusetts, had a smoke pollution law as far back as 1910. Very little interest was shown until a sooty, oily downpour on ten thousand people in a square mile reactivated some local citizens who were dumped on by what apparently amounted to a unique combination of weather and stack effluent from Boston Edison or less likely a Massachusetts Transit Authority (MTA) power plant. Lester Goldner sketches an interesting account of air-resource management policy formation in a part of the east coast megalopolis long before the more vigorous federal air quality legislation.[4]

In the Boston area, concern over air pollution resulted in the adoption in 1959 of a resolution by the Massachusetts legislature ordering a study by the Legislative Research Council of air pollution in the metropolitan Boston area. In May, 1960 a large area of South Boston was covered by a downpour of a black oily substance. The 1959 study and this dramatic episode led to the enactment of a comprehensive air pollution control law in 1960 which replaced a rather weak and limited statute of 1910.

In examining the air pollution problem in terms of the process of formulating public policy, certain general considerations stand out: There are tremendous differences in air pollution problems among the various communities and areas of the country. The significance of a single pollutant or group of pollutants in a particular locale will depend upon such factors as the topography and meteorology of the area, the number and types of sources involved, the quantities of pollutants emitted, the density of the population, and where it is located relative to the sources. The variety of sources creating air pollution problems is almost as great as the variety of activities characteristic of modern life. Some examples of such sources most of which were identified as existing in the metropolitan Boston area are: (1) industrial sources—steam power plants, industrial heating and refuse burning, construction operations, metallurgical operations, junkyards and scrap-metal recovery plants, chemical industries, paper mills, food-processing plants, tanneries, rubber goods plants, textile mills, and other general manufacturing operations; (2) domestic sources—backyard burning of rubbish, home heating, household and apartment incinerators; (3) municipal sources—refuse burning at open dumps, municipal incinerators, sewers and sewage-treatment plants, road dusts, and construction operations; (4) transportation sources— automobiles, trucks, railroads, airplanes, ships. Each community presents a specialized problem, and the sources and pollutants which may be of concern to one geographical area will not necessarily be a problem to another.

Indifference of some groups in the Boston metropolitan area to situations which would be quite disturbing to others was undoubtedly for many years a factor in the apathy toward air pollution control even where the situation was obviously

---

[4] Lester Goldner, "Air Pollution Control in the Metropolitan Boston Area: A Case Study in Public Policy Formation," in The Economics of Air Pollution; edited by Harold Wolozin (New York: W. W. Norton Company, Inc., 1966).

bad. An attorney involved in the investigation of the 1960 Boston sootfall incident and the drafting of subsequent legislation stated that he grew up in the South Boston area, a heavily industrialized "workingman's" district. He stated that even as a boy he could recall the terrible dirt and soot in the area. His mother complained of the curtains on the windows becoming black after a few hours, of the layers of dust and dirt which would accumulate on the windowsills and the exterior and interior walls of their house. However, according to him, this condition was accepted and tolerated by the people in the area as one of the "givens" of city life; when they complained or grumbled about it from time to time, it was always among themselves and it never became a matter to take to the local politicians. This acceptance of the grosser and more visible manifestations of the problem, coupled with the difficulty of comprehending the adverse effects of invisible contaminants, accounted, in his opinion, for the ease with which the General Court continued to fail to provide sufficient appropriations for air-pollution control. This indifference to what the experts would defined as a real problem, although particularly striking in a "workingman's" area, is probably an operative factor in any urban dweller regardless of the socio-economic class of the area in which he resides. Dirt in the city's air and streets is accepted by many as an inherent part of city life, and by a process of desensitization, it may escape notice completely.

The first law pertaining to air pollution in the metropolitan Boston area was enacted largely at the urging of the Boston Chamber of Commerce in 1910. It was amended several times subsequently and provided the basic jurisdictional framework for the present Metropolitan Air Pollution Control District. The 1910 act gave to the State Board of Gas and Electric Light Commissioners the responsibility for smoke inspection and abatement in Boston, Brookline, Cambridge, Somerville, Everett, and Chelsea. The authority of the Board was limited to policing the emission of visible smoke from chimneys and other types of smokestacks, including those of locomotives. The law did not empower the Board to adopt rules for the enforcement of smoke control; instead, the legislation established the permissible degree of emissions for all types and classes of stacks, set forth the

Figure 7-4. Open burning ordinances are seldom enacted and enforced vigorously in the Eastern Seaboard region. Weather conditions along the populated East Coast cities tend to promote the assimilative capacity of eastern airsheds. When eastern air stagnation does occur, then problems typical of the western United States do arise. (U.S. Dept. of Housing and Urban Development)

methods of observation and enforcement, and prescribed penalties. The Board was given the power, after serving notice and conducting a hearing, to order any person or corporation to stop or abate the emission of smoke observed to be in violation of the act.

The legislation was at the time, and remains to this day, a unique arrangement in the field of air pollution control. It is remarkable for the method of creating the District by state fiat; for the lodging of the control of operations in a regular department of the state government; and especially for the method of financing, under which the cities and towns incorporated in the District were, without any direct representation in its control, required to finance its operations. The San Francisco Bay Area Air Pollution Control District, created in 1955, was also established directly, by the California State Legislature, without requiring the concurrence of the counties involved.

Enactment of the 1910 law was largely in response to complaints by the Boston Chamber of Commerce and other groups who were suffering economic loss resulting from smoke damage to merchandise and buildings. Responsibility for administration of the law was placed in the agency concerned with the regulation of public utilities because the railroad and power companies at that time were the principal offenders.

Since 1910, the law has been amended several times. In 1928, twenty-two more communities were added to the District; subsequently three more jurisdictions were added. In 1954, the Division of Smoke Inspection, which had been responsible for administering the smoke-control law, was transferred from the Department of Public Utilities (the successor agency to the old Board) to the Department of Public Health. The transfer of this function to the Department of Public Health was in conformance with the national pattern which had emerged in which air pollution control authority at the state level has been vested in the health departments. Furthermore, the Department of Public Utilities interposed no objection to this transfer; on the contrary, it was quite willing to be rid of a function which was minuscule in size, somewhat tangential to its major functions and interests, and generally viewed as an unrewarding stepchild of the department.

Thus by 1954, after a period of forty-four years, the original smoke-abatement program, which had jurisdiction over six municipalities, was enlarged to cover thirty-one cities and towns in the metropolitan Boston area. Responsibility for the program was transferred from the Department of Public Utilities, which had viewed air pollution primarily as a problem of nuisance abatement, to the Department of Public Health, which, with its sensitivity to air pollution as a health problem, viewed air pollution as including invisible contaminants as well as visible smoke. However, the authority of the Department was still limited to the enforcement of a smoke-control law, which had been rendered obsolete in the forty-four years intervening since its enactment by great changes in the nature and understanding of the problem and the available technical administrative methods of meeting it.

Insofar as public policy formulation is concerned, the dominant theme is widespread public apathy. Apparently there are substantial groups of people throughout the area who are very severely affected by localized air pollution problems and who vent their extreme unhappiness on the local authorities or occasionally on the state Department of Public Health. However, in the nature of the situation, their complaints would be much more effective if they were brought to bear on the legislature and if their efforts were organized and sustained. Presumably in the operative system of decision-making, these people comprise one of the disadvantaged, inarticulate groups which lack both the resources with which to bargain and access to the people who do bargain. In contrast, the groups which tend to oppose effective control action, because their economic interests are at stake, are highly organized and articulate. They have command of substantial material incentives (jobs and money) with which to bargain, and are strategically located and have easy access to the various decision-making institutions and persons.

The striking fact about the situation is that, although the need for taking more aggressive action to control air pollution in the Boston area to avert present and potentially serious hazards is widely recognized by many knowledgeable and "influential" persons, the only significant action which has been taken in decades was largely the result of a fortuitous accident, the sootfall episode in South Boston, rather than the efforts of any one or any combination of these people. If, as it appears, further needed action will require another such sootfall episode, or another Los Angeles, or another Donora, Pennsylvania, in which seventeen persons died, serious questions are raised as to whether modern industrialized and urbanized America can long afford its present system of decision-making.

Atmospheric Resource Situations in New York City

New York City statistics on air pollution stagger the mind. The long-term effects of air pollution on the cardio-respiratory systems of New Yorkers are yet to be determined in terms of *mutagenic* evidence. But there is an abundance of alarming information about New York-Newark air conditions that makes the resident or the visitor to the area a little reticent to breathe too deeply. Each of us draws about thirty-five pounds of air into our lungs each day. When we live in New York or visit New York there are some "extras" that are not as available up in the Adirondacks: they include our share of the New York annual 70,000 tons of particulate matter, 400,000 tons of sulfur dioxide, 1.6 million tons of carbon monoxide, and 11,000 tons of lead. In Manhattan, the sulfur dioxide content in the air is often as high as 0.12 parts per million (320 mg/m^3), which is four times the 0.03 parts per million mark established by the Environmental Protection Agency as an acceptable level in 1971. *The Wall Street Journal* (May 26, 1970) reported that "many people in New York breathe high concentrations of carbon monoxide over the entire day. New York state guidelines warn that levels should not exceed fifteen parts per million more than 15 per cent of the time during an eight hour period. But after four months of measurements in midtown Manhattan, it was determined that carbon monoxide levels remained above that level all day every day. (The 1971 EPA National Ambient Air Quality Standards show nine parts per million as a maximum eight hour concentration not to be exceeded more than once a year.)

The account goes on, "During daytime hours when traffic is heaviest, the carbon monoxide level in Manhattan often soars to between twenty

Figure 7-5. The polluted New York City skyline is a reminder of the constant threat of future killer smogs when inversion conditions develop. (U.S. Bureau of Outdoor Recreation)

five and thirty parts per million having an impact on the lungs equivalent to that of smoking two packs of cigarettes a day. (Carbon monoxide has an affinity for hemoglobin 210 times greater than oxygen and therefore inhibits oxygen transport in the red blood cells and ultimately effects response time and other physiological conditions.) In some areas of the city, such as the Lincoln Tunnel and the approaches to the George Washington Bridge, the carbon monoxide level reaches an astronomical one hundred parts per million—more than eleven times the "safe" level by national ambient air standards.

Yet John Esposito's *Vanishing Air* task force has told us that New York City's Department of Air Resources must be ranked among the best control agencies in the United States. The city spends about $.50 per person per year to control pollution. Nevertheless, in 1969 the atmosphere of New York was bombarded by more man-made contaminants than any other big city in the country. Were it not for the prevailing winds, New York would have suffocated long ago. When these winds fail, a thermal inversion falls on the city. Such an occurrence in 1953 took two hundred to three hundred lives; less severe but similar episodes followed in 1962, 1963, 1966, and 1970.

Pulmonary emphysema, a disease related to air pollution, is the fastest growing cause of death in New York City. In the last ten years the death rate from emphysema has increased 500 per cent. During the same period chronic bronchitis deaths have increased 200 per cent and lung cancer rates in New York are among the highest in the nation.[5] Asthma, usually associated with spring and summer allergies, in New York City peaks in fall and winter when air pollution levels are also at their peak. The poor suffer the most according to every private and governmental report that deals with relationships between air-pollution hazards and socioeconomic conditions.

The author would make the observation that generally the poorest residents live in or nearest to the most polluted air conditions compared to the citizens of highest economic circumstances. Let us think of who lives in the residential areas nearest the most polluted water, under the immediate approach pattern for the large airport, near the solid waste disposal facilities or city dump, or who lives in areas of heaviest air pollution or traffic noise, congestion, and highest emission levels. Many American cities have a prevailing westerly-northwesterly wind direction. Perhaps it is only a coincidence that the most prestigious neighborhoods tend not to be in the downwind fallout pattern from urban wastes but rather in the west and northwest portions of the large cities. It is a hypothesis the reader may wish to check out in his own city.

In October 1968, New York Mayor John Lindsay established a four stage "Air Pollution Control Alert System." The first stage, "forecast," is called when a Weather Bureau Advisory predicts high air-pollution potential for the next thirty-six hours. Stages two (alert), three (warning), and four (emergency) are triggered as carbon monoxide, sulfur dioxide, and particulates reach designated levels. Before any automobile is banned from the streets, any factory is shut down, or before garbage incineration is stopped, emergency conditions must be declared. The emergency levels are set so high that experts believe that New York City will never reach that stage of the alert system. Even the 1966 Thanksgiving Day episode that killed 150 to 175 people would not have qualified.

Plagued by corruption and understaffing, the New York Departemtn of Air Resources, although one of the nation's best, investigates only about 15 per cent of all the complaints it receives. Less than 2 per cent of these investigations result in the issuance of summonses. Complaints are handled poorly, which is incredible considering that air pollution inflicts more damage on New York City than fires and crimes combined, and probably kills as many people as well. Ralph Nader's study cites three basic sources of air pollution in New York City:

1. There are about 135,000 domestic oil burners and 17,000 public and private incinerators that almost without exception operate illegally. Collectively, they spew into the city's air 69 per cent of all the sulfur dioxide emitted in the city, 70 per cent of all the soot or particulate matter, 44 per cent of all the oxides of nitrogen, 8 per cent of all hydrocarbons, and 4 per cent of all carbon monoxide. All of this is worsened by the short chimneys that direct most of these noxious pollutants to the people's breathing levels.

[5] Esposito, op. cit., p. 204.

2. Next are the ubiquitous internal combustion engines that have replaced smokestacks as the greatest producers of air pollution in the city. In all, 1,609,800 tons of noxious fumes—about 60 per cent of the city's total air pollution—are spewed into the city each year by cars, trucks, and buses. The tunnels under the East River with their poor ventilators hold automobile fumes like traps. Despite the direct correlation between slow moving automobile traffic and the amount of hydrocarbons in the air, Manhattan's streets are clogged with delivery trucks that block traffic flow. Parenthetically, it should be mentioned that in many western U.S. cities, the automobile's percentage contribution to pollution is much higher. In the Los Angeles area gasoline rationing has been proposed to reduce the pollution from automobiles. On a nationwide basis other suggestions for achieving reduced pollution include: the use of lead-free gasoline and additive-free gas, the use of low-compression engines so that low-octane fuel can be burned more efficiently with less pollution, and electric automobiles.

3. A third problem in New York is Consolidated Edison Company. Statistics show that the nation's largest power company has reduced its sulfur dioxide emissions by 50 per cent since 1965 and its particulates by 35 per cent. However, neither of these actions can substantially cope with or improve the effects of an ancient, inefficient, and chronically overloaded electrical generating system much beyond the present efforts. In 1969 the Department of Air Resources issued fifty summonses to Con Ed. Furthermore, Con Ed fails to mention anywhere the most lethal of all its air pollutants, oxides of nitrogen, which amounted to 108,300 tons in 1969. Nitrogen oxides are some of the critical components of photochemical smog. One must try to comprehend the magnitude of wastes being produced by New York's second biggest industrial polluter: Con Ed says it burns 1.18 billion gallons of fuel oil, 3.7 million tons of coal, and 79.2 billion cubic feet of natural gas to produce electricity in its fossil fuel plants. A shift away from bituminous coal to oil and natural gas is underway, in part as an effort to utilize less than 1 per cent sulfur content fuels. This trend is obvious when one looks at figures five years previous to those just given that show that Consolidated Edison used 10 billion tons of soft coal and 800 million gallons of oil with sulfur contents up to 4 per cent in 1965.

The problems of sulfur dioxide pollution are tangled in difficulties of economics and technology. Attempting to eliminate or reduce sulfur dioxide emissions from power plants and residential and commercial facilities by using trapping and purifying devices on smokestacks is an expensive venture that requires expenditures of literally hundreds of millions of dollars for a major polluter. New York's Commissioner of Air Pollution Control believed that the sulfur emissions could be reduced by using low sulfur content fuels. Fuel oils range from a heavy sulfur content grade six, to grade two, which has a low sulfur content and is the type commonly used in home heating units. Grade one fuel oil is kerosene. Readers interested in sulfur-dioxide aircraft pollution are reminded that 80 per cent of jet fuel is composed of kerosene fractions.

It would seem that the city's Department of Air Pollution Control has aggressively tried to combat its worsening atmosphere. The department began an experiment in the fall of 1966 in which only low sulfur content fuels were burned for heating purposes. The pilot project was successful, demonstrating that such fuels were practical even for large utilities such as Con Ed. When confronted with the evidence, Con Ed relented and began using low sulfur content fuel in late 1967.

In addition to using low sulfur fuels, another method of sulfur dioxide reduction that requires an input by the individual users is the technique of adding a material such as powdered limestone to the flue gas after combustion. This precipitates sulfur oxides into solid forms. Along these same lines is a technique whereby the flue gas is passed through a chemical processing plant. The Bureau of Mines has set up an experimental plant where alkalyzed alumina is used to absorb oxides of sulfur. Atomic International uses a molten mixture of carbonates as an absorbent, and Monsanto Chemical Company uses a catalytic oxidation process in which the flue gas is separated from fly ash and passed over a catalyst bed containing vanadium pentoxide (V_2O_5), which oxidizes sulfur dioxide (SO_2) to sulfur trioxide (SO_3). The SO_3 in turn combines with water vapor and cools into sulfuric acid (H_2SO_4). Both elemental sulfur and sulfuric acid are easily recoverable by this process, which, because both are very much in demand by industry, will enable the owner of such an operation to partially defray the costs of its utilization. Lastly, there are methods whereby long-chain hydrocarbons such as coal can be converted to gas prior to combustion. Once in this state, sulfur can easily be removed.

The Mayor's Task Force on Pollution was also concerned that the city's air was gaining over 230,000 tons of particulate matter each year. To reduce this amount, new measures had to be taken. New York's Commissioner of Pollution Control began a project to compile a "comprehensive emissions inventory" of every industrial plant in the city. He intended to see that every incinerator in the city whether industrial, municipal, or residential be brought to a point where it would emit 90 to 95 per cent less particulate matter into the air. Under a new city code, the commissioner was empowered to close down all incinerators that did not meet these standards, beginning in May 1967. In 1958, Los Angeles instituted a similar program and, in a single week shut down over 1.5 million incinerators.

As a result of a European trip where air pollution abatement programs were studied, the commissioner proposed that garbage be burned by the public utilities for power production. The fly ash and cinders could then be extracted and used in the production of cinder blocks. This procedure could reduce the city's cost of rubbish elimination and also reduce the fuel bills of the utilities. He also recommended that thirty-eight pollution measuring stations gather information from every area of the city and relay that information to a central computer at Cooper Union where it could be combined with weather data to predict the onset of smog conditions.

These are but a few of the factors in the city's war on air pollution. But

246   the stricter codes in New York City must be followed by similar codes on a regional basis, because wind and meteorological conditions will continue to cause pollutants to drift over New York from other point sources along the Eastern Seaboard and neighboring industrial states under massive inversion conditions.

Air Resource Difficulties in Washington, D.C.

The capitol of the United States presents images that rank among the most noteworthy in the world. Pierre L'Enfant's plans project the elegance and formality of a national government headquarters. Washington serves as a national depository in the areas of art and literature, theater, engineering, and science. Nearly every national organization has offices in Washington in order to participate in the nerve center of activity that characterizes a nation's capital. As an urban organism, it has had problems similar to other metropolitan areas but it usually tries to put its better efforts forward. Georgetown and Capital Park Southwest have attracted worldwide attention for their restoration of old areas of a city and nearby Columbia, Maryland, and Reston, Virginia, are examples of American new communities. Despite its unique urban environmental location, the Watergate residential-hotel complex gained more fame in 1973 for political espionage than it ever has for architectural design and close proximity to urban amenities.

As an urban showpiece one might hope that the treasure of atmospheric resources would be safeguarded with the same tenacity that is applied for the protection of other human needs such as in the Bill of Rights. But the air quality record is not one that America looks to with pride. In fact, several other items on an environmental checklist (such as water pollution, solid waste disposal, and transportation) have not been dealt with effectively until a crisis emerged. Designed as a pedestrian and horse and buggy city, Washington has been strangled by the internal combustion engine. Many urban areas such as New Haven, Boston, and New York have relatively low car per area ratios. Washington, to its great embarrassment and confusion has more cars per square mile (4,200) than any other city in the United States. Like the automobile-victimized cities of Detroit and Los Angeles, about 65 per cent of the downtown land area is devoted to the moving and storage of the automobile. The human costs of this percentage are agonizing when we recognize that almost 60 per cent of the inner city population does not own an automobile. Yet in 1969 and 1970 the District of Columbia government and the highway lobby in Congress led by Kentucky Congressman William Natcher devoted their efforts to promoting the construction of a six-lane bridge across the Three Sisters Islands in the Potomac, which would move Virginia's traffic congestion into the downtown of the capital. Natcher, as a member of the District Subcommittee of the House Appropriations committee, wields great influence over the

Figure 7-6. Washington, D.C., expressways have tended to dehumanize the city that was originally designed on a pedestrian scale. Consider the alternative uses of land that the highway lanes now consume if the Metro had come 25 years earlier and been placed underground along this expressway swath. The vehicular pollution emissions and traffic noise create an unpleasant barrier between the residential areas on the left and federal office buildings on the right. (U.S. Dept. of Housing and Urban Development)

Figure 7-7. Bicycle commuting is a realistic alternative in the Washington, D.C., area. Paved bicycle paths are available as one follows the landmarks clockwise around this photograph. It is a simple matter to bike from the Key Memorial Bridge (left side of photo) into Georgetown along the Chesapeake and Ohio Barge Canal Towpath to Rock Creek Park bike route or to continue along in front of the Watergate Hotel and Kennedy Center for the Performing Arts to the Lincoln Memorial and Washington Monument. It is also possible to bicycle directly to the Washington National Airport on a paved path or to return to Arlington, Virginia, in the foreground along the Potomac River. (U.S. Dept. of Housing and Urban Development)

248   city's destiny. He threatened to stop all mass transit proposals for Washington including a desperately needed subway system, unless President Nixon and Department of Transportation Secretary Volpe gave him a written promise to defend the bridge against all legal attacks. This was produced.

The most disturbing part of the bridge project is the massive upheavals of the landscape of the Potomac River, the Lincoln Memorial, and Reflecting Pool and Tidal Basin that the accompanying freeway would require. (Washington hopes to spend $11 million on the bridge and $65 million on the freeway under or around the Lincoln Memorial.)

The Air Pollution Control Division for the District Department of Public Health has been ineffective. Restricted by a minute staff and a reticent chief, the division has not prosecuted a single violation in its careful neutrality on air-pollution issues.

John Esposito contends that

Washingtonians do not need statisticians to tell them what air pollution does to their property. Anyone who has spent a summer in the District knows how difficult it is to keep houses, cars, clothes, and windowsills unsoiled. But most would be surprised to learn that even the Library of Congress and the National Gallery of Art have thus far been unable to shelter their treasures from the corrosive effects

Figure 7-8. While large funds are being expended for highway projects in Washington, there is a desperate need for investments in improved housing, better education, better health care, and jobs for the people living within view of the Capitol Building. (U.S. Forest Service)

of the city air. And few Washingtonians are up early enough in the morning to witness the daily scrubbing required to keep the White House white. As to vegetation effects, the Department of Agriculture's Plant Industry Station in Beltsville, Maryland, about ten miles from the District, has observed air-pollution type injury on beans, cucumbers, Chinese cabbage, sugar beets, spinach, tomatoes, sweet corn, oats, wheat, barley, red clover, petunias, chrysanthemums, orchids, maples, elms, and pines. The health of the cherry trees, like the health of the poor, is still awaiting scrutiny.[6]

It will be a useful exercise to compare air quality conditions before and after the Metro (Washington's new mass transit system) is in operation under similar weather and population conditions. Most transportation planners and air management professionals who are not affiliated with the automobile industry see little room for the internal combustion engine in the centers of our great metropolitan areas.

Washington, more than any other large metropolitan eastern city, has begun to provide facilities that can make the bicycle a realistic alternative for commuting to work and to civic and recreation functions. The special incentives for cyclists include labeled and paved bicycle paths that are isolated from automobile thoroughfares. Bicycle paths connect downtown Washington with Maryland through Rock Creek Park and another path parallels the Chesapeake and Ohio Barge Canal along the historic towpath. Washington's National Airport has a bicycle path leading from the terminal area along the Potomac River with connecting routes to Arlington, Virginia, and downtown Washington. People who commute to Washington or other cities by air are able to pack their bicycles in courtesy cartons as baggage (a small handling fee is involved because of the oversized container required), unload at the terminal, and pedal to their downtown office. The author has found this arrangement to be very satisfactory on numerous business trips to Washington.

It is apparent that Washington will have to do more for the country than she has been able to do for herself in terms of relief from automobile pollution and congestion. Undoubtedly, federal legislation will be required and subsidization given to alternative power systems for automobiles such as the steam engine, the gas turbine engine, the gas cycle or Stirling engine, and the electric car. Nearly three-fourths of the air pollution of the Eastern Seaboard cities is emitted by automobiles and trucks. It is shocking to realize that traditionally dollar expenditures from the federal government to control other forms (in addition to the car) of pollution are about one hundred times greater than funds used to investigate alternatives to the internal combustion engine. Less than 3 per cent of the total research funds is spent on ways to improve controls for the internal combustion engine which the reader may remember has dropped to a national average of less than 12.2 miles per gallon under normal driving conditions and with the

[6] Esposito, op. cit., p. 224.

Figure 7-9. A recreational bicycle and footpath parallels the Chesapeake and Ohio Barge Canal from downtown Washington for dozens of miles up the Potomac River. This scene is at Lock No. 20. (National Park Service)

Figure 7-10. Midtown Washington, D.C., is equipped with bicycling trails for commuting and recreation. (National Park Service)

pollution-control devices attached and working. Untold millions of air-pollution control devices are detached for improved mileage or are never maintained properly to perform as the law requires.

Noise Pollution

Let us conclude our Washington illustration on a relatively optimistic note with a brief discussion on noise pollution. The atmosphere serves as a receptacle for many wastes—particulates, carbon monoxide, sulfur oxides, nitrogen oxides, heavy elements and, of course, noise—or sounds that are not desired by the recipients. Washington, like every part of the Eastern Seaboard region and any large urban area for that matter, has the full range of noise pollutants. There is surface transportation noise, construction noise, industrial noise, aircraft noise and indoor noise from appliances, temperature control systems noise, and the penetration of outdoor or external noise from poor acoustical design and shoddy workmanship of basically poor noise-resistant construction.

Noise pollution could very well be the major environmental contaminant in the 1980's and 1990's similar to the attention given to air and water pollution in the 1960's and 1970's. A serious information gap exists on what the effects of increasing noise levels are on human physiology and behavior. The recent research is not comforting. The incidence and premature onslaught of deafness has been well documented. Studies are presently underway to further investigate the noise-created health effects of cardiovascular, glandular, respiratory, and neurologic disorders in large urban populations. Actual dollar costs in human health and property damage are rather speculative although cost estimates for "engineering noise control in one industry average $26 per decibel reduction per employee. That is,

Figure 7-11. Even with federal regulations, aircraft noise and exhaust emissions tend to be pervasive urban air problems. People who live and work in flight patterns are subjected to the most constant aircraft pollution. The Washington Monument is almost obscured by smog. Stricter controls hold hope for future improvement in air quality. (National Air Pollution Control Administration)

reducing the noise level by ten decibels in a work area of 100 people would cost 10 × 100 × $26 or $26,000.00"[7] The federal report concludes that "there is no doubt that recognition of the noise problem in America has arrived late. With the exception of aircraft noise, the United States is far behind many countries in noise prevention and control. Consequently, there is need for focusing serious attention on abatement measures. An ultimate goal should be the achievement of a desirable environment in which noise levels do not interfere with the health and well-being of man or adversely affect other values found in a solitude or wilderness experience that he regards highly. The federal government must play a major role in achieving this objective. The problem is a public concern, and its alleviation frequently will require actions that transcend political boundaries within the nation."[8]

Washington was the first major American city that curtailed aircraft noise by making power adjustments, and modifying flight patterns, and times of departures and arrivals. Aircraft approaching or leaving Washington National Airport essentially use the Potomac River airspace that somewhat reduces jet noise over residential, commercial, and government office areas. Normal air traffic is curtailed at 11:00 P.M. until 7:00 A.M. in order to decrease aircraft noise pollution for sleeping Washingtonians.

One of the first comprehensive federal reports on noise described the solutions to the noise problem with unusual ambiguity as it said that

Research on noise has been conducted over a long period of time. As a result our technology has reached the stage where, with few but important exceptions, we can cope with almost any indoor or outdoor noise problem provided that we are willing to go to sufficient lengths to do it.

Unfortunately, the state of our knowledge is such that these lengths frequently are impractical or uneconomic, with the possible exception of building design. Consequently, more information is needed in the application of noise abatement techniques to transportation; building methods and materials; appliance, machinery and equipment design and construction; and the substitution of quiet alternate approaches for noisy methods of accomplishing tasks. Additional information is also needed on the non-auditory effects of noise on humans and animals.[9]

Overall, it appears that the causes of noise pollution are proliferating in a way similar to traditional air- and water-pollution point sources with a 2 per cent annual increase in perceived noise levels in decibels in the average American kitchen. It will be interesting to observe how this growing pollutant is controlled by governmental action, private initiatives, and individual consumer behavior.

[7]Committee on Environmental Quality, U.S. Federal Council for Science and Technology, "Noise—Sound Without Value," in Thomas R. Detwyler, *Man's Impact on Environment* (New York: McGraw Hill Book Book Company, Inc., 1971), p. 186.
[8]Ibid., p. 187.
[9]Ibid., p. 187.

Radioactive Atmospheric Pollution

With the heavy demand for electrical energy in the Atlantic Seaboard states, a large number of nuclear-fueled power plants have been built and are being planned for the eastern megalopolis. From the coast of Maine to the coast of Florida and on nearly every major river, nuclear facilities are operating or are in the planning stages. Thermal pollution of air and water instead of radioactive wastes has captured most of the public interest and courtroom proceedings when a question of nuclear power plant operation is raised. One thing that is safe to say is that radioactive pollution from the use of nuclear fuels is the newest air contaminant of all. Increasing energy demands, especially in the Eastern half of the United States, and the finite supply of Arabian oil and natural gas prompted the development of the longer term nuclear energy sources. (If the reader asks, what about nuclear fuel processing plant contamination and spent nuclear fuel disposal, he is asking the right questions.) The special dangers of atmospheric radioactivity are staggering. The American public is told by nuclear plant contractors and utilities that the likelihood of reactor meltdowns or other nuclear accidents is highly remote. But with more than fifty-four nuclear power plant units already built and dozens of others being planned, the probability of a single mishap increases. Accidental contamination of the atmosphere by radioactivity either from processing plants (which are primarily in the Western United States) or from nuclear power plants (most of which are in the Eastern Seaboard states) increases with greater dependency on nuclear energy is one assumes that the nuclear facilities presently exercise maximum precautions. Then there is the very serious problem of spent fuel storage that no one has yet resolved.

Highly radioactive waste products must be contained *permanently*. One ton of processed fuel produces anywhere from forty to several hundred gallons of waste. Strontium-90, an isotope present in radioactive waste, has a radioactivity level that decreases by half every 28.1 years. This isotope at many concentrations could still be lethal after decaying for 280 years. However, ten half lives are generally enough to reduce most radioactive sources to nearly harmless levels. There is no way known to reduce the toxicity of radioisotopes. They must decay naturally, which means virtually perpetual containment. Over 75 million gallons of waste are now in storage in some 200 large steel, earth, and concrete tanks. It must be understood that we are not talking about a period of a few years, but of a period of time longer than that for which most governments and cities have endured. It must also be understood that this material is so potent that a few gallons released in a watershed could cause death and chaos on a scale comparable only to the havoc of modern warfare.

Iodine-131 is one of the inevitable products of nuclear reactions. Its half life of 8 days is exceedingly short compared with the half life of plutonium

Figure 7-12. Nuclear power plants and other thermal pollution sources on the Eastern Seaboard have installed cooling towers and very high stacks in order to dissipate heat and other pollutants from the facility and the immediate site of origin. Under widespread high inversion conditions that do occur, tall stacks are not effective. (Environmental Protection Agency)

which is 24,400 years. Nevertheless, it has been discovered that radioactive iodine is one of the most hazardous of all fission products because iodine is concentrated in the thyroid gland where very delicate endocrine processes take place. When human and other animal thyroids contain constant (even though) low levels of iodine-131, this phenomenon suggests that the source is exhaust gases from nuclear reactors and associated fuel processing plants. Caution should also be the password for tritium, an active isotope of hydrogen that when absorbed in place of the very common nonradioactive hydrogen might have dangerous effects. Tritium has a half life of 12.5 years. However, krypton-85, which has a half life of about 10.6 years, seems to be the radioisotope of greatest concern to daily atmospheric contamination. J. R. Coleman and R. Liberace of the Radiological Health Division of the United States Public Health Service stated in an official report dated November 1966 that removal of krypton-85 from reactor wastes involved costly techniques that are reasonable only if very small volumes of flow rates are used—a condition that does not apply to the big reactors now built or scheduled to go into operation. And so instead of spending money to remove krypton-85, and thus raise the cost of "cheap electricity" to a realistic price that embraces health standards, reactor operators elected to let the gas go into the air. Other dangerous radionuclides from a conventional nuclear plant with their half lives are cobalt-60 (5.27 days), zinc-65 (24.4 days), chromium-51 (27.8 days), and cesium-137 (30 years).

Curtis and Hogan in their publication, *Perils of the Peaceful Atom* have written

Although some radioactive elements seek particular tissues and organs when taken into the system, krypton-85 with its tendency to dissolve in fatty tissue is distributed fairly evenly throughout the human body, raising overall internal radiation and the attendant chances of cancer induction, genetic damage and shortening of life. . . . Considering, therefore, that krypton-85 is but one of a compendium of some two hundred radioactive isotopes produced by reactors, the reassurance that carefully monitored releases of low-level radioactivity into the environment are not harmful is nonsense.[10]

How Urban Areas Modify Their Local Atmospheric Resource

One of the best ways an urbanite can relate to the megalopolitan and global problem of air resource management is to inquire how his or her own city affects a specific part of the earth's envelope of atmosphere. Urban microclimate research in recent decades has shown that large cities tangibly affect precipitation, radiation, visibility, wind, humidity, and most important, temperature. Of course, most of these factors are interrelated. There is ample evidence that significant local atmospheric conditions are created by urban "metabolism," which differ from the surrounding countryside. "Thermal mushrooms" are created over large cities in stable weather conditions but under a gentle prevailing wind, the caplike formation is pushed or extended in a downwind pattern that could be called a "thermal plume." Atmospheric thermal plumes also contain abnormally high concentrations of particulates, sulfur dioxides, or other urban airborne effluvia. Some of the following urban climate conditions have been documented in Philadelphia, New York, Washington, and other American, Japanese, and European cities.

Urban microclimate differences of precipitation, radiation, and visibility are especially related to the increased particulate matter generated by a typical urban area. In many cases the total tonnage of particulate material pumped into the atmosphere is not as critical as the size of the particles. A gram of carbon in microgram-sized particles is one thousand times more dispersed than if it were put into the atmosphere in milligram-sized particles. Now if the same weight of both sized carbon particles are going to be deposited in the same volume of air (let us assume the urban airshed container remains constant), then the smaller sized particles (microgram) will create greater problems of visibility and radiation reduction; they will

[10] Richard Curtis, and Elizabeth Hogan, *Perils of the Peaceful Atom* (New York: Ballantine Books, Inc., 1969), pp. 192–193.

Figure 7-13. Heat produced from various urban activities creates an island or mushroom effect over a large city during stagnant air conditions. When pollutants are present, they often become entrapped—most often under inverted temperature stratification, which prevents normal mixing of surface and other layers.

tend to promote increased precipitation because more hygroscopic nuclei are available for condensation and greater penetration into the alveoli and other respiratory tissue is expected. Particulates, on the annual average, are about ten times greater over urban areas than over rural environs according to James T. Peterson in his authorative survey of meteorological literature.[11]

Total radiation is generally reduced by 15 to 20 per cent and ground level wind speeds are 10 to 20 per cent less than surrounding rural areas where the only significant variable is urbanization. It is hypothesized that because the built up urban area ruffles the wind currents or, more technically speaking, exerts increased frictional drag on air flowing over urbanized land, the heat mushroom or heat island causes horizontal thermal gradients.

Research on temperature microclimates of cities has shown that a city is warmer than its nonurban environs, sometimes with differences up to 20°F. The mean annual differences show large city temperatures 4°F. higher

[11]James T. Peterson, "The Climate of the City," in Thomas R. Detwyler, *Man's Impact on Environment* (New York: McGraw Hill Book Company, Inc., 1971), p. 131–154.

Figure 7-14. The cooling towers are installed to prevent thermal pollution of receiving waters. However, as the air surrounding the bases of the 400-foot tall towers is drawn through the curtains of water, heat is transferred from the water to the atmosphere. (Environmental Protection Agency)

Figure 7-15. Huge cooling towers are being built in many Eastern Seaboard cities in conjunction with industrial facilities and electric power generation plants. (Environmental Protection Agency)

than the nearby countryside with the highest temperature associated with the highest density parts of the city. Usually greater precipitation is generated downwind from urban areas because of increased particulates that serve as nuclei for water vapor condensation.

High concentrations of pavement, impervious rooftops, and large concrete surface areas absorb and store larger amounts of solar radiation than do the vegetation and soil types in nonurban peripheral areas. At night the lag time for release of the heat accumulated in daytime heating keeps nighttime air warmer than the hinterland. With the relative roughness of most urban surfaces, wind is reduced as mentioned previously, and this fact also reduces the heat dispersal, especially in cooler periods when man-made heat from space heating, industry, transportation, and other energy losses assumes important proportions. Associated with the higher urban temperatures are lower (usually about 5 per cent) relative humidity readings in central city areas compared with suburban and nearby rural land. This seems to be a function of vegetative cover differences and lower evaporation rates because of more rapid runoff conditions and generally higher urban temperatures.

Measuring the Healthiness of Urban Atmosphere

If some readers have the feeling that the information base for making some of the generalizations about atmospheric resources in the Eastern Seaboard region is in need of improvement, the feeling is well founded. **257**

The air quality sampling stations are severely inadequate. Air monitoring stations number less than 1 per cent of stream gages in the United States that sample river and flood conditions. The reliability and usefulness of information collected is also subject to question in many urban areas across the United States.

Considerable progress has been made over the recent decade of sampling. Too often "shirt collar" indexes and once-a-year grab samples were used to determine the healthiness of urban atmospheres. *The Ringlemann visual smoke test* has fallen into disrepute in the scientific community, but it remains in many local air pollution control ordinances. One of its disappointing features was that it was difficult to use at night. The reader should try to visualize holding a color-coded card up against the alleged violator's smokestack plume in the night sky. This, of course, assumed that the inspectors worked at night or weekends when the intentional violators do their burning.

Several exercises are available to persons interested in determining how thorough and how useful air quality control activities actually are in any given community. The following is a checklist of suggestions that may vary in importance depending on the unique characteristics of the airshed, the climate and topographic conditions, the quality and quantity of pollutants and, of course, what degree of air quality the reader and his community subjectively desire.

1. What air quality parameters are sampled?
2. Are all of the important parameters being monitored?
3. What frequency and what degree of accuracy is prescribed?
4. How many "full service" sampling stations exist in the urban area?
5. Do the locations of the air sampling stations cover a representative cross section of the community and take into account prevailing wind directions, possible microclimate incongruities, or other important localized variables?
6. Is the local or regional air-pollution agency staff well trained and supervised?
7. Is a public interest citizen advisory committee attached to the air pollution control agency?
8. Have maximum funds been obtained from federal, state, regional, and private sources for the necessary line operation, research, and education-information functions?
9. Have violations been dealt with in a fair manner?
10. Have "high performance" examples been given proper public acclaim and credit for exemplary operations?
11. Have the critical air quality indexes been translated into a form the general public can understand and use to take the appropriate action?
12. Do current air-quality conditions get reported with the daily sports results, market conditions, and weather statistics (which they are)?

Figure 7-16. Washington, D.C., like other large American cities, has devoted great areas and great sums of money to automobile facilities, storage, and highways. Usually over half of the inner city poor, however, do not own an automobile. (U.S. Forest Service)

13. Does the city have an air-pollution and noise-pollution code that safeguards the public health and welfare at least as stringent as national ambient air quality and noise level standards?

14. Is there a local or regional air pollution "hot line" that can be used to report apparent violations and to dispatch inspectors to point sources of air contamination and alleged noise level violations?

15. Do the violation penalties exceed the cost of continued violation? Is there enough economic incentive in the fine for a violator to stop polluting the air?

16. Does the school system have a thorough and well-taught unit or series of learning experiences from kindergarten through high school dealing with the problems and solutions of urban atmospheric resources? Are adult classes available in environmental education and environmental advocacy?

If the reader is able to honestly answer all these questions in an affirmative way, his local air quality has improved or will soon improve. If he cannot, the responsibility for improvement rests, in some manner, on his shoulders and on the shoulders of the largest corporations in America.

Take another breath. Those thirty-five pounds of air we take in each day should be the best we can manage. If we don't like what we're getting, writing our Congressman will not help. Take one of the questions that produced an unfavorable answer and let that be a personal project with a group of similar-minded people. Perhaps there is an important question that should have been asked that wasn't. Whatever your approach, the reader may want to pick up his telephone and dial 411. That seems to be a universal number for the information operator in the United States; ask the operator for the local air pollution control agency telephone number. When speaking to the agency, ask some of the questions from the list or others as they pertain to the reader's local situation. After the reader and his group start to work out some affirmative answers, he will have begun to deal with an improvement in the respiratory system of an urban organism.

CHAPTER 8

Energy Resources

Energy, like resources of air, water, timber, and wildlife, is usually taken for granted by individuals. Perhaps energy is assumed to be much less of a problem than the other classic resources because of its historic availability at very low costs. More than that, energy, regardless of its various forms of delivery or uses, comes to each of us with supreme subtlety and convenience. When a power failure occurs, we may contemplate for a fleeting moment the costs of being with or *without* our abundant supply of energy. Energy, by definition, is a measure of our ability to do work in the broadest sense of the word.

Even when an electrical outage occurs, it is assumed to be a very temporary phenomenon. Almost no thought is given to our energy sources when the supply is interrupted. The reader could recall the last time he experienced an electrical power failure and the thoughts that crossed his mind. Were some of the first mental flashes questions such as these:

When will the lights go back on?
How long will it be before I can reset the clocks?
I wonder if the things in my freezer or refrigerator will thaw out?
What could have caused this power failure—a vehicle hitting a pole? A workman striking an underground transmission line? A transformer fouled up or flooded?
Maybe it was sabotage, or are they blackmailing us to force higher utility rates or more transmission lines?

Still conspicuously absent in most areas is a question about the adequacy of the total distribution system that supplies the demand placed upon it by customers of the megalopolis. It is common knowledge that U.S. electrical consumption is increasing at nearly 9 per cent per year. It is also widely recognized that the majority of our power supply comes from finite, totally exhaustible, nonrenewable fossil fuels. One source put the 1973 breakdown as follows: "At present nuclear fission plants supply about 1.6 per cent of the electricity consumed in the United States. (Of the remainder, fossil fuel plants supply about eighty-two per cent and hydroelectric plants about sixteen per cent.)"[1] Despite this information, the average individual seldom questions the adequacy of fuel supplies. Instead, a common first response to any real or perceived energy problem is how we might increase our current supply by opening new coal, gas, oil, and oil shale deposits. Although the energy extraction companies lead the way in this questioning, the curious feature is that energy regulatory agencies, quasipublic utilities, and other "public serving" agencies or organizations also think in terms of improved extraction and transmission. What also should be asked are questions about decreasing energy use and increasing the efficiency of necessary consumption to the maximum that technology can provide.

The prolific consumption of electric power in cities of the present and cities of the future is demonstrated with the largest and smallest settlements as well as the oldest and newest communities. The potential sources of energy for the urban population include a wide range: nuclear, fuel cell, fossil, solar, wind, tidal, hydro, and combinations of these. For purposes that are consistent with the objectives of the book, this chapter depicts the problem of energy resource use and management in a way that will enable the urban resident to better comprehend how energy sustains the individual and his needs within a large urban settlement. Equal attention is devoted to exploring what future practices may be called for so that the human needs of a city are accommodated in the face of resource shortages brought about by lack of energy use planning in our postindustrialized urban systems.

CASE IN POINT: THE EASTERN SEABOARD

The transformation and utilization of natural resources by a human settlement has no better example than the one of energy resources and the megalopolis of the Eastern Seaboard of the United States. Here, more than in any other area, are the conflicting complexities of demands for electrical energy and the maintenance of environmental necessities.

This region of the country with its seventeen states from Maine to Florida serves as an example of a system that has increased in size and complexity

[1] Derek P. Gregory, "The Hydrogen Economy," *Scientific American*, Vol. 228, No. 1 (January 1973), p. 13.

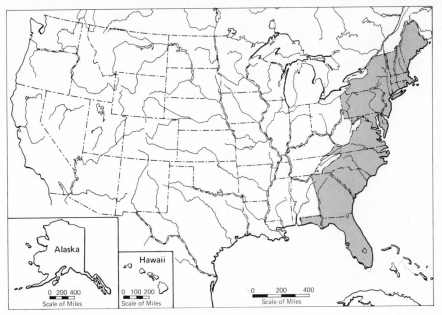

Figure 8-1. The Eastern Seaboard states are used as a regional illustration in the presentation of air resources.

with a corresponding increase in energy requirements. Like biological systems, human settlements of increased complexity lose increasingly greater percentages of energy through conversions. Biological systems of multiple trophic levels and complex human settlements in an industrialized megalopolis both show greater percentages of energy transformation than do the less complex biological organisms and the more simple agrarian systems. Whether or not the true standard of living (which is usually confused with a standard of consumption) increases as the percentage of human energy is replaced by energy supplied from fossil fuels is a question being asked with more seriousness now than several generations ago when the social and environmental costs appeared less heavy. More succinctly stated, what increase in the standard of living or the quality of life does an electric carving knife add over a manual cutter or a four-hundred horsepower vehicle over a one-hundred horsepower vehicle? Furthermore, the increment of additional energy necessary to raise the standard of living in New York, Boston, or Washington, D.C., means a denial of some equivalent opportunity cost to a rural American or an Indian reservation, or a reduced standard of living to someone else in an underdeveloped nation. When one inspects various social indicators of the standard of living in the Eastern part of the United States, he will find shocking and very curious disparities between mineral-rich states such as West Virginia and Kentucky, and high energy-consumption states such as Maryland, Massachusetts, and New York. Table 8-1 provides selected indexes that tend to give a compara-

264 tive idea of standards of living in eight Eastern states. The urbanized people are relatively comfortable and become more so. No relief is available to people of less urbanized states as one can deduct from the per capita state tax burden that could serve as an income redistribution mechanism. If another great hope is through the educational process, Table 8-1 shows how highly urbanized states compare with less urbanized states such as Maine, Kentucky, and West Virginia. It is a tragedy of human resource misallocation when one sees the public school expenditures per pupil or average annual salaries of public school teachers in "low-urbanized" states.

If any single event in America and specifically the Eastern Seaboard states forced us to ask the more comprehensive questions of energy conservation and distribution, it was the famous northeastern power blackout of November 9–10, 1965. Thirty million people and eighty thousand square miles were without electricity in all or parts of New York, New Jersey, Pennsylvania, Connecticut, Vermont, New Hampshire, Maine, and Rhode Island

Table 8-1. Social Indicators of Standard of Living: Eight Eastern States

	KY.	W. VA.	ME.	MD.	MASS.	N.Y.	N.J.	FLA.
% of Population Urban (SMSA)[1]	40.0	31.3	21.6	84.3	84.7	86.5	76.9	68.6
Telephones / 100 people	40	38	44	56	60	65	43	54
% High School Dropouts	30.3	28.6	21.5	20.9	16.5	6.2	25	26.8
(Median Years) Educational Attainment of Adult Population	8.7	8.8	11.0	10.4	11.6	10.7	11.2	10.9
Average Annual Salary of Public School Teachers	$7675	$6908	$7244	$8815	$8750	$9800	$8122	$8900
Public School Expenditure per Pupil	$612	$521	$547	$775	$977	$1400	$659	$728
Physicians/ 100,000 People	100	102	127	170	205	202	171	169
Infant Mortality/ 1000 Births								
White	20.7	25	22.4	19.2	19.2	18.5	21	18.8
Non-white	31.3	43.3	16.3	37.4	34.6	32.7	39.2	37.2
Per Capita Personal Income	$3060	$2929	$2857	$3712	$4156	$4797	$3044	$3910
Per Capita State Tax Burden	$200.64	$223.58	$264.54	$324.87	$368.55	$291.00	$323.55	$234.21

[1]U.S. Bureau of the Census; Census of Population and Housing, 1970, United States Summary. Other information from: *The New York Times Encyclopedic Almanac 1972; N.Y. Times;* 1971.

between eight and one-half and thirteen and one-half hours. During those hours, our dependency on electrical energy was revealed in many personal ways, and probably few other "peaceful" events in our technological age directly affected so many inhabitants of urban areas. The northeast power outage stimulated years of study and investigation that eventually led to a national energy policy. Had it not been for that event, many more years might have slipped by without public interest or awareness in energy resources and their delivery systems.

Should Energy Resources Be Nationalized?

The recent research about energy resource reserves reveals an adequate supply assuming the United States and the world demands do not continue to increase geometrically. Instead of a crisis about a shortage of absolute fuel resources, in the short run we are much more likely to face crisis conditions brought on because the private and public sectors refuse to bear increased social, environmental, and economic costs of power production and distribution. The metabolism of megalopolis—on the Eastern Seaboard or anywhere in the world—becomes a responsibility with which a laissez-faire market system cannot cope. Should the energy industry be nationalized, if, in fact, a crisis is about to occur because of the free-market mechanism of resource allocation? Even if it should be done, could it be done—especially now that the transportation systems serving urban areas are coming under increasing governmental management and control, having been forced into bankruptcy by automobile and energy companies. The federally sponsored interstate highway system is a direct subsidy to the energy-inefficient automobile. Waterborne transportation has essentially been nationalized under the stewardship of the U.S. Army Corps of Engineers. Other examples of heavy federal influence include a river basin region in the form of the Tennessee Valley Authority, the airways through the Federal Aviation Administration, as well as the Interstate Commerce Commission, the Federal Trade Commission, and other efforts of the Department of Transportation that regulate movement of goods and people. Not every federal operation is successful. Amtrak, a government operated rail system, for example, struggles for survival under federal sponsorship.

The welfare, health, safety, security (and whatever other parameters for the quality of life) of most urban Americans are dependent on a reliable flow of electrical energy. It certainly would appear appropriate for a federal jurisdiction to take a lead responsibility in allocating national energy supplies instead of trusting the private energy companies with public welfare. Since the profit objective is the compelling incentive for every energy company, it is not appropriate or reasonable to expect a privately owned, stockholder-controlled oil, gas, or coal company to put goals of social welfare in front of profit objectives. Nationalization of energy resources and their generation and distribution systems is not a panacea, however.

266 Federal bodies, such as the Tennessee Valley Authority, transfer environmental and social costs beyond their jurisdiction by purchasing cheap strip mine coal to the north and east of the TVA area where strip-mine reclamation regulations are lax or unenforced. William Bryan, the Northern Rocky Mountain Environmental advocate in Helena, Montana, has reported that the TVA is in the process of trying to purchase strip-mined coal in the Northern Plains.

Power Grids

The utilization of electricity in the Eastern Seaboard region should be every American's concern for the simple reason that 97 per cent of the United States' power generation is hooked into five regional grid systems, which will become a national grid network. The largest assemblage of interconnected systems, involving more than one-half of the nation's generating capacity, covers all of the United States east of the Rocky Mountains (except Texas) as well as two provinces in eastern Canada. Three thousand, six hundred power companies are involved in the eastern hook-ups that buffer the consumer from daily or seasonal peak demands in

Figure 8-2. Geothermal generated electrical energy from this Northern California facility of Pacific Gas and Electric could theoretically find its way into a national grid system. The prospect is negligible, however, for geothermal power to alleviate a national energy shortage. (Pacific Gas and Electric Co.)

scattered parts of the country. It is theoretically possible for hydroproduced *kilowatts* from Grand Coulee Dam or geothermal kilowatts from California's Pacific Gas and Electric to find their way into East Coast homes and factories, in addition to the power produced by a Consolidated Edison or Potomac Edison coal, nuclear, or gas-fired unit along the East Coast.

The Inefficiencies of Urban Energy Conversions

A large city is notorious for wasting every resource as the raw material is processed and reprocessed for final consumption. Energy is no exception. Regardless of the specific energy resource (for example, hydro, fossil fuel, or nuclear), conversions take place as energy is utilized for doing work. The conventional intermediary forms of energy that are "unlocked" from the sun's original energy placement include thermal, mechanical, and electrical. Electricity, in turn, is converted into household, commercial, or industrial forms of thermal, chemical, radiant, mechanical, and even electrical energy. Except for thermal energy, which is used for space heating, most energy sources are converted to mechanical energy. Mechanical energy is used directly for transportation (about 25 per cent of the U.S. energy demand) and for generating electricity. As a secondary form, chemical energy is available in storage batteries and dry cells. The radiant energy produced by electric lamps ends up primarily as heat. It should be emphasized that considerable losses occur with each conversion and with all electrical transmissions.

In response to the increasing demands of a burgeoning population and the doubling of U.S. electric needs every six to ten years, the United States' power industry has experienced a 7.2 per cent annual growth rate during the last fifty years.[2] The steam electric stations that are being built to accommodate these demands convert water to steam from heat that is obtained from a fossil-fuel or a nuclear reactor.

One way to understand the inefficiencies created by urban conversions or degradations of energy is to follow a unit of coal or gas or oil with its characteristic *B.T.U.* rating and calculate the energy losses from conversions and transmission. The consumption of 340 million B.T.U. per capita (in 1970) is equivalent to energy contained in about 13 tons of coal or 2,700 gallons of gasoline. Since 1900, technology has helped us increase by a factor of 4 the efficiency with which fuels are consumed. However, very substantial inefficiencies still exist, as in the case of the automobile, which is only 25 per cent efficient. Incidentally, in terms of miles delivered per gallon of fuel there has been a gradual decline over the past 25 years so that today's average automobile can travel about 12.2 miles per gallon. Air conditioning, pollution control devices, and extraordinarily negligent operation by the

[2] "Debate on the Thermal Issue Continues," *Environmental, Science, & Technology*, 3:6 (May, 1969), p. 425.

Figure 8-3. Viewing Manhattan by night graphically illustrates an urban area's intensive reliance upon electricity as well as man's extravagant waste of his energy resources. The United Nation's 39-story Secretariat Building is in the foreground. (New York Convention and Visitors Bureau)

driver (quick starts and stops) are primarily responsible for this reduction. For several years, this observer has suggested a tax on horsepower and penalties for rapid acceleration.

One of the least efficient but important uses for electricity is in providing light. The General Electric Company has estimated that lighting consumes about 24 per cent of all electrical energy generated, which is about 6 per cent of the nation's total energy budget. The common incandescent light bulb transforms 95 per cent of the electricity into heat (infrared radiation) and only 5 per cent into visible light. Even with the improved efficiencies of fluorescent and high-intensity lamps the average efficiency is about 13 per cent. But here is the important item: to obtain an overall efficiency for converting chemical (oil, gas, or coal) or nuclear energy to visible light, one must multiply this percentage times the average efficiency of generating power, which is about 33 per cent. With this in mind, the next time the reader's airplane circles in at night on a landing pattern over Boston, Philadelphia, New York, Baltimore, Washington, Atlanta, Miami or over any large metropolitan area (especially at Christmas time) he should remember that he is looking upon a net efficiency conversion of only about 4 per cent! (13% × 33% = 4.29%)

Here then is an example of how technology (unknowingly) went about temporarily "bailing us out." Because of the increase in use of the more efficient high intensity and modern fluorescent lamps, the United States was able to triple its supply of lighting between 1960 and 1970 while only doubling the consumption of electricity needed to produce it. Several technological breakthroughs are expected that will mitigate the power production problem (created by overconsumption) including the fuel cell and magnetohydrodynamic generators. For the reader interested in the overall picture of energy and power, the September 1971 issue of *Scientific American*[3] magazine and the AAAS articles in *Science*[4] are excellent sources of information.

Thermal Pollution

The efficiency of a nuclear power plant is no more than 30 per cent for the complete cycle from fuel to electricity, even before the energy is shipped out on high voltage transmission lines whose losses run in the order of 15 per cent. For the nuclear plant alone this means that nearly 70 per cent of the latent energy in the fuel is wasted as heat in the cooling water and is passed off either to a local body of water or into the atmosphere via rather expensive cooling towers such as Consolidated Edison's Palisades power plant was forced to build in a recent Michigan law suit. Fossil fuel power plants expend up to 60 per cent of their energy source as waste heat.

As Claude Summers clearly states in the September 1971 *Scientific American* "the actual heat load placed on the water or air is much greater, however, than the difference between sixty and seventy percent suggests.[5] For plants with the same kilowatt rating, a nuclear plant produces about fifty per cent more waste heat than a fossil-fuel plant. The reason is that a nuclear plant must 'burn' about one-third more fuel than a fossil fuel plant to produce a kilowatt-hour of electricity and then wastes seventy per cent of the larger British Thermal Unit input." Thus, although the nuclear power plants have the advantages of not polluting the air with smoke or using our depletable fossil fuels, which often need to be transported great distances, one large cost of these advantages is the additional thermal discharge that nuclear plants release.

The energy demands projected for the year 2000 will require a generating capacity of 1.8 million to 2 million megawatt (MW)—seven times the present capacity.[6] This new installed capacity will entail 1,600 units of the same size of today's 1,000 megawatt plants; 200 square miles of land; 3 million cubic feet of water; and a lifetime supply of either 10 million tons

[3] *Scientific American*, Special Issue on Energy and Power, Vol. 224, No. 3 (September 1971), published by Scientific American, Inc., New York.

[4] *Science*, Special Series on Energy and Power, Volume 177, No. 4052 through Volume 178, No. 4061 (8 September 1972 to 10 November, 1972), published by The American Association for the Advancement of Science, Washington, D.C.

[5] Claude M. Summers, "The Conversion of Energy," *Scientific American*, Vol. 224, No. 3 (Sept. 1971), p. 153.

[6] Emmanuel V. Sorge, "The Status of Thermal Discharge East of the Mississippi," *2nd Thermal Workshop, U.S. International Biological Program; Chesapeake Science*, Vol. 10 (Sept.-Dec. 1969), p. 131.

of uranium or 100,000 million tons of coal. This level of energy production will also utilize almost twice the total national freshwater run-off and in so doing daily yield enough waste heat to warm 107 cubic miles of water by 20°F.

East of the Mississippi, there is a trend toward a major concentration of nuclear power plants along the Eastern Seaboard and in the Great Lakes region. Of special concern here is the accumulation of plants in localized areas of Long Island Sound and the Hudson River. In addition to the 40 million people who live within the northeast megalopolis, New York State's marine district also contains some of the most productive marine waters and estuaries in the region. (In 1968 it led all other East Coast states in harvest of hard clams; an estimated 1 million anglers contributed $10 million to the local economy; in commercial seafood production the region yielded 44.9 million pounds of finfish worth $2.9 million and 14.4 million pounds of shellfish worth $11.4 million.) The predicted total volume of heated discharge into the Sound from existing and planned plants is at least 7.2 million gallons per minute. This discharged water will be heated 20° to 30°F. higher than the normal temperature of the Sound.[7] In addition to the plants that discharge into Long Island Sound, others discharge into the Hudson River at Indian Point, which, although technically outside of the Marine District, are important because they discharge into areas of the river that are primary spawning and nursery grounds for many marine fishes. By 1985, one-fourth of all surface water will pass through condenser units. Despite the magnitude of this use of our freshwater resources, relatively little is known about the effects of heated discharge upon aquatic organisms.

Currently ecological studies are underway at two plants on Long Island Sound. Financed by the utilities, their objective is to predict the impact of the power plants. Biologists collected forty-one species of fishes from among the variety of marine and freshwater species in this estuarine area. The studies that are underway will require three to five years of field research and will provide important information about Long Island Sound. Commercial fishermen seek shad, flounder, striped bass, mackerel, blackfish, and occasionally sharks and codfish in this area. Schools of silversides, menhaden, and other forage fish provide the link in the food chain between plankton and carnivorous fishes. Eggs and larvae of twelve species have been collected in the Sound. Shellfish too are important members of the marine community; hard clams, soft clams, oysters, and mussels have been part of the harvestable resources.

The aquatic community is delicate and complex. A natural body of water changes temperature slowly, and cold-blooded aquatic animals have never evolved an ability for temperature control. The heat in their environment determines their internal temperature and thus the biochemical pace of

---

[7] Albert C. Jensen, "Thermal Pollution in the Marine Environment," *The Conservationist*, 25:8–13 (Oct. 1970), pp. 9–10.

their lives. Difficulty occurs when rising temperatures cause biological processes to overtax themselves, which may cause failure to respire properly or internal disorders that lead to illness of death. More serious, although perhaps lacking the dramatic impact, are the permanent ecological changes that thermal pollution precipitates. One oceanographer has estimated that within the next twenty years, a regional warming will occur from the aggregate effect of the electric generating plants in the western portion of the Sound.[8]

We do know that temperature is the primary control of biochemical reaction rates. If water temperature increases, respiration rate increases, but oxygen availability decreases. The imbalance between increased respiration and decreasing availability of oxygen produces a stress situation. Oxygen consumption of aquatic organisms doubles with every $10°C$ rise in water temperature. Changes in seasonal temperature produce a change in life cycle. For instance, a clam living in the heated effluent of a power plant may spawn out of season. Its eggs and larvae would probably be swept into cold water by currents only to perish there.

Since there is to be increased pressure on the aquatic environment from industry wishing to use water for cooling purposes in order to meet increasing demands, it is mandatory that we establish thermal tolerances for all species that may be exposed to thermal pollution. There are ways that the temperature differential between the effluent and the receiving waters can be reduced. Such methods cost money, but if urban Americans continue to demand increased electricity, the time may well be near when we shall have to shift our priorities and make some choices, any of which will be costly, ecologically, economically, or both.

Only economics forces us to waste the power plant heat in the tributaries and estuaries of the Delaware, the Susquehanna, the Potomac, the Connecticut, and the Hudson rivers. When the environmental costs reach a magnitude and a certainty that are worthy of public concern, then perhaps these large volumes of low-grade energy will be widely utilized. Other countries have found commercial uses for the waste coolant water, and eventually, uses such as space heating, heating a year-round warm-water fishery, and maintaining ice-free shipping channels may even be attempted on a large scale along the East Coast. However, the potential environmental damage from thermal pollution needs careful assessment.

It would seem that the recent electrical brownouts and blackouts in the Northeastern United States, the opposition and injunctions against new nuclear power plants, the outcry against environmental degradation, and the finite nature of our nonreplenishable fossil fuels indicated both a need to evaluate our present directions in attempting to meet our energy demands, and a need to better assess alternative possibilities. With this in mind, the reader is invited to read what a former University of Michigan student and Director of the Ann Arbor, Michigan Ecology Center, Michael

---

[8] Ibid., pp. 12–13.

Schechtman, had to say about energy resource policies of the Eastern Seaboard and one realistic alternative in the foreseeable future—solar energy. His comments comprise the next two sections of this chapter.

Energy Resource Policies of the Eastern Seaboard

The question of energy resources for the Eastern Seaboard region is not a problem of localized dimension. Rather, it is a question of both national and international scope. In the first place, the resources upon which the Eastern Seaboard depends are not localized in origin, but in fact come from a variety of national and international sources, and, as such, can be affected by the winds of national and international political and social conditions. Secondly, the particular mix of energy resources used is determined by price, which in turn is determined by national and international factors much beyond the control of the Eastern Seaboard region.[9] Some of these factors are: (1) technological innovations that reduce the costs of various energy sources; (2) the control of decision-making processes of industries vis-à-vis their research efforts to make such technological innovations; (3) the allocation of federal funds and efforts in the field of energy source development and related fields that would have impact on their usage; (4) the manipulation of railroad rates (more commonly known as the regulation of railroad rates); (5) new discoveries of fuel deposits; and (6) imposition of import quotas and tariffs. Another factor that transcends the localized boundaries of the Eastern Seaboard region but, which affects it nevertheless, is the competitive international demand for energy resources. As our own population and level of consumption grow; as world population grows; as various international economic and power blocks compete for the fossil fuel resources; as agrarian nations industrialize and generate a substantial new energy demand that previously was negligible; and as newly industrialized nations seek to further their gains and increase their wealth and welfare, thereby magnifying their energy demand; the price of nonreplenishable energy resources will be subject to a multitude of upward pressures. Therefore, in viewing the question of energy resources for the Eastern Seaboard region it is necessary to maintain a national and international perspective.

The future of energy resource utilization on the Eastern Seaboard involves two major areas of consideration: (1) an assessment of the needs of the population, and (2) an evaluation of the best way to meet those needs. Presently the United States population level is in excess of 200 million

[9] For example, the rail rates granted coal unit trains affect the threshold at which nuclear energy becomes competitive. Also, standards for the emission of noxious effluents or gases from combustion are reflected in the greater attractiveness of natural gas as against coal and fuel oil.

bodies; it is expected to reach 240 million by 1980 and 330 million by the year 2000. Landsberg and Schurr, in a study published in 1968,[10] projected that in terms of energy consumption, we will move from a level of 45.3 quadrillion BTU consumed in 1960 to approximately 79.2 quadrillion BTU in 1980, and 135.2 quadrillion BTU by the year 2000. More recent data from the U.S. Bureau of Mines indicates an even higher projected level for the year 2000, approximately 162.6 quadrillion BTU.[11] Although nuclear energy is projected to play an ever increasing role as an energy source, the majority of energy—over 70 per cent—is projected to be furnished over this time period by nonreplenishable fossil fuels. In regard to the breakdown of this energy consumption, ". . . the outlook is for a rapid increase in energy consumed in transportation, and an almost equally rapid increase in energy taken by industry. Among industries, the chemicals, including petroleum refining, are a particularly dynamic element. Energy needs of the primary metals, other than aluminum, would appear to display less force, because of both the more slowly rising demand for the metals themselves and the increasing productivity of energy in the smelting and processing of metals. The lowest rate of increase is likely to prevail in commercial and especially residential consumption."[12] These projected needs and trends can and will vary substantially in accord with significant changes in population growth and consumption life style patterns. For example, the future role of mass transit and whether or not it will be electrically powered, potentially will have tremendous impact on petroleum demand as well as air pollution and traffic congestion. It is more than possible that there will be a number of these significant changes as both concern for environmental quality and competition for diminishing nonreplenishable fuels grow.

In evaluating the best way to meet these projected energy needs, I see four major parameters of discussion: (1) changing the nature and the extent of our energy demand; (2) creating policies that will yield in the long run the greatest economic utility; (3) creating policies that will generate the least possible environmental degradation; and (4) creating policies that will provide for the very best possible utilization of all our resources. There are two points I must make that are very important considerations to keep in mind. The first is that generally there is a substantial time lag between the time at which a policy decision is made, and when it is implemented,

[10] H. H. Landsberg, and S. H. Schurr, *Energy in the United States: Sources, Uses and Policy Issues* (New York: Random House, Inc., 1968).

[11] G. A. Mills, H. Perry, and H. R. Johnson, "Fuels Management in an Environmental Age," in *Environmental Science and Technology* Vol. 5, No. 1 (January 1971).

[12] At the present time utility sales in the residential service class have risen to nearly 30 per cent of all electricity sold and have become the largest single revenue producer of electric utilities, accounting for more than 40 per cent of sales revenue. In terms of total energy consumed by the residential sector, 9.0 quadrillion BTU were consumed in 1960, 14.5 quadrillion BTU will be consumed in 1980, and 18.2 quadrillion BTU will be consumed in year 2000, all of which indicates a substantial increase in demand; however, the percentage of the total will decrease from approximately 20 per cent in 1960 to approximately 14 per cent in year 2000. (Source: Landsberg and Schurr, op. cit.)

and an even greater time lag between when implementation takes place and when the transition has been completed and all desired consequences have been effected. Because of these time lags, there is a certain insistent urgency to formulate the best possible policies while at the same time to evaluate and improve the efficiency and effectiveness of the institutions that administer these policies. The second point is that because of factors such as the costs of capital investment; inflation; politico-economic organizational procedures, strategies and alliances; and the magnitudes in which we are dealing; the decisions and policies made now may be irreversible to a considerable extent in ten to fifteen years future time. Thus as we formulate an energy resource policy in the context of an environmental quality program, it is necessary to maintain a long-term perspective and to consider all possible significant parameters. Furthermore, the critical decisions that we put off today (such as the question of zero population growth) may lead us by default in directions posing even more critical and difficult decisions for tomorrow.

The question of changing the nature and extent of our energy demand is not purely a technological question, but rather, to a very large extent, is one of values. Perhaps this kind of question is one that should not fall within the scope of this work; I am not sure. However, I find that it is a question that I cannot ignore. It disturbs me very deeply that many people will take a very active stand and demonstrate vigorously against the air pollution of Detroit Edison or Boston Edison, or seek injunctions against new nuclear plants that threaten thermal pollution, but do not and will not align themselves with equal fervor in an effort to attack and reform the root causes of our environmental crisis—our value system and our consumption patterns—the very values and consumption that necessitate the power plants against which we demonstrate so adamantly. There are a great number of psychological phenomena involved here that help explain, but do not justify, our lack of commitment in dealing with the root causes of our environmental crisis. Briefly stated, they are: (1) desiring to seek a simple solution rather than investing the time, energy, and commitment necessary in tackling a complex solution; (2) seeking a convenient scapegoat to place the burden of blame upon; (3) seeking a ready and acceptable target as an outlet for venting the frustrations, rage, and feelings of impotence encountered in trying both to live in contemporary society and to deal with the horrifying miasma of our environmental crisis; (4) seeking to externalize the guilt inherent in accepting personal responsibility; and (5) avoiding the consequences inherent in accepting personal responsibility, that is, the making of personal sacrifices, such as limiting family size, giving up unnecessary household conveniences, consuming less, using public transportation more often, and so forth. All these psychological dynamics notwithstanding, if this society were to meet the crisis of its values and life styles head-on, and make the necessary adjustments, then we could considerably lessen our projected future energy demands.

In formulating a policy for energy resources utilization that in the long

Figure 8-4. The human costs of fossil fuel extraction in the strip mines of Appalachia are staggering. For a people who gave so much of their land, their labors, and their resource base to raise the American standard of living, the people of the Cumberland Plateau were left very little.

run will yield the greatest economic utility, it is necessary first to ascertain the extent of these energy resources. Our fossil fuel supply is indeed limited. The current level of coal consumption could continue for four or five hundred more years; the reserves of oil and natural gas will be exhausted even sooner. By the year 2200, approximately 30 per cent of total power will come from energy sources other than those available today.[13] The very fact of the finite nature of our fossil fuel supply indicates ultimately that a full transition must be made to energy sources other than fossil fuels. The question which I raise at this point is whether or not there is greater economic utility in making that transition sooner, as opposed to later. I contend that the earliest possible transition would provide the greatest economic utility in the long run for the following reasons: (1) it would reduce capital investment in equipment that will ultimately become dis-functional and most likely unusable, equipment such as fossil fuel power plants, additional oil tankers, an excessive number of oil rigs both onshore and offshore, an excessive number of railroad cars for coal and pipelines; (Measured by the dollar value of its plant and equipment, the electric power

[13]P. E. Glaser, "The Future of Power from the Sun," *Power* (August, 1968).

276 industry is the nation's largest by a wide margin, with gross capital assets worth around $70 billion.[14] Furthermore, in annual capital outlays on new plant equipment, the energy industries are a leading segment of the economy. Their outlays account for about one-fifth of all business new plant and equipment expenditures.[15]) (2) it would reduce the capital investment necessary in the industries that would produce these products; (3) it would reduce the capital investment necessary for pollution control devices and for the industries that make them; (4) it would conserve and free up the resources—metals, minerals, and energy—that would have gone into the production of all these capital goods; (5) it would reduce the necessary exploration for new reserves; and (6) it could conceivably eliminate (or at least substantially reduce) the research and development of such supplemental processes as the extraction of oil from oil shale deposits, the conversion of coal to gas and liquid fuels, and the conversion of cellulose to low-sulfur oil.

The growing awareness and concern for environmental quality give special impetus to the parameter of creating a policy that would result in the least possible environmental degradation. The following results could be obtained by an early transition away from fossil fuel dependence. (1) The preservation of the "natural" integrity of land areas in which fuel deposits might be found. (2) Freeing up these land areas for alternative uses such as wildlife preservation and recreation—uses that potentially would allow for more ecologically sound management. (3) Reducing acid mine wastes and leachings from other mining wastes, including radioactive ores. (4) Reducing dependency on offshore oil wells, thereby lessening the possibility of leaks. (5) Lessening oceanic trafficking of oil, thereby lessening the possibility of spills. (6) Reducing the amount of transfer of oil from shore to ship and ship to shore, which has been the single most damaging source of oil pollution in harbors and inland waterways. The reduction of power generation from fossil fuel combustion sources would significantly reduce air pollution and other unwanted by-products. Ultimately we shall have to shift away from the fossil fuels when the economic, social, and energy investments necessary to acquire them exceed the economic, social, and energy benefits accrued from them. Moreover, the alternative energy sources that replace the fossil fuels will have to be developed at some time to a state of the arts whereby the economic, social, and energy investments necessary to utilize them are at least comparable to or less than the economic, social, and energy benefits accrued from them. The critical point is that the sooner the state of the arts for alternative energy sources are developed, the sooner the transition can be made; our concerns and desires for a quality environment can be realized in part, and our efforts to maximize that quality will be significantly enhanced.

[14] Landsberg and Schurr, op. cit.
[15] Resources for the Future, Inc., *U.S. Energy Policies: An Agenda for Research* (Baltimore: The Johns Hopkins Press, 1968).

The final parameter for formulating an energy resources policy considers the optimal goal of having the very best possible utilization of all our resources. The economic and ecological facets of this parameter have already been explored; however, there are other elements involved vis-à-vis their best possible use. For example, our supply of natural gas liquids as a chemical raw material far outweighs its importance as an energy source; however, our present energy demands necessitate giving a higher use priority to the natural gas liquids as an energy source. (In a sense, it is like employing Arthur Rubenstein to chop wood to be made into piano legs, rather than employing his talents to play the piano.) Moreover, a sensible policy would seem to be one that would preserve a portion of our fossil fuels as an insurance for potentially important uses not yet discovered. For example, incredible demands on future coal resources will be made by synthetics, which gain increasingly widespread use in our society and whose major source is coal. As previously implied, if the transition were made at the last possible date, a substantial amount of our metal, mineral, and energy resources would be invested in nonrecoverable products that would become useless, or in products that would be recoverable only after additional inputs of energy and other resources. An earlier transition would mean that these resources, for which there already exists a very strong international demand, would then become more readily available for such important uses as mass transit and housing. Moreover, the earlier transition would free up the multitude of human resources that would have been employed in all the various occupations necessitated by the utilization of fossil fuels as our primary energy source. Finally, there exists the realm of aesthetic values. An early transition could reduce the unsightly panorama of offshore oil rigs and also reduce the numbers of coal and oil shale strip mines whose ravages can be repaired but whose land can never be made the same.

An Alternative—Solar Energy

The discussion by now has more than adequately revealed my bias for immediate research on alternate energy sources. Among potential sources such as nuclear fusion and geothermal energy, there also exists the possibility of utilizing solar energy. "Power from the sun is not, of course, a new concept. In 1901, the sun's energy ran a $4\frac{1}{2}$ hp. steam engine in Pasadena. Twelve years later, a larger solar engine near Cairo, Egypt, was built to generate 50 horsepower. Since then, man has built many energy systems to use solar heat. Examples are solar water heaters, solar distillation plants, and solar ponds, along with solar-powered engines."[16] In addition, solar energy is a nonpolluting energy source that will last as long as life as we

---

[16]Glaser, op. cit.

278 know it continues on the earth. Therefore, capital investment to exploit solar energy would not be channeled into limited use facilities, but rather into facilities with an unlimited lifetime. Moreover, the amount of energy from the sun is immense. "Solar energy falls on the land areas of the world at roughly one thousand times the annual rate of total world energy consumption estimated for year 2000.[17] The question of utilizing solar energy is not one of attractiveness, but rather one of technology.

A very promising use of solar energy that is presently applicable is that of space heating. According to Landsberg and Schurr's data from 1968, space heating in the United States accounted for close to 60 per cent of residential energy consumption in 1960. The projection for 1980 is approximately 48 per cent; for the year 2000, 42 per cent. Given the fact of a population increase by an additional 100 million persons by the year 2000, and the fact that a sizable majority of that increase will take up residence in the Northeastern United States and the Great Lakes basin—areas that have long, cold winters—the total demand (but not the per capita demand) for energy for space heat will increase significantly over the next thirty years. By using solar energy for space heating, we can make a substantial reduction of the fossil fuel drain and its associated problems of environmental degradation.

The notion of using solar energy to heat one's house is immensely practical, since "The solar energy annually falling on the roof of a typical American house is nearly ten times as great as the annual space heat demand of that house."[18] By using computer simulation techniques, Lof and Tybout were able to determine an economic and effective mix of solar heating by means of a collection system that absorbs the heat energy from the sun, stores it, and releases it to the house as needed, and a supplementary heat source. The supplementary conventional heat source was required since (1) it is very costly per unit of heat received to provide for extremely high heating demands through solar equipment alone; and (2) there must be a provision to accomodate any solar deficits. Projected costs were determined to be generally lower than electric space heat and within the range of heat costs from conventional fuels where fuel prices are high. Lof and Tybout summarily stated that "solar heating results, as computed for optimum designs, bear out the belief that in suitable climates, solar space heating could be available even today at costs below those of electric space heat on most places where the latter is in use. If further collector manufacturing improvements are achieved as hypothesized, and as seems probable in view of the history of productivity change, solar heat may well fall within the range of heat costs from higher priced mineral fuels."[19]

Furthermore, in taking into consideration inconsistencies and inaccuracies in our economic system of monetary valuation, they added that "if

---

[17] G. O. G. Lof, and R. A. Tybout, "Solar House Heating," *Natural Resources Journal*, The University of New Mexico School of Law Vol. 10, No. 2 (April 1970).
[18] Ibid.
[19] Ibid.

public control were extended seriously to restrain present consumption of liquid fuels on behalf of future consumption, prices would increase and solar space heat would be the more attractive."[20] The advantages are clear: solar energy does not pollute, it is not a nonreplenishable resource, its use conserves resources that are nonreplenishable, and potentially it is cheaper than conventional space heating. Lof and Tybout concluded that "the most suitable areas for solar house heating are those with moderate to severe heating requirements, abundant sunshine, and ideally, heat needs throughout most of the year."[21]

Without doubt, this applies most readily to the northeastern United States and to the Great Lakes basin. The constraints to this method of space heating are as follows: (1) houses that are to be located close to one another must be of similar height; (2) trees must be placed very carefully to avoid interference with the collection process; (3) houses that have a different slope than the collector must make an additional investment for a corrective mounting; and (4) the collector must have a southern exposure. Heavy accumulation of snow poses yet another potential problem.

In order to promote maximum utilization of solar space heating, it is necessary for government to provide some inducement (I will later discuss the role of government in more detail, with its history of intervention and involvement) for big business to begin production of solar heat collector systems on a scale that could take full economic advantage of mass production techniques. Moreover, there is a need to publicize and advertise the economic viability and ecologically desirable features of this method of space heating, and to encourage its use. Special tax incentives could be invoked in order to promote the use of solar space heating in new housing until such time that its use becomes common practice. For example, the monetary worth of the collector system could be exempted (or even deducted as a further incentive) from the assessment for taxation evaluation. The same could be applied for businesses which used solar space heating, with the added incentive of allowing rapid depreciation write-offs.

The case that has been made in favor of solar space heating can in similar fashion be made for solar hot water heating. In addition to conventional residential uses, using solar energy to heat water to a range of 40°C. to 60°C. for bathhouses and laundries is an economic and practical commercial application. In 1960 there were an estimated 350,000 solar hot-water heaters of all types in use in Japan and 10,000 in Israel. Moreover, solar-water heating systems are in use in other parts of the Mediterranean, in Australia, in Florida, and elsewhere. Swimming pools can be kept at very comfortable temperatures by capitalizing on solar energy. The same kinds of incentives as described could be incorporated into an attempt to promote the use of solar hot-water heating.

[20] Ibid.
[21] Ibid.

280   A number of other applicable uses of solar energy already exist. Solar energy is very suitable for direct distillation of small quantities of pure water from salt water. Although a sizable amount of capital investment is required for larger quantities of water, it is more profitable in the long run to use regenerative solar distillers, which are a combination of a solar installation producing seven to fifteen atmospheres of steam and a conventional distiller.[22] It has been projected that as experience is gained, the costs of producing distilled water will become competitive with standard water supply procedures in certain American localities.[23] Although none of the literature mentioned it, I suspect that the same kind of operation could be applied to the reprocessing of liquid waste residues from industrial processes. In the area of high temperature industrial processes, the Army is already operating in Natick, Massachusetts a large solar furnace capable of producing temperatures up to 5,000°F. Cooking and food processing are yet other areas where solar energy has been successfully utilized on a small scale.

Although the previously described applications of solar energy are both viable and promising, the most important consideration is whether or not solar energy can be converted to generate electricity on a meaningful scale. Scientific knowledge is presently sufficient to devise ways of generating electricity using solar energy; however, the technology involved has not been adequately developed to do so on an economically competitive basis. One method of generating electricity with solar energy is by the direct conversion of heat to electricity via electron transfer from a hot plate 2,200°F. to a plate 1,000°F separated by a thousandth of an inch.[24] A second possibility would be to obtain power from sun-produced temperature differences in the waters of the Caribbean or the Gulf Stream. In this plan the colder lower layers would act as a heat sink, and a floating power plant would do the conversion.[25] A third and particularly novel possibility involves equipment orbiting the earth at an altitude of 22,300 miles that would intercept sunlight on a huge flat collector. Organic compounds with semiconductor properties would convert the solar energy to electricity, which would then be beamed down as microwaves to a receiving antenna on earth. Calculations based on an 80 per cent conversion efficiency (theoretically possible) indicated that a collector weighing 330,000 pounds exclusive of support would have been sufficient to supply the 1966 power needs of the Northeast United States.[26] A fourth possibility entails the use of large curved mirrors and lenses to collect and concentrate the sun's rays, creating enough steam and pressure to run turbines. This could be most

---

[22] UNESCO: *Wind and Solar Energy: Proceedings of the New Delhi Symposium,* Paris, France (1956).

[23] "Solar and Atomic Energy: A Survey," *Studies in Business and Economics,* The University of Maryland (March 1959), Vol. 12, No. 4.

[24] Ibid.

[25] Glaser, op. cit.

[26] Ibid.

effectively done in the areas of the Western states where sunlight is extremely plentiful and land is relatively inexpensive, such as in parts of Nevada. Reassurances from engineers as to the technological aspects of long-range transmission, high voltage potentials, transformer stations, and intergrid exchanges make this possibility especially attractive.[27]

I rest my case. The one remaining question is what role should the federal government play. Although others may argue that the government's role in a free market economy should be as restricted as possible and should not be one of an initiator, it is my contention that by virtue of a history of involvement and intervention—including depletion allowances, import quotas, price regulation, allocation of research and development funds, and official policy positions—the federal government is primarily responsible for the energy resources situation as it exists today. For example, the federal government's role in allocating research and development funds and setting policies and priorities were the determining factors in the development of nuclear fission as a viable and economically competitive energy resource. This is more like the rule than the exception, for in a historical context:

The legacy of the 1930's is thus to be found in the crucial role of the federal government today in the nation's electric power industry as regulator of the privately-owned industry; as a source of low-interest loans to the rural cooperatives; as builder, owner, and operator of giant hydroelectric facilities and more recently of thermal power plants in the TVA; as the owner and operator of widespread transmission facilities; and as wholesale marketer of electric power generated in federally owned facilities to rural cooperatives, municipalities, other public bodies, and also to privately-owned facilities.[28]

Thus within a historical context of intervening in accord with the determined best interests of the country, the federal government must now carefully assess our current energy resource policies and priorities, and create new policies that in the long run will yield the greatest economic utility, the least possible environmental degradation, and the very best possible utilization of all our resources. I am confident that such policies would mean an early transition away from dependence on fossil fuels, and quite possibly movement toward the large-scale utilization of solar energy.[29]

Other Alternatives

Other energy sources of the inexhaustible variety must also be considered, even if today's technology does not immediately make them economically feasible. Most of the world's consumption of energy from fossil

[27] "Solar and Atomic Energy: A Survey," op. cit.
[28] Landsberg and Schurr, op. cit.
[29] This is the end of Schechtman's comments.

282 fuels from the beginning of man until today has taken place within the last thirty years. More specifically, of the eight hundred years of coal mining, more than 50 per cent of the coal burned has been stripped of dug in the last twenty five years. Petroleum has been pumped out of the ground for about one hundred years beginning with Drake's well in Pennsylvania but more than one-half has been pumped and used in the last fifteen years. As one can readily see, we have made tremendous shifts from fuel wood to coal to petroleum as major energy sources. When technology produces a controlled fusion reaction, presumably in the next twenty-five to thirty-five years, it is said that the energy available then will be relatively limitless, but thermal loadings due to cooling requirements will be proportionately greater than at present. In the immediate future a scaling down of electrical demand should be coupled with some of the following alternatives in addition to wind and solar sources.

Tidal Power

The use of tides is often mentioned as a modest source of power particularly for the Eastern Seaboard region. The most successful prototype for harnessing the gravitational forces of the sun and moon is a tidal (240 megawatt) power station at LaRance on the Rance River in France. At this unit the tides of the English Channel are trapped behind a dam on the river. At low tide, water is released and flows through turbine gates back to the sea, thus creating electrical power from mechanical energy. As the tide moves toward a high tide position, reversible turbines generate energy on the flood tide. Four surge intervals exist over the twenty four-hour period.

In areas where coastal configurations create very pronounced tides, such as the Bay of Fundy where differentials exist of up to thirty feet, at the narrow entrance to Chignecto Bay considerable promise for hydropower generation exists. Along the eastern coastline, one of the best sites for the application of this principal is at Passamaquoddy Bay, Maine, in the Saint Croix River-Bay of Fundy area. In 1919 Dexter P. Cooper submitted the first plan for a tidal power plant at this site. (See Fig. 8-5.) Utilizing Passamaquoddy Bay as a high pool and Cobscook Bay as a low pool, water could be taken at high tides, trapped in dam gates, then released into the lower pool through gates where turbines are placed to generate electric power. Water is also released into the ocean again through more gates at low tides.

Interest in the tidal project was expressed again in 1963 with an additional modification. The Saint John River would be used in conjunction with the bay plan using conventional hydroelectric methods. The entire system would produce 1 million kilowatts for local area loads, which is approximately enough power to supply most of New England from Boston northward. The $1 billion cost estimate for the project was made more than a decade ago so substantial changes could be expected in that figure. Another significant change since the project was last proposed is the requirement of an environmental impact statement for large federal projects. Very provocative questions would need to be asked about the effect of "detidalizing" the estuary and tide zone organisms whose habitat would be affected by the massive project. Quite a different cycle or regime would be imposed on the organisms including the anadromous fish such as the Atlantic salmon, and these effects should be analyzed. The changes on human communities in the general project area during construction (and afterwards) warrant equally intensive study before the full array of costs-risks-benefits can be put in perspective for rational environmental management and energy demands. Because of the international scope of the Passamaquoddy Bay and Upper Saint John River Project, an additional layer of trade-offs would need to be considered.

The very mention of an environmental impact report tends to irritate many energy company and utility company personnel. As the urbanite considers eastern power projects that have come into conflict with conservationists, the struggle with high voltage transmission lines, most nuclear fueled and fossil fueled electrical generation plants, sulfur dioxide emissions from power plant stacks, and radioactive wastes from nuclear plants have essentially all been dwarfed by the classic controversy between defenders of the scenic Hudson and Consolidated Edison over the Storm King pumped storage facility. That struggle will not be replayed here.

Pumped Storage Facility

The concept of creating an artificial lake and filling it each night in order to produce a head of water to turn turbines for peak load demand is an alternative that has been used in several Midwestern and Eastern situations. The concept of a pumped storage facility makes use of "surplus" power that is available from steam generation units at night when industrial, commercial, and residential demand is low. This power is used to pump water from a nearby natural body of water to a reservoir above the turbines where it can be stored until a peak demand period. The advantages of pumped storage include the immediate availability of on-line electricity, avoiding a time lag of warmup which is characteristic of steam plants. The power company uses "idle" capacity at off peak intervals to refill the reservoir and in a sense store energy for delivery at profitable peak demand periods. Reversible turbines are used for pumping the water up to the reservoir (at night usually) and for generating electricity during daytime peaks. Disadvantages include conflicts in land use regarding the reservoir site, power plant site, and transmission lines and aesthetic considerations. Also, there tend to be eutrophic conditions initiated while the water is in storage plus disturbance to aquatic communities in the vicinity of the outfall or flue area.

To look at the ecology of energy is one of the best ways to understand the ecology of cities. Our total dependency on solar energy is quickly apparent when we trace energy in food to photosynthesis and fossil fuel to the trapped organic material that captured sunlight. Even hydropower is made possible by the sun's heating of water bodies that promotes evaporation (or lifting) of water so that it can fall on higher elevations. This water which, is deposited at elevations above a waterwheel or turbine, is, of course, potential mechanical energy that can be harnessed to do man's

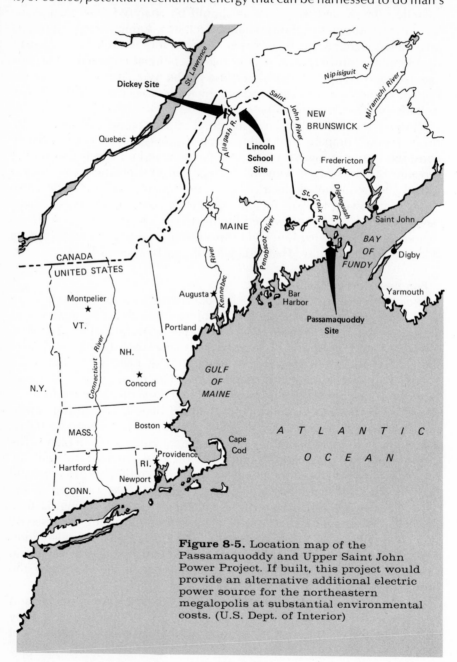

Figure 8-5. Location map of the Passamaquoddy and Upper Saint John Power Project. If built, this project would provide an alternative additional electric power source for the northeastern megalopolis at substantial environmental costs. (U.S. Dept. of Interior)

work. Every observer of urban ecology should also be able to retrace the route that was taken and the forces that were put into motion when an electric light is turned on. We each should be able to do the same exercise with a glass of water of any other daily urban commodity. Let us see where the light bulb route takes us.

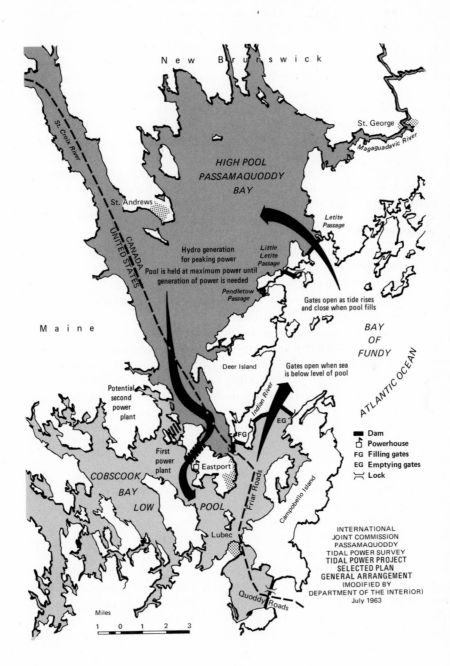

New Brunswick

St. Croix River

St. George

Magaguadavic River

HIGH POOL
PASSAMAQUODDY
BAY

St. Andrews

Letite
Passage

CANADA
UNITED STATES

Hydro generation
for peaking power

Little
Letite
Passage

Pool is held at maximum power until
generation of power is needed

Maine

Pendletow
Passage

Gates open as tide rises
and close when pool fills

BAY
OF
FUNDY

Deer Island

Gates open when sea
is below level of pool

ATLANTIC OCEAN

Potential
second
power
plant

Indian River

EG

FG

First
power
plant

Eastport

Friar Roads

■■ Dam
⌂ Powerhouse
FG Filling gates
EG Emptying gates
⋈ Lock

COBSCOOK
BAY

LOW

POOL

Campobello Island

Lubec

INTERNATIONAL
JOINT COMMISSION
PASSAMAQUODDY
TIDAL POWER SURVEY
**TIDAL POWER PROJECT
SELECTED PLAN
GENERAL ARRANGEMENT**
(MODIFIED BY
DEPARTMENT OF THE INTERIOR)
July 1963

Quoddy Roads

Miles

1 0 1 2 3

The Route of a Light Bulb's Energy

The idea is to retrace the path of the kilowatt or more accurately the 250 watts (and amps) from our light bulb to where it may have come from, emphasizing the ecological and social implications of turning on the light. Our ultimate goal in this mental calisthenic is to carry out an environmental assessment beyond what a utility generally publishes in its literature.

We must remember that when 20 or 30 million people turn on the evening light, the aggregate demand for that one use is millions of kilowatts. Let us assume also that the electrical energy required to illuminate an evening lamp comes off the "on line" supply and does not draw on peaking power that is usually supplied by hydro or other peak power generation sources. The chances are excellent that as we retrace the pathway of the electricity from the lamp back through the wall socket, then the circuit of our apartment, house, or office, we will eventually get out of a subdistribution line. After continuing through transformers, we move to the stepped up voltages, more substations, and into high voltage transmission lines. Eventually our search takes us to a power generation plant whose turbines are most probably driven by fossil fuel.

It is reasonably common to see huge piles of coal at an eastern electric power plant. Up to 40 per cent of the energy in the coal is converted from chemical energy to mechanical energy. The majority of the coal's energy is lost as heat. The coal fires the boilers whose superheated steam drives a turbine to produce electrical energy.

All along the route back to the primary energy source, we could have elaborated on environmental consequences. There are major environmental questions as to where high-voltage transmission lines are placed and whether or not to enlarge present utility line corridors. Conflicts over land use usually arise when proposals are made to place overhead high voltage transmission lines in hinterland areas where recreation or low density residential zoning is in effect. Atmospheric emissions, noise, thermal loads on air and water, and land use all appear in the environmental impact statements of power plants.

But we must return to our energy retracing trip. Our journey had taken us to the coal pile at the power plant. In the past the coal was usually transported by ship, barge, or unitized trains from the mines of Kentucky, West Virginia, Tennessee, Pennsylvania, or Ohio to the power plant in or near the metropolitan load center. To an extent changes in technology and environmental legislation have altered the older patterns. Air quality standards have been established in airsheds with a special emphasis on improving the urban atmosphere. Coal-fired power plants produced considerable loads of carbon monoxide, carbon dioxide, sulfur dioxide, hydrocarbons, and especially particulates requiring electrostatic precipitators, desulfurization processes, and other pollution abatement devices to be

Figure 8-6. Overhead high voltage transmission lines create visual impacts that are usually not in conformity with residential and "natural area" land uses. Aesthetically designed poles and nonreflective materials, which are offered by some utilities, cost up to $40,000 per mile more than traditional transmission construction. (Pacific Gas and Electric Co.)

Figure 8-7. Coal is loaded by conveyor into long trains at this eastern Kentucky mine. (Bethlehem Steel Corporation)

Figure 8-8. Huge front loaders, 28-ton coal trucks, and other heavy duty equipment provide the technological breakthroughs and eliminate labor costs of strip mine coal.

pressed into action. Consequently, a flurry of mine mouth power generation (especially in the Western U.S.) has begun to occur. By producing electrical power at the rural site of an underground or strip mine, large urban populations are spared the *direct* pollutants; furthermore, these "remote" sites often have greater leniency either in the language of the pollution control law or in its enforcement. Other technological breakthroughs include improvement in high voltage electrical power transmission procedures that enable shipment of electricity instead of coal, and a revolution in strip mining equipment, which is having national implications.

Despite these patterns, which exist primarily in western power generation, tremendous electrical energy production, especially in the eastern seaboard, still depends on coal from Appalachia. Even the Tennessee Valley Authority with its vast network of hydroelectric plants, and more recently the nuclear power plants, produces over 50 per cent of its electrical energy from coal ruthlessly strip mined in Appalachia as well as in Montana and Wyoming. Thus we have retraced the energy to light our lamp, in this quasihypothetical situation, back to a coal mine in eastern Kentucky or West Virginia, both of which happen to be among the top coal producing states in the United States. Since the greater percentage of coal mined today is strip mined,

Figure 8-9. Many residents of the eastern megalopolis tend to forget that the energy for their lights, air conditioners, appliances, and other conveniences very likely came from a coal strip mine similar to the one above this eastern Kentucky cabin.

we shall look at some of the environmental costs of this operation, remembering that the word *environmental* as used here includes social, political, economic, and ecological implications.

As one begins to understand the ecology of energy, one is struck by the complexity of forces that are at work to supply an urban region with the power it uses. Our improbable journey has taken us to the coal counties of the Cumberland plateau. It is primarily resource areas such as the Cumberland plateau out of which our cities are built and powered. Timber barons logged the virgin forests to help build eastern cities in the eighteenth and nineteenth centuries. High-grade coal from the hinterlands of Appalachia produced the coke and coal for Pittsburgh's steel mills and coking ovens which in turn helped produce much of the steel and other urban material for our present twentieth century East Coast megalopolis. And today the lights that shine from Maine to Florida are glowing, in part, from energy taken from coal counties such as those in the Cumberland plateau. The verb *taken* may sound a little strong so perhaps we should look back to see what laid the foundation for an almost parasitic relationship that may exist between a huge eastern city and her energy source.

Figure 8-10. Until about 1960 almost all the coal mining in the Appalachian mountain chain was underground or deep mining. A five-man operation keeps this mine producing under conditions of economic uncertainty and questionable safety. The coal buggy is driven into the $3\frac{1}{2}$ foot high tunnel that goes into the mountain for 1,800 feet.

Figure 8-11. Up to 40 tons of coal a day are brought out of this underground mine from a seam 38 inches thick. Notice the inoperative ventilation fan in the background.

290

The Appalachian Story

In the early industrialization period of the East, timber and mining company representatives obtained timber and mining privileges from land owners, many of who were illiterate, by using a legal instrument called the "broad form" deed. When the land owner signed such a deed, in most cases, he was giving the mineral rights of his land to the mining company for sometimes as little as $.10 to $.50 per acre, a disgracefully cheap price for coal. To compound the loss to those original land owners, oil and gas have recently been tapped below the coal seams. Other provisions of the deed often included language in fine print which said that the mining company would not be held liable for damage done to surface conditions, water resources, or other factors as a result of the mining activity. Records in the county deeds office in the poorer counties show that many of the broad forms were signed with an "X."

One must keep in mind that up until about 1960 almost all coal mining in the Cumberland plateau was underground or deep mining. A small opening was created in the hillside and shafts penetrated the seams of coal that enabled workmen with pick and shovel to extract the layers of bituminous coal. The working conditions ranged from backbreaking and very hazardous to deadly with the "built in" risks of cave-ins, methane explosions, and black lung disease. A West Virginia Coal Association spokesman testified than not enough is known about pneumoconiosis to justify "hasty action" although the U.S. Public Health Service has called black lung

Figure 8-12. The life of the underground coal miner is always periless—this one is just a little more so, what with the threat of black lung disease, unemployment, and no compensation for his stripped land in the background.

"serious and of unrecognized magnitude," with one hundred thousand miners currently affected. The United States was the last major coal-producing nation to enact an official government standard for coal-mine dust.

Further changes took place when modernized mining equipment replaced miners and increased coal output. Then the 1969 Federal Coal Mine Health and Safety Act was passed revising the federal code of health and safety regulations for the nation's coal miners, improving the miners' conditions but also forcing marginal deep mine operations to close. The shift became conspicuous from underground mining to surface or strip mining but the broad form deed was still in effect.

In order to meet the urban power demand, it was shown that the soil and rock *overburden* could be removed exposing the horizontal seams of coal using equipment exactly like that used for massive road construction. In some cases several hundred feet of overburden were bulldozed from the top of a mountain and then the exposed coal was scraped up by huge front loaders, dumped in twenty four-ton coal trucks, and taken to tipples for railroad distribution out of the "hollows."

In most strip mining operations in the mountains, the mountainside is cut open to expose a seam of coal that is commonly twenty four to forty two inches thick. A contour terrace is cut and the vegetation, soil, and rock are pushed down the hillside. Large augers are moved to the seam and

Figure 8-13. In the larger underground coal mines automated equipment such as this continuous mining machine speeds the extraction process. Notice the whitish appearance created by the application of rock dust to reduce coal dust dangers. This 42-inch high working area is 4,500 feet underground near the West Virginia-eastern Kentucky border. (Bethlehem Steel Corporation)

Figure 8-14. An auger bores into the coal seam and pulls the coal out for loading into trucks. The overburden is cleared away in order to allow new penetrations of the auger into the horizontal coal seam. Holes are usually backfilled to reduce acid mine drainage problems. (Bethlehem Steel Corporation)

the drills withdraw up to 60 per cent of the coal from deep within the hillside. Once the mining operation has moved on it is extremely difficult to reclaim the mountainside. Some soil technicians say it is totally impractical on slopes with a gradient greater than 15 or 20 per cent. As one might guess, when the topsoil and vegetation are not returned to the scar left by a strip mine, several environmental problems set in.

When the rains come to the Cumberland plateau, which receives up to seventy inches per year, the exposed soil materials are carried into the valleys below. Mountainsides literally move—some so quickly that cabins are swept away. Farmland in the valley bottoms are inundated by increased flooding, and channels and reservoirs fill with silt at accelerated rates. Water passing over exposed mine workings combines with the sulfurous oxides and creates problems of acid mine drainage. However, the settlers in the "hollows" are powerless to stop such ruin, for their great grandfathers signed away their mineral rights in a *broad form deed* for perhaps $.50 an acre while allowing a coal company over the years to extract coal with an average value of $30,000 from each acre. Even with the recent and very modest severance taxes, the ravages to human pride and environmental abuse continue. Back roads used by the mining trucks crumble away, and school and medical facilities in the area are among the worst in the United States. The Kentucky coal counties of Perry, Letcher, Harlan, Pike, and Knott have led the nation in adult illiteracy, highest birthrate, highest per capita **293**

294 welfare payments, highest unemployment, and other indicators of social costs promulgated by chronic economic, political, and environmental disruptions in the presence of one of the richest natural resource regions in North America. By looking at the ecology of energy one uncovers the unhappy inequities that take place when the local people do not have an effective voice in managing their local resources.

In fact, the people of the Cumberland plateau exhibit a high percentage of land ownership, but the mineral rights are in the hands of oil, coal, gas, steel, and railroad companies headquartered in the large Eastern cities. As the local land owner continues to pay taxes on his land ruined by strip mining, the energy conglomerates inform the urban consumer that there is an energy crisis. What we don't hear about are the social costs of producing more and more elctricity. What is really needed is a full enforceable campaign by the private and public sector on how to conserve our total energy resources. In the meantime, the lamp burns on and very little effort has been made to minimize the social costs of mineral extraction or to improve the efficiency of energy consumption in metropolitan areas. Still less attention is placed on alternatives to fossil fuels such as hydrogen-fuel energy sources, solar, breeder, and fusion or even supplemental sources available in small percentages from tidal, wind, and *geothermal* sources.

Looking Toward the Future

What will it take for the urban public of the Eastern Seaboard, or for that matter the public anywhere, to become motivated to make better use of the present energy resource? It is puzzling to observe that a relatively insignificant amount of pressure has been put on the consumer by the utilities or by governmental energy regulatory bodies to conserve electricity. By "bodies" are meant the state public service and utility commissions, the Federal Power Commission, the Atomic Energy Commission, the Bureau of Mines, and the federal and state environmental protection agencies. Most of the public and private energy research money is going into oil shale extraction, nuclear "stimulation" of natural gas, gasification of coal, increased imports, more complete extraction through oil field *unitization,* strip mining, and recharging old gas and oil fields.

If a true energy crisis is imminent, much more coordinated and coercive action is warranted by public agencies—that is, if they have the long-term welfare of the general public and the nation as a whole in mind and not only the vested interests of the energy industry. If there is truly a threat to the health of our environment and our economy due either to an inability to distribute electricity or to produce energy from presently known sources, then some rather vigorous national policies and programs should be put into motion.

Certainly the Eastern Seaboard region makes a prime location to experiment with special efficiencies that can accrue by the placement of jobs,

Figure 8-15. Here is a strip mine ten years after it had been reclaimed. Rains and the steep gradient resulted in a landslide. This illustrates the problem of strip mine reclamation on steep slopes.

Figure 8-16. Some energy-related companies forget about the social costs external to their immediate mine, well, or other site of operation. Coal trucks often leave local roads in a sad state of disrepair after the mines close.

Figure 8-17. The strip mines of the eastern United States give most of their coal to steam plants that supply electricity for the Eastern Seaboard region. Most eastern and midwestern urban electric customers have never seen the full impact of that service on the people and the land of the Cumberland Plateau and other coal-producing areas. Notice the 60-foot exposed head wall from an old strip mine and how the overburden was bulldozed down the slope. If a pasture could be established on the huge terraces, it might be a good place to raise beef cattle!

Figure 8-18. Perhaps supplementary wind energy will be rediscovered as a power source in energy-short areas like the eastern megalopolis. On the Greek island of Mykonos these windmills continue to grind grain and intrigue American visitors.

leisure activity, and the location of commercial centers and residential units in closer proximity to one another so that energy consumed by transportation can be reduced. Bonuses should be given to those who use the most energy-efficient and environmentally conscientious modes of transportation. Dr. Paul Yambert of Southern Illinois University points out that federal income tax actually penalizes small (four-cylinder) car ownership. We should have given out penalties long ago to energy-inefficient systems when reasonable substitutes are available. The East Coast, and all of the United States for that matter, should place a tax on horsepower in the automobile with their 25 per cent (or less) efficient engines as mentioned earlier. Mandatory, effective commercial and residential insulation should be required for every structure, old and new, if there is really an energy crisis.

Simple innovations are possible to immediately implement energy savings: (1) Consider either a ban or a redesign of fireplace construction. Think for a moment of the 85 per cent heat loss up the chimney that in turn sucks more cold air into the room and quickly up the flue. (2) Forbid rapid acceleration of motor vehicles from a stopped position and high speeds, which are two of the least efficient phases in the operation of a motor vehicle. Gradual decelerations should also be used whenever possible. (3) One example is the combustion of organic waste whose highest value could be for hot water or heat production in densely populated neighborhoods or center city areas. Prototypes of vacuum tube collection and garbage incineration systems have been in operation more than a decade in the Stockholm suburb of Sundbyberg. Improved versions have been incorporated in apartment complexes in Hallonbergen, Storskorgen, Sollentuna, Osterhaninge (3,900 apartments), and Bagarmorsen. At local levels, other less complex procedures are available, but seldom pursued such as the use of trees and shrubs to cool living and working areas in the summer and to moderate the winter cold, especially when combined with optimal sun

Figure 8-19. The installation of insulation as shown in this new home saves energy in two ways: by reducing the need for air conditioning in hot periods and by reducing the need for extravagant heating in the cold season. Generous insulation also provides acoustical advantages from external noise conditions.

298   exposure (for example, wide south-facing windows) in designs and positions for homes.

If there is truly a national energy crisis, substantial numbers of people who have flexibility in their place of residence, place of work, or place of recreation could be given special incentives to migrate to the northern or cooler portions of the Eastern Seaboard region when higher energy demands are placed on air conditioning and other artificial cooling systems in the warmer or southern Atlantic Coast states. Similarly when heavy demands are placed on energy for space heating and other severe cold weather energy needs, special incentives would go to those who traveled southward where less energy would be required for heating and other cold weather demands. It is assumed that the "energy-saving migrants" will use the most energy-efficient mass transit systems available. At the moment the author sees almost no effort devoted to consumer education about what colors of cars or houses are most energy-efficient nor does he see any pricing mechanisms to discourage wasteful electrical consumption (the largest power consumers pay the smallest unit price for electricity) as we all "live better electrically."

When the energy crisis does come, however, it will come first to the large megalopolitan areas—undoubtedly the Eastern Seaboard region. It may come in contrived shortages or breakdowns because of poor distribution and generation planning. Often that does take place when the needs for profit come before the real needs of people. Whether or not the power brownouts or grayouts are contrived or real, they will undoubtedly force up the price of electricity (especially to the smallest consumers) in order to guarantee profits to the stockholders of the "public" utilities. The urban populations that are far removed from the primary energy sources and almost totally dependent upon electrical energy will be the most vulnerable in the event of a real shortage or real energy crisis.

As one contemplates future human settlements, it is clear that energy resources serve as a major integrative input. The basic ekistic elements of Nature, Man, Society, Shells, and Networks each are involved with the production, distribution, and recycling of energy in its multiple forms from a Kreb's cycle to a hydropower project. The future success of urban entities will depend on how effectively energy is used and conserved. Perhaps it will take either a false or a real crisis of national proportions before we squarely address the energy resource questions in our consumption-oriented, postindustrialized energy-dependent nation of cities. Until then it would be prudent for us all to revise our habits now in order to live better a little less electrically.

Mineral Resources

Human Settlements as Mineral Resource Magnets

For more than eight thousand years, man has concentrated mineral resources from the hinterland into his towns, villages, and cities. Only lately has the accumulation of minerals (metals, fuels, building materials) in the gigantic metropolis grown to a size that reminds the urban-surburban dweller that a *finite* resource eventually requires substitution, recycling, and reduction of consumptive uses.

Look around any place where man has established a permanent settlement. What mineral resources are represented? The ingredients of every towering urban structure were extracted from mines, quarries, and gravel pits. And for every glimmering light in the urban night, there is a cost imposed somewhere else on the earth's landscape. The electricity needed to make the tungsten filament glow is generated from a fossil fuel or from hydropower produced by a dammed river valley or flooded canyon. The metal components may have come from a western mine and the glass for the bulb may have once been part of a sand dune.

The reader's eye does not have to wander off this page for him to see the use of minerals, for the ink on every printed page requires minerals for processing and production. The paper itself in its transformation from poplar and spruce logs or even recycled paper required an incredible inventory of minerals including metals—especially when one considers the chemistry of the paper and the loading, cooking, screening, drying, wrapping, packaging, and marketing steps that depend upon massive paper mill machinery.

The illustration of metallic and other mineral resources that were gath-   **299** ered together to produce the common printed page serves to focus on the overall problem of mineral resource management in terms of urbanites. As population migration continues to move toward large metropolitan areas in the U.S. and elsewhere, the concomitant flow of mineral resources required to sustain the urban population is overlooked as other less subtle events dominate the public's attention. Furthermore, the large city dweller is usually so insulated from the mine and the metallurgical processing operations that he never recognized some of the basic dilemmas of mineral resource depletion.

The Growing Mineral Crisis

Metropolitan man is well removed from the 30,000 to 32,000 nonfatal mine accidents and the 475 to 500 mine disaster fatalities that occur annually in the United States. Because the metals and other minerals glisten about the urban dweller in apparent excess, he undoubtedly fails to recognize the critical shortages that the United States faces in several minerals. These same critical minerals in many cases seem to occur almost naturally in the superstructure of American human settlements.

The *First Annual Report of the Council on Environmental Quality* speaks of our diminishing minerals:[1]

"Even taking into account such economic factors as increased prices with decreasing availability, it would appear at present that the quantities of platinum, gold, zinc, and lead are not sufficient to meet demands. At the present rate of expansion, silver, tin, and uranium may be in short supply even at higher prices by the turn of the century. By the year 2050, several other minerals may be exhausted if the current rate of consumption continues."

In the spring of 1972, a report for The Club of Rome's Project on The Predicament of Mankind substantiated many of the fears espoused by the environmentalists and so-called doomsday ecologists. What the M.I.T. dynamic systems researchers did was to mix the inputs of population, growth rates, pollution, technology, and naturally available resources. Although this author takes exception with several procedures and findings, he agrees with their projections which emphasize the critical shortages of nonrenewable resources, especially metals and minerals. An inspection of Table 9-1 shows the expected period of resource availability under several potential use patterns.

Table 9-1 lists some of the more important mineral and fuel resources, the vital raw materials for today's major industrial processes. The number following each resource in column 3 is the static reserve index, or the number of years present known reserves of that resource (listed in column 2) will last at the *current* rate

[1]*First Annual Report of the Council on Environmental Quality* (Washington, D.C., U.S. Government Printing Office, 1970), p. 158.

Table 9-1. Nonrenewable Natural Resources[1]

1	2	3	4			5	6	7	8	9	10
	Known Global Reserves[a]	Static Index (years)[b]	Projected Rate of Growth (% per Year)[c] High Av. Low			Exponential Index (years)[d]	Exponential Index Calculated Using 5 Times Known Reserves (years)[e]	Countries or Areas with Highest Reserves (% of world total)[f]	Prime Producers (% of world total)[g]	Prime Consumers (% of world total)[h]	US Consumption as % of World Total[i]
Resource			High	Av.	Low						
Aluminum	1.17×10^9 tons[j]	100	7.7	6.4	5.1	31	55	Australia (33) Guinea (20) Jamaica (10)	Jamaica (19) Surinam (12)	US (42) USSR (12)	42
Chromium	7.75×10^8 tons	420	3.3	2.6	2.0	95	154	Rep. of South Africa (75)	USSR (30) Turkey (10)		19
Coal	5×10^{12} tons	2300	5.3	4.1	3.0[k]	111	150	US (32) USSR- China (53)	USSR (20) US (13)		44
Cobalt	4.8×10^9 lbs	110	2.0	1.5	1.0	60	148	Rep. of Congo (31) Zambia (16)	Rep. of Congo (51)		32
Copper	308×10^6 tons	36	5.8	4.6	3.4	21	48	US (28) Chile (19)	US (20) USSR (15) Zambia (13)	US (33) USSR (13) Japan (11)	33
Gold	353×10^6 troy oz	11	4.8	4.1	3.4[l]	9	29	Rep. of South Africa (40)	Rep. of South Africa (77) Canada (6)		26
Iron	1×10^{11} tons	240	2.3	1.8	1.3	93	173	USSR (33) S. Am. (18) Canada (14)	USSR (25) US (14)	US (28) USSR (24) W. Germany (7)	28

Table 9-1. (continued)

Resource	Known Global Reserves[a]	Static Index (years)[b]	Projected Rate of Growth (% per Year)[c] High Av. Low			Exponential Index (years)[d]	Exponential Index Calculated Using 5 Times Known Reserves (years)[e]	Countries or Areas with Highest Reserves (% of world total)[f]	Prime Producers (% of world total)[g]	Prime Consumers (% of world total)[h]	US Consumption as % of World Total[i]
Lead	91×10^6 tons	26	2.4	2.0	1.7	21	64	US (39)	USSR (13) Australia (13) Canada (11)	US (25) USSR (13) W. Germany (11)	25
Manganese	8×10^8 tons	97	3.5	2.9	2.4	46	94	Rep. of South Africa (38) USSR (25)	USSR (34) Brazil (13) Rep. of South Africa (13)		14
Mercury	3.34×10^6 flasks	13	3.1	2.6	2.2	13	41	Spain (30) Italy (21)	Spain (22) Italy (21) USSR (18)		24
Molybdenum	10.8×10^9 lbs	79	5.0	4.5	4.0	34	65	US (58) USSR (20)	US (64) Canada (14)		40
Natural Gas	1.14×10^{15} cu ft	38	5.5	4.7	3.9	22	49	US (25) USSR (13)	US (58) USSR (18)		63
Nickel	147×10^9 lbs	150	4.0	3.4	2.8	53	96	Cuba (25) New Caledonia (22) USSR (14) Canada (14)	Canada (42) New Caledonia (28) USSR (16)		38
Petroleum	455×10^9 bbls	31	4.9	3.9	2.9	20	50	Saudi Arabia (17) Kuwait (15)	US (23) USSR (16)	US (33) USSR (12) Japan (6)	33
Platinum Group[m]	429×10^6 troy oz	130	4.5	3.8	3.1	47	85	Rep. of South Africa (47) USSR (47)	USSR (59)		31

							Communist Countries (36) US (24)	Canada (20) Mexico (17) Peru (16)	US (26) W. Germany (11)	42	26
Silver	5.5 × 10⁹ troy oz	16	4.0	2.7	1.5	13	Communist Countries (36) US (24)	Canada (20) Mexico (17) Peru (16)	US (26) W. Germany (11)	42	26
Tin	4.3 × 10⁶ lg tons	17	2.3	1.1	0	15	Thailand (33) Malaysia (14)	Malaysia (41) Bolivia (16) Thailand (13)	US (24) Japan (14)	61	24
Tungsten	2.9 × 10⁹ lbs	40	2.9	2.5	2.1	28	China (73)	China (25) USSR (19) US (14)		72	22
Zinc	123 × 10⁶ tons	23	3.3	2.9	2.5	18	US (27) Canada (20)	Canada (23) USSR (11) US (8)	US (26) Japan (13) USSR (11)	50	26

[a] SOURCE: US Bureau of Mines, *Mineral Facts and Problems, 1970* (Washington, DC: Government Printing Office, 1970).

[b] The number of years known global reserves will last at current global consumption. Calculated by dividing known reserves (column 2) by the current annual consumption (US Bureau of Mines, *Mineral Facts and Problems, 1970*).

[c] SOURCE: US Bureau of Mines, *Mineral Facts and Problems, 1970*.

[d] The number of years known global reserves will last with consumption growing exponentially at the average annual rate of growth. Calculated by the formula

$$\text{exponential index} = \frac{\ln\left((r \cdot s) + 1\right)}{r}$$

where r = average rate of growth from column 4
s = static index from column 3.

[e] The number of years that five times known global reserves will last with consumption growing exponentially at the average annual rate of growth. Calculated from the above formula with 5s in place of s.

[f] SOURCE: US Bureau of Mines, *Mineral Facts and Problems, 1970*.

[g] SOURCE: UN Department of Economic and Social Affairs, *Statistical Yearbook 1969* (New York: United Nations, 1970).

[h] SOURCES: *Yearbook of the American Bureau of Metal Statistics 1970* (York, Pa.: Maple Press, 1970).
World Petroleum Report (New York: Mona Palmer Publishing, 1968).
UN Economic Commission for Europe, *The World Market for Iron Ore* (New York: United Nations, 1968).
US Bureau of Mines, *Mineral Facts and Problems, 1970*.

[i] SOURCE: US Bureau of Mines, *Mineral Facts and Problems, 1970*.

[j] Bauxite expressed in aluminum equivalent.

[k] US Bureau of Mines contingency forecasts, based on assumptions that coal will be used to synthesize gas and liquid fuels.

[l] Includes US Bureau of Mines estimates of gold demand for hoarding.

[m] The platinum group metals are platinum, palladium, iridium, osmium, rhodium, and ruthenium.

ADDITIONAL SOURCES:
P. T. Flawn, *Mineral Resources* (Skokie, Ill.: Rand McNally, 1966).
Metal Statistics (Somerset, NJ: American Metal Market Company, 1970).
US Bureau of Mines, *Commodity Data Summary* (Washington, DC: Government Printing Office, January 1971).

[1] Donella H. Meadows; Dennis L. Meadows, Jorgen Randers, William W. Behrens, III, *The Limits to Growth*, A Potomac Associates Book (New York: Universe Books, 1972), pp. 56–60.

of usage. This static index is the measure normally used to express future resource availability. Underlying the static index are several assumptions, one of which is that the usage rate will remain constant.

But column 4 in Table 9-1 shows that the world usage rate of every natural resource is growing exponentially. For many resources the usage rate is growing even faster than the population, indicating both that more people are consuming resources each year and also that the average consumption per person is increasing each year. In other words, the *exponential growth curve* of resource consumption is driven by both the positive *feedback loops* of population growth and of capital growth.

We might define a new index, an 'exponential reserve index,' which gives the probable lifetime of each resource, assuming that the current growth rate in consumption will continue. We have included this index in column 5 of Table 9-1. We have also calculated an exponential index on the assumption that our present known reserves of each resource can be expanded fivefold by new discoveries. This index is shown in column 6. . . . The last four columns of Table 9-1 show clearly that the industrialized, consuming countries are heavily dependent on a network of international agreements with the producing countries for the supply of raw materials essential to their industrial base.[2]

The Club of Rome report has special relevance to our discussion on Rocky Mountain mineral problems for several reasons:

1. Most of the minerals that face serious shortages at present use rates have substantial reserves in the Rocky Mountain states. Under the M.I.T. formula, the following minerals are shown with the years remaining before their depletion at current rates: Coal (111 years), Copper (21 years), Gold (9 years), Molybdenum (34 years), Natural Gas (22 years), Petroleum (20 years), Silver (13 years), and Tungsten (28 years).

One of the devastating revelations that has emerged from the M.I.T. studies and other indexes that monitor and project growth patterns in the exponential rate at which resources are being used in the United States.

Normally one thinks of growth in terms of linear growth—increasing a quantity by a constant amount in a constant time period. To illustrate, a plant that grows one inch every three months is exhibiting linear growth —so is a family that puts $1 a week into a teapot saving the fund for a rainy day. In other words, the amount of increase is not affected by the present size of the plant or amount of money already saved.

If this same plant, however, adds 15 per cent of its total height every three months, or if the same family puts their weekly $1 into a savings account drawing 5 per cent interest quarterly, then exponential growth is involved. That is, the quantity is increasing by a constant percentage of the whole in a constant time period. Exponential growth in both cases results in an increase in the total amount that is much faster than linear growth. Such exponential growth is a common phenomenon in many worldwide systems.

[2]Donella H. Meadows, Dennis L. Meadows, Jorgen Randers, William W. Behrens, III, *The Limits to Growth,* A Potomac Associates Book (New York: Universe Books, 1972).

In *The Limits to Growth* one finds a fascinating French riddle that illustrates the startling suddenness with which exponential growth produces a saturation situation that is of course the theoretical limit to growth.[3] According to the riddle, a water lily is growing on your pond. Doubling in size each day, the plant will cover the pond in thirty days if allowed to grow unchecked. You decide to cut it back when it covers half the pond. When will that be? On the twenty-ninth day, of course. You have one day to save your pond.

If the resource is replenishable or renewable over the short run (that is, water, timber, wildlife) the consumer and resource managers have some lead time to modify their behavior before the reproductive potential or critical mass of the resource base is depleted beyond recovery. With metals and fossil fuels, when the exponential consumption curve slopes toward the vertical with a fixed quantity or limit involved, a suicide course is in motion.

Not only are more suburbanites now using more energy, more metals, and other nonreplenishable minerals in the 1970's, but they are also using them at increasingly faster rates either in spite of or in ignorance of the existing critical mineral shortages. An individual or a nation geared to the growth rates currently in vogue in the United States cannot afford to wait and slow down uses until the supply is 50 per cent depleted. The exponential use rates of minerals include our current uses. If we wait until these minerals are near the point of depletion, we simply will not have the reaction or lead time to compensate for the elimination or demise of a given resource. Furthermore, with several critical metallic resources phasing out of economic reach at about the same time period, additional strain will be placed on remaining resources that will be used with increasing exponential rates! What this suggests is that we must use a new index of resource use and availability. Instead of a static reserve figure, the current growth rate in consumption should be shown in a way that characterizes the pattern of depletion over selected time intervals. When this is done, a more appropriate pricing mechanism could work to reflect true scarcities of specific mineral resources. Instead of rapidly depleting metals being subsidized by other materials that make up a composite commodity—that is an automobile, house, or major appliance—the cost of the metal, let us say copper, should show true market value in order to persuade management to explore substitutes, less costly processing, recycling, and salvage, or beneficiation (the upgrading of low grade ore). The situation with copper is particularly delicate because substantial shifts in the ownership of production facilities have taken place. Within the last four years American control of copper production on foreign soil has changed from 60 per cent to 40 per cent and may continue to diminish. There is a real possibility that more national or local (foreign) control will occur in mineral industries that would erode the position of U.S. dominance over import policies of

[3] Ibid., p. 29.

strategically needed minerals including fossil fuels. Obviously the physical, political, and economic factors are interrelated and as scarcities increase, so do the difficulties of resolving the problem on a shortened period of time.

2. The "bonanza approach" to mineral extraction still prevails in most of the western mining communities and far too little attention has been given to the findings of the Club of Rome Report by the directly affected residents of the Rocky Mountain region. Far greater costs should be placed on the removal of nonreplenishable resources in order that, after the mines or wells close, the region from whence the quick profits are made can sustain itself through diversification of other industry, environmental recovery of mine sites and processing centers, and through other efforts.

3. *The Limits to Growth* shows how prices on minerals rise sharply as their supply nears exhaustion. The largest mining companies or those that are subsidiaries of large corporate conglomerates will be able to remain in operation longer than locally owned operations. As the value of silver, copper, tungsten, and molybdenum increases, one may expect a wider margin of profit, part of which could be used for environmental enhancement. However, under the circumstances of extracting the last quantities of a nonreplenishable resource, the traditional practice has been to take the last crumbs with the least cost. In such cases the mineral operator behaves very much like the slum landlord whose condemned tenament is soon to be emptied by an urban renewal project. Substitutes are provided, but those who have borne the costs, whether it be excessive rents, elimination of mining jobs, or heavy environmental degradation, are seldom the benefactors.

The experience of Appalachian mining has direct lessons for miners of the Rocky Mountain region. Without *severance taxes,* which yield generous revenues to small owners, strict land control measures, air- and water-pollution enforcement, and other factors that help reflect the long-term costs of mineral extraction, large portions of the Rocky Mountain states will be "giving away" minerals to the metropolitan consumers at heavily subsidized prices. Stated differently, when the various pollution control measures are not enforced, the pollution costs fall upon the environment—usually in terms of mine safety conditions, spoilbank pollution of streams, air pollution created by smelters, and others. If most of the pollution costs were paid by the producer and consumer as a part of the price of the product, a more environmentally sound, economically efficient, and probably more socially equitable practice would be initiated. In areas of the Western United States where recreation opportunities and aesthetic conditions of high quality air and water have a unique dollar value, it is all the more urgent for mineral extraction activities to reflect the price of environmental quality management.

4. A final comment on *The Limits to Growth* analysis is to raise a point that was not discussed in that book and for that matter is a seldom mentioned consideration. Mineral consumption (as well as that of energy, food,

Figure 9-1. At 11,000-foot Climax, Colorado, settling ponds and the precipitate from the nearby molybdenum mine fill alpine valleys hundreds of feet deep with spent wastes. The urban appetite for minerals often produces a conflict with wilderness recreation land uses near the point of extraction and processing.

and fiber) proceeds at its greatest rates in urban regions, and urban residents also exercise the greatest control over mineral exploitation. Yet they have the least information and the least incentive to correct the problems at the production site of the process. Since most metals can be recycled and are concentrated during and after use in metropolitan areas, the urban consumer has special opportunities to conserve such mineral resources by utilizing the ecological concept of recycling.

Who remembers the Paley Commission Report of 1952 that was devoted to an analysis on the past, present, and anticipated future of American mineral supplies? More formally this task force was called the President's Materials Policy Commission and its study produced a five volume document entitled "Resources for Freedom." Of course, some of the impetus for this work, as suggested by its title, was to inventory critical mineral shortages and future needs as the result of excessive resource exploitation during World War II. As then, the United States still dominates the stage as the world's single largest minerals consumer; however, underdeveloped nations now are rapidly industrializing. Furthermore, those nations that were industrial giants prior to World War II have now asserted major positions on mineral demands and are increasing their demand for energy and minerals at rates faster than the United States.

There is still another shift that has deep environmental implications for the consumer as well as the extractor and producer of minerals. It can be described in terms of new geographic areas that have equaled or surpassed previous mineral production sites. The Arctic land masses, Australia, Africa, and the Near East have experienced extremely rapid increases in their production rates since World War II. The increasing demand imposed by the urban American's material standard of living promulgates the worldwide mineral exploration and production.

Furthermore, the United States' rapidly increasing demands for mineral resources have forced her to become much more dependent on foreign mineral imports than she was during World War II or in 1950. The United States has shifted away from metal self-sufficiency and concentration on indigenous fossil fuel reserves to very substantial reliance on foreign sources. Figures showing U.S. consumption as a percentage of the world's total consumption of mineral resources are worthy of special attention. The profound question is how much longer the United States can continue to consume 44 per cent of the world's annual production of coal, 42 per cent of its aluminum, 38 per cent of its nickel, 33 per cent of its copper, 40 per cent of its molybdenum, 31 per cent of its platinum (and of that nearly 60 per cent comes from Russia), 33 per cent of its petroleum, and a whopping 63 per cent of the world's yearly supply of natural gas.[4]

Of all the groups of resources in the United States, the urban dweller is undoubtedly very ignorant about the management of mineral resources. From years of consuming metals of relative abundance to a time of large dependency on imported strategic minerals, a sharp change has taken place in the American position of mineral exports and imports.

For example, for twenty-five years, most assessments about mineral use were in annual value of minerals produced and the position of the United States in terms of its self-sufficiency. No mention was ever made of environmental considerations. Very little indeed was written about conservation practices and industry and government said nothing to the urbanite about real and potential problems.

Mineral self-sufficiency is determined by a comparison of production and consumption over a given period. Most fossil fuels, metals, and other minerals are listed according to the quantity and quality of the raw material resource. These reserves are exploitable under prevailing conditions, particularly the factors of cost and price. The picture of relative self-sufficiency compared to other consumers and producers on the world market is not always a case of resource availability. Rather it is an indication of the economic availability of mineral resources in the United States relative to other producers and consumers. Other factors sometimes play a role in mineral self-sufficiency such as technological advancements, available labor, capital, equipment, or even installed capacity, but market supply and demand conditions are the dominant forces.

A standard practice thirty years ago was to show a chart of perhaps forty industrial minerals. In fact, at that time, the United States exceeded her production over consumption in about eleven mineral commodities. The minerals of favorable balance up until 1940 included (in order of most favorable balance) molybdenum, magnesium, phosphate rock, sulfur, helium, petroleum, copper, bituminous coal, anthracite coal, salt, and natural gas. The United States produced between 50 per cent and 100 per cent of her 1940 consumption of the following minerals: iron ore, zinc, fluorspar, lead, rutile (the dioxide of titanium), nitrates, bismuth, mercury, potash, cadmium, bauxite, and vanadium.

[4] Ibid., pp. 56–59.

During the subsequent thirty-year period of continued urbanization, shifts in industrial activities, and several war programs, a sharp change in the "self-sufficiency" minerals has occurred. Warnings had been sounded to expect heavier dependence on foreign mineral imports, and a very interesting set of reactions were set into motion as the demands increased on the minerals that the United States was exporting. Increased pressure was also put upon those minerals that were used in partial and complete dependence on foreign sources.

In 1948 the following minerals came either totally or primarily from foreign nations. As they are listed, consider their everyday uses: chromite, ferro-grade manganese, nickel, platinum, tin, industrial diamonds, quartz crystals, asbestos, cobalt, graphite, arsenic, bismuth, cadium, copper, iron ore, lead, mercury, tantalum, tungsten, zinc, fluorspar, antimony, vanadium, high grade bauxite, and strategic mica.

It should be made clear that the United States has not used up all of these minerals. It is simply more profitable to obtain these minerals from other countries than to rely heavily on U.S. deposits that have higher extraction and/or processing costs. The costs are higher for a variety of reasons: labor, outdated equipment, transportation, low-grade deposits that would require expensive beneficiation, abundance of substitutes, cost of getting to the most difficult deposits such as the steeply pitched anthracite coal seams, and, most recently, the costs associated with increased safety regulations and environmental controls. Because of the multiplicity of cost factors, it is dangerous to generalize that one variable or another is responsible for forcing an American mine to close down.

CASE IN POINT:
THE ROCKY MOUNTAIN REGION

When strikes of oil, gold, silver, tungsten, uranium and other minerals are announced, the word spreads like wildfire and the deposit is often overrun with prospectors who hope to "get rich quick" and then clear out. Historically, the Rocky Mountain region has been characterized by one mineral bonanza after another. The rise and fall of mining settlements from Montana to New Mexico and Arizona are commonplace in the annals of the developing Western frontier. Name a precious or strategic mineral and undoubtedly one can find examples of feverish strikes in the Rocky Mountain empire. Cripple Creek, Colorado, experienced gold fever equivalent to that of the California Gold Rush. Copper remains king in the open pits of Montana. And "The Unsinkable Molly Brown" is testimony to Leadville, Colorado's silver, lead, and now molybdenum strikes that are unequaled anywhere in the world.

Boom towns and ghost towns are created almost overnight by the

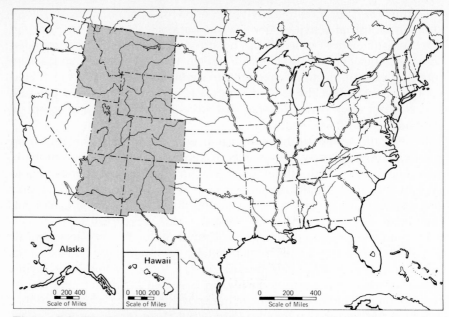

Figure 9-2. The Rocky Mountain region serves as an illustrative area for the discussion of mineral resources. In this area of small urban populations the major mineral extraction activity takes place. Here also are most of America's "boom and bust" towns.

Figure 9-3. Tucked away in the ridges and valleys of the Rocky Mountain region are thousands of ghost towns like Zortman, Montana. Some of them reopen periodically as the price of minerals fluctuates. These mining camps are examples of "extraction communities" mentioned in Chapter 1 in a discussion of urban trophic levels. (Montana Chamber of Commerce)

Figure 9-4. Warren, Idaho, was a booming mining town 100 years ago. Today it is a ghost town tucked away in an Idaho wilderness area in the central part of the state. (Idaho Dept. of Commerce and Development)

changing prices of minerals. Folklore and historical accounts are overflowing with examples. More commonly however, the costs of safety and environmental controls today preclude a small, independent operator from opening a new operation or continuing an old one. Even the largest corporations are thinking two or three times before embarking on an extractive program that has high environmental costs. The hesitancy of the various consortiums of petroleum companies (with giant members such as Atlantic Richfield, Union Oil, Texaco, American Oil, and Gulf) to develop and even fully explore the huge oil shale deposits of Colorado, Wyoming, and Utah well illustrates the impact of environmental constraints. Before full pro-

Figure 9-5. Abandoned mining settlements such as Southern Cross, Montana, dramatize how bustling cities, like vigorous organisms, can die once the resource base that sustained them is depleted. (Montana Chamber of Commerce)

312   duction capital outlays are made, staff ecologists and company economists are being put through extensive cross examination first by company management and eventually by regulatory agencies who have the responsibility to safeguard the water, air, wildlife, recreation land, and various other resources—public and private—which may be injured or negatively affected by the proposed mining activity. However, considering the scope of the known gargantuan deposits of sub-bituminous coal, *lignite,* oil, and natural gas fields in Wyoming, Montana, North Dakota, New Mexico, and Arizona and the uranium and oil shale deposits on the western slope lands in Wyoming, Utah, and Colorado, it seems likely that the Rocky Mountain region will soon experience another mineral bonanza.

The approach to extracting mineral resources, all of which are nonrenewable, is rather different from using the replaceable or maintainable natural resources such as soil, forests, wildlife, and water. For one thing, the amount of mineral deposit is almost always unknown. Even where a

Figure 9-6. Some decrease in population of mining towns is explained by increased automation. Here is part of Anaconda's highly automated Twin Buttes open pit mine near Sahuarita, Arizona. Huge scrapers in the foreground are removing overburden. Here the task is to get to the underlying rock, which can be sulfide ore or oxide ore. After the rock is blasted, it is loaded by power shovel and hauled by truck to primary crushers in the pit.

Environmental controls will represent larger portions of the economic costs of massive land-disruptive mining activities only if an informed citizenry insists upon them. Mining companies do not voluntarily clean up after the profits have been extracted. (U.S. Bureau of Mines)

trace of ore leads to a motherlode, or a wildcat well uncovers an extensive oil and natural gas field, the operator is never sure when the high quality or high concentration will suddenly play out as quickly as it was discovered. This uncertainty about the size and quality of the deposit influences the manner in which the mineral is removed. There is always a hesitancy to invest too heavily in pollution control and safety devices without being certain about the physical "life span" of a given deposit. Consequently most mining and drilling operations are designed to get the highest quality material out at the lowest cost. In the absence of effective public surveillance, many mining and petroleum companies have tried to reduce their costs of operation by sidestepping safety measures, and environmental controls, achieving more thorough recovery, and utilizing lower grade deposits.

Furthermore, normal business ambiguities exist about changing technologies, changing markets, possible substitutes, and a multitude of external factors that play critical roles in the decision to keep a given mine open. With replenishable or maintainable resources, many of the same external cost factors are at work, but a given operator has an excellent idea how many board feet of timber an Engelmann spruce or a Ponderosa pine or a Douglas fir stand will produce under various management practices. Long-term weather records provide a reliable index about the amount of runoff that can be generated from a watershed. The carrying capacity of the range gives the rancher a good "ball park" figure of expected productivity whether it be in pounds of beef or bushels of wheat from a certain acreage under normal weather and management conditions. The problem of uncertainty is raised in regard to mineral extraction not to forgive a mining company but to offer an explanation for past business practices.

Another factor that must be remembered in a discussion about mineral resources and their impact on urban environment is the geographical location of most mineral reserves. The Rocky Mountain region serves as an extraordinary example of great distance between the extraction, production, and general consumption of the commodity. The Rocky Mountain area mineral strike of the nineteenth century occurred essentially in areas of very sparse population. In most areas the prospector was the first permanent resident. Usually he carried in his own provisions and was reasonably self-sufficient during the exploratory and early extraction period. If the uncertainty about the size and value of a deposit was reduced, more claims were staked and the lifeline of supporting services in the form of equipment centers, financial institutions, recreation, and residential facilities was extended to within a commuting distance of the mine or deposit. The cumulative result of having population centers at some distance from the mine site was that the immediate environmental impact of the operation was somewhat mitigated. Yet if the mineral required preliminary or more extensive processing to reduce transportation costs of shipping ore to distant metallurgical centers, severe pollution then took place in or near the mining community. Furthermore, present unregulated smelters did and do wreak

Figure 9-7. The mines located in fragile montane ecological areas usually have a harsh effect on water, soils, and vegetation. Here the Treasure Mine buildings are located near Red Mountain Pass on the headwaters of the Uncompahgre River in Colorado. (U.S. Forest Service)

havoc on the animal, plant, and human populations living in their proximity.

Several reasons come to mind why the oftentimes toxic air and water pollution from smelters, retorts, and refineries are tolerated by residents or even state agencies who have the responsibility to prevent health hazards. The economic constraint of installing pollution control devices is usually offered as the first reason. For a speculative operation with a future of uncertainty the pleas for various financial forgivenesses have been heeded. The depletion allowances that are made available to mineral operations whose output is strategic to the national economy would certainly be nullified if full pollution control devices were made mandatory. Another important reason for the general lack of environmental management in a mineral-oriented settlement is the high degree of transiency among miners and other residents. If the citizens in a "company town" or mining community look upon their residency as a temporary one, there is likely to be very little interest and concern over the necessarily long-range planning for local environmental improvement. One can readily imagine the difficulty of enforcing a strict and effective air-pollution ordinance in one of the zinc smelter towns around Provo, Utah. Most smelters are not even located within a city or town that might have jurisdiction if the ordinance was passed. States traditionally have been resistant to pass or enforce pollution controls that would give a competitive advantage to similar industries in neighboring states. This is particularly true in the highly competitive Western states where mineral-related industries are heavy contributors to the state treasury.

In addition to the uncertainty of the deposit's longevity; the economic, political, and jurisdictional constraints; and the transiency of the miners themselves, there seldom have been major aggregations of population affected by mining operations. This is exemplified by the remote and scattered locations of most mining operations in Idaho, Montana, Utah, Wyoming, Colorado, and New Mexico. However, within the last ten years danger signals have appeared in cities that do not have the topography, local climatic conditions, or adequate runoff to cope with the pollution loads that previously had been tolerated. Among the more established and permanent citizens of urban areas, a growing sensitivity to the quality of their cities' environments has also played an important role. Some careless planning and land use practices have created crises for citizens who heretofore had been pollution-tolerant or unaware of the health and environmental hazards. A most dramatic example of this kind of plunder occurred in Grand Junction, Colorado, where radioactive *tailings* from uranium mine wastes were used as landfill in several commercial and residential areas.

Figure 9-8. A town like Salida, Colorado, is removed from the nearby mines in the mountains. This community is located on the urban ecotone or fringe where agricultural and mining activities overlap. This diversity of economic activity gives the community an additional chance for survival and growth. (U.S. Forest Service)

Figure 9-9. Mine tailings and slag heaps scar many mountainsides in the Rocky Mountain region. The metals were originally extracted and sent to urban areas; today the urbanites come searching for recreation home sites and unmarred open space and find that ecological damage of three generations ago has yet to be repaired. This view is from Colorado's Million Dollar Highway in the San Juan National Forest. (U.S. Forest Service)

A controversy arose over the possible hazards of low level radiation exposure to occupants of the buildings over an extended period of time. As the finger of guilt was pointed toward the Atomic Energy Commission in the investigation, the question of the recapture of low-grade or low-concentration ores was raised with very few, if any, changes in the practices of dumping low grade ores, mine wastes, or spent reactor fuels.

The Urban Dweller's Paradox

As one contemplates the mineral resources of the twenty-first century, one comforting thought is the possibility that technology will permit the mineral industry to rework most of the slag heaps and the abandoned tailing piles, and to extract minerals from previoulsy uneconomical and therefore bypassed reserves. However, this very possibility pinpoints the increasingly complex environmental problems that face the minerals industry. There is a relentless pressure exerted on energy and other mineral resources to keep up with the increasing demand for the finished products to which metals and other minerals make major contributions. Unquestionably the heavier demands for minerals come from the large urbanizing areas of this country and other parts of the world. Some of the heaviest pressure is for the so-called space age and nuclear age metals and energy resources that are found predominately in the Rocky Mountain region. Several of the root problems of mineral resources can be traced to the increasingly large number of urban dwellers who consume more and more metals and energy, yet in their leisure time desire to visit the sparsely populated regions where abundant scenic beauty and rich historical heritage exist. The vacationing American places the Rocky Mountain region high on his list of travels because of the outstanding national parks, national forests, and national monuments as well as other federal and state recreation areas found in that region. It is the urban vacationer, returning home after seeing the despoliation of the mined landscape or the pollution of the air and streams, who inquires of his legislator or his Sierra Club chapter or his newspaper about the acid mine drainage, a despicable tailing pond condition, or seemingly wasteful methane flaring or oil spillage.

Tragically, the urban poor neither have adequate access to the distant recreation areas of the Rocky Mountain region, nor are they the heaviest consumers of energy and minerals (because of incomes that prohibit excessive purchase of appliances and other metal-rich durables.) Thus it becomes the task of the middle and upper income level individuals to fight for improved mining reclamation, hinterland restoration, and various land preservation projects. The comparatively long driving distances to choice recreation sites are difficult for the inner-city poor families to manage, so, in practice, the public recreation land is not equally accessible by all Americans. Denied access to Rocky Mountain and most other national parks because of poor education, low income, lack of jobs, discrimination, unreliable transportation, and other injustices, the "urban industrial peasant" struggles with his day to day problems while the elite have the luxury of challenging mineral leasing practices in the national forests of the Rockies and Alaska, particularly if the abuses occur on or near "their" land.

The circle of the paradox then becomes complete: the mines or the wells were dug and drilled to serve the demands of industrialized urbanizing man. The costs for more cars, more appliances and gadgets, the rails and roads to carry them, and the energy to drive them are forced upon the ecological systems far up on the mountains and deep in the canyons, presumably out of sight and removed from the urban dweller. It is the urban dweller who now discovers the "hidden" price of the cars and gadgets that complement his style of living.

Steel mills and coking ovens have been built near urban areas even in the Rocky Mountain states. Oil refineries have appeared from Denver and Laramie to Salt Lake City. Lenient *variances* issued for industrial and utility pollution control stipulations have been the rule. The end result is that the hinterland and remote scenic environment in proximity to mineral

318   extraction activities is spoiled in a fashion similar to ways the urban environment is ravaged by the processors, fabricators, and manufacturers of mineral commodities.

As we look specifically into the environmental implications of mineral resource management for the average urban dweller, let us consider the specific environmental problems that beset a mineral extractor using typical Rocky Mountain examples. Nine well-known minerals that are commonly found in the Rocky Mountain area are listed with specific environmental considerations that are or should be taken into account to restore environmental quality at the extraction or processing point. Many of the suggestions are derived from 1970 U.S. Bureau of Mines Bulletin 650 called *Mineral Facts and Problems*. When applicable, comments are made about conservation methods to lengthen the use period of the given mineral, for example, substitutes, scrap recovery, and beneficiation.

With gold and so many other metals, it may seem strange that the alternative materials or metals that are listed as substitutes are more expensive, more dependent on foreign imports, or more environmentally hazardous. As explanation, an attempt is simply made to show that there is a physically acceptable alternative without making a value judgment about its economic, political, or ecological feasibility. Some substitutes present particularly difficult problems. Plastics, for example, have created solid

Figure 9-10. Smelter and other related metallurgical processing facilities are not famous for conscientious environmental housekeeping. This copper reduction operation appears to be no exception.

waste disposal problems since they do not decompose, and many plastics, when incinerated, produce highly toxic and corrosive vapors. For other minerals that have distinctly unusual properties, such as mercury and helium, no substitutes are available or known.

Silver

In recent decades, seven silver mines in the Coeur d' Alene district of northern Idaho have supplied at least half of the United States' silver production. Idaho is followed by Utah, Arizona, Montana, and Nevada in the amount of silver mined each year. The largest domestic silver mine in recent years has been the Sunshine Mine near Kellogg, Idaho. It was made famous in 1972 by the worst mining tragedy in the Rocky Mountain region when nearly one hundred miners were killed. Environmental costs of silver production are also very high since 99 per cent of United States production is recovered in the smelting of ores and concentrates; the remainder is obtained by *amalgamation, cyanidation,* and *placer mining.*

Disposal of mining wastes near the mining towns and in the previously unspoiled scenic areas is a major environmental problem for the producing Western states. Scars still remain on other mountainsides and stream banks throughout the Rocky Mountain empire where early silver and gold strikes occurred. Some effort is underway to create disposal ponds to catch mill tailings in Idaho and Colorado especially, but valleys and mountainsides must be sacrificed for this gigantic solid-waste disposal problem.

Smelting of silver ores usually produces excessive volumes of sulfur dioxide and thus becomes a serious air pollution threat. Technology is available to recover sulfur dioxide gas from the smelting and other by-product recovery procedures if the application of that technology can be applied and enforced. Since much silver production is the product or by-product of copper, zinc, and lead, additional comments will appear in conjunction with discussions of those nonferrous metals that are frequently found in the Rocky Mountain region.

One of the common problems associated with silver, gold, molybdenum, copper, and many other minerals is the problem of land disturbance. There are about 226,000 disturbed acres of land as a result of surface and under-ground mining in the Rocky Mountain states according to reports from the U.S. Department of Interior, Bureau of Mines. The past and present hydraulic mining techniques for gold and *alloyed* silver directed powerful blasts of water against the mountainsides or sediment where rich mineral deposits were anticipated. Dredging, panning, and *sluicing* were also common practices. Consequently, surface vegetative cover was disrupted and the less fertile portions of the soil profile and parent rock were exposed. This destruction of the mountain slopes continues today. During typical mountain cloudbursts when erosion is accelerated, the unstable sediment is deposited in streams.

Figure 9-11. This mountainside, scarred over 100 years ago, bears witness to the length of time required for vegetative recovering in the Rocky Mountain region. The environmental pollution of this abandoned mine near Rico, Colorado, is aggravated by acid mine drainage shown in the foreground. (Environmental Protection Agency)

The reason the spent rock or spoil does not become stabilized is that, of mine sites examined in the West, 47 per cent of the spoil ranged from pH 3.5 to pH 5.0. If the pH is less than 4.0, the soil is ordinarily lethal to plants and if the pH ranges from 4.0 to 5.0, it is very difficult to establish vegetation. Aside from the excessive salts of copper, zinc, and lead that can be toxic to fish, wildlife, plants, and other parts of the food chain, rainfall is not often conducive for establishing vegetation on steep gradients associated with mine slag heaps or disturbed areas.

In the case of silver, it is fortunate for ecological reasons that most mining is from the underground deposits. However, improved safety practices and improved controls on the disposition and reclamation of mill tailings and smelter wastes are much needed.

Several technological innovations of recent years have temporarily mitigated the crisis of silver shortages. Improved mining technology has enabled the deep Idaho silver mines to operate at depths greater than five thousand feet where adverse heat and pressure would have prevented extraction under old methods. Metallurgical research has shown how silver can be economically obtained from low-grade copper ores that are not profitable for copper production. Considerable silver is also available through reclamation. In a project on the recovery of metal from municipal incinerator wastes, the U.S. Bureau of Solid Waste Management discovered that *fly ash* derived from the burning of wastes is a potential source of silver and gold with silver values in some samples as high as twenty ounces per ton. In addition, it is possible to salvage considerable silver from electronic scrap. A further modest extension of the world's silver supply is xerography, the electrostatic duplicating process which serves as a substitute for previous methods of using silver in photographic film and related photocopying processes.

Not all of the most effective mineral resource management practices are devised by metallurgical engineers. Process changes with environmental considerations taken into account usually help. But in some instances political and administrative decisions that affect the supply and demand serve as potent protectors of the environment at the mine site and in the consumer's local area. For example, an effective conservation measure for silver was the 1963 repeal of the Silver Purchase Act of 1934. The new policy permitted the sale of treasury silver stock that once backed $5 and $10 certificates. Also substitutes for silver in certain coinage alloys have permitted more silver to be utilized for electrical, electronic, and other industrial purposes. Stainless steel has become a popular substitute for sterling silverware and electroplate, although silver tableware is still a chief category of silver use.

Zinc

The American human settlements are presently consuming 26 per cent of the world's supply of zinc. The United States is one of the four top suppliers of primary zinc with its 10 per cent "contribution." American cities literally eat up more than 1.5 million tons of zinc per year, with the largest consumer being the transportation industry. Die casting, *galvanizing,* splash guards, electrical transmission equipment, household appliances, corrosion resistant plumbing, computers, industrial machinery, and power lawnmowers all rely heavily on zinc. The rubber, paint, ceramic, and textile industries are constant users of zinc in pigments and compounds. One of the typical problems created by Rocky Mountain mineral production is that the ores and concentrates of the Southwest and mountain states are shipped to the Eastern and Midwestern consuming areas. The refining plants are not always located near the Eastern cities or consumers; but regardless where the smelters are, without strict pollution control devices, the dust and fume contamination can be very serious. Oxides of copper, zinc, and other heavy metals have caused considerable damage to fauna and flora in Utah, Idaho, Colorado, and Montana. Researchers are currently at work with tracers to collect evidence of how toxic levels from smelters and refining processes enter man and other animals.

Most of the Western zinc is the result of co-product or by-product production. For example, manganese is a co-product of zinc-lead-manganese-silver ores at the Butte, Montana, mines. The major pollutants, which under proper environmental management can be listed as by-products of Rocky Mountain zinc plants include sulfur, cadmium, lead, germanium, thallium, indium, and gallium.

Most zinc-related ore extraction is done underground without massive damage to surface areas. However, where milling operations take place either near urban centers or in areas where urban populations tend to migrate for recreational pursuits, critical conflicts can occur. This competition for urban space and open space free from solid waste and large holding ponds is certain to be an issue of serious proportions in the years just ahead. The Bureau of Mines summarizes the refining problem: ". . . tailings piles represent a land-use conflict problem in some of the more heavily populated areas. . . . Electrolytic zinc refineries present no solid waste problems since slimes are usually shipped to lead or copper smelters for further processing. (This sounds like the way most electric utilities and the AEC deal with the spent radioactive waste fuel issue—it is shipped off for disposal.) *Retort plants* produce residues that require disposal, however, and plant stacks can give off sulfur and other fumes which can add to the air pollution problem of urban areas."[5]

Improved *flotation* and *reduction* processes have yielded up to 96 per cent recovery from zinc concentrate ores. Few substitutes have challenged the effectiveness of zinc's anticorrosion qualities in the cladding of iron and steel products. The mines in the United States meet only a fraction of the country's zinc needs. In 1969, the United States imported 327,000 short tons of zinc. Where weight is a consideration, aluminum, magnesium, and plastics can be used in place of zinc. In chemical and pigment uses of zinc, aluminum, magnesium, titanium, and zirconium have begun to serve as substitutes.

Copper

Copper is another mineral that the United States primarily imports even though it has been the largest copper producing country in the world since 1893. However, the U.S. production of copper as a per cent of the world production is decreasing from 25 per cent in 1960 to 19 per cent in 1968. Almost all of the U.S. copper is mined in the five Western states of Arizona, Montana, Nevada, New Mexico, and Utah, with twenty-five mines in these Rocky Mountain states accounting for nearly 95 per cent of the U.S. output. Important by-products of the smelting and refining process are gold, silver, molybdenum, nickel, selenium, tellurium, arsenic, rhenium, iron, lead, zinc, sulfur, cobalt, antimony, and bismuth.

[5] *Mineral Facts and Problems,* Bureau of Mines, 1970, p. 823.

Figure 9-12. Bagdad Copper Corporation mine and mill near Bagdad, Arizona. Ore from this mine first is transported to a primary crusher, then conveyed to a storage pile, and reconveyed to a fine ore crusher, whence it goes to the mill. Fine ore crusher and mill are at center, upper left. Tailing area is white band above mill at upper left, and mining waste piles are at a parallel elevation, upper right. (U.S. Bureau of Mines)

Severe environmental problems include those associated with the problem of surface mining. Land use conflicts arise not only from the open pit operation but from the disposal of solid wastes from processed ore as well.

The discharge of toxic and obnoxious gases and fumes has yet to be effectively dealt with, industry-wide. Heightening of stacks is not a proper solution although it has been commonly practiced. Sufficient water supply in the Western production states will also mount as an environmental problem. Electrolytic and *hydrometallurgical* extractive processes instead of the conventional *pyrometallurgical* methods will make major strides in pollution abatement of copper-refining activities.

Breakthroughs in *beneficiation* processes have been the biggest boon to copper conservation. Consequently, the amount of copper ore that the United States imports has decreased from 83,000 short tons in 1960 to 4,000 short tons in 1969. The quantity of copper metal imported by the United States has also decreased from 177,000 short tons in 1960 to 139,000 short tons in 1969. In 1970 copper recoveries from concentrates averaged about 83 per cent. For those who might be complacent with this achievement, it should be pointed out that of the 1 to 2 million tons of copper in ores,

Figure 9-13. Old species and newly hybridized forms of sedges and grasses are raised on beds of spent molybdenum waste. The tailing ponds can be seen in the background. Thousands of years of soil building need to be telescoped into a short period of time as spent shale, spoil banks, and other mine wastes areas are reclaimed.

the 83 per cent recovery means that 200,000 tons of copper are discarded annually in tailing piles. Copper scrap recovery is very important.

Because copper is essentially indestructible, the industry can reclaim copper from obsolete equipment and a vast number of urban uses. Scrapped trolley lines and interurban electric railways provide substantial quantities of usable copper for recycling. (In most cases, one would probably prefer to have the interurban railway sustained and modernized for urban environmental benefits instead of converting the copper and other recyclable metals.) Economists consider copper's "use cycle" to be approximately forty years and some believe that at least 60 per cent of the copper put into use can be eventually recovered.[6] They also say that of all the copper the world has ever used, three fourths of it has been used in the last forty years. Presumably the world is now well into its second use cycle of copper and therefore the flow of copper scrap could be expected to be much greater than during the first forty-year expansion period. Unfortunately, the mechanisms for recycling metals such as copper have not been used effectively. It will therefore take increased environmental costs and

[6]G. A. Rousch, *Strategic Mineral Supplies* (New York: McGraw Hill, Inc., 1939).

foreign and domestic political and economic pressures to utilize the copper scrap that constitutes a mine above the ground in the midst of our metropolitan settlements.

More vigorous research and application of findings is needed on the restoration of vegetation from open pit operations and where holding ponds have accumulated large deposits of spoils. As mentioned earlier, the spoils tend to offer a rather adverse environment for native vegetation. Several botanists and soil specialists in the Western states have collaborated in their efforts to hybridize species of grasses and other vegetation so that vegetation can be restored by hybridized pioneer species. One test plot is at the Climax, Colorado, molybdenum holding pond site and another is at the Parachute Creek oil shale pilot project operated by Colony Development Corporation near Grand Valley, Colorado. It is expected that a general succession of grasses and shrubs will take place. Prior to this effort, most open pit activities, slag heaps, holding pond residues, and other disturbed mining conditions expose the soil, barren of vegetation, and thus pose a continual source of unwanted (and sometimes toxic) sediment into neighboring mountain lakes, streams, and rivers.

This is the region that most American urbanites will want to use for leisure activities on an increasing basis in the years ahead. To allow the mining activities to continue without ample environmental safe-guards is a luxury that America can no longer afford.

Molybdenum

Molybdenum leads the list of minerals that are found exclusively or predominantly in the Rocky Mountain region. The largest known molybdenum deposit in the world is located at Climax, Colorado. Copper porphyry ores in Arizona, Nevada, New Mexico, and Utah have molybdenum reserves as do the *vanadiferous shale* depostis of Montana, Idaho, and Wyoming. No appreciable amounts occur anywhere else in the United States. The major use of molybdenum is, in many cases, a conservation practice in itself: as a major alloying element to increase corrosion resistance, toughness, and strength in steel, chromium, tungsten, manganese, and nickel production.

Nearly one-third of the molybdenum consumed in the United States is used in the manufacture of transportation equipment, especially in automobiles, rail transport, and aircraft engines. Other major uses include its presence in the manufacture of industrial equipment and machinery, in a wide variety of alloy uses and in the electrical generation, food processing, and chemical production industries. Substitutes for molybdenum, depending on specific purposes, include chromium (for piston ring coating in the internal combustion engine) and tungsten and nickel in heat resistant portions of jet engines. These and other alternatives for molybdenum are not produced primarily in America and usually have much higher prices

Figure 9-14. The molybdenum mining town of Climax, Colorado, is totally dependent on the mine located in the mountain in the background. (U.S. Forest Service)

Figure 9-15. These Climax, Colorado, molybdenum tailing ponds are said to have a minimal amount of land disturbance by government officials. The company involved is trying to develop vegetation that will stabilize the area.

and substantial import regulations. Consequently, very few conservation practices are suggested by industry or government spokesmen for molybdenum although the United States maintains a 55 million pound stockpile of this mineral. Such a reserve seems especially odd since the United States produces about three-fourths of the free world's molybdenum supply. Less than 2 per cent of the molybdenum produced is recovered as scrap.

It is somewhat disturbing to review recent United States Bureau of Mines reports (1970) on the environmental disturbances that result from molybdenum mining and processing. Their 1970 Bulletin 650, entitled *Mineral Facts and Problems* reports that "the problem of land disturbance is minimal." No mention is made of the hundreds of acres devoted to the disposal of mine waste in a uniquely beautiful part of Colorado that has high recreation potential. It should also be reported that the Climax molybdenum mine personnel are seeking to hybridize certain species of cover plants in order to stabilize the tailing pond residues that are a by-product of the molybdenum extraction mining. Fortunately, the recent caving techniques or the older "room and pillar" mining leave less of a scar on the landscape than that created by the devastating effects of copper mining. The latter often yields molybdenum as a co-product or by-product.

Yet another environmental problem that more directly affects urbanites is the conversion of molybdenite to molybdic oxide. This process involves roasting that releases sulfur oxides into the atmosphere, particularly in the Eastern and Gulf states where the major molybdenite processing facilities are located. Water and air pollution problems at the mine site continue to plague most molybdenum extraction operations.

Lead

As the second largest metallic pollutant of an urban atmosphere next to iron, lead takes on a special role in a discussion of mineral resources for urban dwellers. After Missouri, which accounts for about 50 per cent of the 360,000 tons of lead domestically mined, come the Rocky Mountain states of Idaho, Utah, and Colorado. Arizona, New Mexico, Montana, and Wyoming also show promising reserves of lead. The lead mined in the United States provides only a portion of the total U.S. needs. In 1969 this country imported 115,000 short tons of lead ore (a decrease of 23,000 short tons from 1960) and 288,000 short tons of lead metal (an increase of 67,000 short tons from 1960). The lead mined in the United States is only 14 per cent of the world's lead production.

Worldwide, lead is used primarily as an alloy with other metals such as antimony and tin. The construction industry, communications industry, and ammunition manufacturers have been heavy users of lead in the past. About one-third of the lead consumed in the United States is used in chemical compounds for the production of tetraethyl lead, metal protective paints, pigments, oil refining, rubber, insecticides, and storage batteries.

By far today the major use of lead in the United States is for transportation, either in the construction of automobile storage batteries, gasoline lead additives, solders, brass alloys, greases, or corrosion resistant paints. The modern automobile batteries used in most American cars each contain about twenty pounds of lead with an average life expectancy for the battery of less than three years. Tetraethyl lead $Pb(C_2H_5)_4$ is a heavy, colorless liquid that contains 64 weight per cent lead and is the active ingredient of the antiknock compound added to gasoline to improve the efficiency and effect the economy of high compression automobile engines. In recent years, as the dangers of lead fumes in the air have been realized, environmentalists have exerted some pressure on oil companies to produce low-lead and no-lead gasoline compounds. Progress in this area has been slow because of claims that automobile engines are harmed by such no-lead fuels.

As one reflects upon these products, their tremendous impact on the urban resident becomes more obvious. It should be noted that the human body may suffer lead damage to the liver, kidney, reproductive system, and the brain and central nervous system. It is an organic form of lead, namely alkyl lead, which is highly toxic and enters the brain and nervous tissue, causing mental retardation and other central nervous system disorders. Recent research has revealed that children are especially vulnerable to lead poisoning. Low income families in particular have suffered the agonies of lead poisoning, for their homes which are painted with the old lead-based wall paint are often in states of disrepair. This peeled and chipped paint is a major source of highly toxic lead that is ingested by children of low income families who consequently may show symptoms of lead poisoning. In addition, the 350 million pounds of lead added to the atmosphere annually—up to 75 per cent of which comes from motor vehicle emissions—is a source of severe damage to children and adults alike who live, work, or play in close proximity to automobile traffic and breath the lead-choked fumes. Again, low income families are especially vulnerable since the majority of city expressways are routed through low income neighborhoods.

In contrast to almost all other minerals, it appears that the highly toxic effects of lead affect a far greater number of urban dwellers at or near the point of consumption rather than at the point of extraction and—or production. Lead smelters are or should be equipped with efficient dust and fume collection systems. Lead mines are underground, and safety devices and practices must be put into operation according to federal law. Mine wastes are usually returned underground so that water, land, and atmospheric pollution at the mine are inexcusable. Thus the thirteen thousand lead miners and production employees who reside in sparsely populated areas could enjoy reduced environmental hazards of lead toxicity common to huge areas of human settlement where tremendous quantities of lead are vented into the atmosphere.

Innovations in the years ahead may reduce the present 4 per cent growth rate in the use of tetraethyl and tetramethyl lead (now almost 300,000 tons per year!) as an antiknock compound in gasoline. Some of the contingencies that may influence a reduction of lead use include a higher grade crude oil and higher octane production; increased dependency on electrified rail, gas turbine, diesel engines, and electric cars that do not require antiknock gasoline; increased air travel; and lead damage sustained by catalytic mufflers and other air-pollution control devices required of internal combustion engines by the mid and latter 1970's.

Substitutes for lead as an antiknock ingredient include nickel and platinum, but they do not have the cost advantage, (assuming one does not compute the social and health cost imposed on man and the environment by lead). A slightly better alternative to lead in gasoline includes the development of low-compression engines that do not need lead derivatives in their fuel. Titanium and zinc are rapidly replacing lead as a pigment additive in interior and exterior house paints. Ultimate combinations of materials that provide stored electrical energy include cadmium, nickel, mercury, silver, and zinc. In the construction industry where corrosion resistant piping and related materials are used, polyethylene, galvanized steel, copper, aluminum, and organic derivatives have served as substitutes for lead. Where corrosive chemicals are involved, stainless steel, plastics, titanium, and cement serve as recent substitutes with generally less devastating and less toxic ecological impacts on man and his environment. Scrap lead presently supplies nearly one-fourth of the domestic demand and as metal recycling centers become more commonplace, this figure is expected to increase. What does one do with his empty toothpaste tube, his dead acid-lead battery, or his replaced lead plumbing?

Uranium

In a discussion of mineral resources of the Rocky Mountain region and their environmental impact on urban man, perhaps no mineral has had the alarm sounded any more vigorously by environmentalists than the one that rings for uranium. It is appropriate then for a very brief outline to be presented since the chief sources of uranium ore in the United States are found in the sedimentary deposits of the Colorado plateau. The Colorado plateau as described here, as well as in the paragraphs to follow dealing with vanadium and oil shale, embraces about 150,000 square miles of western Colorado, eastern Utah, northeastern Arizona, and northwestern New Mexico. Much of this particular region is known as the "Four Corners Area" because of the perpendicular symmetry of the boundaries of the four contiguous states. Parenthetically and of growing importance, this area is experiencing tremendous pressures from the recreation public—primarily urbanites from east and west coasts and Midwest metropolitan regions.

The nonmilitary use of uranium is almost entirely devoted to electric power generation. An estimated 3,300 tons of uranium were used in light water power reactors in 1972, compared to a few hundred tons for mining, desalting sea water, and as radioisotopes in the fields of agriculture, medicine, and industry. Presently there are no alternative materials or substitutes for uranium as a nuclear fuel. However, thorium is expected to complement U-238 during the next decade. Energy from fusion in thermonuclear devices has been proposed but this essentially unlimited source of energy is still in the future in terms of commercial application. The danger of radiation is of special concern from the mining of the ore through all the processing and various phases in the fuel cycle including the disposal of fuel elements themselves. Contrary to what the Atomic Energy Commission and the Department of Health, Education and Welfare have told the public, until now inadequate methods of handling air, water, and solid wastes have been used. Research from medical teams and others not directly affiliated with the Atomic Energy Commission have shown some seriously questionable practices employed in deep well disposal (for example, the Rocky Flats Arsenal located midway between Boulder and Denver, Colorado,) and in the airborne and waterborne wastes from privately financed reactors. Since 85 per cent of the original radioactivity remains in the milling wastes, extreme care must be taken with this particular solid waste problem. Using the slag for commercial and residential landfill as was done in the Grand Junction area of western Colorado appears to have been a most unwise practice.

Perhaps the most vexing environmental problem in America and throughout the world over the long run is the question of what to do with the waste materials from nuclear reactors as they accumulate as gases, liquids, or solids and at various radiation levels. The technology to deal with this problem is neither at hand nor in sight. The half life of the common reactor fuel, plutonium, is 24,000 years. Some observers are very critical of the ocean dumping and burial site procedures especially since the containers of the continually boiling radioactive fluids have a considerably shorter total life than their very dangerous contents. (See Chapter 7 for details of reactor wastes.)

Another environmental hazard exists that is perhaps more critical ecologically than any chemical pollutant over the long time span. This is the waste heat that is a by-product of the nuclear power plant. Government sources show that in the early 1970's nuclear plants discharged approximately 50 per cent more heat into a river or lake environment than modern fossil fuel plants of similar size. The waste heat has a potentially deleterious effect on the environment by reducing the oxygen levels in the receiving water, by increasing the rate of metabolic and chemical activity in the heated aquatic environment by a factor of two or three for every 10°C. increase in temperature. Some biologists contend that the breeding, spawning, and hatching cycles of many ecosystem-sustaining organisms will be thrown out of seasonal phase that will put the organisms in lethal competition with other unchanged environmental resistances and biological predators. Some limnologists are concerned that the thermal pollution will accelerate eutrophic aquatic conditions that already have been accelerated by municipal and industrial wastes near rapidly growing urban regions.

Even to the resident of the relatively sparsely settled Rocky Mountain states, the prospect of excessively heated river, lake, or reservoir water from nuclear or fossil fuel power plants has become an unwelcome factor mixed with the advantages of rich energy sources in the shales, sandstones, and other sedimentary rocks of the mountain region. At present, most of the minerals that are usually found in chemical combination with uranium are either partially recovered or not recovered at all. Considerable deficiencies and economies could be gained if more attention was paid to the co-product and by-product extraction of radium, molybdenum, vanadium, selenium, and scandium. In fact, only the highest grade uranium ores are utilized at present and tremendous beneficiation potential is being postponed—a characteristic of the "bonanza approach."

Figure 9-16. The reflection of the sun shines symbolically on a holding pond at a uranium processing mill near Uravan, Colorado. Note the proximity of the river to the right of the pond earthenworks, which seem to be subject to erosion. (Environmental Protection Agency)

332   Often the cry goes out that the profit motive that drives the private sector of the economy does not give adequate attention to the sometimes intangible factors of pollution control and environmental management. However, the case of uranium production illustrates that even under strict government control and regulations, serious negligence has been committed in dealing with environmental consequences of radioactive extraction procedures at the mine, processing at the mill, disposal of tailing wastes, long-term radioisotope accumulation in the natural environment, and disposal of spent fuel from nuclear power plants. One would have hoped for somewhat better conservation practices with public ownership and supervision. Here is a case where the American public fared no better, if as well, if the activity had grown under private controls. Even as this is written, the AEC is attempting to get exemption from filing environmental impact statements under the National Environmental Policy Act of 1969 for nuclear power plant construction and operation.

Vanadium

The space-age, nuclear-age metal, vanadium, is found predominately in the Rocky Mountain region. Whether as a by-product of phosphorus production in Idaho or as a co-product of the uranium-vanadium deposits of the Colorado plateau, these sources in addition to deposits in Wyoming, Utah, New Mexico, and Arizona have named the United States as a net exporter, the leading consumer, and the world's leading producer of vanadium. Its uses are principally in high-strength, low alloy steel products such as oil and gas pipelines, bridges, aircraft industry uses, nuclear reactors, metal working machinery and power tools. Urban dwellers undoubtedly take vanadium compounds for granted in the preparation of lusters for pottery, glass, and porcelain; in the production of synthetic rubber; in the processing of colored film; and in the production of plastics and color fixatives in paint and ink. Some vanadium catalysts have been proposed to alleviate automobile exhaust and smog pollution.

Several metals are interchangeable with vanadium as grain refining additives in steel making. Manganese-titanium and molybdenum-silicon steels serve as examples. Vanadium, molybdenum, and columbium metal and alloys compete in nuclear plant applications, and platinum is a proven substitute for vanadium as a catalyst.

Vanadium is produced from the Colorado plateau principally as the co-product of uranium, and therefore the environmental problems of radiation hazard and air and water pollution are similar to those of the uranium extraction and processing industry. In the milling process, the liquids from the solvent and water leaching operations are sent to tailing ponds for settling. Also aesthetic problems are created when the large, low-grade deposits of the Colorado plateau are mined with the open pit method that is the usual practice. Residue and slag recovery ranges from

70 to 85 per cent, but no purposeful effort is now made to recover vanadium from iron and steel scrap.

Very little research has been done on the toxicity of vanadium in the original environment. It is known, however, that when the route of exposure is the respiratory tract, vanadium may accumulate in the lungs and high concentrations of the metal may damage human gastrointestinal and respiratory systems. Research in 1971 has indicated that exposure to lower concentrations of vanadium has resulted in the inhibition of cholesterol synthesis in man. As is the case with many of the recent space age minerals and metals, increased levels in the environment pose questions with unresolved answers. In the case of vanadium, levels have been increasing in recent years, as fuel oils containing vanadium and other toxic compounds are burned and as increased industrial use continues. A more careful vigil must be maintained to protect large populations in metropolitan as well as less developed mining communities.

Gold

During World War II, most domestic gold mines in the Rocky Mountain states of Montana, Colorado, Idaho, Utah, New Mexico, Nevada, and Arizona were forced to close in order to divert manpower and equipment to other more critical industries. A fixed price of $35 per ounce was placed on gold, and for years gold fever vanished except among the amateur placer miners who frequent the streams near places such as Cripple Creek or Ward, Colorado. However, in 1973, gold on the international open market rose well over $120 an ounce and resulted in a new flurry of opening old gold mines and panning for gold.

Figure 9-17. Early prospectors in the Rocky Mountain region used pans to separate the heavier gold nuggets from the lighter silt, gravel, and sand of mountain streams. (U.S. Forest Service)

Figure 9-18. Large scale placer gold mining was carried out using a dredge to expose stream gravels as in this operation near Fairplay, Colorado. (U.S. Forest Service)

Figure 9-19. After the gold dredging operations move on, the micro-environment of the stream and riparian community suffer from the disruption. This creek flows into the North Fork of the Salmon River in Idaho and shows the condition *75 years* after the gold dredging took place. (U.S. Forest Service)

Approximately two-thirds of the domestic gold output comes from gold ores and placers; the remainder is recovered essentially from copper and other base metal by-product operations. The copper and gold extraction process is primarily open pit with its traditional land use problems of surface soil and vegetative disruption, wildlife and forest upheaval, and general aesthetic abuse. In addition to potential air pollution from smelters, there is the visual scar on the Western landscape as well as the problems associated with tailing pond establishment and subsequent water pollution difficulties. Obvious water pollution problems are created by the dredging of stream muds and other gold-bearing bottom deposits. Powerful hydraulic blasts of water render considerable instability to the delicate aquatic ecosystem, which is usually associated with high mountain gold placer operations.

Unfortunately, no metal or alloy possesses all of the desirable characteristics of gold for its specified uses in jewelry, dental equipment, electronic components, medicine, and aerospace hardware. Partial substitutes for these uses are available, however, in platinum, silver, nickel, aluminum, stainless steel, and nickel-chromium.

A concluding and happy note about the conservation of gold: metallurgical recoveries of gold from concentrates are as high as 95 per cent and its relative indestructability and its societal value provide built-in mechanisms for saving and recycling this metal.

Oil Shale

The final mineral to be presented in the series of important Rocky Mountain metallic and nonmetallic resources has unique environmental consequences for the Rocky Mountain region as well as for the entire United States. Fortunately, oil shale is still at the speculative stage of development. An array of environmental concerns including potential air and water pollution poses major hurdles to be overcome before full-scale commercial production of oil shale can begin. Other critical factors include the spoilage of recreation canyonland country from the subsequent tonnages of processed or spent shale and the potential buildup of supporting industrial facilities in urban areas.

The world's largest known deposits of hydrocarbon are located in 16,500 square miles of the Green River formation, which includes adjoining portions of Colorado, Utah, and Wyoming. The presumably present 2 trillion barrels of oil pose environmental problems of an equally gargantuan scale. It is appropriate that a discussion of Rocky Mountain minerals include oil shale especially in light of future energy needs, future recreational needs, and future environmental controls, all of which come into consideration for the urban dweller in every portion of the United States. Not only is

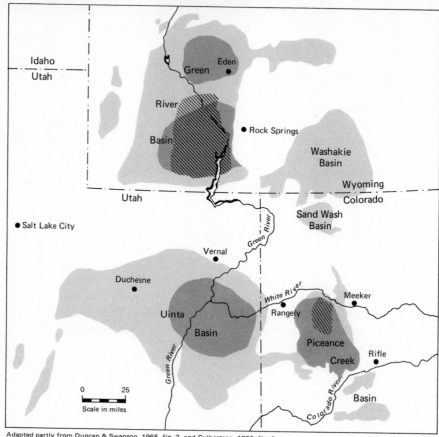

Adapted partly from Duncan & Swanson, 1965, fig. 3, and Culbertson, 1966, fig. 1.

Explanation

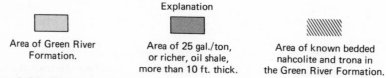

| Area of Green River Formation. | Area of 25 gal./ton, or richer, oil shale, more than 10 ft. thick. | Area of known bedded nahcolite and trona in the Green River Formation. |

Figure 9-20. The vast oil shale and natural gas deposits of the Green River Basin (Wyoming), the Uinta Basin (Utah), and the Piceance Creek area (Colorado) may extend the U.S. energy supply if economical methods of mining and retorting can be developed. (From *Hearings Before the Subcommittee on Legislation of the Joint Committee on Atomic Energy*, Congress of the United States, 90th Congress, Second Session on Commercial Plowshare Services and Related Background Material, July 19, 1968, Washington: 1968, p. 63. Originally adapted partly from Duncan & Swanson, 1965, fig. 3, and Culbertson, 1966, fig. 1.)

oil shale found in other states of the West including Alaska, but also 200 to 800 billion barrels are estimated reserves currently buried in marine sediments occurring from Texas to New York and from Michigan to Alabama. A further reason for national interest in the oil shale of Colorado,

Utah, and Wyoming is that 80 per cent of that oil shale land is owned by the federal government.

Thus the federal government is in a unique position to demonstrate environmentally sound management of a vital but depletable resource. This is an opportunity that was not previously possible when the mineral bonanzas of the West were "up for grabs," and when very little attention was directed to ecological matters or long-term efficiencies of mineral production. Even though uranium and its co-product, vanadium, were mined and processed under strict government regulation, this phenomenon took place during a wartime period and consequently had special issues of national security and national defense as important components of the management and development decision of those minerals.

Paramount among the environmental problems of the oil shale industry of the future is what to do with the shale after the average twenty-five gallons per ton of shale have been "squeezed out." Recent research reports show that commercial oil shale plants will process at least ten thousand tons of shale per day. The disposal of spent or processed shale in nearby canyons raises serious questions about land use priorities and air and water pollution. Furthermore, the question arises: how can Americans make better use of present and less environmentally damaging energy resources such as solar, tidal, geothermal, and other fossil fuels. Research is underway to discover ways of reducing the solid waste disposal problem associated with

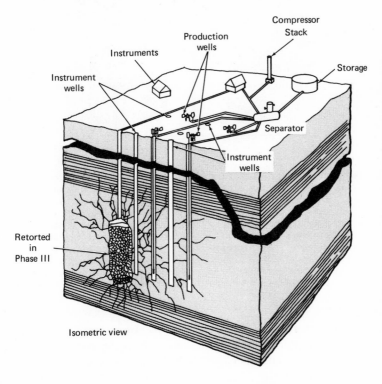

Figure 9-21. Fracturing the oil shale and retorting the oil in place with an underground nuclear explosion has been done on a pilot basis in the area near Grand Valley, Colorado. (From *Hearings Before the Subcommittee on Legislation of the Joint Committee on Atomic Energy*, Congress of the United States, 90th Congress, Second Session on Commercial Plowshare Services and Related Background Material, July 19, 1968, Washington: 1968.)

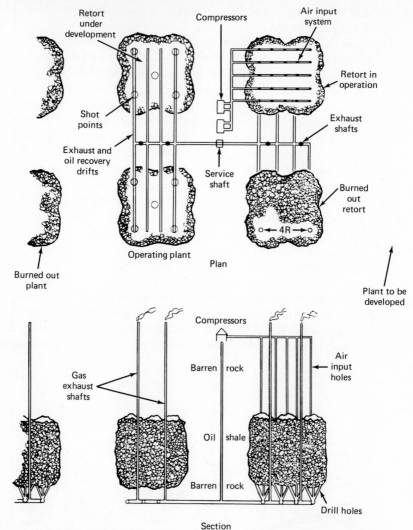

Figure 9-22. Gas and oil stimulation from underground nuclear explosions fracture and retort the oil shale in situ. Wells are drilled to capture the gas at the bottom of the crushed core and other drill holes are placed to the top of the crushed core in order to drive out retorted oil and gas with compressed air. Exhaustive environmental impact analysis should guide development of this mining procedure before experiments like this are permitted to go commercial. (From *Hearings Before the Subcommittee on Legislation of the Joint Committee on Atomic Energy,* Congress of the United States, 90th Congress, Second Session on Commercial Plowshare Services and Related Background Material, July 19, 1968, Washington: 1968.)

oil shale production. Efforts have been directed to compaction, terracing, and revegetation that would hopefully maintain the spoil deposits from blowing or washing down canyons close to the mine site where the proc-

Fragmented rock in
collapse chimney

Fractured rock

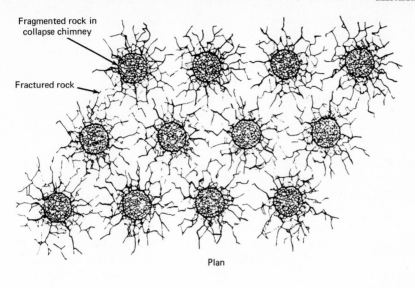

Plan

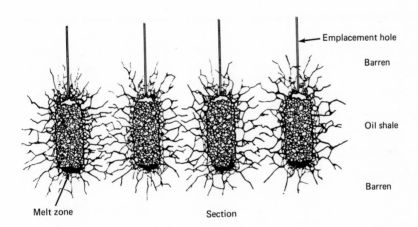

Emplacement hole

Barren

Oil shale

Barren

Melt zone   Section

essed shale would ordinarily be deposited. Crushing of the rock and retorting with its release of organic contaminants are other steps in the process
that raise concerns among oil shale developers and environmental protection personnel. In the early 1970's *in situ* fracturing of shale and retorting
within the formation and subsequent by-product recovery have been the
subject of experimentation. New and serious environmental questions,
however, are raised when nuclear explosions are used for the *in situ* crushing and retort process. Room and pillar, cut and fill, and block caving seem
to be the most reasonable mining procedures at present, but very little
mention is made of returning the processed shale to its original cavities
underground.

Before the present decade, most of the questions about the development

340   of Rocky Mountain oil shale focused on the relative competitive position of petroleum from imports and other national sources including the Alaskan Prudhoe Bay deposits. Technological breakthroughs and various other fossil fuel depletion allowances affected long-term investment to promote oil shale development.

Co-product recovery of alumina in the form of dawsonite is not favorable as deposits of bauxite, but with satisfactory extraction methods the tonnages involved would double the free world supply of alumina now known in bauxite. Also tremendous quantities of soda ash are found in the nahcolite-bearing oil shale of the Colorado Piceance Creek basin. The urbanite who uses more and more energy wherever he lives must recognize that the oil shale deposits of the Rocky Mountain region pose very substantial opportunity costs in ecological and environmental terms.

The present ranching towns of the Rocky Mountain region in proximity to oil shale deposits could grow into cities, oil shale pilot production facilities could grow into large industrial complexes, and the recreation, timber, wildlife, and especially watershed production lands would then face severe degradation, even with the most advanced environmental controls in use today.

In addition to the traditional factors in developing a mineral resource, the environmental impact plays an increasingly important role—in fact, in the case of oil shale, environmental factors will probably be the most critical variable as urban Americans begin to establish some balance between a quality urban existence made possible by tremendous volumes of energy to save human exertion and an attractive quality environment in the hinterland where more urban Americans want to spend more time than ever before.

NEPA's Role

One final dimension to the mineral resource problem of the Rocky Mountain region must be added here. According to the provisions of the National Environmental Policy Act (NEPA), which was passed in 1969 and activated January 1, 1970, every major federal activity or project must be described by an environmental impact statement that is reviewed by the Council on Environmental Quality and several other federal agencies involved in environmental control. Mineral extraction and development that predominately take place in the Western states on federal land comes under the jurisdiction of this federal law. Section 102(2)(c) of the Act stipulates that any activity in which major federal funding is involved must file an account of what the expected environmental costs and benefits of a given project will be and what alternative methods of achieving the same objective are available. It is presumed that the alternative strategies are listed with an assessment of ecological disruptions or other environmental costs so that the public and Congress can make decisions that include environmental conditions as well as whatever political, social, and economic guidelines that had directed them previously.

Mineral Recycling

One alternative for extensive Western mineral development is to consider mineral sources where the disruption to recreation land, ranching, and wildlife or other land uses is considerably less. In some cases increased mineral extraction should be replaced by increased mineral salvage and mineral recycling.

The President's Council on Environmental Quality in its 1970 Annual Report concluded the section of Natural Resources by stating: "There is room for the development of substantial industry in recycling. Recycling of minerals would also appear to be desirable in view of a lessened environmental impact. The amount of waste products that must be disposed of is reduced, and the energy requirements for recycling appear to be less than those required for primary production. In the longer term, there appears to be no adequate substitute to recycling."[7]

Many minerals are found as trash in quantities worthy of reclamation and recycling. Table 9-2 lists significant metals together with figures for the U.S. production, the amount of production from scrap sources, and the additional amounts estimated to be found in municipal solid waste.

Iron is currently the only material recovered in significant quantities from trash. A large portion of this metal is reclaimed as tin-coated steel cans that are used in chemically recovering copper from ore-processing solutions in the Southwestern United States. Over 100,000 tons of cans are used annually in this way in the United States, but this tonnage is only about 2 to 3 per cent of the tin cans thrown out each year. The potential use of cans by the copper industry varies with a good chance of an increase: yet it is only a small portion of the available annual supply of six or seven million tons.[8]

Significant increases in the recycling of steel cans will require return of steel to steel mills. Heretofore, steel companies have been reluctant to recycle steel cans for a number of reasons. The presence of other metals in these cans, such as tin and lead, has been a complicating factor. Chromium is gradually replacing tin as the can coating, making cans a more feasible source of scrap iron for steelmakers. Stringent air-pollution laws serve as a further deterrent to large markets for scrap iron. The open hearth furnaces that until 1964 produced 98 million tons of steel in the United States fell to 60.9 million tons in 1970 as the basic oxygen process rose to 60.2 million tons. The open hearth process can take a heavy (45 per cent) scrap charge, but is far dirtier than the basic oxygen furnaces that will

[7]*First Annual Report of the Council on Environmental Quality,* op. cit., pp. 158–159.
[8]Robert R. Grinstead, "Bottlenecks," *Environment* Vol. 14, No. 3 (April 1972).

Table 9-2. Current and Potential Recycling of Resources in Trash[1]
(Millions of Tons)

Resource	U.S. Annual Production		Estimated Additional Amounts Available in Urban Solid Wastes	Sources*
	Total	From Scrap		
Iron and Steel	130	36	10–14†	1
Aluminum	3.8	1.0	1.0–1.2	2
Copper	3.2	1.4 ⎫		
Zinc	1.9	0.4 ⎬	0.5	3
Tin	0.08	0.023	0.03	4

* Refers to sources of information:
  1. *Solid Waste Report* (Jan. 25, 1971), p. 35. *Chem. 26.*, (May 1970), p. 40.
  2. Sullivan and Stanczyk, *Chemical and Engineering News* (March 2, 1970), p. 14.
  3. Sullivan and Stanczyk, *Chemical and Engineering News* (April 6, 1970), p. 38.
  4. R. H. Taylor, *Compost Science* (May-June 1971), p. 25.
  † Of which cans make up about two-thirds.
  Note: Information on primary production of a number of materials is available in the U.S. Bureau of Mines Yearbook, 1969. Scrap utilization information is available from the National Association of Secondary Materials Industries. Much of the data in column 3 are to be found in National Institute for Resource Recovery, Bulletin, Vol. 1, No. 1 (Oct. 1971). Another source is the *Fourth Annual Report of the Council on Environmental Quality* (Sept. 1973), pp. 202–205.
  [1] Robert R. Grinstead, "Bottlenecks," *Environment*, Vol. 14, No. 3 (April 1972). Adapted from Table 1, p. 4.

take only 30 per cent scrap.[9] More recently, some small steel mills have started using the electric melting furnace that can take a 100 per cent scrap charge. Another problem is that the cost of scrap iron at a steel mill, $10 to $20 per ton, is often little more than the cost of transporting and handling the cans. Iron and steel scrap is more expensive to ship than iron ore. Still another complication is a shortage of gondola cars to ship scrap to the mills.

Abandoned automobiles are one of the most conspicuous solid waste disposal problems. An estimated 20 million cars are strewn throughout the countryside, and every year an additional 8 million are retired from use, 15 per cent of which are abandoned.[10] Of the 8 million junked automobiles each year, about 7 million are recycled by iron and steel scrap processors. A study by the Bureau of Mines in December 1969 placed the recoverable metallic values in a composite automobile as follows:

2614 lbs. bundle iron	. . . .	$24.44
429 lbs. cast iron	. . . . . .	9.06
32 lbs. copper	. . . .	11.34
54 lbs. zinc	. . . .	3.39
50 lbs. aluminum	. . . . .	6.27
20 lbs. lead	. . . .	1.44
	Total	$55.94

[9] Michael K. Drapkin, "Antipollution Laws Are Forcing Steelmakers To Close Old, Dirty Open Hearth Furnaces," *The Wall Street Journal* (December 1, 1970), p. 36.
[10] Ann Tasseff, "Solid Wastes Programs and Research," *Environment Reporter*, Monograph #6; Vol. 1 No. 33 (Dec. 11, 1970), Bureau of National Affairs.

Figure 9-23. Junk automobiles and car graveyards are an unsightly and conspicuous waste of mineral resources. The kinds of metals used in autos are also on the list of imported strategic minerals.

Figure 9-24. An automobile junkyard near Albuquerque, New Mexico. This 1972 photograph suggests that there is a backlog of scrap cars and metal even in the active metal processing states of the Rocky Mountain region. (Environmental Protection Agency)

344　Although the automobile represents a valuable source of these metals, increased recycling faces a number of problems. The scrap industry believes it has the capacity to process every junked automobile in the United States. CEQ's annual report suggested that abandonment might be substantially reduced and junked automobiles be put more promptly into the scrap cycle if they could realize penalties for abandonment and improvement of state titling and transfer laws that currently make it virtually impossible to obtain a title for an abandoned automobile.

The major nonferrous metal found in trash is aluminum at a level of about 1 million tons per year or about 25 per cent of the current usage in the United States. Other major nonferrous metals are copper, zinc, tin, and lead. The relatively high value of all these metals seems to assure markets for their reuse. However, no significant amounts of these metals are currently reclaimed from trash, although the recovery of aluminum through recycling centers has been estimated to account for about 5 per cent of the aluminum discarded in municipal waste collections.

The Bureau of Mines is also studying the development of new and improved technology for recovering and recycling metals and minerals from waste sources in industrial, mining, metallurgical, and chemical processing operations where commercial methods are inadequate, inefficient, or non-

Figure 9-25. Presently there are social and economic incentives promulgated by the auto manufacturers to encourage getting rid of your old car prematurely. Once the car is junked, there are institutional disincentives, not engineering problems, which slow car metal recycling. (Environmental Protection Agency)

Figure 9-26. Scrap autos are crushed for shipment to a compression feeder where they are shredded. (Environmental Protection Agency)

existent. Subjects of major research include ways to recover chromium, copper, nickel, zinc, and cadmium from waste electroplating solutions; and methods to recover and recycle the vast quantities of precious metals (gold, silver, and platinum) presently lost in electronic equipment.

Recognition by the government, industry, municipalities, and individuals for the need of reclaiming and recycling the used materials in our solid waste is a step forward. Unfortunately the views of the Council on Environmental Quality are not representative of very many in any of these sectors. Massive obstructions still block widespread recycling. The economic hurdle is large, for the economy of the United States and the world has been built upon easy and relatively inexpensive use of the natural resources. Sophisticated processes have been developed to extract and to process raw minerals—material now increasingly being recognized as not infinite in quantity. However, government tax incentives awarded for depleting raw materials, unfair freight rates that in many instances favor the transporting of new over secondary materials, and the lack of a market for reclaimed materials discourage major recycling attempts. Furthermore, reclaiming and reusing raw materials from refuse requires prohibitively costly process of separation. Even in many communities where individual citizens faithfully separate glass from cans from paper from organic wastes, the transportation of materials from the local recycling station to point of reuse bogs down because of high shipping costs for scrap materials. The resources of municipal wastes are a long way from being accessible—

Figure 9-27. Junk automobiles and other mineral-rich throw-aways are shredded for recycling and eventually find their way back to blast furnaces as a supplement to virgin ore. Here shredded steel is transferred for shipment with a huge magnet. (Environmental Protection Agency)

municipalities usually seek the cheapest means of refuse handling, which tends to be dumping and open burning followed by sanitary landfills. The problem in our affluent country is not one of shortage of raw materials, but rather one of a shortage of landfill sites (or so many citizens see it). This is confirmed by the fact that those cities that have shown the most interest in recycling systems are precisely those with the least landfill space. Of the fifty largest United States cities, some thirty have sufficient landfill

Figure 9-28. Metal recycling centers and waste recovery facilities have become widespread in the United States. The ultimate goal of a national waste recovery policy would be to recycle all metals (and other potentially valuable wastes) that technological and engineering feasibility permits.

Figure 9-29. An ecologically unsound consumption and waste disposal philosophy prevails among most Americans. Basic changes in value orientation must precede a fundamental change in the use and management of finite natural resources such as metals and other nonreplenishable minerals.

space for less than ten years—for twenty-five of these, there is sufficient space for less than five years.[11]

Communities that might explore recycling wait to make sure that it works elsewhere. Handling of solid waste has long been a jealously guarded community responsibility dreadfully ensnared in politics. Broadscale federal legislative reforms and initiative must preclude broadscale recycling that can best be accomplished on a regional basis with joint cooperation of individuals, government, and corporations. Currently it seems that the concept of recycling has been accepted by the United States on an individual basis, but not on an institutional level.

The *Resource Recovery Act of 1970,* which authorized $463 million for an all-out recycling approach to the solid waste problem, was viewed with great optimism at its passage, but was subsequently more or less disregarded by the Nixon administration. Only 16 per cent of the authorized funds were budgeted in fiscal 1972, mostly to fund pilot projects testing technological feasibility.

At present, massive recycling seems economically unfeasible. And in the really long run recycling probably will not prevent mineral depletion. However, as our raw minerals become increasingly rare, their prices will soar until the cost of reclaimed materials will be far preferable. Hopefully, widespread mineral depletion can be prevented. Perhaps social and economic patterns can change in the United States and other "consuming countries" so that a person's needs can be satisfied while minimizing rather than maximizing the irreplaceable substances he possesses and disperses.

[11]Grinstead, op. cit., p. 3.

CHAPTER 10

Wildlife and Fishery Resources

It may seem unusual for a chapter to emphasize wild animal resources in a reference that deals primarily with the resources of cities and man's impact on urban-related environments. However, many human settlements, especially in the Pacific Northwest and Upper Great Lakes areas, were established *because* of animal resources—a promising fishery, or a collection and distribution point for furs and game animals. Oftentimes, other towns evolved and flourished as supply points for ranchers after the *endemic* or native animal species were driven off and replaced by livestock.

Of course, many of the fur trading posts and fishing towns moved up the trophic levels of urban settlements, if we may use a biological analogy coined earlier in Chapter 1. The "producer function" of supplying fish, furs, meat, and other fish and wildlife-derived commodities such as hides and oils brought additional numbers of workers and activities to the small "extraction" village. As the tempo of the fishing increased, canneries ordinarily were set up with other ancillary activities. In fact, diversification of urban functions has traditionally taken place in most of the earliest settlements. However, in Alaska, British Columbia, Washington, Oregon, and northern California the economic life of a coastal community may still be totally dependent on a fishery in a manner similar to the resource-dependent towns mentioned in Chapter 6 (logging camps) and Chapter 9 (mining towns).

Another very specific and compelling reason for exposing the resident of any large metropolitan area to the concepts of wildlife management, and especially those that are observable in the Pacific Northwest region is that many of the ecological principles of wildlife management and the dynamics of an animal population have useful analogies to urban organisms. There is a multitude of parallel events that we can apply to urban **349**

Figure 10-1. The Alaskan community of Beaver, located on the north bank of the Yukon River six miles south of the Arctic Circle is dependent on the fish and other animal resources of the region. The residents of this village are part Athabaskan Indian and part Eskimo. This kind of village represents a "producer" role in a functional classification of human settlements when local fish and wildlife products are harvested and then exported to larger towns and cities. (U.S. Forest Service)

Figure 10-2. Elk River, Idaho, was a producer town that evolved around the Potlach Lumber Company in the 1940's. After local timber was cut over, residents commuted to distant logging camps and came home for weekends. (U.S. Forest Service)

Figure 10-3. Elkhorn, Montana, hit its zenith as a producer of minerals before 1900. Once the resource base of a single commodity "pioneer" town is exhausted, the town runs the risk of extinction or becoming a "ghost town." (U.S. Forest Service)

Figure 10-4. Portland, Oregon, could be cited as a human settlement of the Pacific Northwest region that began as a town dependent on the fishery, wildlife, and forest resources of the region. It has diversified and broadened its functions from primary producer to include various consumption and synthesizing roles in the region. Portland portrays urban succession in a state which has recognized a carrying capacity with respect to urban and nonurban environments. (U.S. Bureau of Outdoor Recreation)

systems in ways that will improve the design, the health, and the stability of the human settlement as it proceeds through the figurative and literal stages of urban succession.

Comparison of Ecological Systems and Urban Systems

Various interpretations of the concept of carrying capacity are found in the wildlife literature and more recently in the context of worldwide resource allocation as proposed in the 1972 Club of Rome study called *The Limits to Growth* by Meadows *et al.* Generally speaking, the carrying capacity is the number of animals of a particular species that the environment can support whereby the animals and their habitat are accommodated in a healthy relatively enduring condition. With the application of this idea to the human species in an urban setting, the term conveys a concept of specific population densities and consumption patterns that conform to the ability of the population not only to provide basic ingredients of survival such as food, water, and cover for itself but there is also the implicit proviso for a supply of amenities that contribute to the vigorous health and maintenance of the population's general welfare. Stated concretely, this would mean adequate social services for educational, recreational, aesthetic, and other culturally determined needs.

Once the carrying capacity of an environment for an animal species or the population of a human settlement is exceeded, at least two important events take place. One is the sudden, or in some cases, gradual degradation of the supporting habitat or environment that produces the basic ingredients for a healthy, vigorous survival at previously established levels. The other critical event is the diminution in the quality and vitality of the organism itself because it is forced to live in a submarginal habitat. Deer may overbrowse *preferential food sources* to the point that the vegetation's recovery ability for the following season is endangered. Citizens in a once attractive settlement such as San Jose, California, may contaminate the atmosphere and pave and develop every part of the natural landscape to the point that the urban container of the Santa Clara Valley is no longer healthy, pleasing, or minimally satisfactory for the majority of residents. The lifelines of support that prop up large metropolitan areas reach out to distant watersheds, precarious energy generation, and remote agricultural production areas. In due time when one megalopolis competes with another or when one urbanized continent competes with another for a limited and possibly decreasing supply of food, energy, water, or other vital resource, a crash situation then becomes a possibility. Hopefully the biological events that preceeded the 1924–1930 mule deer population crash and habitat destruction in the Kaibab National Forest of Arizona can be avoided.

The management tools of game and fishery biology have useful applications such as the protection at vulnerable periods of a life cycle; improvement of cover; assurance of water supply; improvement of food conditions, refuges, and preserves; restocking; predator control; optimum density limiting factors; succession; and climax conditions have useful applications. The reader is invited to identify some useful linkages to human situations. Prudence should be exercised for each application. For example, it would be easy to carry the analogy of predator control vis-à-vis the Department of Defense or a state or local police agency well beyond its useful meaning.

Another biological phenomenon that is not solely the property of wildlife ecologists, but certainly used by them, is the concept of environmental succession. The biological and physical forces of every landscape comprise what is generally considered to be an optimum environment for the organisms that occupy particular *niches* (roles) in predictable habitats (locations). With geological and climatic changes, the flora, fauna, and physical forces including climate develop in a way to achieve some semblance of equilibrium. Man's intervention into the natural chain of events usually disturbs the natural succession—it could be an aquatic ecosystem moving from oligotrophic to eutrophic conditions or a terrestrial community sequence such as a forest or grassland moving from a pioneer to a more stable climax condition.

Man's disruption of biotic succession has taken many forms including logging, introducing exotic species, burning of forest, grassland, or even tundra lichens (which devastated the winter range of the Barren Ground caribou), grazing of cattle and sheep and, of course, waste effluents in marine and freshwaters. There are events other than man-instigated forces that prevent the theoretical climax condition from being achieved. Hurricanes, prairie and forest fires, and animal or plant infestations have been of considerable influence.

The reason that the fishery manager or game manager is interested in biotic succession is that for each category of succession (there are many classifications for the whole spectrum from pioneer and low successional to climax) there are particular species of animals and plants that are associated with a given level of succession. The passenger pigeon was a member of a hardwood forest climax condition. The grizzly bear, musk ox, bighorn sheep, and caribou struggle for survival in western and northern climax communities. The urban analogy is demonstrated in the siege and struggles of capitals of previous empires and human civilizations—Babylon, Jericho, Constantinople, Corinth, Athens, Rome and Berlin. On the other hand Peking, Moscow, London, Paris, Tokyo, Bonn, and Washington seem to be in the running today for various mid or upper successional stages as centers of leadership and government. It is fascinating to discover how the state capitols of Western states have moved prior to the present seat of state government because of shifts in natural resource activities. The forces that tumble a city from a climax position, which is the status of an exciting, "top of the urban trophic pyramid," stable human settlement also have analogies in the strictly biological realm. Droughts, floods, epidemics, and

354   excessive predation can deal fatal blows to human and animal communities. Once the critical mass for biological and, in the human sense, spiritual replenishment is reduced to extraordinary low levels, the survival of that part of the population is endangered. Cities of the Inca and Aztec civilizations and ghost towns sprinkled throughout the American West are human settlement counterparts to the extinct and endangered species of wildlife.

Before discussing specific animal resource problems, various urban interrelationships, and the attempted conservation practices, the picture of *endangered species* should be mentioned as special interest to any urbanite. To understand the present status and anticipate what may be in store for the future, it is worthwhile to see what has happened since urbanization and industrialization became widespread in the United States.

Endangered Species of Wildlife

The International Union for the Conservation of Nature and Natural Resources reports that in 1600 there were approximately 4,226 living species of mammals and 8,684 species of birds. During the last 370 years at least 443 mammal species and subspecies and 636 bird species and subspecies have become extinct or are considered likely prospects for extinction in the near future. Of these figures, no fewer than 100 mammals have disappeared from the earth and at least 258 bird species and subspecies have been eliminated.

The fossil record shows that no animal has a monopoly on immortality. Evolutionary "dropouts" have occurred long before man invented megalopolis or even before the human species came up with the notion of sedentary villages in favor of nomadic hunting and gathering life styles. The maximum lifespan of any species is about 2 million years for birds and about 6 million years for mammals, but the pattern that has recently been established shows that human influence has speeded the aging process of animal species similar to the way in which aquatic succession in the form of eutrophication is accelerated by man's urban influences. There has been direct extermination from pressures of "livestock protection" as well as hunting and trapping for food, furs, feathers, hides, "fun," and trophies. American examples include the sea mink (*Mustela macrodon*), Eastern wapiti (*Cervus canadensis canadensis*), Badlands bighorn sheep (*Ovis canadensis auduboni*), Eastern bison (*Bison bison pensylvanicus*), Eastern cougar (*Felis concolor coughar*), Oregon bison (*Bison bison oregonus*), Florida wolf (*Canis niger niger*), Plains wolf (*Canis lupuo nubilus*), Merriam elk (*Cervus merriami*), and since 1914, the Virginia heath hen (*Tympanuchus cupido cupido*) and the passenger pigeon (*Ectcopistes migratorius*). More than twenty bird species have been driven to extinction in the state of Hawaii by introduced rats, cats, and mongooses and an environment altered by modern man.

Figure 10-5. Rare and endangered species of the western United States include the California condor, photographed in the Los Padres National Forest, California. (U.S. Bureau of Sport Fisheries and Wildlife)

There are serious indirect pressures on wildlife from changing habitat, assimilation of toxic or sublethal substances, and general environmental contamination of organisms and their food supply that have posed a serious threat or spelled actual doom. The perils from pesticide accumulations and other toxic substance buildups are well known for the duck hawk, the golden and bald eagle, the osprey, and other species located at high trophic levels where harmful substances are biologically magnified.

If the history of other parts of the world has a specific message for animal resources, especially climax and predator species of the Pacific Northwest, the question that is pertinent for the most sought after species—including shellfish, mammals, birds, and fishes is not *if* but *when* each will expire. The passenger pigeon mentioned is a well-known American tragedy in the annals of wildlife literature. There are a few success stories such as the fur seal industry of Alaska's Pribilof Islands, the introduction of the ring-necked pheasant, the sea otter, the halibut, isolated herds of Roosevelt elk, and certain phases of the salmon fishing management program. Overall, however, the wildlife conservation picture is grim. The California condor is almost gone. The grizzly bear population in the United States from western Montana to Alaska is probably less than 850 individuals. California's

Figure 10-6. An incompatibility with human activity, especially man's land use patterns, has brought great hardship to species of wildlife like the grizzly bear. (National Park Service)

Figure 10-7. The Rocky Mountain bighorn sheep have suffered great abuse from overhunting by trophy seekers and more importantly from destruction of their natural range by overgrazing of domestic livestock under federal permit. (U.S. Bureau of Sport Fisheries and Wildlife)

Figure 10-8. This Canadian lynx was shot three miles east of the Red Rock Lakes Migratory Waterfowl Refuge, Monida, Montana. Individuals who slaughter endangered species are often difficult to apprehend. A successful wildlife preservation program depends on a citizenry which is knowledgable about the benefits of predator-prey relationships. (U.S. Bureau of Sport Fisheries and Wildlife)

Figure 10-9. This whooping crane chick was successfully hatched June 13, 1967, from eggs obtained from a nest in Wood Buffalo Park, Canada, in cooperative effort with the Canadian Wildlife Service. (U.S. Bureau of Sport Fisheries and Wildlife)

Figure 10-10. During the next several decades several species of endangered animals will be snuffed out because of human ignorance and mismanagement. The kit fox could be one of these. (U.S. Bureau of Sport Fisheries and Wildlife)

state flag and state seal try to immortalize the grizzly bear inasmuch as it was eliminated from natural ecosystems of the state by 1922. The wolf, sharp-tailed grouse, and bighorn sheep disappeared from Oregon. The precarious position of many of the whales cannot be overemphasized. The salmon, shellfish, and other marine animals that found themselves in conflict with human activity such as sewage disposal or dam building are threatened over the long run. The caribou is on the endangered species list in the Pacific Northwest region as are the Columbian white-tailed deer, fisher, Canadian lynx, greater sand hill crane, bald eagle, kit fox, pileated woodpecker, burrowing owl, osprey, white sturgeon of the Snake River canyon, and the upper Snake River species of salmon and steelhead.

CASE IN POINT: THE PACIFIC NORTHWEST

It may seem strange that the Pacific Northwest region is given as an example to capture our imagination about the difficulties of fishery and wildlife management. Why not use the Great Plains where the pronghorn antelope and the bison have been essentially replaced by livestock, jack rabbits, kangaroo rats and ground squirrels? Why not use the Great Lakes

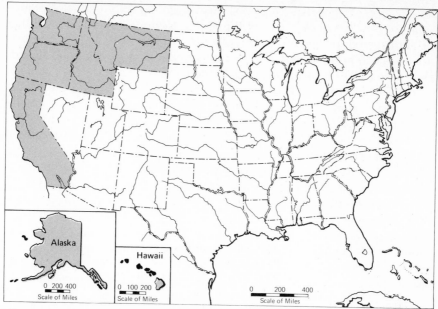

Figure 10-11. Fisheries and wildlife issues of the Pacific Northwest region are discussed in this section.

region where caribou, elk, and wolves have been almost totally replaced by midsuccessional or *"disturbance species"* such as the moose, white-tailed deer, opossum, hare, and ruffed grouse?

The Pacific Northwest area is used as an illustration because in this region there are unique examples of mature or climax animal and plant communities. The musk ox, the Barren Ground caribou, the grizzly bear, the Alaskan wolf, and the bighorn sheep stand out as classic illustrations. This general region serves as the last major reservoir of lessons of biological significance in terms of community succession and population stabilization. At the same time, major portions of the Pacific Northwest face substantial and, in most cases, adverse impacts of local, regional, and nationwide

Figure 10-12. Musk oxen on Nunivak Island, Alaska. (U.S. Bureau of Sport Fisheries and Wildlife)

360   urbanization. With an American citizenry enlightened about the long range values of the "urban reserves" of the Pacific Northwest, it is assumed that the endangered species and the irreplaceable animal and plant community processes can be sustained as a continuing education to urbanites regardless of the location of their human settlement.

An era of industrialization and development is underway in the Pacific Northwest region. At the same time, postindustrialization uses of the environment are competing for the multitude of resources in that region of the continent. Towns are booming as the resource managers of timber, wildlife, minerals, recreation, water, and energy try to address the problem of conflicting uses that are primarily generated by consumers of all kinds in "off-site" metropolitan areas. The strains placed upon salmon and seals, halibut and grizzly bears or wolves and eagles are symptoms of the larger struggle. Highly consumptive urban organisms that have not established carrying capacities for themselves must be integrated with renewable resources that have well-defined limits, tolerances, and production capacities. Failure to integrate will spell the demise of the cities, the resources, and the people who brought on the biological collapse of an endangered resource.

Figure 10-13. The coastal regions of the Pacific Northwest and the offshore marine habitat typify a final frontier for species of whales, seals, shellfish, and numerous commercial and sport fishes. The influence of urban man with his industrial and domestic pollution, his relentless hunger for oil which is transported through these waters, and his coastal development will jeopardize the resource zone unless some basic life style changes take place in America. (National Park Service)

In order to provide the water supply and electrical energy and fossil fuel needs of metropolitan areas of the West Coast, very formidable engineering projects have been built or proposed for the Pacific Northwest region. The rationale for moving ahead with the controversial projects such as the Alaskan pipeline and the giant hydropower dams that appear to pose very serious threats to fish and wildlife was based primarily on the projected demands of water-short, energy-short, oil-and natural-gas short urban areas. The Bonneville Power Administration, the U.S. Bureau of Reclamation and the U.S. Army Corps of Engineers have apparently mustered stronger advocates in urban areas and in the halls of Congress than have the agencies entrusted with wildlife management such as the U.S. Bureau of Commercial and Sports Fisheries, the U.S. Forest Service, or the National Park Service. To be sure, there have been delays on projects as large as the Rampart Dam on the Yukon River or on the trans-Alaska natural gas and oil pipelines based on concerns about wildlife and wilderness habitat, but many informed observers believe that these delays are only temporary.

The Problem of a Common Property Resource

Another factor that must be considered is the problem of a *common property resource.* Even though a human settlement is established in the proximity of a seal rookery; a salmon run; or a migration route of waterfowl, whales, or caribou; there is the question of multiple ownership when multiple locations are used by a species over its entire home range. The problem is aggravated if neighboring states or countries are in disagreement over where and when the animal resource can be harvested, even if there is agreement as to what is the harvestable surplus in a given year. The marine mammals and fishery have been the classic examples of this controversy. The sea otter, the fur seal, and some fish species are examples of a common property resource that has recovered from dangerously low population levels after the nations and individuals involved reached agreement about wise management practices. Without protection or controls over the entire life cycle of a species and over its entire geographic range, the uncontrolled harvest at one point over a sustained period can drop the population below its biological potential to replace itself. Once a downward spiral is set into motion, an unprotected common property wildlife resource is subjected to increased harvest by those who feel they must get the last economic harvest to forestall their increasing per unit cost. Sometimes increased prices, which are often a reflection of increased scarcity, trigger an increased take.

Whenever the catch of whales, salmon, seals, or a similar renewable resource is regulated by the industry involved in the harvest, the regulation often tends to be suspect. This is especially true for the unscrupulous operators who are operating on short-run profit motives and who might not refrain from exploiting a diminishing resource. Some firms are driven

362   by profit motives alone and wish to extract the last possible revenue from a resource because of sunk capital in equipment, gear, processing machinery, and marketing costs. Other operators who are able to sustain a period of reduced harvests would be willing to let the biological potential return to a condition where a profitable harvest could be maintained on a sustained yield basis. An enlightened consumer public might participate in the political decisions affecting such debates if a broad overview can be provided from wildlife and fishery research and if the public is aware of the complexities that surround the management of commonly shared animal resources. Garret Hardin's widely read "The Tragedy of the Commons" is the contemporary classic article on the application of many of these principles to human populations.[1]

The Pribilof Seal Story

One of the most successful resource management examples centers around the Pribilof Islands about three hundred miles off the mainland of Alaska in the Bering Sea. These bleak islands serve as the only breeding ground of the Alaskan fur seal herd, which makes up about 80 per cent of the world's fur seals. The isolated rocky beaches of the Pribilofs serve as the birthplaces of the young seals each summer, and by fall the herd leaves the islands and returns to the sea.

Because of the *polygamous* habits of the fur seal, it is practical to harvest the surplus males without affecting the overall population level of the herd. But this feature was ignored during the early sealing periods. When Russia held possession of the Aleutian archipelago, the seal population was estimated at 2.5 million animals. From 1786 until 1867 when Russia sold Alaska to the United States, no restrictions existed on the number or sex of seals that could be killed by mariners. As many as 140,000 seals per year were taken, and in 1889 the U.S. government forbade the killing of female seals on the islands and established annual quotas of 100,000 seal skins. A rampant period of open sea seal killing took place from 1871 until 1897. The *pelagic* or open sea hunting netted up to 62,000 seals per year and by the 1890's the haul from the Pribilof Islands slumped to about 15,000 animals.

The United States Congress stepped into the picture, and in 1897 passed a ban (which was difficult to enforce) against pelagic sealing. In 1910 the federal government took over all seal hunting operations on the islands. But other mariners, in addition to Americans, continued the open sea slaughter. The fur seal herd had dropped to about 134,000 animals.[2] Shortly thereafter, a four country alliance called the North Pacific Fur Seal Con-

---

[1]Garrett Hardin, "The Tragedy of the Commons," *Science*, Vol. 162 (Dec. 13, 1968), pp. 1243-1248.

[2]Most of the data are from the Bureau of Commercial Fisheries Circular 275 called "Fur Seal Industry of the Pribilof Islands 1786-1965," by Francis Riley, 1967.

Figure 10-14. The Alaskan fur seal demonstrates a classic success story in the annals of American wildlife management. Here is the fur seal in a typical habitat showing vulnerability without proper protection. (U.S. Bureau of Sport Fisheries and Wildlife)

vention was agreed upon by Great Britain, Japan, Russia, and the United States to protect the fur seal. This treaty prohibited all pelagic sealing except by native hunters with primitive weapons. Modifications of the agreement have taken place over the years with Canada and Japan receiving approximately 30 per cent of the annual take. The harvest since the 1911 accord has yielded an average of almost 70,000 skins per year.

Since 1940, biologists from the U.S. Fish and Wildlife Service have tagged over 1.5 million seal pups. Information was sought on migration, mortality rates, and age composition, reproduction patterns, food habitats, and methods of hookworm control. The data that are collected, particularly an accurate inventory of the herd, were used to improve management procedures and attain a maximum sustained yield. It was found that one bull fur seal maintains an average size harem of about forty five cows and the pregnancy rate is about 60 per cent. For several years the population of the herd has been fluctuating between 1.3 million and 1.7 million seals. Factors that inhibit further growth of the herd are the limited summer food supply and the crowding of the rookeries. The future seems promising for

364   this animal resource as long as the females and young seals do not run into overwhelming troubles during their annual 6,000 mile migration down the North American coast.

Pacific Oysters and Clams

Other animal resources that typify a special category of fauna in the Pacific Northwest region are the oyster and the clam.

Oysters

The two main Pacific coast oysters are *Ostrea gigas* and *Ostrea lurida.* Because they are sessile creatures, they fall prey to many different problems. In recent years the pollution from pulp mills and paper mills has greatly harmed the oyster industry. Toxic substances dumped into the estuary and marine habitat retard the rate of pumping and greatly interfere with the feeding mechanisms of oysters. In clean unpolluted water an adult oyster pumps about eighty gallons of water a day. Local environmental factors and seasonal changes can devastate oyster beds even under sustained yield management.

In 1962 oyster production was low because of a wind storm and a disease that killed many three-year-old oysters. Again in 1965 the production dropped because of factors external to the dynamics of the oyster community. In this case, it was the 1964 tsnami that did extensive damage especially in Willapa Harbor. The harvest for that year totaled 9.2 million pounds worth $2.2 million, a decline of 800,000 pounds from the previous year. In 1967, oyster production was 7.7 million pounds valued at $3.2 million, a decline of 88,000 pounds from 1966 but an increase in value of $426,000. The state of Washington produced 85 per cent of the volume. Incidentally the volume of canning of oysters increased because of imports from Japan and British Columbia.

Oysters can provide a large supply of food if farmed in the sea. This is one resource that is relatively easy to manage because of its stationary characteristic. At the present time oysters are overexploited in Puget Sound and predators and pollution are taking a heavy toll of the Pacific beds. By the use of intelligent management, the control of predators, and the reduction of pollution, the oyster beds of the Pacific coast could be greatly expanded.

Clams

Of the Pacific species, the razor clam *Siliqua patula,* is the most important and is used both fresh and canned. It is found on nearly all the sandy beaches from Oregon to Alaska. They are long and narrow and can burrow into sand to a depth of two or three feet. Because they live on the shore between tide lines they are extremely susceptible to pollution. Cooking kills the pathogenic organisms such as *Bacillus typhosus* that are prevalent

Figure 10-15. Pacific Coast beaches provide popular clam-digging and fishing for nearby urban populations. (U.S. Bureau of Outdoor Recreation)

near large cities. The most important fisheries are located in Clatsop County, Oregon; Grays Harbor and Pacific counties, Washington; and Cordova, Alaska. There is a closed season from June 1 to September 1, which is the only management tool in effect.

Clams have been overexploited and seem to be disappearing from the Pacific coast. Production has dropped from over fifty thousand cases a year to fifteen thousand cases per year within the past twenty years. One of the major problems has been the recreational digger; in 1965 about fifty thousand recreational diggers harvested eight hundred thousand razor clams, half of the entire Pacific commercial catch. Laws have been passed limiting individuals to eighteen clams per day but enforcement has been poor. More laws and stricter enforcement are needed to save the Pacific razor clam.

The Caribou of Alaska

The illustration of the caribou has special symbolism in terms of its role as a climax community indicator, the relationship it has with the human members of its ecosystem, and then how it might be managed as a common property resource in the face of modern uses of the Alaskan tundra. When

365

Figure 10-16. Big Alaska moose enjoys a roadside lake in the Alaskan interior. The moose is found in a preclimax succession habitat. (U.S. Bureau of Outdoor Recreation)

Figure 10-17. More wolves are found in Alaska than any other state. Hunting wolves from airplanes has proven to be a practice that is difficult to stop in Alaska. Besides man, the wolf is the caribou's major year-round enemy. (U.S. Bureau of Sport Fisheries and Wildlife)

one first thinks of Alaska, one usually thinks of its wildlife; and of its wildlife the most familiar to us are the great bears—the brown and grizzly, moose, bighorn sheep, and the wolf. Probably no other animals, however, have had such a great sustaining influence on the Alaskan natives as the caribou.[3] For perhaps hundreds of years this animal has been almost the sole support of thousands of Indians and to a lesser extent, Eskimos, whose prosperity or lack of it has been a direct result of the number and availability of caribou. Today, the caribou is valuable for more than sustenance reasons alone. The general citizen's disregard for his environment and forgetfulness about life's interdependencies are punctuated by the precarious position of the caribou.

[3] Gratitude is expressed to Thomas Doerr for his unpublished research paper on the "Caribou in Alaska," which forms the foundation for this discussion.

The caribou of Alaska are generally referred to as Barren Ground caribou, although there are two distinct subspecies in Alaska—Grant caribou, which are of medium build and dark colored, and are found on the Alaskan Peninsula and Unimak Island, and Stone caribou, which are darker and larger than the Grant caribou and are found in the interior and northern parts of Alaska. It is the Grant caribou that is so numerous in the northern, arctic areas and upon which the Indians and Eskimo depend. In addition to the Barren Ground caribou and its subspecies, there are many other species of caribou in the northern latitudes of North America, the most notable of these being the Woodland caribou. But the Barren Ground caribou and its Alaskan subspecies are the most numerous and hence the most important from an economic and sociological standpoint. The principle food of the caribou is lichen or "caribou moss" as it is sometimes called. It grows sparsely on the boggy ground, sometimes taking as long as sixty years to grow to the size necessary for practical caribou forage. This helps to account for the nomadic movements of the herds—few of them ever feed twice on the same winter forage.

Despite the hardship of constant movement, the caribou is well suited for its traveling. It has a heavy double coat, combining dense underfur with long, hollow guard hairs. This provides the caribou not only with very good insulation against extremely cold temperatures but also provides flotation for swimming, during which they can move as fast as five miles per hour. Their very large hooves—roundish and cushioned—act as both snowshoes and paddles. Both sexes have antlers, the only member of the deer family for which this is true. During her life span, the average doe has six fawns. These animals are polygamous, and the average harem during the rut is between twelve and twenty cows. The caribou's only major year-round enemy, besides man, is the wolf—and studies have shown that the majority of kills are of the very old, very young, weak, and sick individuals. The most spectacular attribute of the caribou, leaving aside the astounding racks the bucks develop, is behavioral. It can be truthfully said that the migrations of the caribou are the last events that are reminiscent of the massive herds of buffalo on the Great Plains in the mid-1800's. If this animal had no other redeeming qualities, this alone might merit its preservation.

The casual observer of the Alaskan scene would probably rank the caribou as a big game animal as its most important influence on the economy, but the caribou's greatest influence is as a life source to the Indians and Eskimos. It is on this basis that the caribou has been judged one of the most valuable big game animals in the world. Until fairly recently, it served as the cornerstone of the Chipewyan Indians—known as the caribou eaters, who were almost totally dependent upon it for such basic necessities as food, clothing, tool handles, sinews for sewing, and oil for lamps. The Eskimos were less dependent upon it, basing their economy more on marine mammals, although they turned to the caribou for some important items as winter clothing. Before the advent of firearms, the number of caribou killed by the natives was small, even though hun-

Figure 10-18. Caribou on Adak, Aleutian Islands National Wildlife Refuge, Alaska. (U.S. Bureau of Sport Fisheries and Wildlife)

dreds would often be killed at a single hunt. The natives would spear the migrating caribou herds from canoes and kayaks. They captured them at water crossings or in pounds made of spruce tree fences or columns of stones on the tundra.

The advent of the fur trade upset this caribou-human predator relationship. Longer winter trips were needed to trap more furs and hence larger dog teams. Therefore, larger caches of caribou meat to feed the trappers and their dogs were vital. Along with these changes the rifle was introduced. When Eskimos and Indians first got rifles, they slaughtered the caribou and other animals so enthusiastically that many forms of wildlife were virtually exterminated over large areas—as a result people were in danger of starvation. This, along with the fact that whaling and salmon fishing along the west coast of Alaska was going steadily downhill and the Eskimos who depended on them were following suit, prompted the federal government to try a daring plan. Beginning just before 1900, several attempts were made to introduce domesticated reindeer into Alaska to alleviate the starvation and poverty of the natives. They were taught to care for the herds and, probably more important (after an initial slaughter), they learned not to eat all the available reindeer in a rush. This experiment has met with only

368

moderate success. The Eskimos are a proud people and many of them preferred a hunting life to a herding one. Despite the lack of widespread Eskimo interest, the reindeer boomed on the grazing range left on the Seward Peninsula by the retreating native caribou. Like many introduced populations, (especially those of grazing animals) without natural predation or other forms of environmental resistance, the transplanted reindeer exceeded the carrying capacity of their habitat. From a population of over 600,000 in 1930, they dropped to 26,000 in 1950 and in 1965, 35,000 were left. On Saint George, one of the Pribilof Islands, the reindeer population went from a peak of 2,000 in 1937 to 8 in 1950.

The problems facing the caribou can be generalized into five broad categories: human population, overkill by natives, naturally occurring factors of individuals, degradation of range, and oil. Most large mammals, especially trophy species, are threatened by the encroaching human population in Alaska. The prevailing needless hunting waste of caribou by Eskimos and Indians has been recognized, and vigorous educational steps have been taken along sound conservation lines to correct the situation. Hunting laws have been tightened, and substitute food supplies and storage

Figure 10-19. Whenever additional human populations are brought into the home range of the caribou such as pipeline activity, legal and illegal hunting pressures increase on the caribou and other wildlife species. (U.S. Bureau of Sport Fisheries and Wildlife)

facilities have been established in some villages. Hunting pressure has been further reduced by the opening up of new economic possibilities for the natives. Work in mining and military establishments, in social services, and in aerial transportation has reduced the need for caribou as the main source of sustenance. New sources of employment from the oil industry may even further reduce their dependence on the caribou, if the caribou are still available on a sustained harvest basis. Today there are relatively few natives that depend heavily on the caribou for their livelihood. Naturally occurring factors would include *natural decimating factors* such as catastrophic accidents, blizzards, disease, and predation. Of these, wolf predation is the most substantial, although the wolves, as mentioned earlier, tend to take only the less able-bodied caribou from the herds.

The last two problems for caribou are the most serious and appear to be interrelated more than others. Range degradation is largely a man-caused phenomenon. The *tundra* is an extremely fragile ecosystem. It is made up of very low profile vegetation, mosses, and lichens for the most part, with some small birch or other tree here and there. The organic material in the soil is very thin and highly fragile. Beneath it is *permafrost,* extending down as far as fifteen hundred feet. When this crust is broken, the summer sun melts the permafrost and the area becomes a quagmire. This is the habitat of the Barren Ground caribou. It can be degraded in many ways: fires, overgrazing, and disruption of the top crust are the most important. The discovery of oil on the North Slope has raised a new threat to the caribou in addition to the possible disruption of the tundra crust—the proposed pipelines run through the caribou's habitat and across many of its migration routes. The size of the pipeline could prohibit migrations and if buried underground, the heat from the oil could create a situation not unlike California's famous La Brea tar pits. These two problems exist whether or not there is an oil spill or leak, the possibility of which is speculative. Obviously these problems should be solved before the pipelines are completed. With all these factors entering into the overall picture of the caribou in Alaska, what does the future hold in store for it, or more properly, what do we want the future to hold in store for it?

Actually, the caribou could have a very bright future if certain measures are taken to preserve both its range and its numbers. At the present, the greatest threat to its habitat is the presence of the oil companies that have replaced both fire and overgrazing as the most probable cause of range degradation. In fact, the nomadic nature of the caribou often negated the problems of fire and overgrazing, both being most troublesome to the animal when a severe winter restricted its wanderings. To eliminate the problem of oil and gas extraction activities, the closest possible control over drilling, storage, and transmission is required. Special care must begin with the building of roads and pipelines in order to ensure that the caribou will be able to pass on their migration routes and to prevent disruption of the tundra, turning it into a death trap for any animal that may venture into it. This, along with continued inspection of the work areas and the

Figure 10-20. This aerial view of Stone's caribou suggests the migrating characteristics of the caribou. Pipeline, railroad, highway, and other types of construction and development should take this phenomenon of extensive migratory movements into consideration in order not to block or discourage natural movement of the herds. (U.S. Bureau of Sport Fisheries and Wildlife)

selected route of the pipeline will hopefully maximize the caribou's protection. For the future, new protected areas, better and closer supervision and protection of the herds by the Alaska State Fish and Game department, the new hunting regulations should be instituted. This may, in the case of new preserves, be difficult because of the vast areas of land covered by the herds in their migrations. Where necessary, the federal government should set aside more of its land holdings as restricted preserves. The problem of the natives that are still somewhat dependent upon the caribou could be partially solved in several ways, both of which will necessitate some serious changes. They could try changing their way of life inasmuch as the oil industry promises to offer many new job opportunities for them. Secondly, they could engage in a wild-herd management program where they would not only derive their meat from the caribou but could possibly manage the herds for a profit without the loss of the wildness of the caribou. This is under study and may prove to be a possibility, especially with the advent of the snowmobile as a tool to increase the mobility of the natives as well as providing a necessary transport for the meat. The **371**

Figure 10-21. The perpetuation of the caribou as a climax species in the Pacific Northwest is in considerable jeopardy. Here is a dramatic example of the extent of influence urban man has on a habitat and species which occur thousands of miles from the origin of the influence. (U.S. Bureau of Sport Fisheries and Wildlife)

wildness of the caribou is apparently in no danger by this method because if penned and slaughtered they are frightened and their meat is subsequently tainted. They must be killed on the range. This has presented a problem in that no formal government inspection facilities are available for freezing and processing of the meat to government standards. This is also under study.

In addition to these arguments for the perpetuation of the caribou, there is the rationale of pure aesthetics—what would Alaska be like without the caribou? Some say that northern development has doomed the caribou, and that we should not concern ourselves with its fate, but the meager subarctic forests and tundra underlaid with permafrost offer little use for modern forestry or agriculture. The caribou is the animal best adapted by nature to utilize these habitats. It is suitable for an extensive type of wild-herd husbandry, and if properly managed could continue to provide food and livelihood "on the hoof" to the natives of Alaska and others remote from supplies of domestic beef. But more than that, the caribou-man-tundra interdependency is a living legend that urban dwellers should have as an object lesson in a *biotic climax community* of which man is an integral part. Even though the Isle Royale moose-wolf balance has become a classic in wildlife literature, man's passing participation is that primarily of a backpacker on that national park island. The situation of the caribou tests how well the demands of distant urban consumers can be integrated with a fragile common property animal resource on one of our last frontiers. It will require constant vigilance on the part of government—state and federal, the private sector, and citizens to preserve the caribou, as well as other wildlife in the Pacific Northwest region.

Some readers may question the inclusion of the preceding discussion on the caribou and other wildlife that do not concern urban populations directly on a daily basis. It is hoped that the impact of urban-oriented decisions such as increasing oil exploration and extraction, increasing the number of urban owned leisure homes or recreation developments, and other invasions into the remote hinterland wildlife habitat by urban-generated factors can be seen in terms that are more than symbolic or purely aesthetic. How these wildlife challenges are dealt with will be an insight into urban man's future priorities.

The Fallacy of Bounty Systems

The classic illustrations of irrational game management over the long run are the *bounty* provisions for predator control. Research in recent years has shown that natural predation is a part of the environmental resistance and a *carrying capacity determinant* for animal resources that are generally common property and renewable resources.

The Western and Pacific Coast states were the first to implement bounty systems on a massive scale because of the large amount of land used for hunting, fishing, logging, and grazing. The old Taylor Grazing Act lands, now managed by the Bureau of Land Management, were and are particularly vulnerable to private demands for bounties and predator control programs. Scientific wildlife management is a relatively young profession, and at that time very little research had been carried out on the effects of reduced predator population. There seemed to be no reason to doubt that fewer predators would result in more game and less livestock destruction. As more research findings were collected, however, the theoretical idea of predator control began to be questioned. Yet most of the field experience of predator damage came from individuals who managed large concentrations of wildlife or livestock and their observations have had some indelible effects on fellow stockmen, and state and federal fish and game officials.

In the 1960's Oregon spent up to $400,000 each year in predator control and over $11,000 annually on bounties in an attempt to control the coyote, bobcat, porcupine, red fox, jackrabbit, gopher, cougar, mole, and wolf. (In Oregon the last wolf was killed in 1946.) Data on predator population levels with bounties show that the bounty is an ineffective way of predator control. Furthermore, the system invites fraudulent operations when different states have different laws and varying bounties. Whatever successes are recorded, it seems clear that they are nullified when one considers the fact that once the predator has been destroyed, his food supply must be artificially controlled or destroyed for fear of another "pest" population erupting. If predator control is desired, good ecosystem-wide land management is required.

Domestic sheep losses to coyotes have been estimated at up to $10

374 million per year by ranching and grazing interests, but no one knows exactly how many of the sheep are killed by coyotes or how much mortality is the result of overgrazing and subsequent malnutrition, disease, range destruction, and other sheep-imposed constraints. It is an interesting question where the blame is to be placed since coyotes, like herring gulls, are *carrion feeders.*

If sheep and cattle losses are increasing, the fault more properly lies with the range management and its inability to maintain an appropriate carrying capacity. Where sheep and other livestock are overgrazing the land, especially public lands, the bounty, 1080 poisoning, and other predator control programs that are conducted at public expense should be curtailed. Compound 1080 (sodium fluoroacetate) is a potent rodenticide derived from an organic salt. It is a stable, water-soluble compound that is tasteless and therefore cannot be detected by whatever animal is eating the bait. Compound 1080's action is delayed so that a lethal dose is consumed before any sickening takes place. Furthermore, secondary poisoning is not uncommon. After the initial victim dies, there remain lethal dosages in the viscera and other parts preferred by scavengers. "Eagles fall victim to secondary poisoning following control programs directed at the prairie dog,

Figure 10-22. Elk populations when protected from natural predators, as seen in this photograph, produce surplus numbers that are harvested annually on a permit basis by local hunters. (U.S. Bureau of Sport Fisheries and Wildlife)

coyotes die after eating poisoned mice and other rodents. The target animal, dying, remains a reservoir of death."[4]

In 1969 a survey was made of animal damage on forest plantations in the Pacific Northwest area. The plantations studied were Douglas fir and Ponderosa pine, and it was discovered that most of the damage is done to saplings and seedlings. The damage in order of severity was done by deer (56 per cent), porcupines, pocket gophers, jackrabbits, elk, livestock, small rodents, mountain beavers, and bears. The annual losses to the Weyerhauser Company's young plantation trees run up to $800,000. One might speculate what could have been saved in bounty payments for predators and losses to young trees if a more workable equilibrium could be anticipated for predator-prey relationships. Ten states provide for payments of loss to livestock or other property because of predator damage, but for the most part there is overwhelming sentiment by state agencies against widespread predator control for game management. It seems strange that these payments continue. An alternative to natural predation is to schedule emergency hunts to reduce elk and deer populations that have caused excessive damage to crops. The accumulated evidence in the Pacific Northwest region and elsewhere is rather persuasive that bounties are a poor investment in animal resource management even though the emotional single-visit observer may see a different picture.

A report to the Council on Environmental Quality and the Department of Interior by the Advisory Committee on Predator Control called *Predator Control—1971*[5] summarizes questions that were asked of all fifty state departments of game management or their equivalent. The following questions are pertinent to this discussion on predator control and bounties: "What do present State laws say about the use of poisons and what is the Department stand on the use of poisons?" The response was "Illegal to use poisons—16, special permit required—12, Department personnel—1, legal to use poison—21." Twenty-three state game departments opposed the use of poisons, and selected comments from the six condoning states were as follows:

Idaho does not allow use of 1080 for cases in which the state is involved; Nevada approves poisoning when carried out by Division of Wildlife Services personnel but recognized a problem in illegal use and lack of discretion by private citizens; Oregon favors use of selective baits in arid coyote areas where non-target species will suffer the least degree of harm; Wyoming opposes the use of thallium but currently approves use of 1080 on a selective basis. Alabama does not oppose use of poisons when they are specific on target animals but disfavors large-area application. Arizona believes poisons should be used if they are the most efficient and effective.[6]

[4] Graham, Frank Jr. *Since Silent Spring* (Boston: Houghton Mifflin Company, 1970), pp. 195–196.
[5] Advisory Committee on Predator Control, Stanley A. Cain, Chairman; *Predator Control-1971; A Report to the Council on Environmental Quality and the Department of the Interior* (January 1972).
[6] Ibid., Appendix XIV, p. 169.

376   It was also reported that nine states maintain bounties: Alabama (beaver), Alaska (wolf and hair seals), Arizona (mountain lion, wolf, coyote), Maine (bobcats), Michigan (coyote), Mississippi (beaver), New Hampshire (bobcat and porcupine), South Dakota (bobcat, fox, and coyote), Utah (bobcat and coyote).[7] Twenty states have county-maintained bounties and twenty-three states have no bounties as reported in the 1971 study.

Three recommendations of the report stand out as being rather forceful:

1. We recommend that immediate Congressional action be sought to remove all existing toxic chemicals from registration and use for operational predator control. We further recommend that these restrictions extend to those toxicants used in field rodent control whose action is characterized by the secondary poisoning of scavengers. Pending, and in addition to, such Congressional action, we recommend that the Secretary of the Interior disallow use of the aforementioned chemicals in the federal operational program of predator and rodent control, and that this ruling be made a standard in cooperative agreements with the states. Moreover, we recommend that the individual states pass legislation to ban the use of toxicants in predator control.[8]

2. We recommend to the Federal Aviation Authority that a provision be made for suspending or revoking the license of a private pilot and the confiscation of the aircraft—when he knowingly carries a passenger whose acts lead to conviction for illegal predator control, such as shooting from the aircraft or distributing poisons.[9]

3. We recommend that action be taken by Congress to rule out the broadcast of toxicants for the control of rodents, rabbits, and other vertebrate pests on federal lands, and that the possibility of correlative action be explored for private lands as well.[10]

The Emotional Dimensions of Game Management

It is important to stress the subjective and very emotional dimensions that infuse the dilemma of wildlife and fishery management. Those who wish to maintain game harvesting of one kind or another often possess a strong emotional tie to the land and what it produces for them. Hunters are not always persuaded by research findings of game biologists, especially if the studies infringe on some long-held patterns of behavior. For many outdoor people, an annual fishing or hunting trip with old friends becomes a special ritual that is not easily broken. On the other hand, those who seek the absolute preservation of all members of the animal and plant kingdoms become most adamant about the merits of their position. An unswerving attitude for natural determinism may hold even after an individual or group is told about the ecological merits of controlled burning, artificial propagation, or managed wildlife harvesting.

[7] Ibid., p. 169.   [8] Ibid., p. 5,6.   [9] Ibid., p. 10.   [10] Ibid., p. 10.

Figure 10-23. Some of the most difficult members of the public to convince about rational game management are the "trophy hunters" and "boys in the old gang" who go hunting as part of an annual ritual. The bull moose is portrayed with his conqueror. (U.S. Bureau of Sport Fisheries and Wildlife)

Figure 10-24. Seasonal runs lure the sport fisherman into the breaking surf of the Oregon coast. Part of the lure of Pacific Northwest cities is that the metropolitan resident is within easy reach of most popular forms of hunting and fishing. (U.S. Bureau of Outdoor Recreation)

Figure 10-25. Urban fishing activities along the Pacific Coast attract the daily fishing public. (U.S. Bureau of Outdoor Recreation)

There is a decreasing percentage of the American population actually hunting and fishing in local natural fish and game habitats. If such a trend continues, it is likely that a growing percentage of the population will advocate wild animal management practices in areas such as the Pacific Northwest states where the urban "armchair wildlifer" has never been. Even now, there seems to be a widening conflict of opinion between those who spend most of their leisure time in megalopolis while still exercising considerable influence on the decision-making processes of fishing and hunting procedures, versus those who spend much of their professional time in the field and advocate another fish or game management point of view.

Wildlife in the Metropolitan Environment

The use of wildlife resources in a metropolitan environment is primarily nonconsumptive as compared with the harvesting of traditional back country game that also constitutes "flow" resources. Birds head up a list of the most observed urban wildlife. The emphasis is on identification, feeding, and observing, not hunting. For example, residents of the Washington, D.C., metropolitan area buy over 4,500 tons of wild birdseed each year at a cost of over $1 million. Backyard and balcony bird feeders are a large business in cities and suburbs according to a North Dakota wild birdseed company that grows and ships over 20 million pounds of birdseed a year. Hummingbird feeders that provide nectarlike liquids are also popular. Many urbanites plant supplementary wildlife—luring vegetation such a pyracantha, arbutus, barberry, sunflowers, holly, and mulberry. The *1971 Sunset Western Garden Book*[11] lists plants that attract birds and vegetation that are "deer-proof or close to it" for suburbanites whose gardens and landscaping are overbrowsed by deer. Additional vines and trees that attract birds include Virginia creeper, honeysuckle, alder, birch, dogwood, mountain ash, hawthorn, and sycamore.

Some of the wildlife in an urban area is unseen by people because it is nocturnal. Rats, flying squirrels, bats, opossums, raccoons, deer, fox, frogs, toads, and nighthawks seek their food during the darkness hours. Bats and nighthawks can be seen near the lights of nighttime sports events feeding on airborne insects, whereas early morning hours are best for viewing rabbits, pheasants, quail, and the urban-dwelling amphibians.

During migratory periods waterfowl, warblers, and other bird species often visit downtown parks, open spaces, and large public gardens when adequate supplies of food, cover, and water are available. The common residential community of nesting birds in the cities of the Pacific Northwest includes robins, orioles, tanagers, woodpeckers, mourning doves, wrens, English sparrows, starlings, cardinals, jays, thrashers, thrushes, purple martins, chimney swifts, pigeons, and usually nighthawks who build their nests on flat gravel rooftops.

A major problem with urban wildlife is that monotonous zoning produces inadequate habitat and poor habitat diversity. The basic ingredients of habitat—food, water, and cover—are potentially present in and near every city, but without commitment from state and federal game management specialists and urban planners, almost nothing has been done professionally for urban wildlife management. One breakthrough in this direction is the relatively recent California Fish and Wildlife Plan that includes consideration of city wildlife values and recommends the use of general funds for city wildlife work. Part of the effort to enhance wildlife production will be to inform the general public about the use of pesticides, manicured lawns with no shrubs or no understory beneath the shade trees, and the dependence of animals and birds on feeding stations once they are started. The Milwaukee County park system is a good example to show habitat restoration and citizen education about wildlife problems and possibilities. Many Pacific Northwest region cities such as Victoria and Vancouver, British Columbia, have excellent habitat provisions at present. The large parks and public grounds of Seattle, Olympia, Portland, Corvallis, Eugene, Sacramento, and San Francisco are other examples.

The richest wildlife production areas exist where two or more biological communities (lake, forest, meadow, or stream) meet. This natural edge

---

[11] *Sunset Western Garden Book*, by the Editors of Sunset Magazine and Sunset Books, (Menlo Park, California: Lane Magazine & Book Company, 1971), pp. 132–133.

effect or *ecotone* supplies nesting sites, various feeding areas, brood cover, resting areas, and travel corridors. Whatever the habitat diversity happens to be in a given city (or any area) it is a cushion against wildlife calamity and a bonus for aesthetic and economic values. It is imperative to have year-round water available either in free flowing streams and permanent natural lakes or man-made ponds or fountains. Buried storm sewers, airports, expressways, and parking lots are not suitable habitats for most species whereas untended bluffs, abandoned railroad rights-of-way, vacant lots, property hedge rows, waterfronts, church yards, and cemeteries all hold excellent potential for wildlife development.

Wildlife management in the city requires the understanding by the citizenry when population controls are put into effect in the event of a population explosion. Without predators or other natural control mechanisms operating, an urban wildlife population can become a nuisance. Pigeons, squirrels, opossums, raccoons, skunks, gophers, and deer have sometimes exceeded an urban environment's carrying capacity or a neighborhood's tolerance level. Respect for animals and human safety is also an instructive ingredient of wildlife education when rabid animals and other dangerous species are in any urban vicinity.

Some species of wildlife never could and never should live in the center city because of improper habitat or inadequate space. But in cities where professional wildlife planning is coordinated with other urban planning, funds can be obtained from state conservation departments, from HUD's Open Space Land Program, from several Department of the Interior offices, and from numerous private conservation organizations such as the National Wildlife Federation and National Audubon Society. With the necessary research into urban wildlife ecology and further study of the species that make good wildlife neighbors, urban wildlife managers or specialists could create a new kind of master plan for a metropolitan area that would preserve wildlife habitat, attract new wildlife, and help control problem wildlife.

As wildlife in a metropolitan area becomes a more publicly acknowledged goal, improved urban plans to incorporate wildlife as legitimate residents of new towns and rebuilt communities will be forthcoming. For present cities in the Pacific Northwest and elsewhere in the United States, the heightened sensitivity to fish and wildlife conditions, and management and legislation will occur as urban pollution degrades wildlife habitat and threatens populations of animals and fish that suburban and urban residents have grown to love and appreciate.

Summary of Animal Resource Management Principles

It would be easy to succumb to the temptation of detailing the wildlife and fishery conservation practices that are currently in use. But this in not

Figure 10-26. Snow geese, which have benefited from Migratory Bird Treaties and Wildlife Refuge Acts, are seen here at the Sacramento National Wildlife Refuge, California, along the Pacific Flyway. (U.S. Bureau of Sport Fisheries and Wildlife)

the moment or the place. Authorities are available and very readable for each of the faunal categories the reader wishes to choose. Names such as Leopold, Cooley, D. Allen, Crutchfield, Murie, Craighead, Mech, and Dasmann stand out with distinction for their contributions to the body of wildlife and fishery research. From them we are able to learn the principle and applications of game management: clues about habitat improvement, water needs, adequate cover, fundamentals of home range and territory, edge or ecotone effects, suggestions about predator control, artificial propagation, wildlife refuges and reserves, and the dynamics of animal and plant communities. We should be introduced to important wildlife legislation such as the following, which is adapted from Allen and Leonard.[12]

Legislation Affecting Wildlife and Fisheries
In addition to state measures passed by the various states in recent years, the following federal legislation deserves special mention:

The Lacey Act of 1900 extended certain powers of the Secretary of Agriculture and contained regulations on interstate and foreign commerce in wild birds and other animals. The enforcement features of this act were strengthened by amendment in 1935.

[12]Shirley Allen, and Justin Leonard, *Conserving Natural Resources* (New York: McGraw-Hill Book Company, Inc., 1966).

382   *The Migratory Bird Treaty with Great Britain of 1916* (on behalf of Canada) . . . This treaty or "convention" lists game and insectivorous and other nongame birds, provides for closed seasons which put an end to spring shooting, and agrees that legislation for carrying out all terms will be sought by the contracting powers in their own countries.

The Migratory Bird Treaty Act of 1918 gave full effect to the above treaty of 1916. A similar act was passed by the Canadian Parliament in 1917. The validity of the latter and the constitutionality of the former have been established by court decisions.

The Migratory Bird Treaty with Mexico of 1937 . . . Provisions of this treaty are similar to the one with Canada but also include the interesting prohibition of hunting from aircraft. Appropriate amendment of the Migratory Bird Treaty Act of 1918 was approved in 1936, pending ratification of the treaty with Mexico.

The Wildlife Refuge Exchange Act of 1935 provided for the acquisition of refuge lands privately owned in exchange for federal lands or products from federal lands, when the public interest will thus be served.

The National Forest Fish and Game Sanctuary Act of 1934 granted authority to the President to establish refuges by proclamation within the national forests with the approval of state legislatures in the states involved. This act is important because of the vast area of the national forests and their wild-animal populations.

The Wildlife Coordination Act of 1934 as amended in 1946 was designed to reconcile objectives of various bureaus in the construction of flood control, power, and irrigation works in any river valley. . . . Some progress was achieved in attempting to reconcile the operation (rather than construction) of the Bonneville and Grand Coolee Dams with the conservation of the salmon resources of the Columbia River; but, in general, the results of the law have been disappointing. Since the amendment of the act in 1946, interdepartmental committees have been set up in the Columbia, Missouri, and other river valleys, but they have power only to advise.[13]

There is also the *Pittman-Robertson Act of 1937,* which imposes a 10 per cent federal tax on ammunition and sporting goods that are used by states for wildlife research and development. The *1950 Dingell-Johnson Law* authorizes a similar levy on fishing tackle for use on fishery research and habitat acquisition. Other federal legislation that directly or indirectly affects wildlife includes the *Wetlands Loan Act of 1961,* which established loans from duck-stamp funds for acquiring wetlands and other habitat for waterfowl; the *Wetlands Inspection Act of 1962,* which supplements the Wetlands Loan Act and specifically facilitates loans for land where technical assistance is necessary; the *Wilderness Act of 1964* (described in Chapter 11); the *Scenic and Wild Rivers Act of 1968,* which preserves free-flowing streams from further physical encroachment or development; and the *Marine Mammal Protection Act of 1972.* The intent of the latter act is to conserve animals such as whales, polar bears, walruses, sea otters, and seals; it essentially establishes a moratorium on hunting or importing the marine mammals, but the permits that allow for exemptions are worrisome to many wildlife observers.

[13] Ibid., pp. 254–256.

The fishery management practices that are thoroughly discussed in the fisheries management literature include seasonal and gear regulation, catch limits, spawning habitat restoration, stocking, and disease and competitor control. Reasonably successful fishery commissions have been established on the Pacific and Atlantic coasts. They usually regulate a particular fishery such as halibut or salmon. But as with other major resource regulation decisions the consumer, in her or his city fish market, is in the vulnerable position of being totally dependent on dozens of decisions that precede the moment of final sale and final consumption. Unfortunately when the price of seafood goes up or when the quality goes down, the victim who appears most helpless is the urban consumer located far from the sea and its management problems of a resource with complexities of international magnitude.

Time for a New Look

The author does not mean to belittle or minimize the importance of the vast tonnages of salmon (and other fish), the shellfish, and the wild game that are harvested in the Pacific Northwest and are found on foreign and American tables. Neither does he wish to sell short major sources of pet food, protein derivatives, and, of course, the industrial and commercial uses of fish and game resources.

However, the days of the *potlach* are over. A new look at the animal resource base of the Pacific Northwest is called for if some integration of capability and urban demand is to be attained. In relative terms, the Pacific

Figure 10-27. The changes of habitat, the pressure of human populations, and the excessive hunting that reduced the bison population of North America have lessons for the management of many species of wildlife today. (U.S. Bureau of Sport Fisheries and Wildlife)

Figure 10-28. Proposed site of the Rampart Dam on Alaska's Yukon River. This project was defeated or at least shelved for the time being partly on the basis of anticipated destruction of waterfowl, fishery, and wildlife habitat.

Northwest states will probably be subjected to greater pressures from hunters and commercial and sport fisherman than any other region of the United States. Undoubtedly, equal pressures will be exerted by the lumbering profession, by land developers, and by recreation seekers. The *urban reserves* presently used by waterfowl, game, fish, shellfish, and other wildlife are becoming the major target for a new spectrum of leisure time activities, such as river float trips, big game and trophy hunting, hiking, backpacking, all terrain vehicle uses, downhill and cross-country skiing, and snowmobiling plus photographic safaris. Other urban-generated demands upon energy resources (hydro and fossil fuel), water supply, metals and other minerals, sawtimber, and seafood have begun to challenge the capability of the resource base of the northwestern states in a way that jeopardizes the survival of all the climax fauna and begins to threaten midsuccessional and low successional species as well. Threatening projects include the North American Water and Power Alliance, the trans-Alaskan pipeline, Prudhoe Bay and North Slope oil and gas extraction, the Snake and Columbia River hydropower and irrigation projects, and the multitude of harbor improvement, dredging, power plant, waste disposal, and offshore mineral extraction operations along the Pacific Coast.

Wildlife Management Analogues as Payoffs to Urban Dwellers

The lessons for human settlement enhancement and survival are in part available with the human experiences of the Pacific Northwest region and its wildlife resources. Hopefully, the gradual or even sudden man-caused collapse of a species is not carried out with malice of intent. Rather, when the demise of a habitat or its animal populations takes place, it occurs out of human ignorance and human apathy. That is the hope and the reason

Figure 10-29. (upper left) The musk ox is fighting extinction. (U.S. Bureau of Sport Fisheries and Wildlife)

Figure 10-30. (upper right) The pronghorn antelope is a barometer of the range condition. (U.S. Bureau of Sport Fisheries and Wildlife)

Figure 10-31. (middle left) This mountain goat was released on Kodiak (Island) National Wildlife Refuge, Alaska, by plane in hopes of establishing a population in a supportive habitat. (U.S. Bureau of Sport Fisheries and Wildlife)

Figure 10-32. (lower left) The future of the mountain lion is uncertain in the Pacific Northwest region. (U.S. Bureau of Sport Fisheries and Wildlife)

386   for trying to bring the message of wildlife resource management to the attention of urban dwellers who occupy a climax position in human ecosystems. In many cases the urban dwellers of climax communities within a large metropolitan area such as Nob Hill in San Francisco, Beacon Hill in Boston, and Georgetown in Washington, D.C., seem to display a disproportionately high degree of interest in protecting biological climax environments, endangered species, predator organisms, and wilderness areas. Perhaps it is a total coincidence or perhaps it is a function of a rural childhood on country estates, gentleman farms, or summer camp exposures to wildlife. Perhaps it is a result of having more financial resources, self-interest, and leisure time than other urbanites. It may even be a matter of empathy, conscious or unconscious.

Wildlife biologist and author, Raymond Dasmann describes the phenomenon of biotic succession in a way that can help us relate wildlife history to human events when he states:

the most difficult problems are presented by those animals that are obligate members of a climax community or wilderness area. Since man has modified the landscape, the area suited to these animals has dwindled. Where once they were the most abundant creatures, now they are scarce. Some, such as the passenger pigeon of the hardwood forests, the wild aurochs and wild bison of Europe, and the larger predators of Great Britain, are now extinct. Others, such as the caribou,

Figure 10-33. Members of human climax communities, such as in the established neighborhoods of San Francisco, seem to have a great interest in preserving biological climax communities. Perhaps it is a coincidence or perhaps a subconscious empathy exists between these people and their counterparts in other biological communities.

Figure 10-34. Olympic National Park, Washington, serves as a reservoir for endangered species and provides habitats of ocean and forest, meadow and mountain. (National Park Service)

musk-ox, bighorn sheep, and grizzly bear, are now reduced in numbers. The basic problem for their conservation is that of maintaining undisturbed conditions. Since we do not always understand the factors that led to the development and maintenance of natural vegetation, we face difficult situations. In the national parks of America, for example, where efforts have been made to provide complete protection for the vegetation, the results have often differed from expectations. The exclusion of fire, for example, has created forests that differ from those that were present when the parks were formed . . .

If we are to maintain climax wildlife, we must maintain large wilderness areas in which all the factors present before civilized man entered the scene are allowed to function. Where hunting pressure by primitive man was a part of the original balance, it must be substituted for by some equivalent cause of mortality. Otherwise, game populations will go out of balance. Where fires were natural in the past, they must be allowed to burn today.

Where stable habitat conditions can be maintained, it is possible to maintain stable populations of game over an indefinite period of time. Stability here is used only in a relative sense, for some climax populations will normally fluctuate greatly. Nevertheless, with a stable habitat these populations can be expected to remain, and management plans can be based on their continued presence within an area. Where population control is to be exercised by hunting, such populations should be held in careful balance with their food supply, thus both preserving the habitat and providing for a constant high yield.[14]

[14] Raymond Dasmann, *Wildlife Biology* (New York: John Wiley & Sons, Inc., 1964), pp. 84–85.

Figure 10-35. Fire as a natural force for long-term habitat maintenance in wildlife management has been recognized recently in a more positive light. This fire started by lightning in the Bitterroot Valley of Montana burned over 28,000 acres of insect-infested and over-mature lodgepole pine. (U.S. Forest Service)

Urban dwellers, individually and collectively, who are participants in the resource we call a city need to determine what kind of yield is expected and possible. Those expectations and possibilities can be guided from the lessons and experiences that are available to us in the fish and wildlife communities—communities that seem to represent the best analogues to our own various urban management situations. At the same time, urban and suburban residents should acquaint themselves with the wealth of wildlife that, despite all man has done, resides downtown and within our largest metropolitan regions.

Figure 10-36. Lessons about community survival abound in the history of plant and animal communities. Perhaps the time will come when those who are interested in the survival of human cities will inspect what has happened to species like the black-footed ferret, one of the rarest mammals of the United States, which peers from the entrance of a prairie dog burrow. (U.S. Bureau of Sport Fisheries and Wildlife)

CHAPTER **11**

Recreation and Open Space Resources

CASE IN POINT: THE PACIFIC COAST REGION

The recreation demands made by the urbanites of the Pacific Coast region may be typical of those that will be expressed by most Americans in the twenty-first century. Because of the monotony of bedroom communities or the drearisome conditions of commercial and industrial areas, the money-rich, environment-poor urban dweller will desire and claim a right to leisure time pursuits in a different, relatively pollution-free environment. Those who seek and can afford the unique recreation experiences of solitude and physical and mental rejuvenation will grow in numbers as present urbanization conditions reduce the possibility of satisfying certain recreation needs within the metropolitan vicinity. Recreation activities external to the city that have shown considerable growth in recent years include cross-country skiing, backpacking, snowmobiling, scenic and wild river use, bicycle touring, photography, surfing, and scuba diving. Predictions of recreation demands stated in the Outdoor Recreation Resources Review Commission Report of 1962 are being realized. Two of the major findings that continue to be true are that driving for pleasure and water-related activities are the two most popular forms of recreation for Americans. The lure of ocean, forests, desert, lakes, and mountains is an overwhelming temptation for solitude-seeking metropolitanites of the Pacific Coast region or other Americans who are not accustomed to living in proximity of the tallest trees, the tallest mountains, the most productive tidepools, and many other superlative outdoor recreation possibilities.

In large measure, the available Western open space and wilderness areas

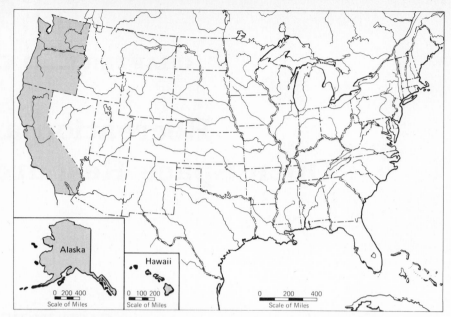

Figure 11-1. The Pacific Coast states typify American urban-related recreation and open space resource questions.

Figure 11-2. Water-related recreation is one of the most popular forms of leisure time use in America. The Pacific Coast region offers the ocean in addition to lakes and streams. This father and son pictured near Lake Tahoe, California, have probably come here to escape suburbia instead of trying to obtain a food supply from the stream. (Environmental Protection Agency)

Figure 11-3. The Pacific Coast with its breakers, beaches, and forests has a special lure for urbanites. This is the Oregon coast but the same kind of attraction for recreation seekers is found from California to Alaska. (U.S. Bureau of Outdoor Recreation)

Figure 11-4. Pacific Coast tidepools like this one along Olympic National Park, Washington, have the richest collection of marine biota in the United States. At low tide people come to rediscover old treasures of the sea as an unforgettable use of leisure time. (National Park Service)

Figure 11-5. One of the unique features about the Pacific Coast region is that the urbanite who is searching for recreation and open space can drive from tidepools to glaciers or snow-covered Sequoias in half a day. (National Park Service)

Figure 11-6. The current trend is to use open space more intensely in order to accommodate growing pressures from additional numbers of recreation seekers. Popularity in surfing on the Pacific Coast is an example. (U.S. Bureau of Outdoor Recreation)

Figure 11-7. This evening campfire circle, which includes two snowmobiles, illustrates an additional conflict and pressure on open space resources in terms of spaces and times not previously in heavy demand. (U.S. Bureau of Outdoor Recreation)

392

Figure 11-8. The highest quality national parks, such as those in the Pacific Coast region, attract great numbers of visitors who will contribute to the parks' deterioration as unique national resources unless better management is applied. Vernal Falls and Nevada Falls are reached by heavily traveled trails—some of which are paved here in Yosemite National Park. (National Park Service)

located from Alaska to California have great appeal to the majority of Americans. In their quest for relief from their monotonous, crowded, polluted urban containers; city dwellers are ironically creating urban organisms in the choicest national parks and recreation areas. It is a growing tragedy that, as the highest quality and most attractive natural areas (such as the national parks) become urbanized through heavy use, the custodians of the public landscape are permitting the same mistakes to occur in the areas of natural ecological delicacy that were tolerated in the traditional city until a crisis of air, water, traffic, noise, and other pollution problems erupted.

393

The City of Yosemite

It was a crystal clear November evening. Our tent was pitched on the far loop of the 240 unit Upper Pines Campground that was near total vacancy. The paved walk to Vernal and Nevada Falls and an intersection of the John Muir trail was illuminated from the moonlight reflected off the first snowfall. The "City of Yosemite" was asleep for the season. But like a grizzly bear for which the valley was named, a heartbeat thumped on through the winter, mostly down at the "Village."

In the Yosemite Village Hotel lobby the Park Service naturalist was giving the Saturday night program. Music from a nearby bar filtered in. Latecomers to the program peeked curiously in on a wedding reception in the banquet hall next door. The cafeteria had just closed but the gift shop and apparel store were still open. Large signs on the hotel lobby doors announced "Hotel Guests Only," to be counterbalanced by the ranger-naturalists' assurances that the park programs are open to everyone. The contrasts, startling as they were, dramatized the paradox the National Park Service

Figure 11-9. Lights at night from the "City of Yosemite" in Yosemite National Park. Yosemite Village provides most modern conveniences equivalent to an urban area of 60,000 people, which is the population on a busy summer weekend. However, waste treatment control facilities are inadequate. (National Park Service)

Figure 11-10. When the Valley and the "City of Yosemite" come out of relative hibernation, the winter recreation enthusiasts, such as downhill skiers, skaters, cross country skiers, snowcat riders, snowshoers, and regular winter tourists, are replaced by the summer surge of visitors. (National Park Service)

Figure 11-11. Yosemite's Tenaya Lake and other remote areas higher in the Sierra Nevada are being sought out as refuges for the wilderness seekers in winter and summer. Permits may soon be required for admission to the most popular wilderness areas in order to prevent oversaturation or people pollution of fragile habitats. (National Park Service)

Figure 11-12. For the thousands of tourists who come only to Yosemite Valley there are tastefully designed signs that rival those of any metropolis. The "City of Yosemite" has produced its own Village Mall, as this 1973 sign announces.

has of providing for the public benefit and enjoyment without impairment of the wilderness or interfering with nature's cycles. The task becomes increasingly impossible to accomplish in the most popular national parks.

The crowd that overflowed the hotel lobby was made up of about half campers and half tourist guests from the ultramodern accommodations at Yosemite Village. The Park Service ranger talked about the impact of 60,000 daily visitors to Yosemite Valley during the rush seasons. In amazement, the author asked about the waste-water treatment facilities and the problems of waste disposal. The goal is to provide tertiary treatment for National Park visitors in the Yosemite complex but arrangement for the disposition of future solid wastes was typical of many "city fathers"—uncertain. Someone else wondered about the human influences on plant and animal populations. We were told that the valley, which is seven miles long, one mile wide, and at least three thousand feet deep under natural conditions would support two bears. With human interference, somewhere between forty-five and sixty black bears rummage the campgrounds and garbage containers. It is a totally unnatural natural situation.

After winter passes and the Badger Pass ski center closes, the "city of Yosemite" comes out of hibernation. Hotels and lodges at various points

Figure 11-13. Parking lots overflow beyond capacity as urbanites along the Pacific Coast escape from the crowded city and are attracted to a popular site like Yosemite. Those who want solitude will need to hike far beyond the crowds. (National Park Service)

Figure 11-14. Double deck buses are provided for visitors to Yosemite National Park. This free shuttle alternative to the automobile picks up and drops off passengers at numerous points of activities on a schedule more frequent (often every five minutes) and more reliable than mass transit systems in other American urbanized areas. The free shuttle buses use low pollution propane gas. Perhaps some park visitors will try to transplant the idea in their home towns. (National Park Service)

398   fill completely. Shopping areas and restaurants do land-office business. The beep and creep traffic congests the valley with its noise, its fumes, and its occupants. Horses are brought onto the trails and the stereo tape reverberations echo from El Capitan to Half Dome and back. As in other cities, some people in the form of backpackers try to escape. But the summer backpackers must go deeper and deeper into the High Sierras to avoid the heavily trodden paths of other exported urbanites.

The automobile has done to the City of Yosemite what it is doing to every American city that experiences an inversion layer. The huge volume of traffic, most of it stop and go, poisons the air trapped by the precipitous valley walls carved by glaciation thousands of years ago. So the National Park Service has done what every city must do sooner or later. A switch was made to cleaner, more efficient transportation. Pleasant, quiet, low-pollution double-decked buses and bicycle traffic were given priority over the automobile in the heart of Yosemite City. The day will undoubtedly come soon when no private automobiles are allowed in the valley. Some effort is underway to question the practicality of polluting campfires in the valley. The day will probably come when a staging area exists outside the "city limits" and everything (tent, food, and lightweight equipment) one brings into Yosemite Valley will come in and go out on one's back. Hopefully, an environmentally appropriate mass transit system will whisk one to his trailhead. The park's appeal to many lies beyond the valley in ap-

Figure 11-15. The most unique and attractive national parks tend to attract the heaviest visitation. As another alternative to the automobile, bicycles are encouraged on the valley floor of Yosemite National Park in order to reduce congestion. (National Park Service)

Figure 11-16. Campgrounds such as this one in Yosemite National Park take on an appearance of a densely populated urban neighborhood. In recent years all the major campgrounds post a "No Vacancy" sign on summer weekends. The tragic question is, who is left behind in the hot (usually polluted) center city? (National Park Service)

Figure 11-17. The half day drive from California's two largest metropolitan areas to Sequoia National Park puts this western park in line for increased "local" visitation as well as more use of this biological spectacle from national and international visitors. (National Park Service)

Figure 11-18. Federal land holdings with fragile alpine meadows, such as Olympic National Park shown here, will face considerable pressures from the urban public who seek solitude and an unpolluted environment. (National Park Service)

Figure 11-19. A surprising number of Americans who visit a wilderness area—even a canoe wilderness area—come as *spectators*. Research has shown that large numbers of people come to the edge of a wilderness area if they can simply watch the mountain climber, the white water canoeist, or the backpacker and not necessarily participate in the physical experience themselves. (U.S. Bureau of Outdoor Recreation)

proximately 1,193 square miles of relatively undeveloped Yosemite National Park. If the Yosemite back country has a "No Vacancy" sign, one might consider one of the other twelve national parks of the West Coast region. National parks in the Pacific Coast states that face great urban pressures include Sequoia, Yosemite, Redwood, Kings Canyon, Lassen, Crater Lake, Mount Rainier, North Cascades, Olympic, and Mount McKinley. Haleakala and Hawaii Volcanoes National Parks also confront comparable problems despite their separation from the mainland.

In a discussion of recreation resources, the number of square miles or acres is usually brought up. However, these figures do not give an accurate portrayal of park congestion. The case of Yosemite illustrates that a well-publicized spectacle such as Yosemite Falls or El Capitan or Half Dome is what at least 98 per cent of the park visitors come to see. The situation that recreation researcher Bob Lucas found in the Boundary Waters Area Canoe Wilderness is applicable to most of the Pacific Coast park areas. Lucas, a U.S. Forest Service recreation researcher based at Missoula, Montana, found that more than half of the visitors to the Quetico-Superior Canoe Wilderness area saw the park essentially through their automobile windows. Echo trail—the only automobile access that borders a southern corner of the 14,000 acre canoe wilderness carries many observers and very few participants in the recreation facilities.

The Parks and Man's Changing Life Style

Heretofore, the remote areas of the large national parks have not been heavily visited. With the increased population and growing appeal of backpacking, more and more park "users" come as full participants instead of being park "observers" and the "remote" areas are beginning to strain under their impact. The facilities of remote areas will need to change. As hikers and backpackers go into wilderness areas in greater numbers and for longer periods of time, the support facilities of waste water disposal, drinking water supply, fire prevention, accident and safety facilities, interpretive, and other services will be required. What we are seeing in our park and recreation land is a subtle colonization of the hinterlands by part-time urbanites.

The reasons the pressure has increased on the open space and recreation facilities include: (1) a general urban urge to escape from the city during periods of leisure time, (2) an increase in the amount of uncommitted or leisure time, (3) an increase in disposable income that is available for recreation-related investments, (4) an improved network of transportation systems—air, rail, and highway for delivery of recreation public to choice areas, (5) a massive promotional campaign by interests (including the National Park Service) who stand to gain by an increase in the use of the national public resources without a responsibility to compensate for the social and environmental costs of park overuse.

Figure 11-20. The waterfront of San Francisco Bay serves as a magnet for leisure time activity. An urban marina increases the range of choice for city residents who choose between driving to a remote park or pausing for peaceful moments in the midst of an interesting urban landscape.

There seems to be an undifferentiated urge to leave the urban area during holidays, vacations, and other periods of leisure time. Exceptions do exist in some of the more vital cities such as many parts of San Francisco and Seattle. On the whole, however, because of monotonous urban planning or decaying neighborhoods or excessive pollution levels (such as noise, visual, and air), urban dwellers seek out a period of respite from the urban environmental costs that have been superimposed upon them.

The Fragility of It All

There is a finiteness about national parks that has strong similarities to the depletable resources of metals and fossil fuels. The national park system was established to preserve unique representations of geological, biological, and other natural processes. Each national park (contrary to national forest or national monument designations) has been set aside because it was the only or the best example of a national natural resource with superlative qualities. If by the very act of giving all of the American public an equal opportunity to visit the outstanding national treasures, the park loses its uniqueness, then the nation has used up an irreplaceable or nonrenewable resource. Once the valley of Yosemite accommodates a daily population of 60,000 residents, the flora, the fauna, the very atmosphere of being there changes appreciably and the resource is being depleted. Load the Russian, the Rouge, or the Salmon rivers with hundreds of wild river trippers per day, and our wild scenic rivers will no longer be wild and scenic. Curiously, one is brought around to the necessity of establishing a carrying capacity for recreation resources like we have had to do for wildlife, timber, water, and air resources. Unfortunately, man's expertise to date in establishing carrying capacities for recreation areas is no better than his level of sophistication and agreement for the same kind of task to cities.

One of the serious problems here is the inadequacy of the research data on actually how much influence soil compaction, firewood scavenging, human-generated noise, and other human-induced pressures have on the flora and fauna of recreation sites, especially those that are noteworthy or popular because of fragile natural features. Another difficulty with crowding is with the changes in values perceived by the visitor. How many people in a wilderness area or on a "wild river" will it take to detract from the "wilderness" quality of the experience? Since we have struggled in vain to determine what the carrying capacity of our traditional urban containers is, perhaps it is too much to expect for the custodians of national parks and other recreation areas to set the trend. On the other hand, perhaps our irreplaceable recreation resource sites are the best places to put out the "No Vacancy" signs before an overshoot of the carrying capacity occurs. The state of Oregon and the city of Boulder, Colorado, have adopted this policy in theory. The National Park Service and the U.S. Forest Service have put this principle into practice, especially in the Sierra and Cascade wilderness regions, by limiting the number of backpackers permitted into certain areas.

The evolution of recreation land acquisition has followed a course very similar to programs for the management of air and water resources. It can truthfully be said that local units of government have lost or relinquished their initiative through neglect. Air and water problems grew so severe at local and state levels without corrective measures that federal mandates were finally required. The provision of outdoor recreation resources has followed a similar pattern. Actually it was logical for the federal government to assume leadership since the vast majority of recreation supply land was in federal and state ownership.

In 1864, when Abraham Lincoln gave the state of California Yosemite Valley and the nearby Mariposa Grove of big trees, it was the first time that any government had dedicated public land for the preservation of scenic value. Eight years later, in 1872, Yellowstone was carved out of territory land and thus qualified as the nation's first national park. After Yosemite and Sequoia were added to the national park system in 1890, cavalry units from the United States Army patrolled the areas for nearly

404 twenty-five years. Their major chore was to evict squatters, ranchers, and literally thousands of sheep, horses, and cattle from the dedicated park areas.

National parks and wilderness areas have always been unpopular with the resident loggers, miners, hunters, and grazing interests. Today developers have joined the opponents. The National Park Service was established by Congress in 1916 to administer sixteen national parks and twenty-one national monuments and less than four hundred thousand visitors that year.

A retired Borax mining official, Stephen Mather, wrote to the Secretary of Interior in 1915 to complain how the parks were being operated. Mather was invited to come to Washington as an Assistant Secretary of the Interior to do something about his complaint. He was made the first National Park Service Director and launched a very successful campaign for improvements and additions to the system. The national park system grew slowly. National monuments, historical parks, national seashores, national recreation areas, and national scenic trails were added as visitation increased. In 1940, 17 million visits were recorded; in 1965, 121 million; and in 1971, 201 million.

Figure 11-21. The Grizzly Giant was part of the Mariposa Grove of Sequoias that were transferred to the State of California in 1864 by Abraham Lincoln. It was the first time any government had dedicated public land for preservation of scenic values. Today this area is part of Yosemite National Park, California. (National Park Service)

Figure 11-22. The Golden Gate National Recreation Area serves a potential nearby urban population of over five million people in the San Francisco Bay metropolitan area. The charm of great cities around the world is always accented by strategically located open spaces.

It is interesting to note that since its beginning more than fifty years ago the park service has encouraged people to visit the parks, and it still continues to advertise for more visitors. Hopefully, before long it will recognize that efforts should be devoted to keeping the parks from being destroyed by overuse. The park service slogan "There's always a vacancy" is no longer true. As each of the sparkling jewels in the necklace of Pacific Coast parks becomes more and more urbanized, it becomes less and less a legacy worth saving for the benefit of posterity. Perhaps, the Pacific Coast parks and recreation areas such as the Golden Gate National Recreation Area and the recently added Alaskan parcels will resist the urbanization that has been transplanted in the first National Park—Yellowstone. The Third Annual Report of the Council on Environmental Quality reported that "within the 5 per cent of the area of Yellowstone National Park that receives most of the visitor use, the developments include 750 miles of roads, 2,100 permanent buildings, 7 amphitheatres, 24 water systems, 30 sewer systems, 10 electric systems with 93 miles of transmission lines, and a number of garbage dumps. There are 54 picnic areas, 3,143 campsites, and 17,000 signs. Hotel and cabin accommodations are available for 8,586 people each night."[1]

[1] *Environmental Quality—The Third Annual Report of the Council on Environmental Quality* (Washington, D.C.: U.S. Government Printing Office, 1972), p. 326.

406 The Pacific Coast region is richly provided with national forests. The major differences between a national park and a national forest are shown in Table 11-1. The multiple use policy of federal forest land serves as a safety valve by relieving excessive recreation pressure as it is placed on the usually more attractive national parks. In addition to providing high quality wilderness and campground recreation facilities, national forests offer hunting

Table 11-1. Differences between a National Forest and a National Park

	United States Forest Service	National Park Service
Objectives	Management and development of all the natural resources and national grasslands under the principle of multiple use for future generations.	Preservation of flora, fauna, geological natural phenomena, and historical events of unique significance for posterity. Interpretation of historical and natural events to enhance appreciation of our evolutionary and national heritage.
Origins	Created as an agency of the Department of Agriculture in 1905 after functioning as the Bureau of Forestry in the Department of Interior since 1891. President Theodore Roosevelt appointed Gifford Pinchot first Forest Service Director.	Established by Act of Congress as part of the Department of Interior in 1916. Initial idea came from Montana Judge Cornelius Hedges whose efforts set aside Yellowstone as first park in 1872 after an 1870 expedition. Steven T. Mather was the first National Park Service Director.
Philosophy	Wise use of national forest and grassland areas with permit regulated logging, mining, hunting, grazing, and recreation concessions. State and private cooperative arrangements include fire control, disease and plant growth research, watershed management, and recreation facilities.	Protection and preservation of ecological processes and historical events is a major focus followed by interpretative and educational programs in the national parks, monuments, recreation areas, historical parks, battlefields, and memorials. No timber cutting, mining, or hunting is permitted whereas limited fire control, plant, and wildlife disease protection exists.
Management	Ten administrative regions are headed by regional foresters, each national forest by a forest supervisor and supported by a technical staff. Forests are divided into ranger districts (50,000–300,000 acres) with a district ranger and a staff of forest rangers who have authority to enforce laws related to land management, such as illegal cutting or poaching. County sheriffs handle misdemeanors on Forest Service land, and violations are tried in state courts. Full staff in Washington, D.C., plus research teams at regional forest and range experiment stations.	Primary Washington, D.C., headquarters with six regional offices and the regional director in charge. Each national park is managed by a resident superintendent plus a staff of park rangers and naturalists. Large national monuments, recreation areas, and historical parks and battlefields have supervisory and staff offices. Rangers may arrest for misdemeanors and violation of park rules within the parks and cases are tried before a nearby federal commissioner.

and other recreation possibilities. Major U.S. Forest holdings in the Western states including Alaska provide opportunities for controlled logging, grazing, mining, oil and gas production, and watershed management for urban markets.

Other federal agencies that are actively involved in providing recreation facilities in the Far West include the Bureau of Land Management, the Bureau of Reclamation, the U.S. Army Corps of Engineers, and the Bureau of Sports Fisheries and Wildlife. State parks of California, Oregon, and Washington are excelled by no other states in the nation. Perhaps they have an unfair initial advantage because of their proximity to ocean, snow-capped mountains, temperate rain forests, and unusual geological phenomena. But they have not been spared pressure by more and more visitors. The fact that millions of Californians were turned away annually from the state park facilities prompted the use of a computerized reservation system called Ticketron. In peak seasons, a prospective state park user must reserve a campsite at least two weeks in advance with the fee paid at the time of reservation. Several million who do not make reservations are turned away annually. Once they have made the journey to a specific state recreation facility and been turned away then they seek out the federal or private recreation facilities if there are any nearby. The time may be not too far off when the only way to ensure equitable use of *all* recreation facilities (federal, state, private, and local) will be through a reservation system, similar to the one now being used by the California State Park System. However, even this procedure has some built-in disadvantages for those who are not able to select their vacation time months in advance.

Figure 11-23. A second home for leisure and recreation has become popular in the Pacific Coast region and in many other scenic areas of the United States. Usually this facility is built for weekend and vacation use. Nearly four million Americans own a second home. (Boise-Cascade Corporation)

408   Private recreation facilities of all qualities have flourished in the last decade. Large timber operations and other large land holding companies have begun to cater to the recreation market. Some provide camping and other facilities. Others such as Boise-Cascade, Georgia Pacific, and Tenneco have entered the recreation real estate business. Chrysler Realty Corporation's Big Sky project located in the Yellowstone Rockies of Montana has a significant impact on recreation and land use planning. Financial backing for the Big Sky project also includes Northwest Orient Airlines, American Airlines, Burlington Northern, and others that do not fall into the category of local entrepreneurs. The concept of a second home or leisure time residence has increasing appeal to those who have flexible vacation schedules. Several families may invest in a seashore, lakeside, or mountain cabin or condominium. Mountain properties in the Cascades and Sierra Nevada (and the Rocky Mountains also) are sometimes jointly owned with schedules of use worked out over the year with the owner families rotating occupancy weekends and holiday periods.

Figure 11-24. Many of the recreation-second homes are equipped with the conveniences and furnishings of a city dwelling. The attraction to this facility is apparently *an escape from* the noise, fumes, pace, and abrasive environment of poorly planned urban areas instead of an *attraction to* more primitive, creative or demanding living. (Boise-Cascade Corporation)

Thus urbanization, in a diluted form, is taking place on public and private recreation lands. The financing of waste-water pollution facilities and other generally provided public services is in a more precarious position than in the traditional city because matching federal funds are not so readily available. There also appears to be a technological need to find new methods for waste treatment means for cottage owners and small isolated mountain or lake leisure homes. Even the national parks, monuments, and U.S. Forest Service facilities have had great difficulty in keeping up to federal and state standards compared to their urban counterparts of similar population size.

The Need to Reevaluate National Recreation Policy

As the recreation problems that await the urbanite who hungers and thirsts to "get back to nature" are multiplying, the time approaches when the United States may need to reevaluate her national recreation policy. Could it be that our national goal cannot be to get every urban American into the hinterland? Traditional recreation management strategies cannot guarantee the safekeeping of the natural environment with the burgeoning population of backpackers overflowing even the most remote areas. Pack trips are more frequent and improved equipment extends the hikers' season and the length of his visit. It now has even become socially desirable and prestigious to get into a wilderness area.

In an attempt to provide for this increased demand for remote areas, Congress passed the Wilderness Preservation Act of 1964, which authorized the creation of a National Wilderness Preservation System. Wilderness was defined as "an area where the earth and its community of life are untrameled by man, where man himself is a visitor who does not remain." Motorized equipment, roads, and other structures are not allowed but as in the national forests, hunting and fishing are permitted in compliance with state regulations. Mining and grazing continue, and mineral exploration is permitted up to 1984. (One wonders what is so magic about 1984 and 1985 when the provisions of the Wilderness Act and those of the Federal Water Pollution Control Act—1972 Amendments go into effect.) To the consternation of preservationists, future mining from patents and claims established before 1984 is also permitted. For the benefit of recreation uses, the provision exists that patents granted in the wilderness areas will not convey rights to any surface mineral resources. Undoubtedly the courts will struggle with that language as mining and recreation conflicts increase.

In 1964, 9.1 million acreas were set aside from 54 areas of national forest land in 13 states. California with over 1,435,700 acres included was one of the three largest beneficiaries of the Wilderness Preservation System. Congressional approval is required for additions to the system. The first additions since the act came when 800,000 acres of federally owned land were

Figure 11-25. An Alaska wilderness near Mount McKinley.

added in 1968.[2] During the Johnson administration, the Redwood, North Cascades, and Guadalupe Mountains National Parks were added. Special bonuses to urban dwellers were the National Wild and Scenic Rivers System and a nationwide system of trails.

The urbanite creates more than the problem of sheer ecological impact when the remote recreation areas are invaded; he raises the entire socioeconomic-political question of whether federal dollars, that is, U.S. Forest Service, Bureau of Land Management, and U.S. Park Service—should subsidize a tiny fraction of the American public. A close inspection of who uses the wilderness area reveals that they are certainly not the urban poor.

Tragically the urban dweller who has been forced to live in the most heavily polluted sections of the city has a proportionately smaller amount of leisure time, a considerably less reliable means of transportation, and a strikingly more modest portfolio of skills and attitudinal motivations for national park or wilderness use than those who are living in the more pollution-free suburbs.

[2]*Congress and the Nation,* Vol. II, Congressional Quarterly Series (1969), p. 472.

Figure 11-26. A Boston vest-pocket park is the only kind of park some urban children will ever see. The chances for families in this neighborhood to visit the great national parks of the far Western states are rather gloomy.

Figure 11-27. Most young inner city residents have never seen a national park or could not afford the equipment to venture into a wilderness recreation area if they got near one. (U.S. Bureau of Outdoor Recreation)

412   Perhaps there is even a disparity between poor urban residents of the Far Western states and inner-city urbanites in other parts of the United States. The slum dweller living in Boston, New York, Philadelphia, Baltimore, or Washington seldom plans a vacation to Yosemite or Sequoia because it is just unrealistic for reasons of distance, time, and other economic constraints. Consider the frustrations, however, for a poor family interested in camping and the treasures of the national parks who lives three to five hours from Yosemite, Kings Canyon, or Sequoia but who is prevented from taking advantage of the park system by the same economic reasons of their eastern city counterparts.

The poor white, Black, or Chicano, or other ghetto dweller simply does not have the proper equipment required and the flexibility of vacation schedules to enable long treks into remote areas or the kind of transportation options to get there even if his daily concerns about job, medical services, educational equity and personal efficacy, and three nondehydrated meals a day for his family were resolved. As so-called "high priority" recreation areas are created in remote areas, the proportion of leisure time facilities and open space for urbanites is decreased.

Figure 11-28. Only a relatively few Americans can afford the time and the expense of the primitive wilderness camping experience. Here two backpackers have penetrated a remote area of the Olympic Peninsula in Washington with the help of lightweight equipment and dehydrated food. (National Park Service)

Figure 11-29. Urban open space can be an eyesore as shown in this first photograph of a Philadelphia corner. Organized efforts of citizens and government officials changed the space as seen in the followup photo. (U.S. Dept. of Housing and Urban Development)

In other words, the opportunity costs or foregone opportunities of buying, staffing, and maintaining a new national park—let us say North Cascades, or Redwoods—are that those millions of dollars were not spent in urban vestpocket parks, waterside parkland development, or other outdoor recreation benefits that might have been directly available to the inner-city poor of Seattle, Spokane, Tacoma, Portland, or, for that matter, San Francisco or Los Angeles. The federal recreation budget is not divided equally for all people in all places. The less obvious point is that whenever a particular environment is saved or a specific public served, it is usually at the cost of someone else's project and probably in another (urban) environment.

Figure 11-30. The same corner at 2400 West York Street in Philadelphia has evolved into an attractive use of small urban open space.
Opportunities are available for the enhancement of many idle lots in the American city. (U.S. Dept. of Housing and Urban Development)

Figure 11-31. Visits to national parks and other high quality recreation areas usually require preplanning, reservations or specialized equipment not ordinarily considered by the ghetto dweller. No state or federal funds are applied to urban overnight camping facilities in the United States; therefore, urban visitors must improvise for themselves. (University of Michigan News Service)

The pastoral landscape at the periphery of metropolitan areas becomes less available to the inner city poor because of subdivision sprawl. Even the swimming hole or pond of the ruralite becomes the focal point of an exclusive tract developer's country estate. The merger of city after city into a megalopolitan expanse swallows up the resistant rancher, farmer, and orchard owner. Rising property taxes force those three and other land dependent operations to "sell out" to subdividers because of a squeezed profit margin. Los Angeles, San Francisco Bay Area, and eventually Puget Sound continue to be examples of low density urban extension with miniscule fractions of the landscape that are dedicated to public open space or recreation facilities. Huey Johnson's San Francisco based Trust for Public Lands is an innovative approach to obtaining open space lands in or near urban areas where the critical needs exist now and where they will increase in the future. Yet here is where the daily demand for the use of the out-of-doors exists. How can we continue to lavish our national recreation budgets on remote high technology demanding facilities when the basic needs of the vast numbers of metropolitanites have hardly a vest-pocket park?

Figure 11-32. Some downtown streets, such as many in San Francisco, lure residents and visitors alike.

Figure 11-33. Small open spaces can be designed to attract urbanites of all ages. Fountains and sculpture are always popular. (U.S. Dept. of Housing and Urban Development)

The Conflict of Urban Recreation Needs Versus Wilderness

Open space resource problems of the Pacific Coast states are illustrated here by two examples: (1) wilderness use alternatives in the Mineral King dispute, and (2) coastal land acquisition and major estuary use conflicts typified in Puget Sound and San Francisco Bay. These fit into a discussion of urban environmental issues because increased open space use or changes in use are direct functions of urbanization. The megalopolitan populations from Seattle to San Diego are exerting demands on desert regions, inland lakes and rivers, mountain recreation facilities, marshland, and offshore islands. The innumerable difficulties confronting local jurisdictions as they attempt to manage open space resources at the city and county level are growing and forcing local governments to seek help.

Second homes primarily for recreation use are consuming great acreages of mountain and coastal land that had previously been "open range" for the recreation public. Thus the wilderness land use, coastal use, and estuary transformation are major issues of the Far West with implications for most other regions of the United States.

Throughout the world, skiing and other winter sports have mushroomed in popularity in recent years. Yet perhaps nowhere do they hold the unique attraction for people that they do in California and the arid Southwest. Here the largest urban areas are essentially without snowfall, but easily within a two to four hour drive from some of the major mountain winter sports resorts. Quiet little mountain towns of two thousand to three thousand increase their population one-hundred fold on the busy weekends of the skiing season, although facilities in the communities are inadequate to accommodate the tens of thousands who migrate to them. (These same migrations to many of the same areas take place during the hot summer months as well.) Responding to the private market forces at work, the normal tendency is to build more ski tows and lodging facilities. Without certain economic safeguards, the involved communities are consequently saddled with providing more police and fire protection, more water-pollution control facilities, more medical services, better transportation accommodations, and, if the population becomes established, enlarged educational facilities.

With continual increasing demands for winter sports facilities, it is apparent that the present ones in the resorts cannot provide for the increased number of users. As expected, the recreation entrepreneur searches for new ski areas to develop. It happened in the Rocky Mountains of Colorado after Aspen, Winter Park, Berthoud Pass, Araphahoe Basin, Loveland Basin, and others became frustratingly overcrowded. It would seem that the trend may be changing, as the common citizen is expressing himself more. California's official spokesman followed Colorado's voter disapproval of the 1976

Winter Olympic games as both states showed concern about environmental degradation and accelerated, unplanned growth resulting from serving as host state to the international recreation extravaganza.

Several other stumbling blocks lie in the path of those who want to enlarge present California Sierra resorts or develop new ones near or in the national forest and national park lands. Most of the stumbling blocks are in the form of individuals and organizations who do not want to stop all growth of winter sports facilities but rather were or are primarily interested in using present and future facilities to their greatest efficiency while showing an ecological sensitivity to the environmental problems that threaten areas of unplanned overuse.

Friends of Mammoth Versus Mono County

Andrea Mead Lawrence is one of those constructive stumbling blocks. She was the first American woman to win two gold medals in the Winter Olympics (giant slalom and downhill in 1952 and 1956). She and a group of her friends became concerned about the issuance of building permits by the Mono County Board of Supervisors for a high-rise condominium. The proposed development was expected to put excessive pressures on the waste-water treatment system of the Mammoth Lakes community as well as create other incongruous land use practices.

As Chairperson of Friends of Mammoth, a citizen's organization to deal with the growth and planning problems of Mammoth Lakes, California, Mrs. Lawrence led a campaign through the courts that resulted in several major steps toward more citizen involvement in the planning process, especially in respect to environmental provisions. Friends of Mammoth gained notoriety in the California Supreme Court decision that upheld the Friends of Mammoth contention that significant private developments requiring a license or building permit must submit an environmental impact statement. This environmental impact reporting procedure has been required of all federal projects or actions as a result of the National Environmental Policy Act of 1969 and of all state governmental projects in California as of November 23, 1970, when the California Environmental Quality Act was enacted. The California Act is a state equivalent of the federal law even as it spells out a format for environmental impact reports.

The environmental impact statement process can serve as a legal mandate for improving the information base of projects involving open space or any environmental influence. The local, state, and federal impact statements essentially require these five elements:

1. The environmental impact of the proposed action.
2. Any adverse environmental effects that cannot be avoided should the proposal be implemented.
3. Alternatives to the proposed action.

418   4. The relationship between local short-term uses of man's environment and the maintenance and enhancement of long-term productivity.
5. Any irreversible and irretrievable commitments of resources that would be involved in the proposed action should it be implemented.

Environmental costs and benefits of any project must be weighed against other costs and benefits (that is, political, social, economic) of the proposed activity. It is presumed that a documentation of the ecological impacts would bring more rationality into the merit considerations of each project as it came before whichever legislative bodies were involved. Friends of Mammoth, after getting a court ruling favorable to their position that essentially asked for a broader base in area planning, then retained an interdisciplinary team of researchers under the coordination of Harvey Perloff of U.C.L.A.'s School of Architecture and Urban Planning to come up with five alternative possibilities for future action. Officials and citizens were interviewed, and the biological and physical environments of Mammoth Lakes were studied. Out of the research effort came a more accurate approximation of what environmental costs and benefits would accrue from several intensities of development.

Mineral King

A more dramatic example of the conflict between mass urban recreation users and the wilderness users is Mineral King, a small alpine valley of hardly three hundred acres south of Sequoia National Park. It is an area of unparalleled beauty as the surrounding High Sierras rise in a spectacular amphitheater of twelve thousand foot peaks while glaciated alpine lakes and streams converge on the valley meadow as the East Fork of the Kaweah River. The tumbling river and the narrow road traverse from the Sequoia National Game Refuge (previously an undesignated portion of the Sequoia National Forest) through the preservation-oriented Sequoia National Park. (See Figure 11-34).

As far back as 1949, the U.S. Forest Service attempted to interest private capital in developing a modest ski area in Mineral King. However, the treacherous road through the National Park was not an all-weather highway and consequently Mineral King lay isolated from Los Angeles and San Francisco skiers. Then in 1965, six bids were accepted by the Forest Service and Walt Disney Productions received a three-year preliminary permit based on their $35 million development proposal. No arrangements had been negotiated with the National Park Service for road expansion, transmission line rights of way, or other impacts created by the expected surge of a mass recreation mecca in nearby Forest Service Mineral King property.

The original Disney proposal hints of substantial urbanization in an area of fragile ecological processes:

=== Roads (existing)
-- - Roads (proposed)
----- Trails
▲ Big trees

Sequoia National Park
and
Mineral King Game Refuge

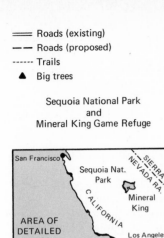

AREA OF
DETAILED
MAPS

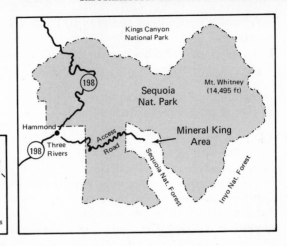

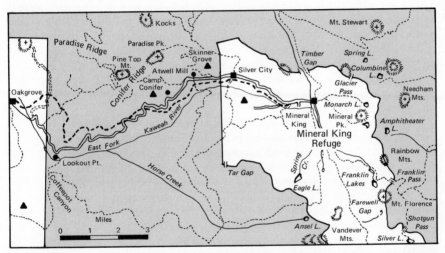

Figure 11-34. Map of proposed Mineral King recreation area in the midst of Sequoia National Park and Sequoia National Forest, California. [Reprinted with permission from Albert Hill and Michael McCloskey, "Mineral King: Wilderness Versus Mass Recreation in the Sierra," quoted in John Harte and Robert H. Socolow, *Patient Earth* (New York: Holt, Rinehart and Winston, Inc., 1971), p. 166.]

1. Estimated number of visitors annually was 2.5 million but reduced to 980,000.
2. A 10-story parking complex for 3,600 vehicles.
3. A 1,030-room hotel complex.
4. Accommodations for 1000 employees.
5. From 22 to 27 ski lifts extending up to 4 miles into the surrounding country.
6. Administrative offices, helioport, hospital, and shops.

7. A nearby convention center with theater, arena, restaurants, and other services.
8. An all-weather highway with passing lanes to handle up to 1,200 cars per hour to connect with state highway 198.

Michael McCloskey and Albert Hill have provided a thorough account on behalf of wilderness maintenance.

At first glance this argument sounds plausible, even appealing. But the thinking behind it is very much like the thinking other developers advance: 'Our electrical consumption doubles every ten years, therefore we must build more power plants.' 'We must continue to build more freeways to relieve traffic jams.'

We are beginning to find out that the new freeways will be crowded too, and that the new power will be used quickly. And as we are finding that anything we provide will find users, we are also finding that our environment gets a bit less tolerable with every new urban freeway and power plant.

Thus we realize that we lose something with every new development as well as gain something. In balancing the losses and gains, we must look at the overall trends in our environment. The quality of the environment is deteriorating because of a host of decisions to move ahead with more development, each of which can be rationalized as based on a proper individual balance between losses and gains. In sum total, however, these decisions push us further and further into an intolerable situation: an environment overloaded with development, with traffic, with smog, and damaged habitats.

To stop the trend toward progressive degradation, there is a growing conviction that we must not only curb population growth but also question the assumptions of those who say we must keep meeting projections of demand. Meeting these projections may be no more than an exercise in building self-fulfilling prophecies. These new developments will be attractive enough to build new clienteles, which can be retrospectively offered as proof that demand was in fact being met. Of course, it is equally arguable that if another option were offered—one involving environmental protection—a clientele could be developed for it too. In this instance, it is entirely likely that inclusion of Mineral King in Sequoia National Park would attract a large body of devoted park visitors. Although one could argue over comparative numbers of visitors under both alternatives, it is quite possible that just as large, if not a larger, sum total of satisfactions would accrue annually to park visitors as to visitors to the resort.

Moreover, once you play the game of meeting projected 'demands,' the question always remains of what you do next once the area fills up. The logic of 'building, building, building' to meet demand suggests that the process must keep on going indefinitely, or at least as long as population keeps growing and entrepreneurs promote new markets. However, it is patently evident in this case that it is physically impossible to keep on going indefinitely. There are just not that many additional sites for major development. Sooner or later, the process of building ski areas must come to an end. With that in mind, we must ask: 'In what shape ultimately do we want to have our mountain landscape?' 'What is the balance between development and preservation that will really best serve society?' If skiing demand in any event is going to be left unsatisfied at some later stage, why let it go on proliferating past the point of proper balance? Shouldn't we really draw the line to keep fragile landscapes, such as the Sierra, in the best shape we now

Figure 11-35. The Valley of Mineral King—a gateway to the High Sierra—preserved up until recently by inaccessibility. Multimillion-dollar development proposals threaten this unique wilderness, which is contiguous to Sequoia National Park.

know how to provide, and keep overpowering projects like Mineral King out?

Another disturbing aspect of the case for the Southern California skiers is the unspoken assumption that there is some obligation on the part of public authorities to provide expanding opportunities for every kind of sport, no matter what the inherent obstacles. Clearly no part of the southern United States is ideally situated to serve skiing. The region suffers from basic climatic disabilities, just as northern regions suffer from disadvantages in not having sufficient opportunities for warm-water ocean bathing.

Nevertheless some California planners seem to feel that engineers should be able to rescue Souther California from all its climatic disabilities, from lack of water, to air, to skiing. If the area is too far from enough water, their answer is re-engineer the state's northern rivers to run them southward. If the area lacks nearby skiing, the answer is to move higher into the Sierra with subsidized access and plans for high volume use to make skiing there financially feasible.

In both cases the resource is bent drastically to rescue a demanding population from the shortcomings of a particular area in which they have chosen to locate themselves. The question can just as well be asked for skiing as for water: 'Why not locate the people in places where these opportunities can be afforded with far less violence to the landscape and its resources?' Certainly, people are not going to move out of Los Angeles in droves just because Mineral King is not built, but preventing its population from reaching farther and farther to abuse resources may gradually make Los Angeles a less and less attractive place to live. This is one way to bring the Los Angeles syndrome to an end.[3]

---

[3] Albert Hill, and Michael McCloskey, "Mineral King: Wilderness Versus Mass Recreation in the Sierra," quoted in John Harte, and Robert H. Socolow, *Patient Earth* (New York: Holt, Rinehart and Winston, Inc., 1971), pp. 178–180.

Figure 11-36. Skiing in Sequoia National Park has traditionally been a relatively undeveloped activity with an emphasis on beginners and family groups. (National Park Service)

Figure 11-37. Olympic National Park's Hurricane Ridge is typical of western national parks that have facilities which some people feel are more appropriately placed in multiple-use national forests or other recreation areas. (National Park Service)

The Mineral King dispute conjures up memories of the Hetch Hetchy battle that concluded when a dam was built in Yosemite National Park in 1913 to create a reservoir of additional water supply for San Francisco.

San Francisco Bay and Puget Sound Estuaries

Another lesson available to the Pacific Coast states as a result of water and land uses that devour valuable open space can be applied to the Western *estuaries* and coastlines. Puget Sound and San Francisco Bay stand out as dramatic examples of how urbanization, if it is insensitive to the ecological advantages of estuary habitat, can eliminate a unique urban resource in terms of microclimate, a key link in marine biological systems, and a provider of incalculable aesthetic benefits.

The coastlines of the Eastern Seaboard and the Gulf States stand testimony to mistakes committed in the absence of adequate information about the benefits that well-planned and thoughtfully managed coastal areas can provide to the urban public. San Francisco Bay, like Mineral King, can serve as a dramatic example of the problem that involves urban pressures on open space and recreation resources.

Figure 11-38. Victoria, British Columbia, exemplifies an attractive use of the Pacific Coast urban waterfront.

Figure 11-39. Bastion Square in Victoria, British Columbia, is an outstanding example of Canadian urban restoration along the Puget Sound waterfront.

Figure 11-40. Victoria's waterfront renewal, using a maritime theme for shops and restaurants, reminds the visitor and resident of the heritage of marine and timber resources of the Puget Sound area.

San Francisco Bay covered 680 square miles 200 years ago. Today it has shrunk to less than 400 square miles. Marshlands that border the Bay have been reduced from 300 to 75 square miles in the last century. San Francisco's Association of Bay Area Governments estimated late in 1972 that if current zoning possibilities were fully implemented, the metropolitan population could grow to 46 million persons. This is the legally established potential growth that is possible without any additional zoning or annexation changes. Today, the San Francisco Metropolitan area (11 county) population is about one tenth that figure, or 4,800,000. If 900 per cent more population is added, it is difficult to imagine the impact on estuary areas, the local

424

Figure 11-41. Over 200 square miles of San Francisco Bay has been filled in for various uses during the last century. Most waterfront development is built on fill that has significantly reduced the size of San Francisco Bay. Illegal filling and highly questionable "special permit" filling continue today because of corrupt practices and citizen apathy.

and state parks, or the existing waste-water treatment systems, the traffic networks or other vital elements that already show signs of saturation at the 5 million population level. Only 18 miles of the 276 mile San Francisco Bay shoreline have been set aside for public parks and access. A total of 96,000 acres of former tidal marshlands have been diked off from the Bay as commercial salt drying ponds and duck hunting preserves (50,000 acres). Perhaps Puget Sound specifically and the rest of the Alaska, California, Hawaii, Oregon, and Washington coastlines can be managed in ways so that these finite resources can provide renewable recreational benefits for the people of America in whose trust they are kept.

To the yachtsman the San Francisco Bay, named after Saint Francis of Assisi, is a weekend haven from an urban workday schedule. It is a refreshing vista for millions of visitors and residents who drive or perch along its bluffs. To the hunter, San Francisco Bay is the major stopover point on the entire Pacific Flyway. To the marine biologists its protoplasmic mud quivers with estuarine life and promises vast future food supplies. To the ornithologist it is the habitat for millions of migratory and resident waterfowl. To the fruit and vegetable growers of the Central, Napa, and Santa Clara valleys, this is the estuary *par excellence* that brings moderate temperatures and moisture to the otherwise xeric inner valleys of central California. For urbanites who may never know the Bay, it is their sewer for industrial and sanitary wastes. The basin of the Bay is the sewer for every ton of atmospheric pollution from every car, every fireplace, and every stack whose effluents saturate the inversion layer that is boxed in by the rim of mountains around the Bay.

425

Figure 11-42. The nearby aquatic open space is one of the features that gives San Francisco its unique natural beauty and at the same time affords abundant recreational opportunity.

Figure 11-43. The marshland and estuaries of the Pacific Coast region serve as valuable wildlife habitat, as seen by the snow geese in the Sacramento National Wildlife Refuge, California. (U.S. Bureau of Sport Fisheries and Wildlife)

San Francisco Bay means something else to other people as Harold Gilliam eloquently points out in his book, *Between The Devil and The Deep Blue Bay*.[4] "To many a developer and land speculator, the Bay is real estate to be filled with dirt and covered with houses and shopping centers and factories. To some city and county planning officials, the Bay offers . . . the chance to create new communities . . . to highway engineers the Bay is an ideal place to build freeways . . . and to local sanitation officials and garbage disposal contractors, who must dispose of thousands of tons of wastes daily, (more than 11,250 tons/day from nearly 5 million people in the Bay Area) the Bay makes an ideal garbage dump or cesspool."

More than a decade ago the battle to save San Francisco Bay began as a thoughtful and serious citizen effort. It was learned that the Berkeley City Council had worked out a plan to fill a formidable expanse of offshore waters. The city owns 4,000 acres and it looked like a great way to increase the tax base and double the size of the city. Bay area conservation leaders catalyzed by Mrs. Esther (Charles) Gulick, Mrs. Kay (Clark) Kerr and Mrs. Sylvia (Donald) McLaughlin mobilized an effort called the Save San Francisco Bay Association. Eventually the original Berkeley plan was torpedoed and the shoreline was landscaped for recreation use. The Save-the-Bay spirit and call for research on full costs and benefits of Bay encroachment spread to other bayside communities. By late 1965, state enabling legislation created the San Francisco Bay Conservation and Development Commission (BCDC) to carry out a comprehensive study of ecological and economic conditions as they effect present and future population in the Bay region. While this master plan was in preparation, the BCDC was empowered "to issue or deny permits, after public hearings, for any proposed project that involves placing fill in the Bay or extracting submerged materials from the Bay."

Since 22 per cent of the bay floor is in private ownership difficult legal problems lie ahead if the owners are deprived of the economic use of their land—"the taking of property". For the first time in 120 years, however, unrestricted filling of San Francisco Bay has come to a halt. Whether or not this urban surrounded resource will be managed for recreation, aesthetic, and open space purposes, wildlife habitat, fish farming, dumping, airport expansion, new town development, or viciously fought over mixtures of all eight, it will be a classic example of how the pseudopodia-like growth of one of America's greatest urban organisms responds to the lessons of urban history and future environmental quality.

The Effects of Overcrowding

None of the federal, state, local, or private outdoor recreation facilities is resistant to the threat of people colonizing even the most distant facilities.

[4] Harold Gilliam, *Between the Devil and the Deep Blue Bay* (San Francisco: Chronicle Books, 1969), p. 29.

428 Increased use of air travel for vacationers brings large numbers of persons who never would have driven. When human settlements grow without proper planning, the ills of urbanization appear even in the most beautiful locations. Serious crime in the National Parks rose 153 per cent from 1966 to 1970, compared to a 71 per cent increase nationally. Costs of repairs to vandalized facilities exceed $1 million annually.

The effect of overcrowding on wildlife in cities produces similar results in the parks and wilderness areas. Air pollution from automobile emissions and other sources is having measurably adverse effects on park ecosystems. Solid waste and waste-water systems for the Pacific parks and other federal recreation areas are not the best examples of waste technology. Sequoia National Park dumps primary treated wastes down a mountainside and the "City of Yosemite" accelerates the eutrophication of the Merced River with phosphates, nitrates, and other by-products of its treated wastes from daily populations up to 60,000. Most of the younger or more remote parks such as Mount McKinley, North Cascades, Redwood, Kings Canyon, Lassen Volcanic, Olympic, Mount Rainer, and Haleakala have less sophisticated waste treatment systems.

University of Michigan recreation scholar, Ross Tocher, has called attention to major forces of attraction that draw urban residents out of the American city. A spectrum of skills and attitudes determine where most people migrate whenever leisure time is available. Metropolitan beaches and parks require the fewest "survival skills." The habitat is reasonably familiar, investment of time and equipment is low, and the potential for human contact is high compared to wilderness backpacking or mountaineering at the other end of the recreation spectrum. As physical and social

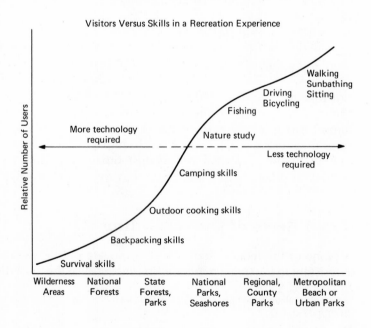

Figure 11-44. With increasing pressure on national and state parks by urban populations, more use is anticipated on remote recreation areas. This requires specialized skills and equipment needed in cross country skiing, backpacking, and wilderness survival.

Figure 11-45. Huge commercial recreation facilities such as Disneyland, complete with its Matterhorn, provide leisure time "escape" sites. The visitor requires no technology to enjoy the experience as contrasted to a mountain-climbing or backpacking trip to the High Sierras or the Alps. (U.S. Bureau of Outdoor Recreation)

conditions of the inner city become more aggravated, the human repulsion of the urban area grows. Even with no particular site of attraction in mind, most American city dwellers use a free day or free weekend to escape. The "escape" from the city is most frequently a drive in the automobile to an area that requires little planning and little technology. In European cities, historical and other cultural treasures serve as very substantial attractions to the center city for local visitors and international travelers. European museums, galleries, city parks, and other leisure time pursuits including the *city center* itself are reached more easily by mass rapid transit and other public transportation than by private automobile as a rule.

A common Pacific Coast vacation is spent camping, hiking, fishing, or hunting. Most camping activity is in the middle of the experience continuum (See Figure 11-46) in terms of skills required. As recreation areas are becoming increasingly used, one's experiences there are decreasingly pleasant. Too often the days of preplanning for a vacation trip result in traffic jams, overflow campgrounds, dirty facilities, and overfished waters. Yet, how few realize that such discomforts are the result of our bringing the city to places of fragile, ecological balance, to places of dynamic interrelationships that are not prepared or designed to withstand the biological and physical pressures being placed upon them.

429

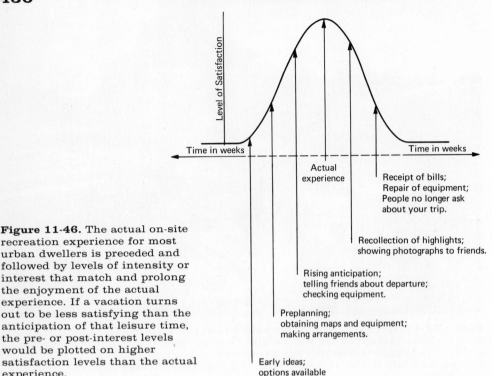

The Recreation Experience Continuum

Level of Satisfaction

Time in weeks

Time in weeks

Actual experience

Receipt of bills; Repair of equipment; People no longer ask about your trip.

Recollection of highlights; showing photographs to friends.

Rising anticipation; telling friends about departure; checking equipment.

Preplanning; obtaining maps and equipment; making arrangements.

Early ideas; options available

Figure 11-46. The actual on-site recreation experience for most urban dwellers is preceded and followed by levels of intensity or interest that match and prolong the enjoyment of the actual experience. If a vacation turns out to be less satisfying than the anticipation of that leisure time, the pre- or post-interest levels would be plotted on higher satisfaction levels than the actual experience.

A closer look at who generates the urban pressure on western recreation areas reveals that it is not only the urbanite. If, by chance, a family or a group of friends finds a truly unspoiled spot of solitude, they certainly do not mount a large campaign to advertise the remote cove along the coastline or undisturbed mountain lake. Instead, those who promote increased outdoor recreation in the Pacific Coast area or any area in the United States or the world are those who stand to benefit from the increased crowds. Comparatively speaking, the National Park Service sponsors few television, newspaper, magazine, or billboard advertisements urging visitors to come to Yosemite, to Hawaiian Volcanoes, to Olympic, or Redwood National parks. Instead it is the travel agencies, the automobile companies, the oil companies, and the airlines who promote and provide goods and services to the recreation minded public.

The 1972 report of the President's Commission on Population Growth and the American Future indicated that 93 per cent of California's population was classified as urbanized.[5] Figures for Washington, Oregon, and Hawaii are respectively 66.0 per cent, 61.2 per cent, and 81.9 per cent. Why are urban Americans "driven out" of their metropolitan areas to recreation

[5] *Population and The American Future,* The Report of the Commission on Population Growth and the American Future, (Washington, D.C.: U.S. Government Printing Office, 1972), p. 27.

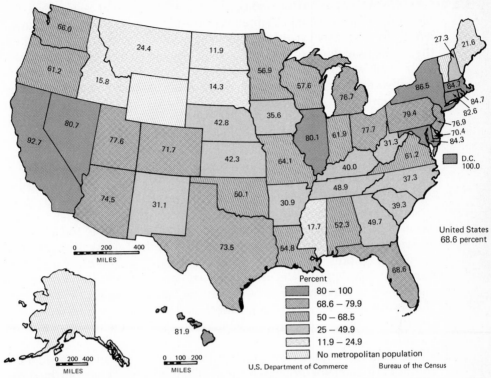

Figure 11-47. The United States' percentage of urbanization by state. (Source: The President's Commission on Population Growth and the American Future, 1972)

areas that are *microcosms* of the city and do not give their urban visitors much opportunity to recreate the body, the mind, or the spirit?

European city dwellers have a rather different approach to their use of leisure time. In the great cities of Europe, the visitor will find facilities for camping that are almost totally absent in all American cities. Curiously, campgrounds throughout continental Europe are often in closer proximity to the sights to see than are hotels. Rome, Paris, Copenhagen, Oslo, Brussels, Cologne, Munich, Venice, Vienna, West Berlin, Stockholm, Milan, Belgrade, Lisbon, Barcelona, Lausanne, and Florence have examples of fine camping grounds near or in the very heart of their cities.

Urban-Based Recreation and Open Space

An entire new thrust is required of urban-based recreation that productively uses urban open space and other potential recreation resources for residents and visitors to America's metropolitan areas. The major zoos or botanical gardens of San Diego, San Francisco, Portland, and Seattle are not adequate to provide the wide range of recreation needs in the de-

431

432 veloping West Coast megalopolis. The major commercial recreation complexes featuring historical simulations, animal specimens, and fantasy worlds (such as Disneyland, Safari World, and Marineland) do not address the leisure time requirements of the local residents who live in cities where these highly publicized attractions are located. Furthermore, private beaches, private golf courses, and private swim and tennis clubs are beyond the economic and geographical reach of most central city residents. However, vestpocket parks or miniparks that are planned by neighborhood groups on small inner-city land parcels add to the recreation resource base available to people of all ages on a daily basis. At nearly any time of day or evening it is not uncommon to find tiny parks in the heart of San Francisco with children's imaginative play equipment in use directly beside elderly chess players working out strategies under the shade of nearby trees.

Some of the larger parks, arboretums, cemeteries, and richly landscaped grounds of public buildings provide screening from noise, traffic fumes, and visual blight. When natural features such as the Lake Washington area of Seattle are present, they add excellent diversity to the cityscape. With proper design, lighting, security measures, and a reasonable number of people, urban parks need not be denied for fear of mugging or vandalism. The availability of islands of greenery and relative solitude serve as a cherished resource for urban individuals who are unable to get away from the city.

The work of Fredrick Law Olmsted stands out as the most outstanding contribution to major urban parks in the United States. "Over one hundred years ago he wrote of pollution and the role of parks in lessening and controlling it."[6] His social purpose and skill in landscape architecture created an unmatched blending of the basic ekistic elements of nature, man, society, shells, and networks in the major urban parks that he designed—San Francisco's Golden Gate Park, Detroit's Belle Isle, Mount Royal Park in Montreal, Boston's Franklin Park, Brooklyn's Prospect Park, and the most famous—New York's Central Park. All of these plus his impressive landscape monuments in more than twelve other cities serve as literal urban breathing spots where carbon monoxide and other air contaminants have been shown to be significantly lower than in nearby man-made environments.

Bike trails, an urban fishery, and habitats for birdlife and urban wildlife such as raccoons, opossums, squirrels (flying and others) and rabbits each hold special appeal for city residents of all ages. High quality city recreation programs are geared to pleasantly developed and equitably dispersed city parks. School districts that develop portions of school sites and campuses as outdoor laboratories render special bonuses to local youth groups and nearby property values, in addition to enriching the curriculum opportunities of the school that has preserved or created the natural area contiguous to the indoor classrooms. It is a sad state of affairs when a public

---

[6]Jane Loeffler, "Open Space, People and Urban Ecology," *Ekistics,* Vol. 35, No. 208 (March 1973), p. 122.

grade school in San Jose, California, must bus its children several miles through residential and commercial developments to a suitable open space where physical education classes can be conducted because there is no adequate play area around their school.

In an earlier era, land was viewed as a commodity to be considered for its maximum market value rather than an irreplaceable natural resource. Today, this attitude is one of the basic problems in the acquisition of future urban land for recreation and open space preservation. In fact, in California and many other Western states agricultural land is taxed for its highest potential value or use. As suburbanization moves toward rural areas and land values increase, property taxes also increase from $100 to $30,000 dollars per acre. Because the farmer can no longer pay the taxes and still maintain his agricultural operation, this arrangement in effect forces the vegetable farmer or orchard owner to sell his land to developers or land speculators. In some cases a few lots at a time are sold to a housing project in order to pay the skyrocketing taxes. Usually in time the entire farm or ranch is converted to subdivision with little, if any, open space preserved for the new residents.

Robert Cahn, environmental editor of the *Christian Science Monitor,* has written about the legal battles that are developing over state and local agency regulations to control consequences of unplanned growth. Cahn, a former Council of Environmental Quality member, writes that some rejected applications for construction of environmentally unsound or destructive projects result in law suits that allege that such action is a taking of private property rights for public use without compensation. However, courts in California, Wisconsin, Maine, and Maryland have sustained state land use controls against owner challenges. "The growth and development of the country will thus be greatly effected by the courts as they seek to determine the adjustments in property rights required in the general public interest."[7]

Palo Alto, California, has adopted an open space policy based on the economic justification that costs for public services required in the development of the foothills would substantially exceed revenues received from such residential development. The Palo Alto open space ordinance for the foothills recognizes that open space is a land use equal in importance to traditional residential and commercial categories.

It is the author's hope that as we have moved through our discussion of the hinterland recreation resources, as we have viewed the increasing congestion of national parks and wilderness areas caused by "escaping" urbanites, and as we have touched on inner city and metropolitan parks and open space, that we have begun to set the stage for a look at urban organisms or human settlements of the future, for in the twenty-first century diverse recreation resources will probably be major attractions in whichever part of the world city one chooses to live.

---

[7] Robert Cahn, "Thwarted Developers 'Are Taking the Fifth'," *Christian Science Monitor* (May 23, 1973), p. 9.

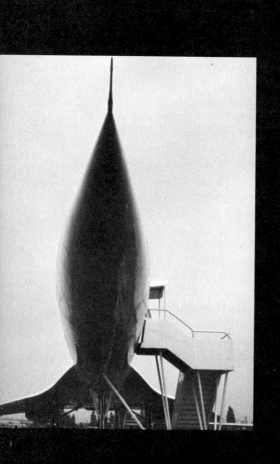

Mechanisms of Future Urban Resources

CHAPTER **12**

Ecumenopolis and Cities of the Future

The Earth As an Island in Space

In order to understand the future, one must have a basic understanding of the past. And to have a serious appreciation for the working of an entire system—whether it be the human body, an aircraft carrier, or a pond ecosystem, one must become familiar with the delicate functions of the many synchronous parts. The challenge to understand *ecumenopolis,* or the world city, can best be understood, in the author's opinion, if man takes leave of the metropolis or megalopolis where he presently lives and goes to an isolated island. There are several important similarities between a remote island as a container for man and Spaceship Earth as a container for the world city.

Except for possible variances in the amount of solar energy that is received on the earth's surface, most other cycles and flows of resources are assumed to be relatively fixed. Resources such as water, air, minerals, and land have a given quantity over planning periods that seldom exceed fifty to one hundred years. Obviously use rates and recycling rates vary immensely, but the raw materials are either in "storage" or in use regardless of what form or place they are in from time to time. With slight modifications, an island that is not in constant contact with larger continental land masses can demonstrate to even a temporary inhabitant the lessons that must be learned if ecumenopolis or, as one Soviet geographer has called it, Planetopolis, is to become an acceptable alternative for future urban existence.[1]

There is a dramatic uniqueness about a distant island as a relatively closed

[1]B. B. Rodoman, "The Organized Anthroposphere," *Ekistics,* Vol. 29, No. 175 (June 1970), pp. 438–443.

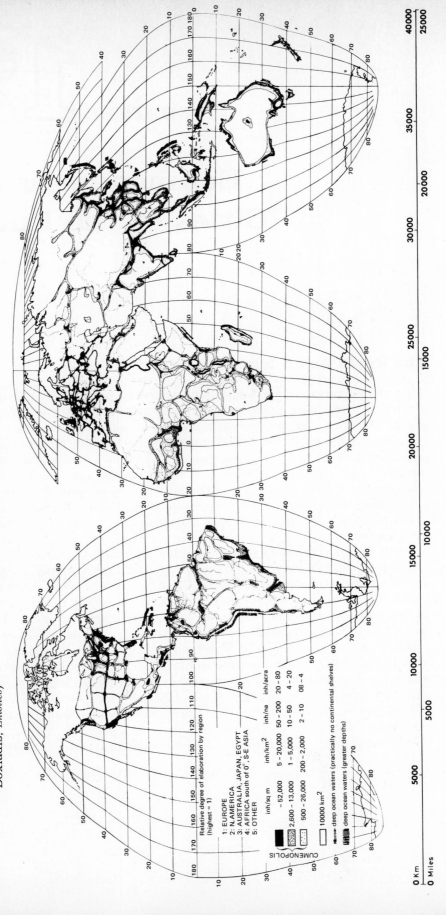

Figure 12-1. A world city or ecumenopolis is predicted by most urban scholars for the twenty-first century. Here is a world map with concentrations of population shown in the most habitable regions or corridors. The vast majority of the earth's surface including the oceans are not suited to urbanization with technology presently available. (from C. A. Doxiadis, *Ekistics*)

Figure 12-2. The delicacy of the earth's resources was never appreciated until mankind looked back during lunar landings. This photograph, which was taken from the Apollo 17 in December 1972, extends from the Mediterranean Sea area to the Antarctica south polar ice cap. Note the heavy cloud cover in the Southern Hemisphere. Almost the entire coastline of the continent of Africa is clearly delineated. The Arabian Peninsula can be seen at the northeastern edge of Africa. The large island off the southeastern coast of Africa is the Malagasy Republic. The Asian mainland is on the horizon toward the northeast. (NASA)

system. If there is habitation on the island and if that island is self-contained in the normal use of the word, the islanders must fend for themselves. The sea provides the perpetual harvest. Conversion of solar energy by the marine life that uses available nutrients is the mainstay of the diet. If the population grows beyond the limits of the beaches, estuaries, and fertile valleys, the supply of native nuts, fruits, and vegetables is exceeded. Instead of encouraging a reduction in population, the American approach has been toward more extensive and intensive harvests of the land and marine life.

Figure 12-3. The Greek island of Sifnos is relatively self-sufficient. The visitor who hikes the rugged terrain of a small isolated island can find a parallel to the dependence mankind has on the finite resources of the Spaceship Earth.

Figure 12-4. Mykonos has grown to be a popular island stop for visitors in the Aegean. Consequently, the island population has tended to shift from a dependence on the fields and the sea to a reliance on tourists for economic sustenance.

Figure 12-5. The fortified walls of Rhodes are reminders of the protection island dwellers sought from pirates and other invaders. In a seige, the self-sufficient defenders in a walled island city pitted their survival against the invaders who brought their supplies by ship.

Curiously, even early settlements separated by major land distances operated very much like islands made remote by water. A monastery had its own well, vineyard, garden, and pasture area. For all practical or impractical purposes, the early monastery was a clositered, relatively self-contained system—a terrestrial island. Nomadic villagers were not only rather self-contained, but they were also portable. Greek, Roman, and medieval cities, which were or could be walled off from attackers as closed systems, survived under siege for long periods. Forced by a similar need for protection from would-be attackers, the cliff-dwelling and mesa-residing Indians of the American Southwest operated in relative isolation for hundreds of years. However, eventually connections began to be made between islands, between monasteries, between remote villages, and sparsely spaced cliff dwellers. As the growth in population continued, more linkages were created, and with them began the succession from extractive activities to commercial service, and eventually the sophisticated urban functions of synthesis and integration.

Remote islands can serve as reminders to anyone who is curious about what recycling really means. If an island is serviced by steamer at periodic but widely spaced intervals, this lifeline convenience, or in the most extreme situations, survival is treated with more respect than in terrestrial-based urban areas. In fact, the comparable lifelines of power, food supply, water, sewerage, and information are taken for granted to the point where most urban residents do not know that they exist or how they function. Unfortunately, it takes a failure or crisis like a blackout or a drought to alert them to the fact that the modern megalopolis is very dependent not only on the fundamental resource base but also on the intricate delivery systems or networks that convey the essential goods and services.

Figure 12-6.
Resourceful Indian cliff dwellers of the American Southwest located human settlements in canyon walls as a protective strategy against invading bands.

442   On an island, the arrival of the supply steamer or cruise ship is an important event. Local villagers crowd the quay or wharf to *first* see what has arrived and *then* to load on board whatever goods are intended for the mainland or the next island port. This is the critical point of flow that is seldom seen or realized by modern metropolitan man. And until he does see or experience the importance of that lifeline, urban man will take less and less care of his "umbilical cords" and the resources in the hinterland or those that have been aggregated in his urban midst.

The island that needs to be visited for our understanding of ecumenopolis should also be of a size and topography that can be traversed by foot over a period of several days. Stated differently, the limits need to be known not only in distances but in carrying capacity. This implies that a determination needs to be made about a given standard of living that would be appropriate for the resources available or potentially within reach of development. Over many generations, the families living on an island of that general description have established some equilibrium that takes into account the expected living standard as balanced against yield from the land and sea, plus imports. Of course, with increased imports the balance could be thrown off but spatial constraints should appear as a negative force to any upsurge in population expansion.

Figure 12-7. The arrival of a steamer at an isolated island is a constant reminder of the dependency on the inflow and outflow of human and other resources.

Figure 12-8. Commodities arriving and leaving a dock dramatize the heavy reliance an urban area has on transportation networks. In the event of a shipping stoppage, paralysis hits an island community that has become totally dependent on networks. The largest cities of the world have become totally dependent on a continual flow of food, energy, and other resources to sustain normal urban functions.

The scene is set. The megalopolitan visitor needs to participate in several specific activities during his time on the island in order to learn the principles of ecumenopolitan living. He needs to draw water from the domestic cistern or from the village well and carry it to his dwelling. Then the metropolitan water supply system can be appreciated with new reverence and enthusiasm. He needs to purchase the fruits, vegetables, bread, and meat on a daily basis to really understand and appreciate refrigeration, packaging, and the incredible chain of events that deliver the wide array of produce to the modern supermarket. And he needs to pause in the streets

Figure 12-9. Looking at a fresh fruit and vegetable stand should raise our awareness of an urban area's total reliance on networks to feed tens of thousands on a daily basis. Unlike a century ago, the dealer depends on dozens of middlemen to bring the commodity to his stand and to you.

444 and participate in the humanity that is there. True, he is a visitor to the island, but he becomes a participant in the balance of existence; a link in the social and physical networks that keep a relatively isolated system functioning. However, the visitor to the island should not pass his transiency off as an irrelevancy in the exercise. For each person is a very short-term visitor to island earth or spaceship earth. Yet in the period of man's tenure as a species his impact has changed the very functioning of the biosphere. As technology continues to give man more leverage against the physical forces that previously had severe impacts, the balance of power so to speak is shifted away from the natural or physical forces to man as an environmental change agent. If the productivity of authors who write about environmental degradation is any index of man's new earth plundering ability, man has begun to play a catastrophic role in recent decades.

If mankind lived on the island mentioned earlier, perhaps this insensitivity to the ecological balance of our environment would not be so flagrant. But the fact is that man *does* live on a planetary island and he hardly knows it. His life support systems do not have a steamer that pulls up to the dock on a regular schedule. At least as yet our "ports" that are the interplanetary launching pads are exporting more commodities than they are importing. But the men who use those ports have, more than any other human beings,

Figure 12-10. If the earth is considered an island in space, here is the "port" for major departures. The Apollo 17 space vehicle, which carried astronauts Cernan, Evans, and Schmitt, waits on Launch Complex 39A for its December 7, 1972, blastoff for NASA's sixth and last manned lunar landing mission in the Apollo program from Cape Kennedy, Florida. (NASA)

Figure 12-11. Those who have hiked on our "neighbor island Moon" have experienced the fundamental concepts of living in closed systems. Hope exists that one of the major lessons of space exploration is to do a better job of managing Earth's resources before major human settlements are forced into closed support systems. Scientist-astronaut Schmitt collects lunar samples during the December, 1972, Apollo 17 mission. (NASA)

sensed the reality of the earth as an island. Those who have circled or hiked on our neighbor island, moon, have experienced the fundamental concepts of living in closed systems in the vehicles of the cosmonauts and astronauts. They also have the advantage of viewing earth with a fresh kind of dependent objectivity. Their eyes have taken the walk around the island and they have been reminded of earth's physical limits and man's physiological limits. Even those who ride in high altitude conventional aircraft observe the veils of atmospheric pollution over *conurbations* and plumes of water pollution in every lake and sea bordered by human habitation.

For thousands of years the connections between the remote islands of the earth were never made. Eventually with development of seaworthy craft, the essential ingredients of a terrestrial settlement were put into a floating container. It could be said that transoceanic vessels were and are portable microcosms of human villages. The spectrum of complexity extends from Thor Heyerdahl's rafts to the luxurious liners and aircraft carriers that house up to three thousand inhabitants. In classical times the galleys and later the Viking ships were often equipped to conquer island settlements, villages along the sea, or other vessels that carried valuable cargo. Thus connections were made and adjustments were apparently made by the seacoast villages to fortify themselves. The hilltop cities in the Mediterranean bear testimony to an era where the naval assault was superior to the terrestrial stronghold.

The best fortified city, which was dependent upon its stores of grain, water, oil, and other commodities, could often outlast the besieging forces who had to return to their villages for renewed supplies. As the lifelines to the besieging army were being restored, the forces from within the walled citadel would have an opportunity to drive off the enemy forces. As long as the internal supplies lasted, the fortress town was safe. But when strong naval forces with the associated "merchant marine" besieged a coastal bastion, the lifeline over the sea could be maintained with considerable ease and advantage. Naval powers came into supremacy and controlled the islands and the coastal towns, and began to link one up with the other over sea routes. Networks of land transportation began to emerge at a later date with engineering sophistication best exemplified by the early Greeks and Romans.

The entire Roman Empire was connected with major roads leading to Rome. History repeats itself as evidenced by the fact that Italy was the first nation to devote a major portion of its national income to a national highway system in the twentieth century. The *autostrada* example was borrowed by Germany in the form of the famous *autobahns* that were also constructed for military purposes. The national interstate highway system in the United States followed the same pattern. It was young Major Eisenhower who in the 1930's participated in a study of the feasibility for a national highway network for defense purposes. Twenty years later as President, his administration launched construction of the interstate system under the guise of security reasons. But we must not become too distracted by interesting tangents. For whatever purposes, transportation nets did begin to connect distant islands and remote terrestrial villages. In fact, every form of human settlement probably has some contact with the larger world. Air travel has completed the connections with the most remote jungle hamlet or mountain village moving us closer to the realization of a world city.

The Interrelationships of Human Settlements

When thus linked together, human settlements around the world are able to exchange information, physical goods, and services. What has not been emphasized enough is that disservices can also flow over these channels.

The pollution loads that are dumped into rivers and oceans affect all users.
The air pollution contributed by Tokyo, Sydney, Los Angeles, or New York
City has a direct relationship to the quality of air in London, Moscow, or
Calcutta. The envelope of the earth's atmosphere is a thin and common
lung for all the inhabitants of Spaceship Earth. It has tremendous rejuvena-
tive powers but its *commonality* is absolute. It may be man's downfall that
the commonality of all natural resources is so subtle that people in separate
islands or separate metropolitan areas operate without understanding the
vital impacts of man's influence on himself and his environment.

Let us visualize what happened when the supply of an essential resource
became very scarce on a given "island." After making certain that no
reserves were immediately available and after learning that that important
resource was available at the next "island," a visit was made to procure
the needed material. The visit may have been in the form of a raid or an
enterprising business exchange or barter. This pattern continues to repeat
itself among today's nations. The struggle between the "haves" and the
"have nots" is only an interim stage in the succession from the isolated
island perception of human existence to the reality of the situation that
is one island, one city, one Earth for all riders of this resilient but finite
planetary vehicle.

With the evidence now available, the commonality of resources and the
interrelationships that have been described in theory here now become
observable in practice. Worldwide networks for monitoring environmental
change have recent, short-term but alarming trends. Heavy metals such as
copper, cadmium, arsenic, lead, mercury, and others infuse throughout the
waters of the world. Telecommunications link every city on every continent.
Even remote villages receive television programs via the satellite network.
John G. Papaioannou, Research Director at the Athens Center of Ekistics,
has been one of the most diligent workers in the area of future megalopolitan growth. His writings in *Ekistics*[2] prophesy a rather gloomy outlook
until the year 2000, after which an increasingly brighter picture is forecast.

Ekistician Papaioannou foresees connections being established between
major megalopolitan areas on each continent where urbanization is in
progress today. As techniques of transportation and communication improve, urban regions will undoubtedly become more and more strongly
connected, he believes. With population growing and with unused habitable space becoming more scarce, the networks of megalopolises will
become larger and "thicker" so that the megalopolis will be replaced
toward the end of the first half of the twenty-first century by the next ekistic
unit; the urbanized region. About a generation later this will be replaced
by the urbanized continent. By that time, the middle or end of the twenty-
first century, urbanized continents will be the prevailing forms of settlement, with some isolated "urbanized regions, megalopolises, and metropolises."

[2]John G. Papaioannou, "Future Urbanization Patterns; A Long Range, World-wide View,"
Ekistics, Vol. 29, No. 175 (June 1970), pp. 368–381.

Ecumenopolis

Only a few links seem to be missing in this rather complex picture to achieve unity all over the system of urbanized areas on the globe. This highest or most complex unit in the hierarchy of settlements is called ecumenopolis, or world city. This term describes what will be a unified settlement system bridged by a connected system of networks over the habitable portion of the earth but not necessarily in continuous development. The connection of the metropolitan and later megalopolitan "islands" (by now they are certainly well integrated so "islands" becomes a poor descriptor) becomes stronger as the complexity increases. The major axes of urbanization exert great influence on the growth and future of even the most complex human settlement. Perhaps it was first phrased by Aristotle in his *Physics I* when he wrote, "Here and elsewhere we shall not obtain the best insight into things until we actually see them growing from the beginning." The suggestion of an island experience for every urban dweller is simply a prescription for that insight. So as time passes, ecumen-

Figure 12-12. The aerial view of Detroit, Michigan, hardly shows that its famous product, the automobile, takes up nearly three fourths of the city's land area for its storage and movement. Dehumanizing and energy-consuming urban sprawl is facilitated by increased access to residence and job by the automobile. No high-speed ground transit is available to this metropolitan region of nearly four million people. (U.S. Dept. of Housing and Urban Development)

opolis will very likely behave as one of its original components—a remote island of habitation in the planetary sea of Winken, Blinken, and Nod. If man and his critical island-dwelling existence is not practiced as the physical laws of nature dictate, ecumenopolis that is already born will never mature.

Maturation of ecumenopolis implies several basic principles—for example, the maximum number of potential human contacts with a minimum expenditure of energy, protective space, and privacy, plus the integration of the maximum variety of physical and cultural diversity. As populations of the world gather into larger and larger human settlements, the trend becomes established for continuous, high-energy urban systems. The influence of these forces will invariably become stronger than any urban pressure we know today. In terms of constraints, the biological and physical laws that spell out an environmental carrying capacity have predominated and will always predominate. The most pervasive influence of human settlements upon the environment and upon the settlements themselves will be the transportation networks.

The Automobile and Urbanization

The ribbons of concrete that lattice the urban environs and the hinterlands beyond have profound influences on drainage patterns and wildlife habitat, and create countless forms of visual blight. But the most devastating impact is in the metropolitan tissue itself. With the 90 per cent federal and 10 per cent local funding arrangement for interstate highway systems, the municipalities bow to the economic persuasion to place the expressway in the least-cost site. Unhappily for the affected residents, the least-cost site is first the low-rent district (usually black, brown, yellow, or poor white neighborhoods) who can expeditiously be dehumanized because they are without political efficacy. The next most vulnerable parcels of land to be consumed by the highway engineers are the public parks and open spaces. Hopefully, in the urban complexes of the future, intangible values of minority neighborhoods and recreational open space will become competitive with or greater than the values attached to building roads. In the world city of the future, rapid mass transportation will be underground. It would be inconceivable that for the numbers of people to be moved, at the economies that could be realized, and at the conveniences available, any major urban mass transit system could be built at surface levels. As man has managed his networks over time, there has logically evolved a practice of placing networks underground.

Water supply systems, drainage canals, and waste water disposal systems have almost always been placed underground in the advanced stages of any civilization. Today, even major urban communications networks are built underground for reasons of efficiency. In the near future, the metallic spaghetti that "separates man from God" will all be housed in hollow

Figure 12-13. Atlanta, Georgia, chokes with auto traffic on Interstate 75. As new expressways are built, more cars seem to fill them. Costs of interstate and other highway construction are especially heavy on the inner city poor who are forced to relocate and on other residents who bear the hardships of traffic noise, air pollution, and neighborhood disruption.

Figure 12-14. Even in a city very rich in history and ethnic neighborhoods, such as Boston, the expressway sliced through the human communities and created an unwelcome barrier between residence and job, between cultural activities and dwellings, between natural open spaces and people. All this road building in Boston took place despite the presence of an underground mass transit system!

Figure 12-15. The hearts of cities should be reserved primarily for pedestrian activity. Proper location for major urban networks is underground as shown in this schematic sketch of the Bay Area Rapid Transit Powell Street station in San Francisco. (U.S. Dept. of Housing and Urban Development)

Figure 12-16. San Francisco was one large American city which chose an alternative to the interstate highway for its urban commuters. The Bay Area Rapid Transit speeds former auto drivers throughout the Bay area. Countless neighborhoods and environmental amenities of which San Francisco is proud were saved by choosing BART instead of the more expensive, more energy consuming, more polluting automobile. (BART)

curbing or in underground conduits that may serve as utility corridors for many commercial and residential services. Tunnels for mass transit will follow the leads of Paris and London whose planners had the courage to build underground systems while American cities were still struggling with electrified surface commuter systems. It is a travesty that some of America's largest cities such as Los Angeles, Detroit, Saint Louis, Philadelphia, Pittsburgh, Baltimore, Dallas, Houston, and Milwaukee have no rapid mass transit system at all. Washington's Metro and San Francisco's BART were courageous and overdue struggles coming at least twenty-five years after they were urgently needed. Author Carrie McWilliams in the early 1920's described Los Angeles as "a collector of suburbs in search of a city." Los Angeles began taking to the suburbs too early in its formative life ever to have firmly rooted an urban center. Older metropolises sprouted suburbs around long-established hubs and then proceeded to choke their hubs with their automobiles. As architect and city planner, Victor Gruen, put it: "We turned our cities into doughnuts with all the dough around the center and nothing in the middle."[3]

One reason, perhaps, that sprawl was considered peculiar to Los Angeles for so long may be found in the fact that the automobile appeared on the scene while the city was still in swaddling clothes. As late as 1880, Los Angeles had only ten thousand inhabitants. It moved through the successional stages to a crashing urban climax. It grew phenomenally the following decade: even so, it had only fifty thousand inhabitants by 1890. The automobile was thus able to fashion the city in fledgling form, and was also able to do so at a high speed because of the compatibility of the early automobile with southern California's climate. The automobile's worst enemies at the time—cold weather and mud—were minimal in an area that enjoyed a long, dry season and basked in warm sun. When the Stanley Steamers began to chug from east to west, they frequently bogged down on the way, but once they got to the San Bernardino Valley and the area that was later to become Los Angeles County, their home was found. The speed of the ensuing courtship of automobile and urban area blurred or confused comprehension of the portent of things to come. There is no longer any doubt that the automobile dehumanized many cities first in the United States and soon after in the rest of the world, and it will continue to do so unless the lessons of our American automobilized urban areas can be told with clarity and honesty.

In Los Angeles, the largest noncity in the world, there was a railway system known to its patrons as the "Pacific Electric." It was, and in its freight carrying capacity still is, owned by the Southern Pacific Railroad Company. But if the Southern Pacific could have kept the Pacific Electric running, it would have. The Southern Pacific, of course, is in business to make a profit. For a good long while, the Pacific Electric was doing exactly that. It was said, in fact, to have been the most profitable intercity electric railway

[3] Mitchell Gordon, *Sick Cities, Psychology and Pathology of American Urban Life* (Baltimore, Maryland: Penguin Books, Inc. 1965), p. 13.

in the world at one time. Some routes, however, began to become un-profitable as early as the mid-1920's and more did so in the 1930's. But World War II with its gasoline rationing and other restrictions on automobile use gave the Pacific Electric a new lease on life. Shortly after the end of the war, the final decline of the Pacific Electric set in. By 1950, the operation was costing the Southern Pacific over $3 million a year despite considerable trimming of its routes. By 1953, the Pacific Electric was already being described by those with short memories and even shorter foresight, as the ancient lemon of Los Angeles. In 1961 service ceased on the last remaining passenger line, a twenty-one mile segment between downtown Los Angeles and the harbor of Long Beach.

The story of the Pacific Electric may be of special interest to Angelenos, but it also bears on the commuting headaches, past, present, and future of residents of practically every major metropolis in the world with the possible exception of aquatic Venice. For one reason, the killer of the Pacific Electric is still on the prowl. It is, of course, the automobile—and all the sprawl and congestion that that vehicle brings with it wherever it goes.

In France, the automobile has even worked a revolution in the nation's culinary habits, by bringing the sale of sandwiches to gasoline stations. The French highway death rate is already so high—two and one-half times that of the United States—that 150,000 people, the equivalent of a city the size of Lille, will die on French highways by the time France completes the fifteen-year highway modernization program that was announced in the mid-1960's.

The automobile's appetite for space in horrendous. The forty-four thousand mile interstate highway system that was born with the passage of Congressional legislation in 1956 (upon its planned completion in 1975) will occupy more land than the entire state of Rhode Island. The fact that 90 per cent of the facilities' $58 billion cost is being born by the federal government and only 10 per cent by state governments is meager consolation for municipalities spared the construction burden but not the tax loss. Two thirds of the entire downtown area of Los Angeles is already given over to the automobile, approximately 33 per cent of it to parking lots and garages and the rest to roads and highways. Each one of the city's interchanges linking one freeway to another consumes approximately eighty acres of real estate; every mile of freeway uses up twenty-four acres. By 1980 Los Angeles is expected to have thirty-four square miles of land devoted to its freeway system. This is approximately the size of the entire city of Miami, Florida.

The average standard-size automobile with a driver but no passengers takes up more than nine times as much space per person in motion as a public conveyance. At rest, it needs as much space as the average downtown office devotes to each employee. "Highways are the greediest consumers of real estate we have," declares William N. Casella, senior associate of the National Municipal League in New York. An official of *McCalls*

magazine estimates that traffic delays cost that publication an estimated $50,000.00 a year in extra driver wages, gasoline, and equipment. After a detailed study the Russell Sage Foundation in New York determined that traffic congestion was already costing New Yorkers at least $350 million a year as far back as 1931. A *New York Times* survey of business and automotive executives recently estimated the national loss, inclusive of executive time lost in taxicabs, delays in freight deliveries, and other waste,

Figure 12-17. One of the metropolitan areas that benefits from BART is Oakland, California. It is informative to see the greater consumption of land and a smaller volume passenger capacity per area that the highway system imposes on an urban area compared to BART's efficient land utilization. BART's track and station are neatly placed in the expressway median strip. Can you imagine what the motorist thinks who is stopped in the daily rush hour traffic jam as the BART trains whiz past? (BART)

was close to $5 billion a year. Bus systems are among the biggest sufferers. To cite one example, Milwaukee figures it has more than forty-five buses in its fleet to compensate for traffic congestion-related delays. That is approximately $750,000 worth of buses to say nothing of the expense of operating them. Lewis Mumford describes the weekday commuting process in major metropolitan areas around the world as "an exchange of urban jam for suburban jelly." It should not take long, however, for the suburban

455

Figure 12-18. The speculative supersonic transport never lived up to its early promises of ecological safeguards and economic feasibility. The question lingers about the propriety of moving very few people at very high speeds at very high costs versus applying the technology of the same engineers to move many people at slightly lower speeds at considerably lower environmental and social costs.

jelly to take on the consistency of urban jam. The plight of Los Angeles, again, may be more than a little enlightening in this respect. Los Angeles is the freeway-building freak of the world. By the end of 1960 it had poured over $900 million into 310 miles of freeways and expressways reaching into Orange and Ventura counties. Los Angeles' rush hour congestion, however, is worse than it ever has been, and with the number of automobiles increasing even faster than the population, it may grow still more intolerable. The nation's highway officials figure that they will need over fifteen hundred miles of freeway to accommodate the vehicles that will be on the road by 1980. By that time Los Angeles will have over $5 billion invested in its freeway system.

Whatever the world city is going to become, one fact remains clear. The automobile does not have a place in the hubs of the megalopolitan areas. The *hinterlands* are the place, if there is one *for* the *automobile*. Mass transit is a survival necessity in the interior of the massive megalopolitan growth areas.

The supersonic transport offers a new problem as well as a new hope in terms of world city transportation. In late 1970, the British-French Concorde supersonic transport had completed over 225 hours of flight testing and 120 flights. It had logged almost 170 hours in the air of which 30 were at supersonic speeds. Neither of the two models, however, have yet flown at the projected *Mach 2 speed* that became possible only recently with the fitting of the more powerful engines. Thus far the aircraft has flown at altitudes up to 47,000 feet and at a speed of Mach 1.5 or about 1,000 miles per hour. In 1973 Trans World Airlines and Pan American canceled options of SST orders primarily for economic costs that did not outweigh the benefits of slightly faster transcontinental flight times. If supersonic flight fares try to cover even a tiny part of the research and development costs, only a tiny minority of world travelers could afford the ride. Another big problem with the Concorde and its sisters is the unknown as well as the known impact on the environment. Sonic booms have a demonstrable affect on the cardiovascular system, the nervous system, and the respiratory system of man. High-altitude exposure effects to crew and passengers are a potentially serious unknown. Perhaps most troublesome is the unknown

Figure 12-19. This British-French Concorde endured a difficult financial research-and-development period. Economic and environmental uncertainties promoted cancellations of early orders from major airlines. These photographs were taken in Paris by the author before the tragic crash of a Soviet supersonic transport in 1973.

458 but suspected impact on *stratospheric* weather patterns and ultimately on the weather and climate of Spaceship Earth.

Even with the increasing number of subsonic jumbo jets such as the 747, the Tristar, stretch DC-10's, stretch DC-8's and the possible widespread use of vertical takeoff and landing craft, present airports cannot hope to provide the most efficient and reliable means of transportation between cities of the future. Resistance to airport expansion is based on safety, social, economic, and environmental arguments. High speed rail and tube transit will probably come into prominence again when airport expansion costs, aircraft noise, and airplane contaminants become unacceptable obstacles for urban populations to tolerate. Recently the technology has advanced to the point where underground tunnels are almost competitive with center city surface transit construction costs. The pneumatic tube with capsules or vehicles operated by vacuum and air pressure differentials has been demonstrated with considerable promise. Additional expressway and other interstate highway expansion meets even more opposition because of the numbers of people and numbers of acres directly affected. Surface transportation efficiencies agreed upon by most transportation planners show the following capacities on a single lane per hour:

Passengers in automobiles on surface roadways	1,600
Passengers in automobiles on expressways	2,800
Passengers in buses on surface roadways	9,000
Passengers in streetcars (trams on rails) on surface roadways	13,500
Passengers in streetcars in subways	20,000
Passengers in local subway trains	40,000
Passengers in express subway trains	60,000

Population Growth and Urbanization

In the first half of the twentieth century, the population of Los Angeles grew thirteen times as fast as the average of the nation's fifty-seven largest cities. Their populations rose 160 per cent in that period while that of Los Angeles rocketed by 2,200 per cent.

Like so many concepts of the present age, from the size of the federal budget to the speed of spacecraft, the rate of urban growth is an exceedingly difficult one to grasp in anything like its full import. No one seems to really know where we are on our *sigmoid growth curve*. Almost everyone behaves as if we are near the bottom of the curve instead of near the top. The dimensions of a growing city like those of an elephant viewed by a mouse begin to be seen only by an examination of many different angles including those of the cosmonauts and astronauts who have come to perceive earth as an island in the sky.

"The Athens of Pericles' Day," Professor James Marston Fitch notes in an article in the *Columbia University Forum,* "was never larger than Yonkers.

Renaissance Florence was smaller than New Haven. Chicago is three times the size of Imperial Rome." The Population Reference Bureau, a Washington, D.C., nonprofit organization of biologists and other professionals who think that the alert should be sounded on man's prolificacy, figures 1 of every 25 people who ever walked the earth from the time *Homo sapiens* supposedly made his debut on the planet, more than 2 million years ago, is doing his walking today. It calculates total human births since that date at approximately 77 billion. The global population in the early 1970's was close to 3.8 billion. It took $16\frac{1}{2}$ centuries for the population to double, from approximately 250 million at the time of Christ to an estimated 500 million when Cromwell was ascending to the rule of Britain in the mid-seventeenth century. It took only 2 centuries for the world population to double again; the total came to 1 billion in 1850. The next doubling took but 80 years; the figure was 2 billion by 1930. It will take half that time—some 40 years—to double the 1970 figure; population prognosticators place the world population at 6 to 8 billion around 2000 A.D.

The United States is expected to grow at about the average global rate; the 208 million people it had at the time of the 1970 census could exceed 360 million during the twenty-first century. Some states, of course, will surge ahead even more rapidly. California will have to make room by 1980 for as many people again as it had in 1960, although it was already the most populous state in the nation by 1963.

The population density of the 13 former colonies in 1790 was 4.5 persons per square mile. That same territory today contains close to 700 persons

Figure 12-20. Increased density is the pattern in this Berlin Housing Development and in other metropolitan areas of Europe and Asia. In America the number of persons per square mile in metropolitan areas is decreasing as affluence and environmental amenities tend to draw residents away from the center city. (German Information Center)

460   per square mile. This begins to approach the population density of the Netherlands, which is the most densely settled country in the world. If present population trends continue, the day will come when there is "Standing Room Only" as the Zero Population Growth clubs throughout America and the world are prophesying. In 800 years, at the present growth rate, an average of only 1 square foot of space would be available for each person in the United States. Children born after 1956 who live out their normal life expectancy can envision the United States as a nation of 400 million people. The country had just under 100 million as recently as 1915. President Richard Nixon in his population address in the late 1960's emphasized that it took America 300 years to reach the 100 million mark; it took 50 years for America to add the next 100 million and it appears that during the next 25 years, the nation will add its third 100 million people. To put it in terms of comparative sizes and growth rates, it would be helpful to look at how many people are being added each year. Metropolitan New York gives birth each year to a city roughly the size of Norfolk, Virginia. New York City and its bedroom communities and Northeastern New Jersey counted 300,000 births in 1960. Norfolk, with just under 305,000 people in 1960, was the forty-first largest city in the United States at the time, larger than Miami, Florida; Omaha, Nebraska; or Akron, Ohio. The 1970 census listed the Norfolk-Portsmouth, Virginia, metropolitan population as 680,000 and it had slid to forty-seventh largest in the 1970 ratings.

The Surge to the City

By 1980, over 90 per cent of the American people will be living in urban areas. The figure in 1920 was 51.2 per cent; in 1970 it was 73 per cent. Five metropolitan areas accounted for 20 per cent of the nation's total population in 1960. One out of every five Americans then lived in either Greater New York, Chicago, Los Angeles, Philadelphia, or Detroit. In 1974 more than 93 per cent of California was urbanized!

At the time of the first United States census in 1790, Philadelphia was the largest city in the land with 44,000 persons. It is interesting to note that before America achieved her independence, Philadelphia was the second largest city in the British Empire. New York City was the new nation's second largest city with only 33,000 inhabitants. Levittown, New York, which didn't exist before World War II, was 50 per cent larger in 1960 than the country's biggest city was in 1790; By 1970, thirty-three metropolitan areas in the United States had more than 1 million residents.

The surge to the city will be even greater in some of the world's under-

Figure 12-21. New York City is only one of several urban centers that make up the megalopolis of the eastern United States. As the original cities become too saturated or too ponderous to function effectively, development of the urban organism moves out to the hinterland areas. (U.S. Dept. of Housing and Urban Development)

462 developed countries than in the United States. Urban growth rates in parts of Asia in the early 1960's and into the 1970's were running 400 per cent higher than those in the West, and the movement to the cities on that great land mass has obviously only just begun. Ths diseases of worldwide sprawl into and around the periphery of cities are likely to grow more universal. Dr. Luther Gulick, Chairman of the Institute of Public Administration, defines the diseases in the following list:

Clogged streets.
Dying public transit.
Spreading blight.
Increasing air and water pollution.
Growing lawlessness.
Diverging educational opportunities.
Neglect of park space and other community facilities such as libraries and
    museums.
A sorely felt lack of comprehensive governmental institutions necessary for
    mustering physical and political support of the community's "most
    elemental requirements."

Or, are cities themselves the disease? Lewis Mumford, in *The Culture of Cities,* indicated that a good many seem to be. He saw the metropolis as an accumulation of people accommodating themselves "to an environment without adequate natural or cultural resources: people who do without pure air, who do without sound sleep, who do without a cheerful garden or a play space, who do without the very sight of the sky and the sunlight,

Figure 12-22. There are "clogged streets" even in San Francisco. Fuel shortages and the high cost of gasoline somewhat curtailed the use of the automobile in 1974. But where traffic congestion persists in a city of excellent mass transit, it is apparent that a change of life style is required and overdue.

Figure 12-23. The inter-urban trains of the Chicago area still run, but it is a "dying public transit." No American mass transit system pays for itself. (U.S. Dept. of Housing and Urban Development)

Figure 12-24. This is a good example of the spreading urban blight. One cannot help but wonder what the suburbs built in the 1970's will look like in 20 years? (U.S. Dept. of Housing and Urban Development)

Figure 12-25. An unfortunate part of every city's life is the increasing air and water pollution. (University of Michigan News Service)

Figure 12-26. Diverging educational opportunities are very evident, especially for those who help produce basic resources for the cities. Opportunities are far from equal for all, although some stumbling efforts have been made to achieve equality in school and health benefits for the rural poor. (U.S. Dept. of Housing and Urban Development)

Figure 12-27. Park space and other community facilities such as libraries and museums are lacking in the neglected inner city.

Figure 12-28. Innumerable areas suffer from a sorely felt lack of comprehensive governmental institutions, which are necessary for mustering physical and political support of the community's most elemental requirements.

466 who do without free motion, spontaneous play, or robust sexual life. The so-called blighted areas of the Metropolis," he says, "are essentially *do without areas.*" If one wishes the sight of urban beauty while living in these areas, one must ride a bus or an automobile many, many miles to touch nature in its unspoiled state. One must travel in a crowded train to the far outskirts or hinterland of the city. Lacking the means to get out, one succumbs; chronic starvation produces lack of appetite. "Eventually," Mumford warns, "you may live and die without even recognizing the loss."

"Men come together in cities," said Aristotle, "in order to live. They remain together in order to live the good life." In many cities today men come together principally to earn a living—and get out of it as quickly as they can, tortuously if necessary, in order to enjoy the pleasures that Aristotle might easily have taken for granted in his day in the Athenian Agora. No longer can one find clean air, a refuge from noise and crowds, a patch of earth, and a glimpse of sky unscathed by high altitude jets or the unpolluted streams in the Athens of today.

This book has been primarily an attempt to stimulate the interest of the general reader and student in some of the principal problems confronting the city in which he lives—or shortly will live even if he does no more than stay where he is. It has, then, one principal purpose—to light up some of the darker corners of city anatomy and city physiology. No attempt is made to deal with every city problem. The present effort would be unmanageable if such an attempt were made. Some of the problems that have not been treated at length such as the growth of racial *dichotomies* in Northern and Western cities in the thick of urban sprawl, are perhaps more

Figure 12-29. "Men come together in cities," said Aristotle, "in order to live. They remain together in order to live the good life." The London waterfront along the Thames is an example of how an old and great city has managed its urban resources to attract residents and visitors alike.

properly treated in volumes of their own; they are not dealt with here, with apology, but the emphasis is to look at selected basic resources that will supply and maintain the city of the future—the World City.

The World City

The cities of the world that for the first several thousand years of urbanization remained reasonably isolated from each other can no longer enjoy (or suffer from) that islandlike existence. Two major changes in the last hundred years have been responsible for the creation of human settlements that are forerunners of the world city ecumenopolis. The population growth of the world with increased expectancies for mobility is one factor. The other important change is the migration of populations into urban areas with increased reliance on goods and services from other urban areas. The hinterlands, however, must provide the basic resources for the survival and maintenance of a megalopolis. Jean Gottmann, Constantinos Doxiadis, Arnold Toynbee, and other scholars of urbanization have depicted the eventual urbanization of continents into a World City. In the twenty-first century it is hypothesized that a plateau will be reached in the world's sigmoid population growth curve. (See Figure 12-30) It is also presumed that an international form of ecumenopolitan administration will be re-

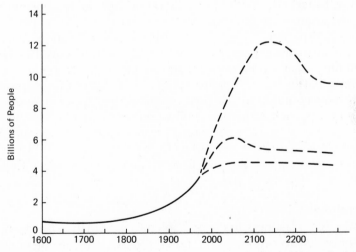

Figure 12-30. No certainty exists among demographers as to what the world's population curve will look like in the future. Most species produce a sigmoid growth curve and it is projected that *Homo sapiens* is in the upslope of the S-shaped curve. The critical question is when the human race will reach a plateau level which is an indication of a quasi-equilibrium between resource supply and resource demand. Three possible projections are shown with an overshoot and a return to a lower plateau on the upper estimates.

468   quired to coordinate the functions of worldwide urban affairs. Eventually the great cities we know today will become huge "neighborhoods of special activity" in the World City.

Once the migration from the countryside to the city is carried out in developing countries as it has in post-industrialized nations, the problems of urban government will be even greater than they are at present. The squatters who come into metropolitan areas around the world have always proven to be a difficult environmental and administrative challenge. The *favelas* of Rio de Janeiro; the hillside shacks of Hong Kong, Rome, Bombay, Calcutta, Shanghai, Moscow, Sao Paulo, and Mexico City; and the ghettos of Chicago, New York, and Detroit all share the common problem of newly acquired citizens who require more public services than the revenue they generate from their means of production or possession of property. Large urban territorial units will be exceedingly difficult to manage with or without a global federation of the sovereign states and megalopolises.

Large metropolitan areas in the United States are facing very serious problems of providing public services to inner city residents and suburbanities. The most noticeable growth in population has taken place in the outlying regions of metropolis. Migration to the central city represents movement of very poor individuals from rural areas. Those from within the city or from other cities eventually try to acquire "a little piece of land" out in the suburb. The suburb is usually another municipal jurisdiction. If this outlying community is without commercial or industrial activity, the taxation for individual landowners is very high compared to the communities with heavy industry or high tax revenue-generating capacity. Furthermore, the unit cost of providing public services such as fire, police, water, sewage, transportation, medical, recreation, and educational facilities is much higher in low density, scattered suburban settlements. The dormitory communities that are part of a large city drain the existing resources to the point that in Fairfax County, Virginia, and Santa Clara County, California, taxes continue to rise but services to the dispersed residents decrease. In fact, each additional family represents a net loss to the municipality in terms of revenues generated versus taxes received. The San Jose Unified School District of Santa Clara County estimated in 1972 that it loses $481 per year per pupil. Contrary to the claims of Chambers of Commerce, growth does not always pay.

Microtowns

Some urban planners find hope for future human settlements in the concept of *"microtowns"* within the World City. The idea of a microtown is based on the concept of a relatively self-contained community that, with the aggregation of other microtowns or other urban units, make up a metropolitan area or megalopolis. The microtown would have the necessary array of urban services available within a ten-minute walk of its residents— shops, theaters, schools, churches, a community center, a library, and other necessary urban amenities. The truly unique urban offerings such as a sports arena or coliseum, a major museum or symphony, a primary seat of metropolitan government, and a major communications center would be within reasonable reach (up to forty-five minutes by mass transit). The microtown, however, provides the human scale for people of all ages. It provides the intimacy of one's personal garden and the opportunity to play an active role in community events and decisions. Its population is probably 35,000 or less. The microtown is also this author's concept of the traditional town or medieval city-state of the seventeenth and eighteenth centuries, with the exception that microtowns are located within the administration of megalopolis or the World City. The microtown is another way of saying that the multiple urban functions need to be humanized at a useful level for urban dwellers. Microtowns are also called superblocks, towns within towns, and *quadros*.

The quadros or huge square settlement units of Brasilia, Brazil; the superblocks of Islamabad, the new capital located in northern West Pakistan; and the large-sized neighborhood of Eastwick in Philadelphia are recent examples of reasonably self-contained clusters of dwelling units, shops, gardens, community centers, schools, and other urban facilities where the pedestrians and residents are of primary consideration. The idea behind these bold experiments in new urban containers is that the urban life returns to a scale of the earliest preindustrialized towns, populations of 35,000 to 50,000. These microtowns are within easy distance of special cultural and other metropolitan amenities that could never be provided by small towns of similar size that are isolated from the great cities of the

Figure 12-31. Reston, Virginia, is situated twenty miles from downtown Washington, D.C. It is one of the recent "new towns" to be built in the United States. European planning principles of a pedestrian orientation were applied with some success in Reston.

world. Some of the microtowns are designed with internal employment for the majority of residents who seek jobs. Stevenage, England, and Reston, Virginia, are often cited as examples of new towns built with industry and other kinds of employment so that their residents do not need to commute to jobs in another part of the megalopolis. Industry and business are not always able to be attracted to the microtown within a metropolitan region and when that happens, workers must commute. The environmental costs of the dormitory town or suburb are much higher when high speed mass transit is not used.

New Towns

In the late 1960's and early 1970's it dawned on American urban planners that the 100 million Americans whose births are expected in the next 30 years will not be housed, employed, transported, schooled, and contented in the overcrowded and decaying cities of the present. It was decided that a national effort would be launched very similar to the Scandinavian, French, British, Dutch, and German plans that called for the construction of new communities either within established urban areas, around the periphery of present cities, or as "free standing" new towns located at some distance from the major metropolis.

The small light that Ebenezer Howard lit at the turn of the century took many decades to become a torch in British new towns. It was Howard's dream that a *garden city* in the countryside could provide the vitality of active town life in the surroundings of the natural environment. Stevenage, Welwyn Garden City, and many others have provided an alternative to those who felt that living in London was more than they could bear.

Several kinds of urban developments have been called "new towns" in the United States and elsewhere. What Howard meant by his garden city new-town concept was a self-contained human settlement predesigned for a specific size and with various urban functions and employment opportunities that could operate in relative isolation from other nearby towns or the metropolis. Great stress was placed on a rural or pastoral surrounding and easy accessibility to work, shops, schools, recreation areas, and civic activities by the resident population. There is also the ever present hope that heterogeneity of employment, social classes, and cultural events could be incorporated into the new town. The "new community" concept in the United States has many similarities in theory except that most of the new community projects and applications show a more conspicuous dependency and relationship to a nearby metropolitan area than do the European examples.

The garden city that Howard envisioned would be separated from the metropolis of London in cultural and political alliances once a string of satellite towns combined efforts to support a specialized hospital, university, museum, or symphony. Ten new towns of 35,000 each, linked by high speed transportation, could enjoy cultural amenities now possible through intensive organization instead of high density population on a single site.

Palo Alto and Berkeley serve as this kind of "Social City" or "Regional City" in an informal way for special cultural functions in the San Francisco Bay metropolis. Lewis Mumford has portrayed the biological implications of the city better than anyone else. For those who would ask if growth and saturation have been considered in Howard's approach, Mumford has this reply:

. . . Howard's greatest contribution was less in recasting the physical form of the city than in developing the organic concepts that underlay this form; for though he was no biologist like Patrick Geddes, he nevertheless brought to the city the essential biological criteria of dynamic equilibrium and organic balance: balance as between city and country in a larger ecological pattern, and balance between the varied functions of the city: above all, balance through the positive control of growth in the limitation in area, number, and density of occupation, and the practice of reproduction (colonization) when the community was threatened by such an undue increase in size as would lead only to lapse of function. If the city was to maintain its life-maintaining functions for its inhabitants, it must in its own right exhibit the organic self control and self containment of any other organism.

Howard sought, in other words, to give to the new kind of city all the advantages that the big city possessed before its inordinate expansion put them beyond the means or beyond the reach of its inhabitants. He saw that, once it has achieved an optimum size, the need for the individual town is not to increase its own area and population, but to be part of a larger system that has the advantage of large numbers and extensive facilities.[4]

Recent events in America have refuted William H. Whyte's charge that it "is an impossible vision" for the new town to have the texture and fabric of the city. It is true that the new town-garden city experiment in America began slowly with Radburn, New Jersey, and the federal green belt towns of Greenbelt, Maryland; Greenbrook, New Jersey; Greendale, Wisconsin; and Greenhills, Ohio; and then faded until the experiments of Columbia, Reston, and the rush of late 1970's new communities. Most of these efforts in the United States and the United Kingdom were intended to relieve urban congestion. However, sprawl of residential developments and scattered business and housing units on low cost land within a sixty-minute commuting distance of the city center brought a peculiar backlash effect. The residents of the sprawled suburb began to miss the normal functions of a city that provided for human contacts, a mixture of activities, and some personal involvement in community decision-making. There was an expressed need for a better educational climate, various civic functions, and other community-wide activities. Curiously, an effort seemed to be gaining momentum that called for an urbanization of the suburb. The sprawlites or as they are more commonly called suburbanites, wanted a branch library, a neighborhood school, a shopping center that had "downtown" stores

[4]Lewis Mumford, *The City in History* (New York: Harcourt Brace Jovanovich, Inc., 1961), p. 516.

Figure 12-32. An integration of natural environments with urban functions is a major objective of the Reston, Virginia, plan. Unfortunately, success has yet to be attained in the area of widespread economic diversity among Reston residents. Other new towns have been planned in an effort to cope with America's growing urban populations.

represented, a community center, and even (despite the increased lot size)—a neighborhood park and recreation program.

Scattered communities and housing projects grew and still are growing without a thoughtful consideration to the urban tax base and without adequate regard for air, water, open space, wildlife, or land resources. Furthermore, with the speculative form of growth that has characterized the 1950's through the 1970's, a very limited choice has existed for many people as to where they could live and the types of housing and environment in which they could live. Moreover, employment and business opportunities for inner city residents are reduced and the distances between the places people live, where they work, and where they find suitable recreation are greatly increased.

Columbia, Maryland, and Reston, Virginia, are examples of midcentury new towns that were begun with private capital, primarily from Connecticut General Life Insurance and Gulf Oil, respectively. The financial difficulties of early day Reston and Columbia have been well publicized. Most of the financial trouble is created by the need for a mammoth outlay of capital

Figure 12-33. Tapiola Garden City, Finland, situated six miles outside Helsinki (which is seen on the horizon) served as a prototype for some of the planning of Reston, Virginia. Pictured here is Tapiola's recreation center located near the town's fountains and centrum. Excellent integration of natural features with urban functions demonstrates how a human community can blend Nature, Man, Society, Shells, and Networks.

Figure 12-34. Ecumenopolis or the World City is forming with new additions like Amsteveel, a suburb of Amsterdam, Netherlands, demonstrating efficient use of urban space. One large unfinished task is to try to estimate the carrying capacity of future urban containers and ecumenopolis itself.

for roads and general community services before the financial returns come back to the private owners at a level that maintains solvency. Ordinarily the national government will underwrite long-term capital expenditures when social overhead costs are involved that help reduce a national problem such as a housing shortage. In some European countries the national government participates in a very supportive way in new community development. In the Netherlands and several Scandinavian countries, the government has even adjusted interest rates in order to favor investment in new towns or gone to the extent of diverting labor to high priority new community construction through preferential building and work permits. Reston and Columbia in this country depended entirely on private capital from oil and insurance companies. For the private sector to have to wait as long as the public treasury for a return on investment is something most stockholders are reticent to undertake.

The economic life of American new towns was given a new lift under Title IV of the *Housing Act of 1968,* which authorized the Department of Housing and Urban Development (HUD) to issue loan guarantees to *private* developers of large-scale new communities. Previously the argument was made that no private entrepreneur could lay out the necessary capital costs for public services—such as roads, sewers, schools, and recreation centers, as well as quality residential units. The concern was that a minimum of twenty to thirty years would be needed before the developer could break even when the new town finally filled to capacity and then generated adequate marginal revenue (not withstanding inflationary trends or other unhappy market conditions). As a result of Title IV, developers found their obligations backed by the U.S. Treasury, and the necessary long-term capital could be borrowed through private debt placements or public offerings of a government note of indebtedness and at much lower interest rates than was previously possible. Up to $25 million was available for a single project plus a total of $250 million for all loan guarantees. Title IV also provided for supplemental grants to local governments for open space and for installation of water and sewer lines in HUD-guaranteed new towns.

Thus the economic building blocks for ecumenopolis are being put in place, one by one, in the United States in ways rather similar to the public-private financing of new towns and new communities in Europe. Title VII of the *Urban Growth and New Community Development Act of 1970* raised the ceiling on total loan guarantees to $500 million and extended the loan possibilities to public agencies such as New York States Urban Development Corporation. HUD was authorized to issue loan guarantees covering all costs of acquiring and developing land incurred by government authorities for projects they sponsor and 85 per cent of the costs carried by private developers. By 1973 HUD had approved ten new communities for federal guaranteed assistance programs amounting to $226.5 million. Seventy more applications and preapplications were in the "hopper" that year alone. The first ten new communities being built under this program are Jonathan, Minnesota; Saint Charles Communities, Maryland; Park Forest South, Illinois; Flower Mound, Texas; Maumelle, Arkansas; Cedar-Riverside, Minnesota; Riverton, New York; San Antonio Ranch, Texas; The Woodlands, Texas; and Gananda, New York. These projects are expected to house 687,000 persons in 223,452 units during the next twenty to thirty years.

City of the Future

As those of us who are living in a metropolis gaze into the proverbial crystal ball, the future does not appear clearly. Some individuals predict grave disasters and eventual doom. Others see continued improvement in human conditions along with continual growth. Still other describe sporadic setbacks in the quality of cities and in the kind of lives urbanites have, these being balanced out by incremental leaps forward with the net result unchanged from the status quo we tolerate at the present.

With the automobile and suburbanization, the city of tomorrow may be a twin city with morning and evening migrations of people moving back and forth from their bedroom communities to their offices, schools, factories, and other activities. The trend seems to be toward placing civic functions and domestic functions in two geographical zones that are thoroughly separated from each other. The contrived student council or typical neighborhood civic meetings are increasingly balms to soothe the restless citizenry instead of meaningful, efficacious steps toward inventing, planning, and implementing goals for the public welfare. Localized blocks or neighborhoods become islands within the megalopolis. For their survival they often feel they must build walls or ramparts of one kind or another in order to protect their own ideas and quality of life. In the process, they forget some of the ecological imperatives—imperatives that apply equally to the human ecosystem such as succession, the strengths of *diversification*, regional *climax*, evolutionary opportunity, tolerance, *limiting factors*, habitat adaptability, and competition-cooperation.

The World City runs the risk and the dangers of becoming a bipolar domestic-civic function. Citizens of ecumenopolis will first tend to work, play, become educated, and perform civic functions in different places. The danger of this pattern is of course that the ecumenopolitan becomes spread very thin among various roles and locations. As a citizen of the world we see more of the whole picture but become frustrated in trying to find where the need is greatest so we can "plug in." At present, there are no institutional arrangements for most people to play an active role in the government and administration of a World City that has been physically born. As continents urbanize and become connected by communications, trade agreements, and other networks, they begin to exchange residents. Perhaps they will not need to evolve administrative arrangements other than on an ad hoc basis. That may be an innovation for the future cities of the world to consider. It would be a radical departure from the past when we always spent great energy and time writing constitutions and building bureaucracies with the conviction that we needed them.

Other pitfalls lie ahead for ecumenopolis. The transiency and mobility of future populations will undoubtedly reduce the degree of commitment among residents. Symptoms of this difficulty are seen in bedroom communities and new towns particularly in the United States. The average American family moves once every five years. With the uncertainty that exists about relocation, the degree of long-term involvement is usually low. The involvement of suburban residents in civic affairs is similar to that of a college student who expects to be on a campus no longer than four to five years. The general feeling is why should I start a project when, who knows, I will be leaving long before anything can really happen. Certainly the magnitude of megalopolitan or ecumenopolitan problems tends to overwhelm the individual who is a perspective participant. Thus we have touched on another problem where the person is so baffled by the size and complexity of an issue that he or she retreats to a scale of operation where some sense of accomplishment is possible. Then we are back to the microtown or community within the larger interrelated World City. Whatever the size or the place, in order to flourish, the city of the future must have variety, economic security, a place where anchors can be set and where the future holds new promise. Whether we realized it or not, the village, the city, the metropolis, and an urbanized continent are large second-order natural organisms situated at "strategic break-even points of man's movement and the transshipment points for his goods."[5] The city of the present and the city of the future transform and synthesize the multitude of human and other natural resources within its influence area. As Buckminster Fuller has said, "the city is a verb." It is dynamic and constantly changing. Ecumenopolis is a much larger verb, and we are part of that process.

[5] Morton Leeds, "City of the Future," *HUD Challenge,* (August 1972), p. 22.

Glossary of Terms

This glossary provides special definitions or explanations only for selected italicized terms found in the book.

Absorption: assimilation; taking in or reception by molecular action, as of gases or liquids.

Acid mine drainage: seepage water that combines with acid forming ions in mine ores such as chlorides and sulfides to produce an acid solution. This acid often finds its way into local streams. Sometimes the pH is as low as 3.5, which is lethal to most stream organisms.

Acre foot: the amount of water needed to cover 1 acre with 1 foot of water. It is equivalent to 325,872 gallons or 43,560 cubic feet of water.

Activated sludge technique: a secondary waste-water treatment process where the effluent is mixed and aerated in large tanks containing populations of bacteria and other organisms that remove large percentages of the suspended solids and reduce the biochemical oxygen demand of the effluent.

Adsorption: collection on a surface in a condensed layer, as when charcoal adsorbs gases.

Air Quality Act of 1967: federal legislation that amended the 1963 Clean Air Act and further strengthened federal efforts. The law continued to give states and localities primary responsibility for control of pollution from stationary sources, but the amendments for the first time provided a system for handling such air pollution of a regional basis. It established the National Air Pollution Control Administration (NAPCA) in HEW, which has since been moved to EPA.

Airshed: the atmospheric region that has interrelationships with specific land-based activities. For example, a metropolitan area located in a valley has a direct impact upon the volume of air confined to that valley and vice versa. Air drainage patterns develop in a fashion similar to a watershed with currents of cool air flowing down mountain slopes or settling in the valley bottom during evening cooling.

Alloyed: mixed with other metals.

Alluvial: soil or other deposits bearing moist, sedimentary matter that are found frequently at the base of slopes, in flood plains, and estuary areas.

Amalgamation: extraction of precious metal from ore by treatment with mercury.

Anadromous species: fish and other aquatic species such as salmon that have the ability to move from saltwater to freshwater swimming upstream against the current to spawning areas.

Anaerobes: organisms not requiring air or free oxygen for life. Thus anaerobic respiration takes place in the absence of atmospheric air or freely occurring oxygen.

Analogy: a comparison of arrangements, either biological or urban, which are similar in function but dissimilar in structure and origin.

Angiosperms: any plant that has seeds enclosed in an ovary.

Anthropocentric: interpreting everything in terms of human experience and values.

Atmosphere: in physics, a unit of pressure equal to 14.69 pounds per square inch at sea level. The envelope of gases surrounding the earth.

Atomic Energy Act of 1954: federal legislation that repealed certain restrictions of the 1946 Atomic Energy Act. It provided for the exchange of tactical information with other nations participating in defensive arrangements with the United States; the exchange with friendly nations of certain restricted data on industrial applications of atomic energy, and also the release of fissionable materials in amounts adequate for industrial and research use.

Atrophy: degeneration from disuse.

Autecology: the study of interrelationships and consequences of a single species and the manner in which it affects and is affected by its environment. Actually tends to deal with population study, for by gaining more information about the individual species and its requirements in nature, we learn more about the community or ecosystem of which it is a part.

Biochemical oxygen demand (BOD): a measure of the amount of oxygen used by microorganisms to consume and transform biodegradable organic material in water. The BOD test is widely used to measure the organic strength of waste water in terms of the number of pounds of dissolved oxygen required to convert a given amount of waste in 24 hours at 20°C.

Biocide: a killer of life.

Biological continuum: the concept of a series of living communities blending gradually one into another from one climate or geographical region into another.

Biological pyramid: one way of portraying the distribution of living organisms in a community. The broad base contains the green plants that receive energy from the sun. The second layer contains the herbivores; the carnivores make up the third layer since they represent a smaller mass, less stored energy, and fewer numbers.

Biomass: that part of a given habitat consisting of living matter, expressed either as the weight of organisms per unit area or as the volume of organisms per unit volume of habitat.

Biota: refers to the living components of a region or site. For example, bark beetles, birds, squirrels, soil bacteria and fungi, and worms and parasites of various types would be some of the members of a pine tree's biota.

Biotic climax community: a biotic community is the complex of living things occupying a particular area. A biotic climax community is the culmination of a series of biological successions that is more in quasiequilibrium with the physical and biological components of an area than an adjacent community.

Bituminous deposit. a mineral deposit containing relatively soft coal with volatile hydrocarbons.

Board feet: a unit of measurement in the lumbering industry. One board foot equals a volume of wood one foot square by one inch thick.

Bottomland: low-lying area near rivers that is subject to high moisture levels. Flora and fauna differ from higher elevation habitats that have better drained soils.

Bounty: money paid for an animal or a specified part thereof, usually those considered to be a nuisance to ranchers or farmers. Bounties have been paid for coyotes, foxes, bobcats, wolves, crows, ground hogs, and mountain lions, to name a few.

British Thermal Unit (BTU): the amount of heat required to raise the temperature of 1·pound of water, 1 degree Farenheit; a unit of heat equaling 252 calories.

Broad form deed: a legal document with sweeping general features. Such deeds have been commonly used by coal mining companies to extract resources and commit land abuse, giving no legal recourse to the land owners for damages inflicted by a strip mining activity (by the TVA as an example).

Carnivore: any organism that feeds primarily on flesh. Most examples are animals. However, insect-eating plants are sometimes put into this category under the specific title of insectivores.

Carrion feeders: organisms that feed upon dead material.

Carrying capacity: the total number of individuals of a species that will live in an ecosystem (or habitat) under certain conditions. An environment can sustain specific demands of an organism or a community during critical periods of its life history. This ability to sustain a healthy equilibrium between the environment and its supportable population is known as the carrying capacity.

Carrying capacity determinant: a factor or factors in an environment that alter the carrying capacity either increasing or decreasing it.

Chapparal: an ecological habitat composed of thickets of shrubs, thorny bushes, and evergreen oaks that have small leathery leaves adapted to the summer drought-winter rain climate typical of chapparal areas.

Chemosynthesis: the synthesis by plants of organic chemical compounds with energy derived from other chemical reactions as from oxidation by bacteria.

Chernozem soil: a type of soil that develops in temperate to cool subhumid environments. These soils are characterized by a distinct calcium carbonate (hard pan) stratum in the C horizon. In the United States a narrow zone of chernozem soil extends west of the prairies from Canada to the Gulf Coast.

Chlorenchyma: plant tissue containing chlorophyll.

Chlorinated hydrocarbon: long-lived chemicals such as DDT that kill a particular object, such as an insect species, and that can persist and inflict damage to other creatures in ground, water, and air.

Civilian Conservation Corps (CCC): a federal program that functioned from 1933–1949 engaging almost 2.5 million young men who primarily worked on conservation projects.

Cladophora: a microcrustacean that is often labeled by the misnomer "water flea." *Daphnia* is a common freshwater genus.

Clarke-McNary Act of 1924: federal legislation that expanded the federal-state-cooperative principle in managing America's forests.

Clean Air Amendments of 1970: federal legislation aimed at setting strict air-pollution standards by making several new provisions: shifted all responsibilites previously designated to the HEW secretary to the EPA administrator; provided for increased research grants, set stringent air quality criteria and control techniques, required that national ambient air quality standards be established, and established the very controversial 1975 motor vehicle emission standards that American automobile makers said they could not meet. Several well-known foreign automobile manufacturers announced in 1973 that their imports could meet the tough EPA standards.

1963 Clean Air Act: federal legislation that authorized many new Department of Health, Education and Welfare activities in support of state and local air pollution programs. Responsibility was given to the Environmental Protection Agency in the early 1970's.

Climax: the most stable or terminal community that will appear in a localized situation and is capable of reproducing itself repeatedly within this same local area. A climax condition is the long-term result of dynamic interrelationships between biological components, climatic conditions, and other physical and biochemical factors.

Coal Mine Health and Safety Act of 1969: federal legislation that revised the federal code of health and safety regulations for the nation's coal miners, improving miners' conditions but also forcing marginal deep mine operations to close.

Commensal: refers to a relationship existing between members of different species in which one organism definitely benefits from the association but the other individual is not benefited or adversely affected under normal conditions.

Commercial timber: timber from which merchantable wood products can be taken in paying quanitites.

Common property resource: a resource where single ownership is either impossible or extremely difficult.

Conservation: an operational collection of ecological knowledge and skill applies in a way to understand and manage as many consequences of an environmental activity as possible in keeping with the expectations of all participants—plants and animals, including man.

Contour farming: farming practice where crops are planted parallel to the contour of the slope that in effect makes each row a miniature reservoir or dam for moving water and moving soil particles.

Conurbations: part of an urbanized continent or massive concentrations of metropolitan areas.

Cord: a quantity of wood cut for fuel (128 cubic feet as arranged in a pile 8 feet long, 4 feet high, and 4 feet wide.)

Council on Environmental Quality: a three-member council plus staff established under the executive branch as a result of the National Environmental Policy Act of 1969. Serves a special advisory role to the President in environmental affairs.

Crop rotation: farming practice of annually changing the crop growing on a particular field in order to maintain the soil's fertility. Usually highly nutrient-extractive crops such as corn, tobacco, or cotton are rotated with legumes that add nitrogen to the soil, or with cover crops such as grains.

Cyanidation: process of extracting gold or silver by dissolving ore in a solution of sodium cyanide.

Decibel: a unit of intensity of sound, equal to 20 times the common logarithm of the ratio of the pressure produced by the sound wave to a reference pressure. A measurement of 50 decibels is considered moderate sound; 80, loud; and 100, the level beyond which the sound becomes intolerable.

Decomposer: those organisms that transform dead organic matter into raw materials that can be used again by the producer level of a food series. The final consumer in any food chain.

Deltaic plain: a geological formation that results from river sediment being deposited near the river's mouth and lower reaches of a river basin.

Demonstration Cities and Metropolitan Development Act of 1966: a federal omnibus urban assistance and housing bill. Highlight of the bill was a three year, $1.2 billion "demonstration cities" plan—a key Great Society measure designed to rebuild entire urban areas by tying together the wide array of existing federal and local programs and new innovations by the participating communities for a coordinated attack on blight. The program was later renamed "Model Cities."

Disturbance species: a species that interrupts the normal successional processes or that appears when normal successional processes have been halted.

Diversification: differentiation which reduces the possibility of shock in a biological community.

Domino theory: a chain reaction series of events, where one event triggers a similar response.

Dust Bowl: the area of prairie and range states that suffered severe droughts and soil abuse in the late nineteenth and early twentieth centuries, resulting in terrible dust storms during the 1930's.

Earth Day: an annual observance begun in 1970, whose purpose is to heighten environmental awareness and problem solving among the general public.

Ecological stability: an equilibrium reached by maintaining a political, biological, and physical balance that is able to be sustained over a long period of time between man and his environment.

Ecology: the study of the interrelationships and consequences of an organism or a community of organisms with its surroundings.

Ecosystem: a collection of biological, nonbiological, and other factors that are functioning in a relationship to each other on a given portion of the landscape. One ecosystem is often distinguishable from another nearby dynamic system by its different members and their interactions with the macroenvironment.

Ecotone: the transition zone between two ecological communities. In the ecotone the conditions for each of the adjacent communities become more adverse and there is often an intermingling of species from both communities. The ecotone may vary in size from very narrow, as where water meets land, to as much as one hundred miles between two continental communities.

Ecumenopolis: the highest and most complex unit in the hierarchy of human settlements, encompassing the total planet; that is the World City or universal city.

Ecumenopolitan: dealing with ecumenopolis.

Effluent: the outflows, sometimes offensive, from sewage treatment plants, industrial facilities, nuclear and coal-fired electric power plants, or other water-using operations.

Ekistics: the science of human settlements. (Ekistical and the other family of derivatives stem from the Greek *oikos* meaning "habitation or being settled.") Ekistics demonstrate the existence of an overall science of urban systems influenced by biological, social, administrative, and technical sciences, economics, and the humanities. C. A. Doxiadis is recognized as the primary spokesman in this developing field.

482

Endangered species: those plants and animals that are in danger of extermination or extinction.

Endemic: native, indigenous, peculiar to the region.

Enteric group: intestinal organisms; usually the helpful bacteria and other micro-organisms that inhabit a digestive system.

Entrophy: quantitative increase (usually of energy) in an enclosed system.

Environmental Impact Statement: a report that must be filed by the responsible agency as a result of the 1969 National Environmental Policy Act. It assesses the environmental consequences and alternatives of a significant federal project or activity. Section 102 (2) (c) spells out the provisions that are interpreted in federal guidelines.

Environmental Protection Agency (EPA): a federal agency that helps to implement features of the National Environmental Policy Act of 1969. The EPA absorbed many pollution control agencies and staff such as the Federal Water Pollution Control Administration and the National Air Pollution Control Administration. William Ruckleshaus was its first administrator.

Epilimnion: the surface layer of water in a lake or pond that is warmed by solar radiation in midsummer. The continual stirring of the upper water layers by winds results in a fairly narrow temperature range near the surface.

Estuary: an inlet or river mouth area where tides ebb and flow.

Eutrophication: development of an abundant accumulation of nutrients that support a dense growth of aquatic plants—the decay often depletes the oxygen content of water. The "third" stage in the life of a lake, the natural process that is rapidly accelerated by intense urbanization and intense agricultural fertilization. By derivation it means "well-nourished."

Evapotranspiration: the movement of water molecules from plant tissues into the atmosphere.

Exponential growth: refers to a quantity that increases by a constant *percentage* of the whole in a constant time period.

Fall line: a point where the elevation changes sharply as a river or stream approaches the coastal plain.

Favelas: South American slum areas.

1948 Federal Water Pollution Control Act: a pioneer piece of federal legislation that provided modest funding for municipal waste-water treatment facilities and research dealing with interstate water pollution problems.

Feedback loop: a mechanism that provides information to the original system or person, often with the purpose of correcting or improving quality of the performance while the system is in operation.

Fission: the act of cleaving or splitting into parts. In biology, the division of an organism into new organisms as a process of reproduction.

Flood plain: that land contiguous to water that has been inundated by that water when its regular channel capacity is exceeded. Rivers in broad valleys usually have a very wide flood plain.

Floodproofing: although perhaps a misnomer, floodproofing refers to structural modifications such as ground level to first-floor pillar construction that reduces flood damage during periods of high water. "Flood resistance" would more accurately describe the engineering and architectural features involved that are attempts at flood damage reduction.

Flotation process: a technique used in separating minerals from the ores in which they are found. The ore is crushed into small particles that are added to a liquid with chemical reagents that form a froth after stirring. The froth can be skimmed off, leaving the mineral in the liquid.

Flow resource: biological resources or replenishable resources that, as long as the reproductive potential or critical mass is sustained, will duplicate themselves over time in a manner that yields a sustained harvest into the future.

Fly ash: fine particles of soot or other particulate material entrapped in flue gases from the combustion of fuels.

Fusion: thermonuclear reaction to form combinations of interacting atoms.

Galvanizing: coating iron and steel with zinc.

Garden city: an urban plan first publicized by Ebenezer Howard that incorporated green space and formal gardens as an integral part of a city plan.

Geothermal energy: derived from the internal heat of the earth.

Grafting: the act of cutting a shoot or bud from one plant or tree and inserting it into the stem or trunk of another where it continues to grow, becoming a permanent part.

Green manuring: the process of plowing under the living plants to maintain a nutrient balance in the soil.

Guffy Coal Act of 1936: (also called the Bituminous Coal Act of 1937.) Federal legislation that authorized the coal industry to bring some order into its operating through "production control." Was an attempt to regulate and control wasteful competition, but was deemed ineffective and allowed to lapse in 1943.

Gymnosperms: any of a large class of plants producing seeds not enclosed in a seed case or ovary, as certain evergreens.

Habitat: the native environment of an animal or plant, or the kind of place that is natural for an animal or plant. It is an area possessing uniformity of physiography, vegetation, climate, or any other quality the investigator assumes is important.

Half life: refers to the decay rate of a radioactive element. It is the time necessary for half of the atoms of the radioactive isotope to disintegrate through fission into a stable form.

Hard biocides: those biocides (pesticides, herbicides, and rodenticides) that resist biodegradation.

Hardwood: technically a broad-leaved tree, regardless of particular hardness of wood, but usually considered to be a tree with wood of relative hardness such as oak, maple, or ironwood.

Herbicide: a substance or preparation for killing plants, especially seeds.

Herbivore: an animal that feeds chiefly on grass or other plants.

Highway Trust Fund: a financing mechanism under the Public Highway Act of 1956 whereby annual flow of revenue from gasoline taxes amounts to approximately $5 billion a year. The 90 per cent federal contribution for interstate highway construction comes from the Highway Trust Fund. In the mid 1970's, mass transit and other forms of transportation have also qualified for financing.

Homology: a comparison of arrangements that share a common primitive origin but differ in evolved type and function.

Horizon: the main divisions of a soil profile, consisting of a lettered series: the A horizon (the topmost organic layer), the B horizon (the layer of considerable leaching and percolation beneath the A horizons), the C horizon (the subsoil layer beneath the B horizon), and the D horizon (the lowest layers or parent material).

Housing and Urban Development Act of 1968: federal legislation that authorized the U.S. Department of Housing and Urban Development to issue loan guarantees to private developers of large-scale new communities.

HUD: U.S. Department of Housing and Urban Development—a federal agency involved primarily in urban affairs.

Hybridization: the crossing of two separate species in order to reproduce a tree with specific desired characteristics such as resistance to disease or drought.

Hydrologic cycle: pertaining to the sequence of water passing into atmosphere as vapor, precipitating to earth as rain, ultimately returning through evaporation.

Hydrometallurgical: relating to the reduction of ores by washing out the insoluble matter with various liquid reagents.

Hypolimnion: the layer of water in a lake or deep pond that is found below the thermocline and extends to the bottom. The water in this layer demonstrates a slow drop of temperature toward the bottom, typically low in oxygen content, and high in carbon dioxide. It may have a stagnant zone with bottom temperatures in the range of 5°C.

Inversion: a weather condition involving thermal stratification usually with a warm lid of air present above the cooler surface air, thus creating a stagnant or stratified condition with little if any circulation of air.

Kilowatt: unit of power equal to one thousand watts. A watt is a current of one ampere flowing across a potential of one volt.

Kilowatt hour: unit of work equal to one watt working one hour.

Knutson-Vandenberg Act of 1930: federal legislation that authorized financing for reforestation of national forest lands.

Land and Water Conservation Fund Act of 1964: one of the most significant recreation bills passed since New Deal legislation. Earmarked receipts from various sources, including user fees charged for the use of various federal recreation land areas such as the National Park System, Tennessee Valley Authority lands, National Forests, and others for acquisition of new park and recreation areas by both the federal and state governments. The objective is to provide a systematic form of aid to the states and federal agencies in acquiring and developing new outdoor recreation resources.

Lateralization: the process of soil development where there is considerable leaching and baking of the soil that removes most nutrients and forms a tough, hard layer high in iron and aluminum salts.

Leeward: the quarter toward which the wind blows.

Leguminous: belonging to the family of beans, senna, and mimosa. These species have nitrogen-producing (converting) nodules on the root system.

Lignite: relatively low-grade brown coal—often woody in texture.

Limiting factors: the condition or conditions that will prevent an organism from successfully invading an environmental area or that prevents the organism from achieving its optimum metabolism.

Littoral zones: that area from the water's edge to a depth of about six meters in a freshwater lake or pond.

Loam: rich, friable soil composed of sand, silt, and clay.

Loessial soils: deposits of soil calcareous in composition deposited by wind.

Loessial terraces: upthrusting banks of yellow, calcareous, windswept loam.

Mach 2 speed: a number indicating the ratio of the speed of an object through a medium to the speed of sound in the medium. Speeds of airplanes are measured in mach numbers. Speeds of one, two, or three times the speed of sound are termed Mach 1, Mach 2, Mach 3, and so on.

Macronutrients: those elements that are most abundantly available and from which plants derive the majority of their nutrition—for example, nitrogen, phosphorus, potassium, carbon, hydrogen, oxygen, sulphur, and calcium.

Marine Mammal Protection Act of 1972: federal legislation intended to conserve animals such as whales, polar bears, walruses, sea otters, and seals. Establishes a moratorium on hunting or importing the marine mammals, but the permits that allow for exemptions are worrisome to many wildlife observers.

McNary-McSweeney Act of 1928: federal legislation that provided for a financial program of forest research.

Megalopolis: a thickly populated region centering around a series of metropolitan centers. For example, the Northeastern megalopolis of the United States includes the metropolitan areas of Boston, New York, Newark, and Philadelphia.

Megawatt (mw): a unit of measurement for electrical energy equivalent to 1 million watts.

Mesotrophic: in the hierarchy of trophic levels, a mild or moderate nutrient abundance.

Metabolic by-products: those things produced secondarily as a result of activities taking place in a particular organism, habitat, or environment.

Microcosms: a community, institution, or other unity believed to be an epitome of a larger unity; in miniature.

Microcrustaceans: a minute crustacean, not easily seen by the naked eye.

Micronutrients: trace elements that are required by plants for healthy growth: such as, boron, copper, chlorine, iron, manganese, molybdenum, and zinc.

Microtown: a relatively small self-contained community that when aggregated with other microtowns, forms a metropolitan area and ultimately a megalopolis.

Minerals Multiple Surface Use Act of 1955: a conservation law of major importance for the public lands whose provisions concerned surface rights (timber, grazing, fish, and wildlife) on lands for which mining claims were made under the mining law of 1872. Designed to prevent mining claimants from making illegitimate use of the surface resources of the claim such as timber cutting, grazing cattle, and building summer homes.

Monoculture agriculture: the farming practice that concentrates on the production of a single species that has proven superior in yield and insect and disease resistance, but usually requires the support of considerable technology.

Monoculture forestry: a forest management practice whereby production of each economically valuable tree genus is limited to a single, genetically superior species, subspecies, or genotype that has been bred to exhibit both a rapid and highly predictable growth rate and physiological characteristics of high economic value.

Monospecies: one group of intimately related and physically similar organisms that actually or potentially interbreed and are less commonly capable of fertile interbreeding with members of other groups.

Morphology: the features comprised in the form and structure of an organism or any of its parts.

Multiple Use-Sustained Yield Act of 1960: federal legislation that specified that the national forests should be administered under the principles of multiple use and sustained yield with the objective of developing five basic resources: outdoor recreation resources, range resources, timber resources, watershed resources, and fish and wildlife resources. Each should be developed to the maximum without unduly subordinating one to the other, seeking a perpetually high level of renewable resources.

Mutagenic: capable of inducing mutation—that is, a relatively permanent change in hereditary material.

Mutualism: a relation between two or more organisms or communities in which each benefits from the other.

National Environmental Policy Act (NEPA): a major piece of federal legislation passed in 1969 that established a national policy for the environment and an environmental advisory staff for the President called the Council on Environmental Quality. One provision of the Act, Section 102 (2) (c) requires the preparation of an impact statement on proposals for legislation and other major federal actions significantly affecting the quality of the human environment.

Natural decimating factors: any direct cause of reduction in population numbers that is related to or concerned with nature.

Naval stores: products (as tar, pitch, turpentine, pine oil, resin, or terpenes) obtained from the oleoresin of pine and other coniferous trees.

Niche: the functional role that an organism plays within a community or ecosystem.

Nitrogen-fixation: the conversion of free atmospheric nitrogen into combined forms.

Nonrenewable resource: substances such as oil, gas, coal, copper, and gold that once used cannot be replaced, at least not in this geological age.

Nonreplenishable resource: natural materials that do not have the potential of being restocked or refilled or supplied again.

Oleoresin: a solution of a resin in an essential oil, as turpentine, occurring naturally in various plants.

Oligotrophic: an early stage in lake succession where the water is low in nutrients and therefore unable to sustain a large biomass. At the same time, the water of oliogotrophic lakes is deep and relatively cold, thus holding high concentrations of dissolved oxygen.

Omnibus Flood Control Act of 1936: first major effort by the federal government to involve a federal agency—namely the U.S. Corps of Engineers—in flood protection activities.

Organic Forestry Act of 1897: federal legislation that specified the administrative needs and obligations of a forest reserve or national forest including the option of selling stands of timber independently of the land parcels.

Osmosis: the flow or diffusion that takes place through a semipermeable membrane typically separating either a solvent and a solution or a dilute solution and a concentrated solution, thus bringing about equilibrium on the two sides of the membrane.

Overburden: all of the earth and other materials that lie above a natural mineral deposit. Also applies to earth and other material after removal from their natural state in the process of strip mining.

Pantheistic: relating to the doctrine that there is no God, and placing a belief in the combined forces and laws that are manifested in the existing universe, especially natural phenomena.

Parasitic: relating to the act of deriving life at another organism's expense. A form of symbiosis that technically defined implies living together.

Pathogen: any disease-producing organism.

Pelagic sealing: the act or occupation of killing, capturing, or pursuing (fur) seals in the open ocean as distinguished from killing them at their breeding places on land.

Permafrost: perennially frozen subsoil.

Persistent pesticides: chemicals that exist for a long time after application and resist degradation over many seasons.

pH: the symbol used in referring to the hydrogen ion concentration of a substance using a scale of 0 to 14 on which 7 represents the value of pure water or neutrality, values less than 7 representing increased hydrogen ion concentration and increased acidity, values greater than 7 representing decreased hydrogen ion concentration and increasing alkalinity.

Photochemical: of or relating to or produced by the chemical action of radiant energy, especially light.

Photosynthesis: the formation of carbohydrates from water (or some hydrogen source) and carbon dioxide, in chlorophyll-containing cells (as of green plants) when exposed to light.

Phylogenetic ladder: a descriptive format to show the natural evolutionary relationships between different organisms.

Phytoplankton: the aggregation of plants (primarily algae) that float aimlessly at various depths of water or are moved too feebly to maintain a constant position against any appreciable water current.

Pioneer species: the aggregate organisms in a pioneer community—the first serial stage to become established.

Placer mining: the process of extracting minerals from sand or gravel by washing with water.

Pollutant: something that pollutes; that is something that makes another medium physically impure or unclean.

Polygamous: having a plurality of wives or husbands or mates.

Potlach: a ceremonial feast where American Indians of the northern Pacific Coast region exchanged (and even destroyed) riches in a rival display of wealth.

Prairie States Forestry Project of 1934: this act provided a brief period of funding and manpower designed to plant shrubs and trees to form windbreaks or shelter belts in the states suffering from heavy wind erosion.

Preferential food sources: those sources of food that are preferred or chosen over others when a choice is present.

Primary producer: an organism that contains chlorophyll and is thus able to combine water and carbon dioxide in the presence of sunshine to yield basic foodstuffs (sugar) for those organisms unable to manufacture their own.

Primary waste treatment: a process that removes the suspended solids or material that floats or will settle in sewage by using screens and other devices. Mechanical or physical separation of solids from supernatant in waste-water treatment.

Project flood: a flood that is at least 10 per cent greater than the highest water level in the past.

Pseudopodia: the appendagelike projections from the cell membrane of an amoeba that resemble and serve as food gatherers—strictly translated: "false feet."

Public Highway Act of 1956: contained a major provision to establish the Highway Trust Fund, which is financed by federal gasoline taxes, and up until recently has been used solely for federally funded highway construction.

Pyrometallurgical: relating to chemical extraction of metals that depends on heat action (as roasting and smelting).

488   **Quadros:** another name for "microtown."

Radio-nuclide: a radioactive nuclide. A nuclide is an atomic species in which all atoms have the same atomic number and mass number; an individual atom in such a species.

Recycling: the salvaging and reprocessing of used materials such as paper, metals, glass, and cloth.

Reduction process: deoxidization.

Reforestation: the replanting of trees in forests that have been denuded by cutting, fire, disease, insects, or other decimating factors.

Refuse Act of 1899: federal legislation that outlaws the discharge of pollutants into navigable waters of the United States or tributaries of navigable waters unless a permit has been obtained from the U.S. Army Corps of Engineers. Municipal sewage is exempted. This act was virtually ignored for almost 70 years, and it was not until December 1970 that the White House required firms and individuals to file for Refuse Act permits.

Resource Recovery Act of 1970: federal legislation that encourages recycling municipal wastes for recovery of material and energy; also contains a provision that the EPA administrator may make grants for innovative disposal systems as well as for planning and training of personnel.

Retort plant: a factory where substances are subjected to distillation or decomposition by heat.

Ringlemann Visual Smoke Test: a method still used that depends on optical comparisons carried out by visually correlating stack smoke with a pollution intensity index.

Scenic and Wild Rivers Act of 1968: federal legislation that attempts to preserve free-flowing streams from further physical encroachment or development.

Sclerenchyma: a protective or supporting tissue in higher plants composed of cells with thickened, lignified, and often mineralized walls.

Secondary waste treatment: a second step in waste-water treatment in which bacteria consume the organic parts of the waste. Accomplished by bringing the sewage and bacteria together in trickling filters or in an activated sludge process. Involves primarily biological activity as compared to primary or tertiary steps that are predominately physical and chemical processes.

Second echelon resource: a resource that uses, synthesizes, and concentrates the basic resources such as timber, water, minerals, or wildlife. Also referred to as a second-derivative resource.

Seiches: the oscillating waves that occur in lakes and landlocked seas because of winds blowing over lakes and piling water up along the lee shore that then rocks back and forth like miniature tidal waves.

Selective cutting: a forest harvesting method in which selected trees are pruned from a forest stand. Thus the ground is always covered and timber removal is regularly practiced. A stable, long-range management practice of this kind is part of a sustained yield program.

Severance tax: an assessment placed on the individual or company that removes a resource such as coal from land owned by a unit of government or another party. The philosophy behind a severance tax is to return to the landowner or local unit of government some fraction of the value of the extracted resource to compensate for environmental or other costs of the mining operation. For example, if the TVA paid a percentage of the value of coal stripped out of

Kentucky, it would mitigate (at least in a tiny way) the one-way flow of wealth to beneficiaries who bear an infinitesimal, small percentage of the total human and environmental costs.

Short ton: a unit of weight equal to two thousand pounds avoirdupois.

Sigmoid growth curve: an S-shaped curve that commonly portrays the rate of growth plotted over time for an individual organism. The initial rapid growth occurs early in the life history of an organism with a plateau or leveling out effect in midlife shown at the top of the "S."

Sluicing: the mineral extraction practice of using a sluice—that is, a long inclined trough or flume usually paved with riffles to wash ore.

Small Watershed Act of 1954: (Public Law 566) federal legislation whose objective is to reduce upper watershed erosion and flooding. An important proviso of the act states that at least 50 per cent of the drainage area of a given project must practice sound soil conservation procedures as stipulated by the Soil Conservation Service.

Softwood: that wood coming from needle-leaved trees such as pines, firs, tamaracks, and spruces.

Soil Bank Program of 1956–1960: a program designed to reduce certain crop surpluses by taking those croplands out of production. Was replaced by other programs in the early 1960's.

Soil Conservation Act of 1935: through the act Congress was empowered to set up soil conservation practices by the federal government and the Soil Conservation Service to implement this policy. The establishment of Soil Conservation Districts and subsidy payments for the prevention of soil erosion and other soil abuses were also included.

Soil porosity: the soil's ability to absorb water and air. Coarser textured soils have larger pore spaces.

Soil profile: a vertical section of soil that shows the stratified horizons A, B, C, and D.

Solid Waste Disposal Act of 1965: a federal act whose purpose was to begin a national research and development program for new and improved methods of solid waste disposal and to provide technical and financial aid to state and local governments in developing, establishing, and conducting solid waste disposal programs.

Static reserve figure: refers to the number of years that known global supplies will last at current global consumption. The figure is obtained by dividing the known reserves by the current annual consumption.

Sterilants: an herbicide designed to completely eliminate a kind of plant and to have a persistent residual effect in the soil.

Stratification (water): a natural phenomenon in bodies of water where the water seeks layers according to temperature ranges. This layering effect creates barriers to horizontal circulation of heat and other pollutants. A similar situation exists with air.

Stratospheric: of the stratosphere—that is, the upper part of the earth's atmosphere, beginning at an altitude of about seven miles and continuing to the ionosphere. Characterized by an almost constant temperature at all altitudes.

Stream channelization: the straightening of natural waterways to speed storm runoff and presumably reduce flood damage.

Strip cropping: farming practice of interspersing wide row crops such as corn, cotton, tobacco, and other vegetables that do not hold soil and water well with crops or vegetation such as hay, alfalfa, clover, and some grasses that do retain soil, moisture, and nutrients.

Subsidence: the sinking of land areas primarily due to the rapid withdrawal of groundwater without natural recharge taking place.

Suburbanization: the process of an area changing from rural to suburban condition. A conversion of agricultural land to residential and commercial uses.

Succession: an orderly sequence of different communities over a period of time in the same particular area.

Surcharge: an additional amount added to the usual charge.

Sustained yield: involves managing a forest so that a timber crop can be harvested each year indefinitely without the forest becoming depleted. However, the amount harvested must be counterbalanced by annual growth increments. The important emphasis is on growth rather than cutting.

Synecology: the study of interrelationships and consequences of a community of organisms with their surrounding environment and vice versa. All plants and animals as well as pertinent abiotic factors are considered.

Synergistic factors: elements that work together.

Tailings: wastes or refuse left in various processes of milling, mining, and distilling.

Tannin: (tannic acid) a yellowish, astringent substance ($C_{14}H_{10}O_9$) derived from oak bark and gallnuts and used in tanning, dyeing, and medicine.

Tennessee Valley Authority (TVA): a novel federal project begun in the 1930's to integrate the resource development of the Tennessee River basin. Although a model federal agency in its conception, recent practices with coal strip mining, nuclear power plant construction, and other controversial resource projects have tarnished the image of the TVA.

Terracing: farming practice used on very steep slopes where earthen steplike embankments are built to increase arable land and to check soil and water runoff.

Tertiary waste-water treatment: a third step in sewage treatment where the flow from the secondary process is subjected to further treatment such as coagulation, filtration, adsorption, desalination, and other processes. Commonly used to remove nutrients such as phosphorus and nitrogen.

Thermocline: in a deep freshwater lake or pond, a relatively uniform layer in a contrasting zone of rapid temperature change. In a typical lake of the temperate zone, this may be a 15-foot stratum about 30 to 45 feet beneath the surface with a temperature drop of nearly 0.7 per cent per foot of depth. In many bodies of freshwater approximately 50 to 65 per cent of the temperature change may occur within the thermocline in the summer.

Topsoil: the upper organic layer or A horizon of soil. The unconsolidated mineral matter naturally present on the surface of the earth that has been subjected to and influenced by genetic and environmental factors of parent material, climate, macro- and microorganisms, and topography, all acting over a period of time, and that is necessary for the growth and regeneration of vegetation on the surface of the earth.

Total systems approach: a comprehensive view of the outputs of industrial, commercial, residential, and public wastes, as well as their linkages (or feedback loops) including physical and social interrelationships.

Tracheid: any of the large, thick-walled, water-conducting tubelike cells found in woody tissue, as of the conifers.

Trophic level: a particular position in the food and energy hierarchy that indicates the organism's relationship with its counterparts in any living community.

Trophy animal: an animal whose unusual size or features tend to make it a sought after display piece by fishermen and hunters.

Tundra: the region on a mountain or in the Arctic between the limit of the trees and the perpetual ice.

Turgidity: the quality of being swollen, rigid, or distended.

United Nation's Conference on the Human Environment of 1972: an effort by the United Nations to increase the communication among nations in the area of environmental problem assessment and to explore ways that developed nations might cope with environmental problems of a worldwide scale.

Unitization: refers to the practice where multiple owners of a single oil deposit or field manage the single unit in a way to maximize efficiency of yield instead of redundant drilling and excessive pumping that might take place with "cut-throat" operators.

Urban: according to the U.S. Bureau of the Census, population residing in groups of 2,500 or more is classified as urban.

Urban Growth and Community Development Act of 1970: federal legislation that raised the ceiling on total load guarantees to $500 million and extended the loan possibilities to public agencies.

Urbanization: the process of an area's changing from rural to urban in character.

Urban Mass Transportation Act of 1964: federal act that authorized a 3-year $375 million program of matching grants and loans to enable states and localities to construct and improve mass transit facilities. The provisions of this bill were continued and expanded in 1966 in S-3700, PL 89-562.

Urban reserves: an area of land that either in a general planning guide or through zoning has been designated for future urban-related development.

Vanadiferous shale: shale with a high vanadium content.

Variances: extensions, forgivenesses, or exceptions to pollution control regulations that are granted by governmental agencies to many industries and utilities.

Water Pollution Control Act Amendments of 1972: federal legislation that greatly increased federal contributions for waste-water treatment plants for municipal regions; established a "nondegradation" clause; and set 1983 as the time when no untreated wastes can enter interstate waters, thus in a sense mandating secondary treatment for all waste waters destined to enter navigable rivers in the United States.

Water Resources Planning Act of 1965: federal legislation that provided for federal and regional coordination of plans for water resource development. The Federal Water Resources Council was established to recommend programs and aid in their implementation.

Watershed: the territory surrounding a river or lake that contributes flow to the river or lake. Also called the drainage basin.

Weeks Act of 1911: federal legislation that provided for the purchase of lands to be managed as national forests at the headwaters of navigable streams and cooperation between federal, state, and local governments in forest fire control in watersheds of navigable streams.

Wilderness Act of 1964: federal legislation that authorized the creation of a National Wilderness Preservation System and established procedures to increase and preserve wild land holdings.

492 **Wildlife Restoration Act of 1937:** federal legislation that gave financial assistance in the acquisition and development of suitable lands for wildlife.

Wild river: a free-flowing stream unobstructed by man-made structures and usually flowing through undeveloped landscape.

Winter kill: the term referring to oxygen depletion in a frozen lake or river where a thick blanket of snow prevents sunlight penetration and consequently curtails photosynthetic oxygen production which is required by aquatic fauna.

Xeric: a condition in a habitat or in succession where moisture is present in the most minimal amounts.

Zooplankton: microscopic animal life found floating or drifting in the ocean or in bodies of freshwater, used as food by fish and other aquatic organisms.

Bibliography

Chapter 1

BACON, EDMUND N. *Design of Cities.* New York: Viking Press, 1967.

CAIN, STANLEY A. *Natural Resource Ecology—Class Syllabus.* Ann Arbor, Michigan: University of Michigan (1965).

CIRIACY-WANTRUP, S. V. *Resource Conservation, Economics, and Policies.* Los Angeles: University of California Press, 1963.

COX, GEORGE (ed.). *Readings in Conservation Ecology.* New York: John Wiley & Sons, Inc., 1969.

DICE, LEE R. *Man's Nature and Nature's Man, The Ecology of Human Communities.* Ann Arbor: The University of Michigan Press, 1955.

DOXIADIS, C. A. *Ekistics.* London: Hutchinson of London, 1968.

GORDON, MITCHELL. *Sick Cities: Psychology and Pathology of American Urban Life.* Baltimore: Penguin Books, 1965.

GRAHAM, EDWARD H. *Natural Principles of Land Use.* New York: Oxford University Press, 1944.

GRAY, L. C. "Economic Possibilities of Conservation." *Quarterly Journal of Economics,* Vol. XXVII (1913), p. 499; by Bunce, Arthur C. *Economics of Soil Conservation.* Ames, Iowa: Iowa State College Press, 1945.

HOWARD, EBENEZER. *Garden Cities of Tomorrow.* London: Faber and Faber, 1946.

JACOBS, JANE. *The Death and Life of Great American Cities.* New York: Random House, 1961.

LEOPOLD, ALDO. *A Sand County Almanac.* New York: Oxford University Press, 1949.

MUMFORD, LEWIS. *The City in History.* New York: Harcourt Brace Jovanovich, Inc., 1961.

ODUM, EUGENE P. *Fundamentals of Ecology.* Philadelphia: W. B. Saunders Company, 1953.

OWEN, OLIVER S. *Natural Resource Conservation: An Ecological Approach.* New York: Macmillan Publishing Co., Inc., 1971.

PARK, ROBERT E., ERNEST W. BURGESS, RODERICK D. MCKENZIE. *The City.* Chicago: University of Chicago Press, 1925.

493

494 PARKINS, A. F. and J. R. WHITAKER et. al. *Our Natural Resources and Their Conservation.* New York: John Wiley & Sons, Inc., 1939.

PINCHOT, GIFFORD. *Breaking New Ground.* New York: Harcourt Brace Jovanovich, Inc., 1947.

VAN HISE, CHARLES R. *The Conservation of Natural Resources in the United States.* New York: Macmillan Publishing Co., Inc., 1910.

WEBER, MAX. *The City.* New York: The Free Press, 1958.

ZIMMERMAN, ERICH W. *World Resources and Industries.* New York: Harper and Row, Publishers, Inc., 1951.

Chapter 2

ABRAMS, CHARLES. *The City Is the Frontier.* New York: Harper and Row, Publishers, Inc., 1965.

ANDERSON, NELS, EDWARD C. LINDEMAN. *Urban Sociology.* New York: Alfred A. Knopf, 1928.

BARLOW, ELIZABETH. "Cut the Garbage." *New York* (Jan. 18, 1971).

DARLING, F. FRAZER. "The Unity of Ecology." *Advancement of Science,* London, 1963.

DICE, LEE R. *Man's Nature and Nature's Man, The Ecology of Human Communities.* Ann Arbor: The University of Michigan Press, 1955.

DOXIADIS, C. A. *Ekistics.* London: Hutchinson of London, 1968.

GEDDES, PATRICK. *Cities in Evolution.* New York: Harper and Row, Publishers, Inc., 1971.

GREER, SCOTT. *The Emerging City: Myth and Reality.* New York: The Free Press, 1962.

GRUEN, VICTOR. *The Heart of Our Cities—The Urban Crisis, Diagnosis, and Cure.* New York: Simon and Schuster, 1964.

GUMPERT, DAVID. "Efforts to Save, Reuse Waste Products Slowed by Variety of Problems." *The Wall Street Journal,* (June 23, 1970).

HOWARD, EBENEZER. *Garden Cities of Tomorrow.* London: Faber and Faber, 1946.

LYNCH, KEVIN. *The Image of the City.* Cambridge: M.I.T. Press, 1960.

MCHARG, IAN. *Design With Nature.* Eugene Feldman, Philadelphia: The Falcon Press, 1969.

MCKENZIE, R. D. "The Ecological Approach to the Study of the Human Community." *American Journal of Sociology,* XXX.

MUMFORD, LEWIS. *The Human Prospect,* edited by Moore, Harry and Karl Deutsch. Boston: Beacon Press, 1955.

MUMFORD, LEWIS. *The City in History.* New York: Harcourt Brace Jovanovich, Inc., 1961.

SCHRAUFNAGEL, F. H. "Chlorides," Report of the Commission on Water Pollution, State of Wisconsin.

SMERK, GEORGE M. *Readings in Urban Transportation.* Bloomington: Indiana University Press, 1968.

SWATEK, PAUL. *The User's Guide to the Protection of the Environment.* New York: Ballantine Books, Inc., 1970.

VON ECKARDT, WOLF. *A Place to Live.* New York: Delacorte Press, 1967.

WEBER, MAX. *The City.* New York: The Free Press, 1958.

WOOD, ROBERT C. "Science and the City." *Smithsonian Annual II: The Fitness of Man's Environment.* Papers delivered at the Smithsonian Institution Annual Symposium, Feb. 16–18, 1967. Washington, D.C.: Smithsonian Institution Press (1968).

Chapter 3

ADRIAN, CHARLES. *Governing Urban America.* New York: McGraw-Hill Book Company, Inc., 1963.

BABCOCK, RICHARD F. *The Zoning Game.* Madison: University of Wisconsin Press, 1966.

BANFIELD, EDWARD C. (ed.). *Urban Government: A Reader in Politics and Administration.* New York: The Free Press, 1961.

CALDWELL, LYNTON K. "Environment: A New Focus for Public Policy." *Public Administration Review* (Sept. 1963).

DARLING, F. FRASER and JOHN P. MILTON. *Future Environments of North America.* Garden City, N.Y.: Doubleday/Natural History Press, Doubleday & Company, Inc., 1966.

FITCH, LYLE C. "Goals of Urban Transportation Policy." *Ekistics,* Vol. 29, No. 170, (Jan. 1970).

GALBRAITH, JOHN KENNETH. *The New Industrial State.* Boston: Houghton Mifflin Company, 1967.

GOLDMAN, MARSHALL. *Controlling Pollution: The Economics of a Cleaner America.* Englewood Cliffs, N.J.: Prentice-Hall, 1967.

GRUEN, VICTOR. *The Heart of Our Cities—The Urban Crisis, Diagnosis and Cure.* New York: Simon and Schuster, 1964.

HERFINDAHL, ORRIS C. and ALLEN V. KNEESE. *Quality of the Environment: An Economic Approach to Some Problems of Using Land, Water, and Air.* Baltimore: Published by The John Hopkins Press for Resources for the Future, Inc., 1965.

HERSON, LAWRENCE J. R. "The Lost World of Municipal Government." *Urban Government: A Reader in Politics and Administration.* New York: The Free Press, 1961.

JARRETT, HENRY (ed.). *Environmental Quality in a Growing Economy.* Baltimore: John Hopkins Press, 1966.

MICHAEL, DONALD N. "On Coping With Complexity: Planning and Politics." *Daedalus,* XCVII (Fall, 1968).

STARR, ROGER. "Power and Powerlessness in a Regional City." *The Public Interest,* XVI (Summer, 1969).

STEIN, CLARENCE S. *Toward New Towns for America.* Cambridge: M.I.T. Press, 1966.

UDALL, STEWART. *The Quiet Crisis.* New York: Holt, Rinehart and Winston, 1963.

U.S. Congress House Committee on Science and Astronautics. *Science & Technology and the Cities.* Compilation of Papers Presented for Tenth Meeting of Panel on Science and Technology, 1969. Washington, D.C.: U.S. Government Printing Office (1969).

WEBBER, MELVIN M. "The Post-City Age." *Daedalus,* XCVII, (Fall, 1968).

Chapter 4

ALLEN, SHIRLEY W. and JUSTIN W. LEONARD. *Conserving Natural Resources.* New York: McGraw-Hill Book Company, 1966.

BARDACH, JOHN. *Downstream.* New York: Harper and Row, Publishers, Inc., 1964.

CLARK, J. R. "Thermal Pollution and Aquatic Life." *Scientific American,* 220(3) : 18–27.

HYNES, H. B. N. *The Biology of Polluted Waters.* Liverpool University Press, 1966.

MACKICHAN, K. A. and J. C. KAMENER. "Estimated Use of Water in the U.S., 1960." *Geological Survey Circular,* 1961.

MOSS, SENATOR FRANK E. *The Water Crisis.* New York: Praeger Publishers, Inc., 1970.

MOWITZ, ROBERT J. and DEIL S. WRIGHT. *Profile of a Metropolis.* Detroit: Wayne State University Press, 1962.

PARKER and KRENKEL. *Biological Aspects of Thermal Pollution.* Nashville: Vanderbilt University Press, 1969.

PARKER and KRENKEL. *Engineering Aspects of Thermal Pollution.* Nashville: Vanderbilt University Press, 1969.

"Physical and Ecological Effects of Waste Heat on Lake Michigan." Prepared by Great Lakes Fisheries Laboratory, Ann Arbor, Michigan (1970).

U.S. Department of the Interior. "Feasibility of Alternative Means of Cooling for Thermal Power Plants near Lake Michigan." Washington, D.C.: U.S. Government Printing Office (1970).

WADE, MASON (ed.). *The International Megalopolis.* Toronto: University of Toronto Press, Eighth Annual University of Windsor Seminar on Canadian-American Relations, 1969.

ZWICK, DAVID and MARCY BENSTOCK. *Water Wasteland.* New York: Grossman Publishers, Inc., 1971.

Chapter 5

CARSON, RACHEL. *Silent Spring.* Boston: Houghton Mifflin Company, 1962.

CAUDHILL, HARRY A. *Night Comes to the Cumberlands.* Boston: Atlantic Monthly Press, Little, Brown and Company, 1963.

CAUDHILL, HARRY A. *My Land is Dying.* New York: E. P. Dutton & Co., Inc., 1971.

GIBBONS, EUELL. *Stalking the Wild Asparagus.* New York: David McKay , Inc., 1962.

GRAHAM, FRANK JR. *Since Silent Spring.* Boston: Houghton Mifflin Company, 1970.

GUSTAFSON, A. F. *Conservation of the Soil.* New York: Maple Press, 1936.

HAPP, C., G. RITTENHOUSE and G. C. DOBSON. "Some Principles of Accelerated Stream and Valley Sedimentation." *U.S.D.A. Technical Bulletin,* No. 695 (1940).

HELFMAN, ELIZABETH S. *Rivers and Watersheds in America's Future.* New York: David McKay Co., 1965.

OWEN, OLIVER S. *Natural Resource Conservation.* New York: Macmillan Publishing Co., Inc., 1971.

RODALE, ROBERT, (ed.). *Health Bulletin.* Emmaus, Penn.: Rodale Press, Inc., published biweekly.

State of Montana, Environmental Quality Council, *First Annual Report* (October 1972).

The Missouri Basin Inter-Agency Committee, "The Missouri River Basin Development Program." Washington, D.C.: U.S. Government Printing Office (1952).

TURNER, JAMES S. *The Chemical Feast.* New York: Grossman Publishers, Inc., 1970.

TVA Division of Forestry Relations, *Tennessee Valley Forests.* Norris, Tenn. (1950).

Chapter 6

"A Forest Service Warning on Timber." *San Francisco Chronicle,* (December 6, 1972).

EDDINGTON, CHARLES. "The Mechanization Explosion." *Forests and People,* XIX (Third Quarter, 1969).

ESPOSITO, JOHN. *Vanishing Air.* New York: Grossman Publishers, Inc., 1970.

"From These Trees." Southern Pulpwood Conservation Association, Atlanta.

GUMPERT, DAVID. "Efforts to Save, Reuse Waste Products Slowed by Variety of Problems." *The Wall Street Journal* (June 23, 1970).

MCARDLE, R. E. "What the South Is Doing Today." *American Forests* (April 1956).

McElwee, R. L. "Genetics in Wood Quality Improvement." *Proceedings of the Seventh Southern Conference on Forest Tree Improvement* (1963).

McKnight, J. S. and R. C. Biesterfeldt. "Commercial Cottonwood Planting in the Southern United States." *Journal of Forestry*, Vol. 66, No. 9 (1968).

Owen, Oliver S. *Natural Resource Conservation, An Ecological Approach.* New York: Macmillan Publishing Co., Inc., 1971.

Sutton, Victor J. "The Pulp and Paper Industry. A Look into the Future." Southern Pulpwood Conservation Association, Atlanta.

Swatek, Paul. *The User's Guide to the Protection of the Environment.* New York: Ballantine Books, Inc., 1970.

U.S. Department of Agriculture Forest Service. *Annual Fire Report for National Forests.* Washington, D.C. (1968).

Webb, Charles D. "Juvenile-Mature Tree Relationships." *Proceedings of the Seventh Southern Conference of Forest Tree Improvement.* Gulfport, Miss. (1963).

Wolozin, Harold. *The Economics of Air Pollution.* New York: W. W. Norton & Company, Inc., 1966.

Chapter 7

Committee on Environmental Quality. U.S. Federal Council for Science and Technology. "Noise—Sound Without Value," in Thomas R. Detwyler, *Man's Impact on Environment.* New York: McGraw-Hill Book Company, Inc., 1971.

Curtis, Richard and Elizabeth Hogan. *Perils of the Peaceful Atom.* Garden City, N.Y.: Doubleday & Company, Inc., 1969.

Goldner, Lester. "Air Pollution Control in the Metropolitan Area: A Case Study in Public Policy Formation." *The Economics of Air Pollution,* edited by Harold Wolozin. New York: W. W. Norton and Co., 1966.

Gottmann, Jean. *Megalopolis, The Urbanized Northeastern Seaboard of the United States.* Cambridge: M.I.T. Press, 1961.

Peterson, James T. "The Climate of the City," in Thomas R. Detwyler, *Man's Impact on Environment.* New York: McGraw-Hill Book Company, Inc., 1971.

The Conservation Foundation, *A Citizen's Guide to Clean Air* (1972).

"Toward Cleaner Air." *League of Women Voters Committee Guide* (April 1972).

Chapter 8

"Debate on the Thermal Issue Continues," *Environment, Science and Technology,* Vol. 3, No. 6 (May 1969).

Glaser, P. E. "The Future of Power from the Sun." *Power* (Aug. 1968).

Gottmann, Jean. *Megalopolis, The Urbanized Northeastern Seaboard of the United States.* Cambridge: M.I.T. Press, 1961.

Gregory, Derek P. "The Hydrogen Economy." *Scientific American,* Vol. 228, No. 1 (Jan. 1973).

Jenson, Albert C. "Thermal Pollution in the Marine Environment." *The Conservationist,* 25: 8–13 (Oct. 1970).

Landsberg, H. H. and S. H. Schurr. *Energy in the United States: Sources, Uses and Policy Issues.* New York: Random House, Inc., 1968.

Mills, G. A., H. Perry and H. R. Johnson. "Fuels Management in an Environmental Age." *Environment, Science, and Technology,* Vol. 5, No. 1 (Jan. 1971).

Resources for the Future, Inc. *U.S. Energy Policies: An Agenda for Research.* Baltimore: The Johns Hopkins Press, 1968.

498 *Science,* Sept. 8, 1972 to Nov. 10, 1972, Vol. 177, No. 4052 through Vol. 178, No. 4061, special series of articles on Energy and Power.

Scientific American, Special Issue on Energy and Power, Vol. 224, No. 3 (Sept. 1971).

"Solar and Atomic Energy: A Survey." *Studies in Business and Economics,* Vol. 12, No. 4, The University of Maryland (March 1959).

SORGE, EMMANUEL V. "The Status of Thermal Discharge East of the Mississippi," *2nd Thermal Workshop, U.S. International Biological Program, Chesapeake Science,* Vol. 10 (Sept.-Dec. 1969).

SUMMERS, CLAUDE M. "The Conversion of Energy." *Scientific American,* Vol. 224, No. 3 (Sept. 1971).

The New York Times Encyclopedic Almanac (1970), *New York Times* (1971).

UNESCO: *Wind and Solar Energy: Proceedings of the New Delhi Symposium.* Paris, France (1956).

U.S. Bureau of the Census, *Census of Population and Housing* (1970).

Chapter 9

Bureau of Mines, *Mineral Facts and Problems.* Washington, D.C.: U.S. Government Printing Office (1970).

DRAPKIN, MICHAEL K. "Antipollution Laws are Forcing Steelmakers to Close Old, Dirty Open Hearth Furnaces." The Wall Street Journal (Dec. 1, 1970).

First Annual Report of the Council on Environmental Quality. Washington, D. C.: U.S. Government Printing Office, 1970.

GRINSTEAD, ROBERT R. "Bottlenecks." *Environment,* Vol. 14, No. 3 (April 1972).

MEADOWS, DONNELA H., DENNIS L. MEADOWS, JORGEN RANDERS and WILLIAM W. BEHRENS, III. *The Limits to Growth* (A Potomac Associates Book) New York: Universe Books, 1972.

ROUSCH, G. A. *Strategic Mineral Supplies.* New York: McGraw-Hill Book Company, 1939.

TASSEFF, ANN. "Solid Wastes Programs and Research." *Environment Reporter,* Monograph #6, Vol. 1, No. 33 (Dec. 11, 1970), Bureau of National Affairs.

Chapter 10

Advisory Committee on Predator Control, *Predator Control, 1971,* A Report to the Council on Environmental Quality and the Department of the Interior (Jan. 1972).

ALLEN, DURWOOD L. *Our Wildlife Legacy.* New York: Funk and Wagnalls Company, 1962.

ALLEN, SHIRLEY and JUSTIN W. LEONARD. *Conserving Natural Resources.* New York: McGraw-Hill Book Company, 1966.

"America's Rare Sea Mammals," United States Department of the Interior, Fish and Wildlife Service, Bureau of Commercial Fisheries, Washington, D.C.: (Dec. 1968).

COTTAM, CLARENCE and ELMER HIGGINS. *DDT: Its Effect on Fish and Wildlife.* U.S. Fish and Wildlife Service, Circular 11, Washington, D.C.: (1946).

DASMANN, RAYMOND. *Wildlife Biology.* New York: John Wiley & Sons, Inc., 1964.

GRAHAM, FRANK JR. *Since Silent Spring.* Boston: Houghton Mifflin Company, 1970.

HARDIN, GARRETT. "The Tragedy of the Commons." *Science,* Vol. 162 (Dec. 13, 1968), pp. 1243-1248.

HARDIN, GARRETT. *Exploring New Ethics for Survival, The Voyage of the Spaceship Beagle.* New York: The Viking Press, Inc., 1972.

McVay, Scott. "The Last of the Great Whales." *Scientific American,* Vol. 215 (Aug. 1966), pp. 3–11.

Riley, Francis. "Fur Seal Industry of the Pribilof Islands: 1786–1965." Bureau of Commercial Fisheries, Circular 275, Washington, D.C.

Sunset Western Garden Book, by the Editors of Sunset Magazine and Sunset Books, Menlo Park, California: Lane Magazine and Book Co., 1971.

Chapter 11

Cahn, Robert. "Thwarted Developers are 'Taking the Fifth.'" *Christian Science Monitor,* Vol. 65, No. 151 (May 23, 1973), p. 9.

Congress and the Nation, Vol. II, Congressional Quarterly Series (1969).

Environmental Quality—The Third Annual Report of the Council on Environmental Quality. Washington, D.C.: U.S. Government Printing Office, 1972.

Geddes, Patrick. *Cities in Evolution.* New York: Harper and Row, Publishers, 1971.

Gilliam, Harold. *Between the Devil and the Deep Blue Bay.* San Francisco: Chronicle Books, 1969.

Hill, Albert and Michael McCloskey. "Mineral King: Wilderness Versus Mass Recreation in the Sierras," quoted in John Harte and Robert H. Socolow, *Patient Earth.* New York: Holt, Rinehart and Winston, Inc., 1971.

Laeffler, Jane. "Open Space, People and Urban Ecology." *Ekistics,* Vol. 35, No. 208 (March, 1973), pp. 121–123.

Osborn, Fredrick J. *Greenbelt Cities.* London: Faber and Faber, 1946.

Population and the American Future, The Report of the Commission on Population Growth and the American Future. Washington, D.C.: U.S. Government Printing Office, 1972.

Whyte, William H. *The Last Landscape.* Garden City, New York: Doubleday & Company, Inc., 1968.

Wingo, Lowdon Jr. (ed.). *Cities and Space: The Future Use of Urban Land.* Baltimore: Johns Hopkins Press for Resources for the Future, 1963.

Chapter 12

Appleyard, Donald, Kevin Lynch, and John R. Myer. *The View from the Road.* Cambridge: M.I.T. Press, 1969.

Doxiadis, C. A. *Ekistics.* London: Hutchinson of London, 1968.

Ekistics, Vol. 29, No. 175 (June, 1970).

Eldredge, H. Wentworth (ed.). *Taming Megalopolis,* Volumes I and II. Garden City, N.Y.: Doubleday & Company, Inc., 1967.

Gordon, Mitchell. *Sick Cities, Psychology and Pathology of American Urban Life.* Baltimore: Penguin Books, 1965.

Hall, Peter. *The World Cities.* New York: McGraw-Hill Book Company, 1966.

Leeds, Morton. "City of the Future." *HUD Challenge,* (Aug., 1972).

Meyer, J. R., J. F. Kain, and M. Wohl. *The Urban Transportation Problem.* Cambridge: Harvard University Press, 1965.

Mumford, Lewis. *The City in History.* New York: Harcourt Brace Jovanovich, Inc., 1961.

National Committee on Urban Growth Policy. Donald Canty (ed.). *The New City.* New York: Frederick Praeger, 1969.

Rodoman, B. B. "The Organized Anthroposphere." *Ekistics,* Vol. 29, No. 175 (June, 1970).

BIBLIOGRAPHY

500   SAX, KARL. *Standing Room Only—The World's Exploding Population.* Boston: Beacon Press, 1955.

SELF, PETER. *Cities in Flood, The Problems of Urban Growth.* London: Faber and Faber, Ltd., 1961.

SPILHAUS, ATHELSTON. "Technology, Living Cities, and Human Environment." *Science and Technology and the Cities.* Compilation of Papers Presented for the Tenth Meeting of Panel on Science and Technology, 1969. Washington, D.C.: U.S. Government Printing Office, 1969.

STEIN, CLARENCE. *Toward New Towns for America.* Cambridge: M.I.T. Press, 1966.

WADE, MASON (ed.). *The International Megalopolis.* Toronto: University of Toronto Press, Eighth Annual University of Windsor Seminar on Canadian-American Relations, 1969.

WARNER. SAM BASS JR. (ed.). *Planning for a Nation of Cities.* Cambridge: M.I.T. Press, 1966.

Index

Italic numbers refer to illustrations.

Absorption, 477
Acid mine drainage, *320,* 477
Acre foot, 477
Activated sludge treatment, 117, 477
Adsorption, 477
Advocacy, environmental, 49, 56
Advocate, role of environmental, 49–51, 53
Air, as a flow resource, 229
Air emissions, nationwide, 230*t,* 237
Air inversion, *254, 256, 484*
   frequencies, 235
   occurrences, 234
   of San Francisco Bay area, 427
   temperature, 230
Air pollution,
   in Boston, 238–41
   costs in U.S., 232, *237*
   effects of specific pollutants, 231*t*
   episodes, 236
   incinerators, 243–44
   legislation, 77, 233–34
   in New York City, 241–46
   open burning, *239*
   personal steps to take in reducing air pol-
     lution problems, 259–60
   relationship to internal combustion engine,
     244
   in San Jose, California, 127
   in Washington, D.C., 246–51
Air pollution control alert system for New
   York City, 243
Air Quality Act of 1967, 233, 237, 477

Air quality sampling stations, 258
Air quality standards, national, 232*t*
Aircraft noise, *251, 252*
Airport expansion, 458
Airshed, 477
Alabama, forest production, 206
Alaskan fur seal, *363*
Alaskan moose, *366*
Alaskan oil pipeline, 370
   effects on wildlife, *369, 371*
Alaskan Prudhoe Bay, oil deposits, 340
Alewife, 88
Allocation, conservation philosophy, 12, 33
Aluminum, 301*t*
   in trash, 344
Amalgamation, 478
American Airlines, 408
American life style, 54, 98–101, *275, 289, 347,*
   464
Amsteveel, Netherlands, *473*
Anadromous species, 88, 478
Anaerobes, 478
Analogous arrangement, 22–23
Anhydrous ammonia, 166
Animal manuring, 170–71
Apollo 17, *439, 444, 445*
Aristotle, 448, 466
Arsonists, southern forest, 222
Asbestos, 89
Association of Bay Area Governments
   (ABAG), 424
Astronauts, view of earth, *439,* 445

501

Athens Center of Ekistics, 447
Athens, Greece, *94, 466*
Atlanta, Georgia, *450*
Atlantic flyway for migratory birds, 63
Atmospheric resources, 229–60
Atomic Energy Act of 1954, 478
Atomic Energy Commission, 76, 316
  EIR exemptions, 332
  regulatory practices, 330
Autecology, 26, 478
Autobahn of Germany, 446
Automobile,
  alternative power systems, 249
  in city center, 90, 259
  damage from salt on roads, 56–57
  emission standards, 82, 233–34
  human costs, 91, 246, 259, *450*
  impact in France, 453
  land needs, 95, 246, 247, 259, *448*
  junk, *342t, 343,* 344, *344,* 345, *346*
  recoverable metallic values, *342t, 344*
  special interest groups, 95
  toll on natural and physical environment,
    88–89, *95*
  traffic, *95*
  urban space requirements, *247, 259,* 453
Autostrada of Italy, 446

Badlands National Monument, 174
Bagdad, Arizona, copper mine and mill, *323*
Bardach, John, 79
Bay Area Rapid Transit (BART), 95–97, *96, 97,
  451, 452, 454, 455*
Bay Conservation and Development Com-
  mission (BCDC), 427
Beach erosion, *128*
Beaver, Alaska, *214, 350*
Beneficiation, conservation philosophy, 33
  copper, 323
Berlin, Germany, *86, 459*
Bicycles,
  in national parks, *398*
  in Washington, D.C., *247, 249, 250*
Big Sky, Montana, 408
Bighorn sheep, *356*
Biocides, 62
Biological continuum, 47, 478
Biological controls, for urban gardeners, 172
Biological indicators of pollution, 132–133
Biological oxygen demand (BOD), 117, *119,*
  478
Biological pyramid, 13, 30, 478
  marine and terrestrial, *25*
Biomass, 478
Biota, 478

Biotic climax community, 478
Biotic succession, 353
Birds, migratory species, 62
  banding, 62
Bison, *383*
Bituminous deposits of coal, 479
Black lung, 291–92
Board feet, 479
Boise-Cascade, 408
Boom towns, 309
Boston, Massachusetts, 386, *411, 450*
  air pollution in, 238–41
  Air Pollution Law of 1910, 239–40
  expressway networks, *450*
  Massachusetts Transit Authority, *94,* 238
Bottomland of rivers, 15, 479
Boulder, Colorado, 403
Boundary Waters Area Canoe Wilderness, 401
Bounty, 373–76, 479
Brasília, Brazil, 469
British Thermal Unit (BTU), 479
Broadform deed, 291, 293, 479
Bronchitis, death rate, 242
Brown, Victor, total solid waste recycling
  efforts, 54
Bryan, William L., 266
Building insulation, for heat loss reduction,
  297, *297*
Bureau of Land Management, 373, 407
Bureau of Reclamation, 183, 407
Bureau of Sport Fisheries and Wildlife, 407
Burlington Northern, 408

Cahn, Robert, 433
Cain, Stanley A., 32
California,
  condor, *355*
  Environmental Quality Act, 417
  fish and wildlife plan, 379
  state park system, 407
  use of Ticketron, 407
Camping, within European cities, 431
Canadian lynx, *357*
Carbon monoxide,
  effects as air pollutant, *231t*
  levels in New York City, 241–42
Caribou, 365–73
  Alaskan species, *368, 369, 370, 372*
  problems threatening survival, 370–71, *369,
    370*
Carrying capacity, 7, 479
  for animal resources, 373
  of cities, 42–44, 442
  determinant, 479
  of soil, 161, *161*

of Spaceship Earth, 447
of urban environment, 352
of water, 114
Carson, Rachel, 184
Casella, William N., 453
Caudill, Harry, 174
Cell membrane, 41–43
    tasks of, 41
Cellulose, 220
Central hardwood forest, 190, *191*
Central flyway for migratory birds, *63*
Central Park (New York City), 432
Change agent, environmental, 50
Chapparal, 479
Chemical cycle, *149*
Chemical ice retardants, 89
Chemosynthesis, 479
Chernozem soil, 159, 479
Chicago, Illinois, *113,* 132, *463*
Chlorinated hydrocarbon, 185, 479
Christianity, 54, 71
Chromium, 301*t*
Chrysler Realty Corp., 408
Circulation,
    of man, 47
    of cities, 47
Ciriacy-Wantrup, S. V., definition of con-
    servation, 32
City,
    as concentrator of resources, 28
    in evolution, 23
    growth of, 14
    input considerations, 34
    as natural resource, 12, 13, 37–38
    output realities, 34
Civilian Conservation Corps (CCC), 74, 207,
    479
Clams, 364–65
Clarke-McNary Act, 200, 210, 479
Clean Air Act of 1963, 77, 233, 480
Clean Air Amendments of 1970, 233, 479
Clear cut logging, 206, 210
Cleveland, Grover, 199
Cliff dwellers of American Southwest, *441*
Climax, Colorado, molybdenum mine, *307,*
    325, *326*
Climax community, 365, *372,* 480
    human, 386, *386*
Climax species, 353
Closed systems, 441
    cities as, 446
Club of Rome, mineral inventory, 300–304,
    301–303*t*
Coal Mine Health and Safety Act, 292, 480
Coal reserves, 301*t*

Coal,
    strip mining, *173, 174, 174, 175, 176, 287,*
        288, 288, 289, 291–95, *293, 295, 296*
    underground mining, *290, 291, 292*
Cobalt, 301*t*
Coeur d'Alene silver district, 319
Colorado, disapproval of winter olympics,
    416–17
Colorado plateau, uranium deposits, 329, 332
Columbia, Maryland, 246, 472, 474
Combined sewer, 114
Commensalism, 13
Common property resource, 361–62, 480
Commoner, Barry, 79
Compost,
    gardening, 170–71
    market for resale, 54
Concorde (SST), *456, 457, 457*
Conservancy districts, Ohio, 58
Conservation, 7, 12, 480
    author's definition, 33
    awakening, 80
    ecological definitions, 32–33
    economic definitions, 32
    evolution of term, 30–33
    general definitions, 31
    movement of 1970's, 81–82
    need for comprehensive urban approach,
        34
    philosophy of regulation, 75
    rural areas and, 75
Consolidated Edison, 244–45
    Storm King controversy, 283
Consumer,
    first order, *25, 26, 27, 28*
    second order, *25, 26, 27, 28*
    third order, *25, 26, 27, 28*
Contour farming, 164, *164,* 480
Controlled burning, 228
Cook County Forest Preserve, 169
Cooling tower, *254, 256, 257*
Copper, 54, 55, 301*t,* 322–25, *317, 318, 323*
    U.S. production, 305
Copperhill, Tennessee, 174
Council Bluffs, Iowa, *137*
Council on Environmental Quality, 135, 340,
    341, 345, 480
    opinion on mineral shortage, 300
Covent, Louisiana, *157*
Covington, Virginia, 222
Cripple Creek, Colorado, 333
Crop rotation, *165,* 165–66, 480
Cumberland Plateau, 174, *175, 275, 289, 289,*
    291–95, *295, 296*
Cyanidation, 480

Dade County, Florida, jetport, 227
Dana, Samuel Trask, 30
Dasmann, Raymond, 386
Decibel, 251–52, 480
Decomposer, 481
Deltaic plain, 152, *157*, 481
Demonstration Cities and Metropolitan Development Act of 1966, 481
Density of urban areas, 459–60
Depletion allowances, 55
Detroit, Michigan,
  auto's land needs, *448*
  mass transit, 90, *448*
  waterfront, *130, 131*
Detroit River, *112,* 130, *131*
Dingell-Johnson Law of 1950, 382
Disneyland, California, *429*
Disturbance species, 481
Doerr, Thomas, 366n
Donora, Pennsylvania, air disaster, 236
Doxiadis, C. A., 35, 36, 41, 467
Dubos, Rene, 79
Ducktown-Copperhill, Tennessee, *22,* 236
Dust Bowl, 159, 481
Dutch elm disease, 188

"Earth Day," 78, 81, 481
Eastern seaboard, regional case studies,
  atmosphere, 229–60, *237*
  energy, 263–97, *263*
Ecological stability, 13–14, 481
Ecology, 26, 481
Ecosystem, 26, 481
Ecotone, 481
  advantages for urban wildlife, 380
Ecumenopolis, 437, *438,* 448–49, 467, *473,* 481
  difficulties of, 475–76
Efficiency,
  of electric light, 268
  of nuclear power plant, 269
Effluent, 481
Ehrlich, Paul, 79
Eisenhower, Dwight D., 74, 446
Ekistic elements, *35,* 35–37, 85, 432
Ekistics, 35, 481
  elements of, 35–38
Electricity,
  failure, 261
  present consumption, 262
  projected consumption, 273, 273n
  transmission lines, *99, 100,* 287
  underground transmission, *100*
Elk, *374*
Elk River, Idaho, *350*

Elkhorn, Montana, *351*
Emphysema, death rate, 242
Endangered species of wildlife, 354–58, *355, 356, 357,* 482
Energy resources, 261–97
  biological transformation of, 29
  conservation procedures, 297
  energy crisis, 294, 298
  fission, nuclear, 38t, 39n, 262
  fossil fuels, 270, 273, 275, 281–82, 286–94, 335–40
  fusion, nuclear, 39n
  future demands, 269
  geothermal, 266, *267,* 483
  hydro-, 25, 283–84
  loss by conversions, 29, 263
  nuclear, 262, 269, 270
  price, factors affecting, 272
  role of federal government, 281
  solar, 277–81, 437–39
  tidal, 282–83
  urban conversions, 267
  use rates, 305
  wind, *296*
Environmental education, 65
  college, 65–68
  community level, 66–68
  precollege or prevocational exposure, 65
  urban resource seminar, 65–68
Environmental impact statements, 56, 91, 340, 417–18, 482
Environmental Protection Agency, 82, 482
  control of air pollution, 234
Environmental reform, costs of, 98
Epilimnion, 126, 482
Erosion, 59
  control ordinances, *158*
  of Great Lakes shoreline, *128,* 129, *129*
  soil, 59, *59, 153, 154,* 155, *156,* 172–73, *172, 197*
  wind, 159, *160, 169*
Eskimo, relationships to the caribou and reindeer, 366–69
Esposito, John, 242
Eutrophication, 124, 482
Everglades National Park, *193,* 223–27, *223, 224, 225, 226*
Exploitation, 12–22, 70–72
  Christianity and, 71
  energy consumption and, 71–72
  of flood plains, 15–19
  of land resources, 14, 22
  by recreational developments, 22
  relationship to human poverty, 61
  of topsoil, 21

of wildlife, 13, 353–58, 360–65, 368
Exponential growth, 304, 482
  of resource consumption vs. linear growth, 304–305
Exportation limits, 55
Extraction communities, *8, 27, 310*

Fairfax County, Virginia, 468
Fall line, 24, 482
Federal Water Pollution Control Act of 1948, 77, 134, 482
Federal Water Pollution Control Act Amendments of 1972, 117, 119–20, 409, 491
Feedback loop, 482
Ferret, black-footed, *388*
Fertilizer overuse, 155
Fifty-year flood, 139
Fire control, forest, *208, 209, 388*
Firebugs, 209, 222
Fishery management, 383
Fitch, James M., 458
Flood control in urban areas, 136–44, *140, 141*
Flood damage, costs of, 16–17, *140, 141,* 177–78, *178,* 183
Flood plain, 15–22, *137,* 138, *140,* 482
Flood problems, "solutions" to, *180, 181, 182*
Flood protection, 64, *140, 181, 182*
Flooding, agricultural, *151,* 157
Floodproofing, 139–40, *140,* 482
Florida Flood Control District, 226
Flyash, 483
Food chains, 29–30
Forest resources, 187–228
  exploitation, 196–97
  fire control, *208, 209*
  hybridization, 218, 484
  industrial revolution and, 205–206
  management, history of, 199–202
  management in urban zreas, 187
  ownership, *198,* 202
  productivity, 201
  products, 200, *204,* 205
  regions of the U.S., *189*
  savings by recycling paper, 53
  tent caterpillar, *213, 214*
Forestry practices, 210–15
Fossil fuel depletions, 275
Fracturing of oil shale *in situ, 337, 338, 339, 339*
Freight rates, effect on recycling, 55
Friends of Mammoth, 417
Fuel efficiencies, 267
Fuller, Buckminster, 476
Fur seal, 362, *363*

Gardner, Massachusetts, 25
Gatlinburg, Tennessee, *17*
Gavins Point Dam, 183
Geddes, Patrick, 471
General Motors, 82, 233
Georgia-Pacific, 408
Geothermal energy sources, *266, 267,* 483
Ghetto vs. suburb, recreation opportunities, 410, *411,* 412, *414, 415,* 465
Ghost towns, 309, *311, 351*
Gilliam, Harold, 427
Glaciation, of the Great Lakes, *122, 123*
Gold, 10, 301*t,* 333–35, *333, 334*
Golden Gate National Recreation Area, 405, *405*
Gottmann, Jean, 467
Grafting of plants, *218,* 483
Graham, Edward H., definition of conservation, 31*n*
Grand Junction, Colorado, uranium wastes, 315
Grand Valley, Colorado, oil shale pilot project, 325, *337*
Gray, L. C., definition of conservation, 32
Great Depression, 74
Great Lakes,
  cities, 124
  dredging, 130
  erosion of shoreline, *128,* 129, *129*
  glaciation, *122, 123*
  impact of NAWAPA, *142, 143*
  megalopolis, *111*
  regional case study, 110–45
  role in settlement, 112
  seiches, 129
Green Bay, Wisconsin, 131
Green belts, urban, *46,* 169
Green manuring, 169, 483
Green River formation, 335, *336*
Grizzly bear, *356*
Groundwater, 108
Gruen, Victor, 452
Guadalupe Mountains National Park, 410
Guffy Coal Act of 1936, 483
Gulf States, regional case study (forests), 204–28, *205*
Gulick, Ester (Mrs. Charles), 427
Gulick, Luther, 462
Gully reclamation, 174–77

Habitat, 14, 483
  maintenance, *388*
Half life, radioactive elements, 134, 483
Hardin, Garrett, 79, 362
Hardwoods, *198,* 483

"Harvesting" human settlements, *24*

Herbicides, 79, 483

Highway Trust Fund, 89, 483
  impact on mass transit, 90
  revenue source, 90

Hill, Albert, 420

Hobart Hills, California, *9*

Homologous arrangement, 22–23

Housing and Urban Development Act of 1968, 474, 483

Houston, Texas, recycling efforts, 54

Howard, Ebenezer, 45, 169, 470–71

Hudson River, nuclear power plant sites, 270

Human resource depletion, *61*

Human settlements, 23, 24
  anatomy similar to animal communities, 35–38, 384–87

Hybridization, forest species, 218, 484

Hydrocarbons, effects as a pollutant, 231*t*

Hydrologic cycle, 107–108, *108*, 484
  urban, *109*

Hydropower, 25, 284

Hypolimnion, 126, 484

Incinerators and air pollution, 243–44

Independence, Colorado, *8*

Injunctions against nuclear power plants, 274

Inland Waterways Commission, 72

Insulation, residential, *297*

Integration, conservation philosophy, 33

International Falls, Minnesota, *189, 190*

Interstate highway system,
  costs, 90, 453
  initial aim, 92–93
  land acquisition, 449
  origin, 446
  size, 453

Iodine-131, 253, 254

Iron, 301*t*

Islamabad, West Pakistan, 469

John Muir Trail, 394

Johnson, Huey, 414

Johnson, Lyndon, 410

Kaibab National Forest, 352

Kansas City, Missouri, 18, *20*

Kellogg, Idaho, Sunshine Silver Mine tragedy, 319

Kentucky coal counties, 293

Kerr, Kay (Mrs. Clark), 427

Kilowatt, path of, 286

Kit fox, *358*

Klamath, California, 18, *20*

Knutson-Vandenberg Act of 1930, 200, 484

Kodiak National Wildlife Refuge, Alaska, *385*

Krypton-85, 254

Lacey Act of 1900, 381

Lake Okeechobee, 225, *225*

Lake physiology, 121–27
  epilimnion, 126, 482
  eutrophication, 124, *133,* 482
  hypolimnion, 126, 484
  oligotrophic, 121, 486
  overturn, 126
  relationship of temperature and oxygen content, 124, 145
  stratification, *125,* 124–25, 489
  summer kill, 127
  thermocline, 126, 490
  winter kill, 126, 492

Lake Tahoe, California, 119, *120, 390*

Land and Water Conservation Fund Act of 1964, 484

Land disturbance, from mining operations, 319–20

Landfill,
  composition of, 53
  space available in U.S. cities, 346–47

Lateralization of soil, 21, 484

Laurel, Mississippi, *206*

Lawrence, Andrea Mead, 417

Lead, 302*t,* 327–29
  as antiknock compound in gasoline, 328–29
  poisoning among low-income families, 328

Legislation,
  air pollution, 77, 233–35
  Air Pollution Law of 1910 (Boston), 239–40
  Air Quality Act of 1967, 233, 477
  Atomic Energy Act of 1954, 478
  California Environmental Quality Act, 417
  Clarke-McNary Act of 1924, 200, 210, 479
  Clean Air Act of 1963, 77, 233, 480
  Clean Air Amendments of 1970, 233, 479
  Coal Mine Health and Safety Act, 292, 480
  Demonstration Cities and Metropolitan Development Act of 1966, 481
  Dingell-Johnson Law of 1950, 382
  forest management, 200
  Guffy Coal Act of 1936, 483
  Housing and Urban Development Act of 1968, 474, 483
  Knutson-Vandenberg Act of 1930, 200, 484
  Lacey Act of 1900, 381
  Land and Water Conservation Fund Act of 1964, 484
  McNary-McSweeney Act of 1928, 200, 484
  Marine Mammal Protection Act of 1972, 382, 485

Migratory Bird Treaties, 382
Minerals Multiple Surface Use Act of 1955, 485
Multiple Use–Sustained Yield Act of 1960, 485
National Environmental Policy Act (NEPA), 134, 340, 486
National Forest Fish and Game Sanctuary Act of 1934, 382
New Towns Act of 1946 (Great Britain), 45
Omnibus Flood Control Bill of 1936, 16, 138, 177, 486
Organic Forestry Act of 1897, 199, 486
Pittman-Robertson Act of 1937, 382
Prairie States Forestry Project of 1934, 487
Public Highway Act of 1956, 89, 487
Refuse Act of 1899, 134, 488
Resource Recovery Act of 1970, 83, 347, 488
Scenic and Wild Rivers Act of 1968, 382, 488
Silver Purchase Act of 1934, 1963 Repeal, 321
Small Watershed Act of 1954, 183, 489
Soil Conservation Act of 1935, 489
Solid Waste Disposal Act of 1965, 83–84, 489
Urban Growth and New Development Act of 1970, 474, 491
Urban Mass Transportation Act of 1964, 491
water pollution control, 77, 134–36
Water Pollution Control Act of 1948, 77, 482
Water Pollution Control Act, 1972 Amendments, 77, 117, 119–20, 409, 491
Water Resources Planning Act of 1965, 491
Weeks Act of 1911, 200, 210, 491
Wetlands Inspection Act of 1962, 382
Wetlands Loan Act of 1961, 382
Wilderness Act of 1964, 382, 491
Wilderness Preservation Act of 1964, 409
wildlife and fisheries, 381–82
Wildlife Coordination Act of 1934, 382
Wildlife Refuge Exchange Act of 1935, 382
Wildlife Restoration Act of 1937, 492
Leopold, Aldo, definition of conservation, 32
Levittown, New York, 460
Lignin, 220
Limits to Growth, as applied to mineral resources, 304–306
Lincoln, Abraham, 403, *404*
Linear growth rates, 304
Litter, 51–55
    costs, 51–54
Litterbugs, 52
Littoral zone, 484
Loam, 19, *150*, 484
Loblolly pine, *197, 208, 215, 216,* 217

Lodgepole pine, *193*
Loessial soil, 152, 484
Loessial terraces, 152, 484
London, England, *8, 42, 46, 86, 466*
Long Island Sound, nuclear power plant sites, 270
Longleaf pine, 205, 207, *208, 211,* 217, 218, 219
Los Angeles, California, 421
    dehumanization by the auto, 452–53, 456
Louisiana forest production, 206
Low-income families, lead poisoning, 328
Lucas, Bob, 401
Lufkin, Texas, 221
Lumber barons, 206

Mach 2 speed, 484
McCloskey, Michael, 420
McGee, W. J., definition of conservation, 31
McLaughlin, Sylvia (Mrs. Donald), 427
McNary-McSweeney Act of 1928, 200, 485
Macronutrients, soil, 166, 485
MacWilliams, Carrie, 452
Madison, Wisconsin, 54
Mammoth Lakes, California, 417
Man, as ekistical element, *35, 36*
Manganese, 302*t*
Marine Mammal Protection Act of 1972, 382, 485
Maryland transportation legislation, 90
Mass transit,
    European systems, 93, *93, 94*
    policy decision making, 90–91
    as survival necessity, 450
    U.S. efforts, 93, *94*
Massachusetts Transit Authority, *94,* 238
Materials Policy Commission Report of 1953, 76
Mather, Stephen, 404
Maximization, conservation philosophy, 33
Mechanization,
    logging, 219–20, *219*
    urban areas, 14
Megalopolis, 40, 467, 469, 485
    dependency on outlying resources, 441–46
    East Coast, 289
    Great Lakes, 110, *111*
    metabolism, 265
    West Coast, 432
Meier, Richard L., 11
Mercur, Utah, *10*
Mercury, 302*t*
Metabolic by-products, 7
Meuse River Valley air disaster, 236
Miami, Florida, airport, 227

Microclimate effect,
  of trees, 187
  of urban area, 255–57, *256*
Micronutrients, soil, 166, 485
Microtowns, 468–70, 485
Mid-Century Conference of 1953, 76
Migration, to central city, 468
Migratory Bird Treaties, *381*, 382
Migratory flyway, *63*
Milwaukee, Wisconsin, 116, 131
Mine disasters, 300, 319
Mine mouth power plants, 288
Mineral consumers, world leaders, 301–303*t*
Mineral consumption, U.S. as percent of
  world total, 301–303*t*
Mineral depletion, 300, 304
Mineral extraction,
  amalgamation, 319, 478
  cyanidation, 319, 480
  dredging, 319
  flotation, 482
  hydrometallurgical, 323, 484
  panning, 319
  pyrometallurgical, 323, 488
  sluicing, 319, 489
Mineral imports to the U.S., 309
Mineral King, 418–23, *419*, *421*
  case against mass recreation, 420–21
Mineral producers, world leaders, 301–303*t*
Mineral production, co-product or by-product, 322
Mineral reclamation,
  copper, 324
  gold, 325
  silver, 321
Mineral recycling, 341–47, 342*t*, *343 344*, *345*,
  346
  cans, 341
  obstructions, 345–46
Mineral reserves, global, 301–303*t*
Mineral resources, 299–347
Mineral self-sufficiency, 308–309
Minerals Multiple Surface Use Act of 1955,
  485
Mining,
  environmental effects, 312–16, 323
  vegetative recovering of land, *320*
  waste disposal problems, 319
  see also Coal mining
Mississippi flyway for migratory birds, *63*
Mississippi River,
  delta region, 21, 152
  drainage basin, 147, *148*, *151*, 172
  regional case study (soil), 151–85
  sedimentation rate, 148

Missouri drainage basin,
  flooding, *137*, *179*, *180*
  saline seep, 165–66
  soil practices, 166
Molybdenum, 302*t*, *307*, 324, 325–27, *326*
  spoilbank, *307*, *324*
Monoculture agriculture, 184, 485
Monoculture forestry, 210–15
  ecological dangers of, 212
Monospecies agricultural practice, 21, 485
Montana Environmental Quality Council,
  165–66
Morgan City, Louisiana, *18*
Mount McKinley, *410*
Mountain goat, *385*
Mountain lion, *385*
Multiple use concept, *422*
Multiple Use–Sustained Yield Act of 1960, 485
Mumford, Lewis, 455, 462, 471
Munich, Germany, transportation alterna-
  tives, 93–94
Municipalities,
  salting of streets, 55–58
  solid waste disposal, 53, 82–84
  waste treatment, 114–21
Musk ox, *359*, *385*
Muskegon, Michigan, waste treatment, 117–
  19, *118*, *119*
Mykonos, Greece, *88*, *296*, *440*

Nader, Ralph, 50, *79*
Natchez Trace National Parkway, 169
National Audubon Society, 226, 380
National Environmental Policy Act (NEPA),
  134, 340, 486
National Forest Fish and Game Sanctuary Act
  of 1934, 382
National forests, 199, 406*t*
National Park Service, 394–98
  differences from U.S. Forest Service, 406*t*
  established, 404
  first director, 404
National parks,
  rates of visitation, 404
  unique characteristics, 402–403
  see also specific parks
National Wilderness Preservation System, 409
National Wildlife Federation, 380
Nationalization of energy resources, 265
Natural gas reserves, 302*t*
Natural resources, classification, 38–39*t*
  exhaustible, 38*t*
  immutable, 38*t*
  inexhaustible, 38*t*
  maintainable, 38*t*

misusable, 38t
nonmaintainable, 39t
nonrenewable, 39t
nonreusable, 39t
renewable, 38t
reusable, 39t
Natural resources,
human, 13
traditional, 13
Nature, as ekistical element, 35, 36
Networks, as ekistical element, 35, 37, 85, 88, 89, 98, 443, 450, 451
New towns, 470–75, 473
Amsteveel, Netherlands, 473
costs of, 474
English, 45–46
Tapiola, Finland, 473
U.S., 469, 472
New Towns Act of 1946 (Great Britain), 45
New York Department of Air Resources, 243
New York City, 268, 460–61, 461
air pollution, 241–46, 242
air pollution loads, 241
air pollution sources, 243, 244
cost of Sunday paper disposal, 52
as New Amsterdam, 44–45
New York State, productivity of marine district, 270
New York Times, cost of disposal, 52
Nickel, 55, 302t
Nitrogen-fixing bacteria, 148
Nitrogen oxides, effects of, 231t
Nixon, Richard M., 78, 460
Noise pollution, 251–52
Nonrenewable natural resources, 25, 301–303t, 486
Norfolk, Virginia, 460
North American Water and Power Alliance, 142, 143, 144
North Cascades National Park, 410, 413, 428
North Pacific Fur Seal Convention, 363
Northern forest, 188–89, 189, 190
Northwest Orient Airlines, 408
Nottingham, England, 93
Nuclear power plant,
efficiency, 269
percent of U.S. energy supply, 262

Oakland, California, 454–55
Odum, Eugene P., definition of conservation, 32
Oil pollution, reduction of, 276
Oil shale, 294, 311–12, 335–40, 336
Green River formation, 335
in situ fracturing, 337, 338, 339, 339

Piceance Creek basin, Colorado, 340
waste disposal problems of processed shale, 337
Oligotrophic lake, 121, 486
Olmsted, Fredrick Law, 432
Olympic National Park, 387, 391, 400, 412, 422
Omnibus Flood Control Bill of 1936, 16, 138, 177, 486
Open pit mining,
copper, 323
restoration of nearby vegetation, 325
Open space resources, 22, 389–433
abuse, 22
reasons for increased demand, 401
for urban populations, 401–405, 413, 415
Oregon, 373, 377, 391, 403
Organic gardening, 171
Organic Forestry Act of 1897, 199, 486
Osmosis, 42, 486
Ottumwa, Iowa, 182
Outdoor Recreation Resources Review Commission Report, 389
Overburden, 174, 296, 486
Overturn, 126, 289, 292
Owen, Oliver S., 38t–39t
Oxidants, effects of, 231
Oxygen consumption, relationship to heat, 271
Oxygen content of water and temperature relationship, 124, 145
Oysters, 364
Ozone, effects as air pollutant, 231t

Pacific Coast forest, 194, 195, 195
Pacific Coast region, regional case study (recreation and open space), 389–433, 390
Pacific flyway for migratory birds, 63, 381, 425, 426
Pacific Northwest, regional case study (wildlife and fisheries), 358–87, 359
Palo Alto, California, open space policy, 433
Papaioannou, John G., 447
Paper,
industry's attitude toward recycling, 54
manufacturing process, 221
pollutant, 51–52
recycling, 52–55, 203
wood requirements, 221
Parkins, A. F., definition of conservation, 31n
Particulate, 57
effects as air pollutant, 231t
percent of air pollution, 245
Passamaquoddy tidal power proposal, 282–85, 284–85
Pelagic hunting, 362, 486

Perloff, Harvey, 418
Peroxyacetyl nitrate (PAN), 231*t*
Pesticides,
 biological magnification of, 62
 chlorinated hydrocarbons, 185
 coordination of usage, 62
 forest management and, 211
 international regulation need, 62
 persistent, 62, 487
 in soil, 183–85
Pesticides, specific,
 aldrin, 184
 BHC, 184
 DDD, 184
 DDT, 62, 62*n*, 184
 heptachlor, 184
 lindane, 184
 phorate, *209*
 1080, 374
 Thimet, *209*
 2-4D, 184
Petroleum reserves, 302*t*
Philadelphia, Pennsylvania, *98,* 412, *413*
 Eastwick area, 469
Philosophy, Oriental and Near Eastern, 70
Photosynthesis, 26
Piceance Creek basin, Colorado, *336,* 340
Pinchot, Gifford, 30, 31, 50, 72, 200
Pioneer species, 47
Pittman-Robertson Act of 1937, 382
Placer mining, *333, 334,* 487
 environmental impact, *334*
Platinum group, 302*t*
Pleistocene Ice Age, development of Great
 Lakes, 121, *122–123*
Plowshare, 134
Plutonium, 253–54
Pollutants, 51, 487
 atmospheric, 230
Pollution,
 biological indicators, 132–33, *133*
 definition, 51
 internalizing costs, 51*n,* 64
 need for national and world-wide standards, 64
 thermal, *125,* 269–71, 330
 see also Air pollution, Noise pollution, Radioactive pollution, Water pollution
Population (human),
 community commitment, 475–76
 contributor to formation of world city, 467
 effect on recreation areas, 401, 416, 421,
 428
 energy requirements and, 267, 269
 growth and urbanization, *101,* 458

growth of global, *438,* 459–60
impact on wildlife, 378
mineral consumption and, 300–307, 301–
 303*t*
Netherlands, 460
New York City, 460
Nixon, Richard, address of, 460
past growth and impact on development
 of early human settlements, 441
related to demand and supply of forest
 products, 202–204
San Francisco Bay area, 424–25
of thirteen colonies, 459
U.S. growth rate, *101,* 459
U.S. percentage that hunt and fish, 378
urbanized in U.S., *101,* 430, *431*
world's sigmoid growth curve, 467
Portland, Oregon, *351*
Potomac River, 248
Poverty, *61*
Power blackout of Novermber 1965, 264
Power grid, national, 266
Power industry, annual growth rate, 267
Power lines, underground transmission, *99,*
 100
Power plants,
 fossil fuel, 262, 286
 geothermal, *266*
 hydro-, 25
 nuclear, efficiency, 269
 nuclear, percent of U.S. energy supply, 262
Prairie States Forestry Project of 1934, 487
Preservation, conservation philosophy, 72–73
 definition, 32–33
President's Commission on Population
 Growth and the American Future, 430
President's Materials Policy Commission, 307
Predator control, 373–76
 Advisory Committee on Predator Control,
 375
 use of 1080 poison, 374
Predators, *25,* 29
Pribilof Islands, Alaska, 362–64
Primary air pollutants, *232,* 233
Primary producers, 26, 487
Primary trophic level, 26–27
"Problem shed," 76
Producer settlements, 27, *27, 350, 351*
Project flood, 17, 18, 487
Pronghorn antelope, *385*
Public Highway Act of 1956, 89, 487
Puget Sound, 423–25
Pulpwood, 218, *219,* 221, *222*
 production, 202
Pumped storage, 283

Quetico-Superior Canoe Wilderness, 401

Radioactive atmospheric pollution, 253
Radioactive isotopes, half-life, 134, 254–55
Radioactive wastes,
  in atmosphere, 253–55
  storage, 253, 330
Radio-nuclide, 488
Railroad,
  effect on development, 88
  freight rates, 55
Rampart Dam, *384*
Reclamation,
  gully, *156, 172,* 174–77
  mineral, 321, 324, 325
  from strip mining, *176, 295*
Recreation resources, 22, 389–433
  abuse, 22
  drawbacks of commercial attractions, 432
  experience continuum, *430*
  facilities of ghetto dwellers, *411,* 412
  land acquisition, 403
  skills, *428*
  socioeconomic-political question, 410
  urban pressures, *428*
  water-related, *390*
Recycling, 488
  autos, *346*
  cans, 341
  comprehensive efforts, 53
  federal efforts, 54
  in Houston, Texas, 54
  metal, 53, *347*
  minerals, 341–47, 342t, *343, 344, 345, 346*
  obstacles, 54–55, 345–46
  paper, 52–55, 203
  urban resources, 441
Redwood, *195, 196*
Redwood National Park, 410, 413, 428
Reforestation, 175–77, 196, 488
Refuse Act of 1899, 134, 488
Regulation and management, conservation
  philosophy, 73–75
Renewable resource, 13, 25, 38t
Reserve Mining Company, 82
Resource,
  base, 10
  city as, 24
  conversion, 28
  definition, 10, 11
  diversity, 25
  economist's definition, 11
  exploitation, 12, 22
  nonrenewable, 82
  planning policy, 76–77

production, *28*
renewable, 82
seminar, 65–68
traditional, 10, 38
transformation, *28*
Resource management, 12, 49, 50, 70
  carryover from local to regional, 58, 64
  comprehensive, 56, 64, 75–76
  coordinated, 64, 65
  districts, 58
  external effects, 64
  incentives, 59–60, 64
  inequities of uncoordinated, 64–65
  integrated, 55, 58
  internalizing costs, 51n, 64
  introduction of new program, 56
  lack of comprehensive urban, 34
  pesticide usage, 62
  regional coordination, 58–64
  TVA, 58–59
  urban, 64–65
  water, 59–61
Resource Recovery Act of 1970, 83, 347, 488
Resources for the Future, 76
Reston, Virginia, 246, *469, 470, 472, 472, 474*
Restoration, conservation philosophy, 33
Reutilization, conservation philosophy, 33
Rhodes, island of, *44, 87, 440*
Ringlemann Visual Smoke Test, 258, 488
Roadside litter, 52
Rocky Mountain forest, 193, *193*
Rocky Mountain region, regional case study
  (minerals), 309–47, *310*
Roosevelt, Franklin D., 74, 75, 200
Roosevelt, Theodore, 30, 50, 72, 73, 115, 200

St. Francis of Assisi, 71, 425
Salida, Colorado, *23, 315*
Saline seep, 165–66
Salinity,
  ground water, 57
  laterlization, 21
Salting of streets, 55–58
  alternatives to, 57
  disadvantages of, 56–57
  effect on lakes, 125, *125*
  environmental impact, 56–57
San Francisco, California, 99, *386, 415, 425, 426, 451, 462*
San Francisco Bay, 423–27, *425*
  filling of, 127, *204, 425*
  impact of urbanization on, 405, 424–25, *425*
  value, 402, 425, 427
San Francisco metropolitan area, population, 424–25

San Jose, California, *204*, 352, 433
Sanitary landfill, 51, 346
Sanitary waste, 113
Santa Clara County, California, 468
Santa Clara valley, as an urban container, 352
Save San Francisco Bay Association, 427
Sax, Joseph, 50
Scenic and Wild Rivers Act of 1968, 382, 488
Schechtman, Michael, 272
Schweitzer, Albert, 71
Scrap iron, 342, 342t
Sea lamprey, 88
Seattle, Washington, 402
Second homes, *407*, 408, *408*, 416
"Second order" (echelon) resources, 12, 22–28
Second trophic level, 28
Secondary air pollutants, 232t, 233
Sedimentation rate, 155
  of Mississippi River, 148
Seiches, 129, 488
Selective cutting, 207, 488
Sequoia National Park, *392*, *399*, 403, 418, *419*, 420, *422*, 428
Settlement, human, 23, *23*, 384–87
Severance taxes, 306, 488
Sevierville, Tennessee, flooding, *15*, 16
Sewage, land application of, 118, *118*, *119*
Sewer, combined, 116
Shells, as ekistical element, *35*, 36
Shelterbelts, 167–69, *167*, *169*
  in urban areas, 169
Sifnos, Greece, *11*, *439*
Sigmoid growth curve, *467*, 489
Silver, *10*, 303t, 319–21
  reclamation, 321
Silver Purchase Act of 1934, 1963 Repeal, 321
Silverton, Colorado, *9*
Slash pine, 205, 217, 218
Sleeping Bear Dunes National Lakeshore, *128*, 129, *129*
Small Watershed Act of 1954, 183, 489
Smelters, toxic materials from, 314, 318
Smog,
  in eastern cities, 235, *251*
  in western cities, 235
Smokey the Bear, 227–28
Snow geese, *381*, 426
Snowmobile, *392*
Social costs, of agricultural chemicals, 185
Social issues compared to environmental issues, 78, 79, 80
Society, as ekistical element, *35*, 36
Society of American Foresters, 214
Softwoods, 198, 489

Soil community,
  breakdown, 153–59
  effects of chemicals, 184
Soil Conservation Act of 1935, 489
Soil Conservation Service, 183
Soil resources, 147–85
  alluvial, 478
  carrying capacity, *161*
  conservation of, 19, *157*
  erosion, 59, *59*, *153*, *154*, 155, *156*, 172, *172*, 173
  erosion control ordinances, *158*
  formation patterns, 151
  horizons, 148, 150, 155, 156, 157, *159*, 161, *163*, *170*, *175*, 177, 483
  in inner city, *63*
  lateralization, 21, 484
  loam, 19
  nutrients, 212, *212*
  porosity, 489
  problems of suburbanization, 147
  profile, 48–50, *149*, *151*, 489
  topsoil, 21, *21*, 159
Solar energy, 277–81, 437–39
  electrical generation and, 280
  solar furnace, 280
  solar hot water heating, 279
  solar-powered engine, 277
  solar space heating, 278–79
  solar water distillers, 280
Solid waste, *8*, 51–55
  content, 53
  disposal cost, 53
  disposed in national parks, 428
Solid Waste Disposal Act of 1965, 83–84, 489
Solid waste management, 52–53, 82–84
  built-in obsolescence, 83
  city as chemical, physical, and energy sink, 83
  federal policy recommendations, 84
  federal role, 83–84
  long-lived products, 83
  municipal costs, 52, 53, 83
  policy changes, 83
  recycling incentives and barriers, 52–53, 84
  state role, 83–84
Sonic boom, 457
Southern Cross, Montana, *311*
Southern forest, 191, *192*, *193*, *197*, *206*, 204–27, *211*, *215*
Southern Forest Resource Council, 210
Southern Pacific railroad, 452–53
Southern pine beetle, *216*
Spaceship Earth, 11, *439*, 444–45
Species elimination, 14, 15

Standard of living,
  relationship to energy consumption, 263
  social indicators of, 263, 264t
Static reserve figure, 489
Steel scrap, use in steel manufacturing, 341–42
Stevenage, England, 46, 470
Stockholm, Sweden, suburbs of, 297
Storm drain, 113
Stratification of lake, 124–25, 489
Stream channelization, 152–53, 181, 489
Strip cropping, 165, 489
Strip mining, 173, 174, 174, 175, 176, 287, 288, 289, 289, 291–95, 293, 295, 296, 312
Strontium-90, 253
Substitution, as conservation philosophy, 33
Suburban sprawl, 471
Suburbanization, 7
Succession,
  aquatic, 124–31
  biotic, 353
  "terminal," 13
  of urban areas, 47, 351
Sulfur dioxide,
  levels in New York City, 241
  pollution control, 245
  pollution problems, 244
Sulfur oxides, effects as air pollutant, 231t
Summer kill in lake, 127
Supersonic transport, 456, 457–58, 457
Sustained yield, 490
  of U.S. forests, 203
Swatek, Paul, 53
Synecology, 26, 490

Tapiola Garden City, Finland, 473
Teach-in on the environment, 80
Tenneco, 408
Tennessee River,
  before TVA, 59
  flood protection projects, 178, 178, 179
Tennessee Valley Authority (TVA), 58, 59, 74, 75, 76, 174, 177–78, 178, 201
  Fontana Dam, 179
  power generation, 288
  reforestation, 207
  social costs of, 266
Terracing, 165, 490
Thermal mushrooms over cities, 255, 256
Thermal pollution, 125, 256, 269–71, 330
  impact on marine life, 270
  from nuclear reactors, 254, 330
Thermocline, 126, 490
Thermodynamics, Second Law of, 29
Third forest, 218, 223

Tidal power, 282–83, 284, 285
Tidepools, 391
Tin, 302t
Tocher, Ross, 428
Topsoil, 21, 21, 150, 490
  loss of, 159
Total systems approach, 76, 490
Toynbee, Arnold, 41, 467
Traffic congestion, costs of, 453–55
Transiency of American families, 476
Transmission lines, high-voltage, 99, 100, 286, 287
Transportation, efficiencies, per lane, per hour, 458t
Transportation, mass transit,
  European systems, 93
  policy decision making, 90–91
  as survival necessity, 450
  U.S. efforts, 93, 94, 96, 97
  urbanization and routes, 85–87
Tree improvement, 216–19
  environmental control, 216–17
  genetic control, 217–19
Tree plantations, southern, 217
Trophic level, 25, 25, 26, 26, 491
Trophy animals, 13, 377, 491
Tropical forest, 191, 193, 214
Trust for Public Lands, 414
Tundra, 370, 491
Tungsten, 303t
Turgidity, 42, 491

Udall, Stewart, 50, 72
Uinta Basin, Utah, oil shale deposits, 336
Umbilical cords, of metropolitan man, 442
United Nations Conference on the Human Environment of 1972, 491
U.S. Army Corps of Engineers, 17, 61, 138, 181, 183
  dredging in Great Lakes, 130
  recreation planning, 407
U.S. Bureau of Land Management, 201
U.S. Bureau of Mines, 303n, 342
  metal recycling efforts, 54, 344
U.S. Bureau of Sport Fisheries and Wildlife, 201
U.S. Department of Agriculture, 54, 61, 62
U.S. Department of Commerce, 61
U.S. Department of Defense, 61
U.S. Department of Health, Education, and Welfare, 54, 61
U.S. Department of Housing and Urban Development, 474
U.S. Department of the Interior, 54, 61
U.S. Department of Justice, 61

U.S. Department of State, international water treaties, compacts, and projects, 61
  Columbia River power production, 61
  Rio Grande irrigation allocations, 61
  St. Lawrence Seaway, 61
U.S. Department of Transportation, 61
U.S. Forest Products Laboratory, 54
U.S. Forest Service, 62, 214
  differences from National Park Service, 406t
U.S. National Park Service, 394–98
  differences from U.S. Forest Service, 406t
  established, 404
  first director, 404
U.S. Soil Conservation Service, 62, 201
Unitization, 491
University of Michigan, 32, 80–81
Uranium, 329–32, 331
Uravan, Colorado, 331
Urban blight, 463, 465
Urban conservation,
  challenge, 40
  conceptual foundations, 40–41
  philosophy, 34
Urban consumption of mineral resources, 316–18
Urban density, 459
Urban emigration, 428–29, 459
Urban growth rates, 42, 458–59
Urban Growth and New Community Development Act of 1970, 474, 491
Urban Mass Transportation Act of 1964, 491
Urban organism, 25, 28, 30
  elements of, 34
  networks, 443
Urban parks, 414, 432
Urban poor, 411, 415
  lacking access to wilderness areas, 412, 414, 415
Urban recreation, positive examples, 415, 432
Urban reserves, 491
Urban residents, forces attracting from cities, 428–29, 459
Urban resource seminar, techniques of, 65–68
Urban soil management, 162
Urban transportation,
  comparison with human circulatory system, 84–85
  in Europe, 93, 94
  federal role, 82–83
  relationship of streets and traffic flow, 89
  in United States, 94, 95–97, 96, 97, 452, 454, 455
  traffic, 95

Urban trophic levels, 27
Urban water pollution, 83
Urban water supply, 59–62
Urban waterfront, 131
Urbanization, 7, 12, 14, 491
  diseases of world-wide sprawl, 462
  in flood plain, 17, 17
  percentages by state, 431
  percentages in the U.S., 460
  on recreation lands, 409

Value system, 12
Van Hise, Charles R., definitions of conservation, 31n
Vanadium, 332–33
Variances, 317, 491
Vest pocket park, 411, 414
  in urban areas, 411, 432
Victoria, Vancouver Island, British Columbia, 423, 424, 425
Vietnam, 78

Walls,
  biological, 41–43
  fundamental tasks, 43
  city, 43–44
  urban, 41, 440
Walt Disney Productions, proposal for Mineral King, 418–20
Ward, Colorado, 333
Wars, effect on conservation, 73
Washington, D.C., 247, 248, 257, 386
  air pollution problems, 246–52, 247, 248, 251, 259
  bicycle paths, 247, 249, 250
  cars per capita, 246
  mass transit study, 92, 247
  noise control, National Airport, 252
  wildlife, 378
Waste assimilation, 114, 121
Waste disposal problem, of processed shale, 337
Waste heat, from nuclear power plants, 271
Waste water treatment, 50–51
  costs, 120
  federal role, 120–21
  land application, 117–19, 118, 119
  primary, 116–17, 487
  secondary, 117, 488
  tertiary, 119–20, 490
Water pollution, 464
  biological indicators, 132–33, 133
  control legislation, 134–36
  detergents, 58
  industrial, 132

management and urbanization, 58, 136
radioactive, 133–34
salting streets and, 57
Water Pollution Control Act of 1948, 77, 134, 482
Water Pollution Control Act Amendments of 1972, 117, 119–20, 409, 491
Water resources, 107–45
    assimilation capacity, 130
    consumption, U.S. per capita, 109
    costs, 144–45, 145n
    cycle, 108, *108, 109*
    federal jurisdiction, 61
    historical role, 110–14
    incentive for settlement, 24
    industry and, *112*
    international water-related treaties, compacts, and projects, 61
    legislation, 77, 134–36
    manager, 51
    metropolitan management, 51–52, 59–60
    recreation, *390, 391, 392, 400, 402, 464*
    regional management, 59–62
    treatment, municipal economies of scale, 60
    treatment costs, 115
    urban uses, *112, 113,* 144
    world supply, 110t
Water Resources Planning Act of 1965, 491
Waterfront renewal, *423, 424, 466*
Waterville, Maine, 25
Weeks Act of 1911, 200, 210, 491
Welland Canal, 88
Welwyn Garden City, England, 45, 470
Wetlands Inspection Act of 1962, 382
Wetlands Loan Act of 1961, 382
Whitaker, J. R., definition of conservation, 31n
White, Lynn, Jr., 71
White House Conference on Conservation, 72–73
Whooping crane, *357*
Whyte, William H., 471

Wild river, 492
Wilderness,
    camping, *412*
    definition, 409
    effect of people on, 403
    management, in national parks, 396
Wilderness Act of 1964, 382, 491
Wilderness Preservation Act of 1964, 409
Wildlife and fisheries resources, 349–88
    in Everglades, *224, 226*
    legislation, 381–82
    management, *383*
    in metropolitan areas, 378–80
    stability, 387
Wildlife Coordination Act of 1934, 382
Wildlife Refuge Exchange Act of 1935, *381,* 382
Wildlife Restoration Act of 1937, 492
Windbreaks, *167, 168,* 169
Winter kill in lake, 126, 492
Wisconsin, salt application on highways, 55
Wolves, *366*
World Bank, 77
World city, *438,* 467–75
World War II, 76
Wyandotte Chemical Corporation, 82

Yambert, Paul, 297
"Yardstick" effect, 74
Yosemite National Park, *393, 394–401, 394, 395, 396, 397, 398, 399,* 403, *404,* 405
    auto, impact of, *397, 398*
    bicycling, *398*
    buses, *397*
    sewage treatment, 396, 428
    Yosemite Valley, *393, 395, 398, 398*
    Yosemite Village, 394, *394,* 396, *396*

Zimmerman, Erich W., definition of conservation, 321
Zinc, 303t, 321–22
Zoning, 55